THE PERSONALISM OF EDITH STEIN

Studies in the Carmelite Tradition

THE PERSONALISM OF EDITH STEIN

A Synthesis of Thomism and Phenomenology

ROBERT McNAMARA

The Catholic University of America Press
Washington, D.C.

Copyright © 2023

The Catholic University of America Press

All rights reserved

Library of Congress Control Number: 2022946859

ISBN: 978-0-8132-3747-3

eISBN: 978-0-8132-3748-0

אהיה אשר אהיה

—*Exodus 3:14*

To my mother, *in memoriam*.
To my father, *in spem*.

As kingfishers catch fire, dragonflies dráw fláme;
As tumbled over rim in roundy wells
Stones ring; like each tucked string tells, each hung bell's
Bow swung finds tongue to fling out broad its name;
Each mortal thing does one thing and the same:
Deals out that being indoors each one dwells;
Selves—goes itself; *myself* it speaks and spells,
Crying *Whát I do is me: for that I came.*

Í say móre: the just man justices;
Kéeps gráce: thát keeps all his goings graces;
Acts in God's eye what in God's eye he is—
Chríst—for Christ plays in ten thousand places,
Lovely in limbs, and lovely in eyes not his
To the Father through the features of men's faces.

—*Gerard Manley Hopkins*

CONTENTS

Preface ix

Acknowledgments xvii

Abbreviations xix

Introduction xxiii

Prolegomenon: A Preparatory Analysis xxxix

Part I: Human Nature 1

    Chapter One: Point of Departure in the "Life of the I" 5

    Chapter Two: Human Unity and Bodily Formation 43

Part II: The Human Individual 87

    Chapter Three: The Material Individual in General 91

    Chapter Four: The Human Individual in Particular 126

Part III: The Human Being's Relation to God 171

    Chapter Five: Philosophical Knowledge of God 173

    Chapter Six: The Personal Form of the Analogy of Being . . . 204

Conclusion: Being a Person 247

Epilogue—Stein's "Thomistic Personalism"? 261

Bibliography 267

    Primary Sources 267

    Reference Sources 270

    Secondary Sources 270

Index 285

χάριτι δὲ θεοῦ εἰμι ὅ εἰμι . . .
 —*1 Corinthians 15:10*

PREFACE

"Person" signifies what is most perfect in all nature.

—*Thomas Aquinas*[1]

The twentieth century was marked by two contrary movements that profoundly shape our contemporary understanding of the human person and our corresponding appreciation of human dignity. The first, primarily political, was found in the horrifying abuses carried out against persons of certain religious and ethnic groups throughout the course of the Second World War. The second, primarily philosophical and theological, was found in a deepened understanding of the human person illumined by a diverse range of twentieth-century thinkers and broadly identified as "personalism." These distinct and contrary movements—one ideological and political, debasing the person, the other philosophical and theological, revering the person—intersect in the life and thought of St. Teresia Benedicta a Cruce, more widely known by her given name, Edith Stein, a Jewish convert, Christian philosopher, and Carmelite sister murdered by the National Socialist regime in 1942. Stein lived through the horrors of the twentieth century and left behind works of great significance for the Western tradition, several of which provide significant contributions to the movement of personalism, in both its philosophical and theological kinds. Throughout her less than thirty years of scholarly productivity, Stein wrote phenomenological and metaphysical treatises covering such varied topics as ontology, psychology, education, and politics; provided large, annotated translations of works of Sts. John Henry Newman and Thomas Aquinas; engaged in detailed analyses of Christian theological doctrines; and penned spiritual reflections suffused with Carmelite mysticism inspired by the works of Sts. Teresa of Avila and John of the Cross.

---

1   ST I, 29.3, co.

But nowhere is her thought more insightful than in her frequent in-depth investigations of the being, nature, and life of the human person. When it comes to the human person Stein's thought is both subtle and comprehensive. Among a diverse range of personalist topics, she analyzes the personal character of human nature and the individual identity of the human being, the expansive nature of the spiritual soul and the personal significance of the living-body, and the inherently communal dimension of human life together with the created person's unparalleled relation to the personal God. Not only are these topics and closely related others repeated areas of direct investigation in Stein's works, but she also touches on such anthropological and personalist themes in a thoughtful way throughout her extensive and varied writings.

Indeed, Stein's whole life with its uncommon course of development and her particular philosophical interests is marked by appreciation for the dignity of the human person. Stein was born into a practicing Jewish family in the German city of Breslau (now the Polish Wrocław) on October 12, 1891, the Day of Atonement (*Yom Kippur*), the holiest of days in the Jewish religious calendar. Stein's devout mother considered the date of her birth significant—and indeed, it distinctly impressed the course of Stein's life, up to and including her eventual martyrdom. In a prescient letter of 1930 she wrote, "After every encounter in which I feel the powerlessness of my direct influence, the urgency of my own holocaust intensifies."[2] Stein bore this truth with an ever-deepening understanding as she matured personally and religiously, and it affords for us a rich interpretive key to her life and thought, even surfacing in her philosophical and theological writings as she progressively comes to understand the human person as "bearer"—a decisive insight of Stein's thought as a whole, which fully matures during her years as a Christian thinker. The youngest of eleven children, Stein was a gifted child who found herself at home in the schoolroom and the life of the mind. She succeeded well in her primary and secondary education before enrolling in the University of Breslau in 1911 for the study of German and history, while also embracing a defined interest in the newly developing discipline of psychology. Yet, dissatisfied with her basic course of studies and the as-yet inadequately developed nascent science of psychology, and having discovered Edmund Husserl's recently published *Logical Investigations* (1900–1901), Stein transferred to Göttingen University to study the newly introduced philosophical method of phenomenology under the instruction

---

2   SBB I, nos. 83, 108.

of Husserl himself, surrounded by his many gifted and enthusiastic students, chief among which was the talented teacher Adolf Reinach. She eventually completed her doctoral dissertation *On the Problem of Empathy* (1917) under Husserl's supervision and later became his personal assistant, collating and editing his philosophical writings and introducing newer students to the method of phenomenology.

As it did for many of her contemporaries, phenomenology deeply impressed the young Stein and it became her principal mode of investigation for the entire course of her philosophical career. This remained true for her even after her temporary break from philosophy following her conversion to Catholic Christianity and subsequent in-depth engagement with the metaphysical tradition of the *philosophia perennis*. Returning to philosophical investigation in the late 1920s, Stein began the task that would consume her philosophical research for the remainder of her life—namely, the potentially fruitful encounter of Husserlian phenomenology and Thomistic Scholasticism. Through the confrontation of these historically separated philosophical movements, Stein intended to contribute to the considerable task of working out a fruitful synthesis of modern and medieval thought, the philosophical schools predominating in the German academy and Catholic universities of her day, and ultimately discovered this task to be her philosophical "mission in life."[3] After teaching for a number of years—first at a Dominican school in Speyer, then at a Catholic pedagogical institute in Münster—and having failed to secure a professorship in philosophy at the Universities of Göttingen and Freiburg—initially because she was a woman, then because of her Jewish ethnicity—Stein entered the Carmelite Order in Cologne (the Carmel *St. Maria vom Frieden*) and devoted herself to the service of God, a service that was to be accomplished also philosophically. As a Carmelite nun, under the direction of her superiors, Stein penned her final philosophical work and magnum opus, *Finite and Eternal Being* (1936–37), an ambitious phenomenological and metaphysical work that she presents as an effort to provide a comprehensive Christian philosophy, subtitling the work "An Attempt to Ascend to the Meaning of Being." Throughout the work Stein engages the metaphysical thought of St. Thomas Aquinas and the Christian tradition while continuing to employ the phenomenological method in order to cast light on the meaning of being, its finite λόγος (*logos*) in the many different λόγοι (*logoi*) of beings,

---

3   SBB I, no. 245, 269–72.

together with the ultimate ground of all meaning in the eternal Λόγος (*Logos*).⁴ The text was not published during Stein's lifetime—again as a consequence of her Jewish ethnicity—and the manuscript was left behind in the Carmel of Echt, Netherlands, when she was arrested by German military police on August 2, 1942, and transported to Auschwitz-Birkenau for execution on August 9.

Just as she had in her philosophical and theological writings, Stein witnessed the coordinating centrality of truth throughout her life, up to and including her untimely death at the hands of the Nazi regime. Truth was the guiding beacon that enlightened the path of her personal life and stood as the firm reference point coordinating the course of her philosophical investigations. As a fruit of this fidelity to truth, Stein's life and thought echoes powerfully through time, both in terms of the integrity of her life given freely unto death, which renders her a figure of growing devotional interest among Catholic faithful, and in terms of the depth of her philosophical insight, which continues to inform philosophical discourse up to the present day. This steadfast adherence to truth radiates in all areas of Stein's thought, but is perhaps most notable when her philosophical investigations lead to positions that stand opposed to the conclusions of her two principal masters, Husserl and Aquinas. Though Stein found in both thinkers sure guides in the life of the mind and discovered in their writings the authentic resonance of truth—precisely inasmuch as each in their own way sought to uncover the λόγος of being—she remained faithful to the truth itself as the final arbiter in philosophical matters. Indeed, this fidelity is itself an embodiment of Stein's understanding of philosophy and the specific calling of the philosopher. The philosopher, she argues, ought to be oriented toward truth in *first-person* engagement with the world, even while performing philosophical investigation as a communal venture, and must engage with the reality of human life, community, and culture so that the truth of philosophical investigation would return to enlighten the personal and social dimensions of life. Stein's philosophy is then a genuinely personalistic philosophy, both because her practice of phenomenological philosophy consistently reveals the personal subject as its definitive cornerstone and because the human

---

4   The Greek λόγος (and its plural λόγοι), most often translated as "word" following the scriptural translation of the Gospel of St. John, is preferable to any attempted translation, precisely inasmuch as the Greek concept embraces all meaning, whether found in things, thought, or word, and the corresponding tight correlation of all meaning in things, thought, and word in the centering linchpin of thought about things expressed in words.

person and human sociality appear in her works as central themes of repeated investigation. The personal orientation of her philosophy is also evident in the way Stein's life informed her philosophical interests and engagement, and conversely in the way her philosophical studies shaped her personal life and its course of unfolding. The practice of philosophy was no mere academic exercise for Stein but arose as a genuine *philosophy of life*—a philosophy borne from life lived with personal authenticity, before then informing the path of personal life and experience—which meant that Stein performed philosophical investigation in an intensely personal way. As a result of this personal focus, together with her corresponding fidelity to truth, her philosophy lends itself to being personally appropriated in a way that uniquely informs philosophical investigation and clarifies the meaning of being a person.

I first became interested in Stein's thought during my undergraduate studies in philosophy when I attended the first international conference of the newly founded *International Association for the Study of the Philosophy of Edith Stein* (IASPES). Prior to this academic encounter I found the person of Stein herself intriguing and her singular life more than compelling. Yet, whenever I attempted to read any of her works, I was plunged into a seemingly impenetrable tangle of complex inquiries, inquiries for which I had no apparent entry point. Fortunately, the presentations of the scholars at this conference cracked the surface for me, I purchased a copy of *Finite and Eternal Being*, and I set out upon what would become a progressive immersion in Stein's thought. Having already closely studied the writings of Sts. Thomas Aquinas and Karol Wojtyła / Pope St. John Paul II, I was somewhat prepared for my encounter with Stein's particular brand of phenomenology and metaphysics and quickly grew enamored with her philosophical perspective, with the kinds of questions she asked, and with the mode of her philosophical investigation. When I later undertook doctoral studies, I did not have to think twice about the general sphere of research: it was to be the human person in Stein's writings. And since my first philosophical passion had been the thought of Aquinas, I was intent on examining the Thomistic character of Stein's mature philosophical anthropology and personalism. This dual study, which took Stein together with Aquinas, was important for me not only because of Aquinas's towering position in the Catholic intellectual tradition, but also because Stein herself recognizes this imposing presence and enters into a profound give-and-take with his writings. What I found especially gripping was the way Stein engages the writings of Aquinas from the newly developed perspective of phenomenology and thereby reconsiders Thomistic teachings through a contemporary lens, one cognizant of the many philosophical and cultural developments since the time of Aquinas, while also vigorously engaging with the wisdom of the Thomistic tradition.

Engaging Thomistic thought phenomenologically enables Stein to present the human person in an expansive, richly nuanced manner, one that attends to the significance of the experiencing subject without at all ignoring the objective metaphysical structure of the person. Such attention to the subjective aspect of personal being brings fresh insight to the metaphysical anthropology of Aquinas and the Thomistic tradition in a way not unlike that also introduced by Wojtyła in his own phenomenological and Thomistic writings. Indeed, Wojtyła vividly captures the importance of this duality of approach when he says,

> The experience of man cannot be exhausted by means of 'cosmological' reduction. We must consider *l'irréductible* [the irreducible], what in every man is unique and unrepeatable, through which he is not only 'in particular' this man—an individual of a species—but through which he is *a person: a subject*. Only then is the image of man correct and complete."[5]

---

5 Karol Wojtyła, "Subjectivity and 'the Irreducible' in Man," in *Person and Act: And Related Essays*, trans. Grzegorz Ignatik (Washington, DC: The Catholic University of America Press, 2021), 536–45: 542; emphasis added. Here and in the following, care needs to be exercised in understanding the meaning of "subject" and "subjective," a meaning which has little to do with subjectivism in a negative moral sense. In what follows, I take "subject" and "object"—as their common suffix indicates—to be correlative terms, where, properly understood, a subject cannot be had without an object or an object without a subject, since each by definition is implied by its correlative opposite. Most broadly considered, a subject is that which is directed toward an object, whether the subject be a person, animal, power, act, etc., and an object is that toward which a subject is directed, whether the object be a thing, person, act, etc.; then, more narrowly, a subject is some*one* who is directed toward some*thing*; and the *thing* toward which some*one* is directed is his object. In this particular context, and also in what follows, the human person is understood to be a rational and sensitive subject of conscious experience and spiritual activity, and the various persons, things, acts, and events toward which the person is directed are his objects, objects of knowledge, love, activity, etc. One can then also say that the human person is objectively a subject, and that the subjective life of the person is something objective, since the subjectivity of the human person can be taken as an object of knowledge, love, etc. It should be noted that Aquinas certainly understood the human person to be a subject in the sense just

As with Wojtyła, Stein sees the need to complement the metaphysical objectivity of Thomism with the subjective perspective provided by phenomenology. Both recognize that taking either perspective in isolation from its complementary opposite would lead to a foreshortened presentation of the human person, one that would inadvertently emphasize one dimension of what it means to be human at the cost of its fitting complement. Such a presentation would ever risk being misunderstood as a presentation of the whole and, consequently, present a skewed conception of the human person. With both perspectives taken together we find a fuller, truer account of what it means to be human, one that is attentive to the human being as a natural object with a defined actual and ontological structure, and to the human being as a conscious subject with a unique mode of personal life. This simultaneity of attention is particularly important in understanding the human person in the contemporary world, precisely since this era heavily privileges the subjective aspect of personal life without grounding this experiential dimension in the objective givenness of human nature and the actuality of human life.

In this book I explore Stein's presentation of the human person, giving due regard to both dimensions of her mature thought, the objective and the subjective, by analyzing her engagement with the metaphysical anthropology of Aquinas in her later phenomenological personalism. In so doing, I highlight certain notable features of Stein's mature personalism while also situating her anthropology against the backdrop of the Thomistic tradition, thus manifesting her unique contribution to the anthropological tradition of the *philosophia perennis*. For this exploration I focus on several interconnected spheres, those related to the meaning of being a person and the structure of human nature, the personal unity of the human being and the personal formation of the living-body, the problem of the individual being and individuality of the human person,

---

detailed, yet one should also recognize that new attention to personal subjectivity in the modern era brings certain important features of personal subjectivity to the fore, features that are of themselves significant, and which will be significant in the analyses of Stein's engagement with Aquinas in what follows. For an insightful, even if brief, outline of personal subjectivity, see Karol Wojtyła, *Love and Responsibility*, trans. Grzegorz Ignatik (Boston: Pauline Books and Media, 2013), 3–7; and for a more in-depth analysis with other foci, see John Crosby, *The Selfhood of the Human Person* (Washington DC: The Catholic University of America Press, 1996), esp. the chapter on subjectivity, 82–133; and the shorter, Mark K. Spencer, "Aristotelian Substance and Personalistic Subjectivity," in *International Philosophical Quarterly* 55, no. 2 (2015): 145–64: 145–46.

and the question of the human being's unparalleled relation to the personal God. Throughout, I attempt to stay true to Stein's self-declared "mission in life" by investigating her conception of the human person through the lens of the interplay of Husserlian phenomenology and Thomistic Scholasticism. With Stein's sure guidance, I show that these alternate perspectives are reciprocally complementary and mutually informative in attaining a fully comprehensive understanding of the human person. Moreover, by attending to the human person from the vantage point of both together, we not only come to appreciate something of Stein's distinctive conception of philosophy, but we also begin to perceive what she herself saw when she looked upon the human person—a unique subject of personal life and conscious experience, eminently individual in being and qualitative distinctiveness, a created analogue of the personal God. It is my hope that this study will render Stein's thought more widely known, especially among Thomistically inclined thinkers, and that it will ultimately provide impetus to turn to her writings and therein discover the true depth of her vision of the mystery and dignity of the human person.

October 12, 2022

ACKNOWLEDGMENTS

I am grateful to all those who have encouraged and advised or otherwise helped me to complete this book with its beginning in my doctoral dissertation. In particular I would like to thank my supervisorial team, Mette Lebech and Marian Maskulak, who were generous with their time, expertise, and sure and incisive guidance at all stages of research, as well as my doctoral examiners Fr. Christof Betschart and Stephen Yates, who examined the work with charity and kindness and who asked questions during my defense that I am still mulling over. I wish to thank the staff of the Maryvale Institute and Liverpool Hope University, especially Mary Mills, Harry Schnitker, Andrew Morris, and Gergely Juhasz, for their dedicated service to me and the doctoral candidates at the Institute and University, and also the Brigittine Sisters at Maryvale for their devoted care for our spiritual and material needs. I give thanks to my fellow doctoral students at Maryvale, especially Dan Schneider, Fr. Justino Cornejo, and Fr. Marcello Navarro, with whom I shared many an enjoyable evening decompressing over dinner and drinks.

    I am grateful for the intellectual fraternity of my colleagues at Franciscan University of Steubenville, particularly those of the philosophy and theology departments, and especially William Newton, Javier Carreño, Meghan Schofield, Maria Wolter, Brandon Dahm, and John Crosby, from whom I received much intellectual stimulation, scholarly counsel, and critical commentary of my writing. I am uniquely indebted to William Newton for initially entrusting to me the privilege of teaching the students at Franciscan University and to these same students from whom I am ever learning the craft of teaching. I give thanks to my colleagues at the Aquinas Institute of Ireland, Fr. Conor McDonough, William Newton, and Gaven Kerr, for their fraternity and encouragement over the years, and for the many budding Thomistic scholars I encountered at our annual summer schools. I am grateful to the many academics I have met at numerous Steinian and Thomistic conferences who have helped me grapple with the challenging thought of Stein and Aquinas, especially Walter

Redmond, David Twetten, Christof Betschart, Sarah Borden Sharkey, Jadwiga Guerrero van der Meijden, Nicolò Lorenzetto, René Raschke, Elodie Boublil, Claudia Mariéle Wulf, Emanuele Caminada, Martina Galvani, Francesco Alfieri, and Cecilia Giudice.

I am thankful to Javier Carreño, Meghan Schofield, Maria Wolter, Alex Plato, and Josef Seifert, whose comments on different portions of the manuscript, and suggestions for the inclusion of further material, bore improvements throughout, and especially to Jadwiga Guerrero van der Meijden for assessing the whole manuscript and making many valuable recommendations while also identifying a number of areas where further refinement was necessary. I would like to give thanks to two reviewers of the manuscript for The Catholic University of America Press, for their especially close reading of the text and the many incredibly helpful recommendations they made for improvements. I am grateful to the *American Catholic Philosophical Quarterly*, *Philosophical News*, and *Be&Be Verlag* for permission to reprint substantial portions or later iterations of portions of earlier articles on Stein's conception of human unity and bodily formation, and of the human individual.

Finally, I wish to thank my family and friends who endured my everyday distraction throughout the years of research for their faithful support and unfailing encouragement at all stages: my sister Sharon, my brothers Kevin and Jason, and most especially my beautiful wife Caroline and our four children, Vivian, Jack, Catie, and Oran, who endured my absence—at least in mind—at various stages of research and writing, and who are day by day helping me to understand *how to be a person*.

ABBREVIATIONS

Full bibliographic details are provided in the appended bibliography.

Edith Stein

AMP	*Der Aufbau der menschlichen Person*
BEI	*Bildung und Entfaltung der Individualität*
DF	*Die Frau, Fragestellungen und Reflexionen*
EES	*Endliches und ewiges Sein*
EPh	*Einführung in die Philosophie*
GT I	*Geistliche Texte I*
IG	*"Individuum und Gemeinschaft," in Beiträge zur philosophischen Begründung der Psychologie und der Geisteswissenschaften*
KDS	*(Übersetzung) Alexandre Koyré, Descartes und die Scholastik*
KW	*Kreuzeswissenschaft*
LJF	*Aus dem Leben einer jüdischen Familie und weitere autobiographische Beiträge*
MT	*Miscellanea thomistica. Übersetzungen—Abbreviationen—Exzerpte aus Werken des Thomas von Aquin und der Forschungsliteratur*
NFG	*"Freiheit und Gnade" und weitere Beiträge zu Phänomenologie und Ontologie*
PA	*Potenz und Akt*
PE	*Zum Problem der Einfühlung*
PK	*"Psychische Kausalität," in Beiträge zur philosophischen Begründung der Psychologie und der Geisteswissenschaften*
SBB I	*Selbstbildnis in Briefen I: 1916–1933*
SBB II	*Selbstbildnis in Briefen II: 1933–1942*
SBB III	*Selbstbildnis in Briefen III: Briefe an Roman Ingarden*
US	*Eine Untersuchung über den Staat*
WGE	*Wege der Gotteserkenntnis*
WIM	*Was ist der Mensch?*

WP	"Was ist Philosophie? Ein Gespräch zwischen Edmund Husserl und Thomas von Aquino," in *"Freiheit und Gnade" und weitere Beiträge zu Phänomenologie und Ontologie*

Edition

ESGA	*Edith Stein Gesamtausgabe*

Thomas Aquinas

Works of Aquinas are referenced using internal divisions of his texts (with paragraph or line numbers where appropriate).

CT	*Compendium theologiae*
DEE	*De ente et essentia*
DME	*De mixtione elementorum*
InDA	*Sentencia libri De anima*
InMeta	*In duodecim libros Metaphysicorum Aristotelis expositio*
InPA	*In libros Posteriorum analyticorum expositio*
QDA	*Quaestiones disputatae de anima*
QDP	*Quaestiones disputatae de potentia*
QDSC	*Quaestio disputata de spiritualibus creaturis*
QDV	*Quaestiones disputatae de veritate*
Quodl	*Quaestiones de quolibet*
SCG	*Summa contra gentiles*
Sent	*Scriptum super Sententiarum*
ST	*Summa theologiae*

Editions

Leonina	*Sancti Thomae Aquinatis, Doctoris Angelici, opera omnia, iussu impensaque Leonis XIII P.M. edita*
Marietti	*Thomae Aquinatis, opera omnia*

Aristotle

Works of Aristotle are referenced using Bekker line numbers; for Aquinas's commentaries of Aristotelian texts, the Aristotelian reference is given in brackets.

DA	*On the Soul (De anima)*
Meta	*Metaphysics*
PAn	*Posterior Analytics*

A Note on Translation

Though a number of Stein's texts are available in published English translations, in order to ensure uniformity with my own translation of *The Structure of the Human Person* (*Der Aufbau der menschlichen Person*), which is not yet available in English, and to guarantee consistency across her various works, I translate all direct quotations of Stein's texts; to likewise ensure consistency across the works of Aquinas in various translations, I translate direct quotations of his texts. However, all quotations from both authors have been closely reviewed against the published English translations available to me, all of which are listed in the appended bibliography. I would like particularly to thank two Stein scholars for their translation work, Walter Redmond and Marian Maskulak, Redmond for making available his soon-to-be published translation of *Finite and Eternal Being*, and Maskulak for making available her draft translation of part of chapter 7 of *The Structure of the Human Person*. If I had not received these two translations early in my research, before I accomplished basic German reading proficiency, my task of understanding Stein's involved texts would have been far more challenging and laborious.

A Note on Cover and Closing Materials

The introductory poem by Gerard Manley Hopkins is taken from *Selected Poems*, ed. Bob Blaisdell (New York: Dover, 2011), 46; the introductory quotation by St. Augustine of Hippo is from his *Soliloquies*, 2.1.1, found in *St. Augustine's Cassiciacum Dialogues*, vol. 4, trans. Michael P. Foley (New Haven, CT: Yale University Press, 2020), 53.

> "O God, ever the Selfsame:
> may I know myself, may I know Thee."
> My prayer is done.
>
> —*Augustine, Soliloquies 2.1.1*

INTRODUCTION

> Behind all that the human being does stands a guiding *Logos*.
>
> —*Edith Stein*[1]

St. Edith Stein's philosophical maturation takes place in direct dialogue with the Christian philosophical tradition, primarily through extensive and prolonged engagement with the thought of St. Thomas Aquinas. In her thorough study and translation of certain key texts of Aquinas, as well as the study of representative texts of the Thomistic tradition, Stein engages Thomistic teachings while continuing to employ the phenomenological method of investigation. As a result, by the end of her life Stein had woven an intricate metaphysical tapestry integrating insights gained via the phenomenological method with teachings received from Aquinas and the Thomistic tradition. I explore one aspect of this assimilation by analyzing Stein's engagement with Aquinas and Thomism in her mature philosophy of the human person. The human person is a recurring theme of inquiry throughout Stein's works, already present in a defined way in her early more purely phenomenological writings, and it endures as a focal point as she transitions to a consideration of metaphysical themes. Indeed, Stein's practice of philosophy itself has a defined personalist character, inasmuch as she holds the personal subject to be its cornerstone, a knowing (and loving) subject placed in the natural world together with other personal subjects in variously constituted social groupings. In this introduction, I outline this personalist character of Stein's thought in general—from her early phenomenological works to those later decidedly metaphysical—in order to situate the investigation of the Thomistic character of her mature personalism in the proper context of her broader philosophical interests. I also provide an outline of the scope of the present study, an introductory note on method and

---

1   AMP, 2.

methodology, and a guide to the analysis as it unfolds, indicating the specific areas explored and the gradually "developing picture" of the human person uniting each area under investigation.

The Personalist Character of Stein's Philosophy

Stein's first four philosophical treatises—*On the Problem of Empathy* (1917), *Psychic Causality* (1922), *Individual and Community* (1922), and *An Investigation Concerning the State* (1925)—detail various aspects of the personal subject's insertion into the experienced world, a world that is constituted for the knowing subject together with other personal subjects, through the mediation of the body and what is bodily, and according to a value-motivated mode of object constitution.[2] Each work approaches a distinct philosophical problem—the act of empathy, the lawfulness of psyche and spirit, the individual as a member of community, and the organization of the state—yet never in such a way that the analysis remains remote from the personal subject as such.[3] Rather, by

---

2   See PE, PK, IG, and US. For Stein, the experienced world is that into which the conscious subject is inserted and, consequently, that which is given in experience for the conscious subject as an objective world. This understanding of world has certain similarities to Husserl's later presentation of the "life-world [*Lebenswelt*]" while also possessing a clearly defined existential valence from the outset. The identity of the world and the various different kinds of worlds detailed by Stein, "inner," "outer," and "above," are treated in more detail below; see chapter 1, "Point of Departure in the 'Life of the I.'" In phenomenology the objective givenness of the world (and its objects) requires the act of "constitution," where constitution is understood as the way objects are disclosed for the conscious subject in and through the synthesizing activity of consciousness. The act of constitution should be understood as *disclosive* of the objects given in experience, according to their meaning and value, rather than as *constructive* of these objects, and it should be taken as a motivated activity, where "motivation" is understood as the distinct lawfulness of consciousness that determines the conscious subject in (the succession of) acts of constitution relative to the meaning and value of the objects so constituted. For further detail on the act of constitution and its motivational character, see below, esp. l–li, lx–lxi, and lxvi–lxviii.

3   In investigating the problem of empathy, Stein reveals that the embodied person encounters the objective world together with other bodily subjects, in part through knowledge of other persons' subjective experience of the world; in investigating the distinct lawfulness of the psyche and spirit, she unveils the personal spirit as a being that relates to the world according to a motivated intentionality that is especially responsive to values; in investigating the insertion of the individual into a relational network of personal subjects, she discloses the different forms of common living possible

considering each philosophical problem in turn, Stein progressively hones her understanding of the constitution of the personal subject and thereby unveils a gradually expanding and deepening conception of the human person. In just this way, Stein underscores the preeminent significance of the personal subject together with his distinct path of personal unfolding, while concomitantly highlighting the inherently social dimension of human life as personal. Stein shows that values play a determinative role in both spheres, first in terms of the essential relation of the personal individual to values, where persons (and only persons) are understood to be value-valent beings, then in terms of the shared common relation of persons to values of certain kinds, where the kinds and range of values shared by persons determine the character of their interpersonal relations.[4] Indeed, throughout these works Stein mounts

---

for embodied personal subjects, and the objective determination of these relational networks in virtue of their differentiated relation to values; finally, in investigating the structure of the state, she discloses the basis of the state in the personal freedom of its individual members, and the relation of the state to values inasmuch as the state is determined by the freedom of its personal subjects and conditioned by the exercise of this freedom relative to values.

4   Stein's early phenomenological conception of value has parallels with that of Dietrich von Hildebrand, as both recognize the essential relation of persons and values, both grant to value recognition an affective character (even if not exclusively affective), both distinguish moral values from other kinds of values, and both recognize the formative significance of value in the life and development of the individual. Yet, whereas Stein's mature understanding of value takes shape in a way that lies in continuity with a Thomistic understanding of the good and the human person's recognition of and striving after the good, even if involving certain decisive developments beyond Aquinas and Thomism, von Hildebrand situates his understanding of value and personal responsivity in some degree of tension with the standard Thomistic presentation of the good and human striving for the good through the appetitive powers of the soul, in particular criticizing the Thomistic conception of human affectivity and the essential relation of the good and desire. For von Hildebrand's theory of value, see esp. Dietrich von Hildebrand, *Christian Ethics* (New York: David McKay Co., 1953), chaps. 5–6, 15–17; and Dietrich von Hildebrand, *The Nature of Love*, trans. John F. Crosby (South Bend, IN: St. Augustine Press, 2009), chaps. 1, 2, 5, 7, and also John F. Crosby's "Introductory Study" in the same work, xiii–xxxvi; and for von Hildebrand's critique of a traditional philosophical understanding of affectivity, see *The Heart: An Analysis of Human and Divine Affectivity*, trans. John F. Crosby (South Bend, IN: St. Augustine Press, 2007). For further detail on Aquinas's conception in contrast to von Hildebrand, see Michael Waldstein, "Dietrich von Hildebrand and St. Thomas Aquinas on Goodness and Happiness," in *Nova et Vetera* 1, no. 2 (2003): 403–64.

an increasingly compelling case that the values encountered by the personal subject play a decisive role in his development, unlocking, expanding, and deepening his personality while also coordinating the relations of persons in overlapping social groupings—whether they be mere masses of individuals gathered together, coordinated associations with purposes and ends, or organic communities of life lived in common.[5] Thus, notwithstanding the different themes explored in these early works, the central concern of Stein's early thought is the *personal subject*, or more precisely stated, the personal subject as a member of community, united to other individuals by virtue of a common orientation to value—together with which, of course, is the preeminent value of the person.

Stein's attention to the person and interpersonal relations is complemented in her later educationally focused works, all of which are devoted to securing the proper development of the human person within the family and society. This attention to the person not only appears in her many popular talks and essays on education (1928–33) and women (1928–33), but is also central to the paired series of lectures on philosophical and theological anthropology, *The Structure of the Human Person* (1932) and *What Is the Human Being?* (1933), prepared and (partially) delivered by Stein at a Catholic pedagogical institute in Münster, Germany, in the early 1930s.[6] In these pedagogical works Stein proffers a philosophical and theological conception of the human person that she argues ought to inform the educational venture of Catholic institutes, and indeed educational institutes more broadly, by providing an anthropology adequate to the nature and individuality of the human person. This anthropological foundation for education bears significance for Stein inasmuch as she recognizes that the human person is naturally set on a path of development toward personal maturity, a path she understands as the developmental *unfolding* of the human person. The proper unfolding of the person requires a well-defined anthropology, both philosophical and theological, as its guiding foundation, to enable rather than frustrate this process. And since this takes place through the involvement of others in the educational sphere, even while it is the person himself that realizes this potency, all educational intervention must be established on the ground of a true conception of the human being if it is to contribute to the unfolding of the individual. Indeed,

---

5   The terms mass (*Masse*), association (*Assoziation*), and community (*Gemeinschaft*) are technical terms for Stein, and her understanding of each can be found in the early treatise, IG.

6   See BEI, DF, AMP, and WIM.

Stein maintains that to the degree the educational venture flows from an erroneous or flawed conception, to that same degree it is destined to fail by distorting or thwarting the course of unfolding of the educated individual. And so, in her anthropological works Stein both constructively critiques the predominating assumptions of the German-speaking world of her day—those of idealism, depth psychology, and existentialism—and proposes an alternate anthropology grounded in Christian metaphysics as that which provides a true framework for education.

Considering the collective character of these educational works, taken together with her earlier, more purely phenomenological explorations, it is evident that Stein seeks to understand the human person in a refined and comprehensive way, such that her corresponding philosophical conception of the human person can rightly be described as *personalist* in character and content. When the mature Stein proceeds to works of general ontology and metaphysics—*Potency and Act* (1931) and *Finite and Eternal Being*—or to theological and spiritual treatises—*Freedom and Grace* (1921), *The Way to Knowledge of God* (1940–41), and *The Science of the Cross* (1942)—her attentiveness to the significance of the person endures.[7] Though the fields of investigation in these listed works are more general in kind and content, the human person remains within the observable perimeter of her investigations and is frequently drawn to the foreground as the object of direct study. Stein never leaves the problem of the person behind in her philosophical explorations, not only because, as earlier indicated, she recognizes that the person is implicated in philosophical investigation as its subject but also because she believes that the human person provides something of an interpretive key to every general metaphysics, insofar as the human individual embodies a summation of the natural created world—a microcosm of the cosmos—with a corresponding capacity to recapitulate the entirety of the natural world within the soul in acts of knowledge and love. This is apparent in *Finite and Eternal Being* when Stein bookends her entire investigation with attention to the human person, beginning with the first-person perspective characteristic of her "Augustinian way" of philosophizing, and concluding with an analysis of the meaning of being an individual, culminating in an examination of the created person's unparalleled relation to the personal God.[8]

---

7   See PA, EES, NFG, WGE, and KW.

8   In accord with the aim of this book, in what follows I gradually unpack key dimensions of the personalist character of Stein's mature thought.

In various interconnected ways, then, even in these later, more general metaphysical and theological works, Stein consistently attends to what it means to be a person, whether it be in terms of the ontological structure of human nature and the dynamic unfolding of the human individual, or in terms of the interconnected network of interpersonal relations and the insertion of the individual subject into the natural world. Accordingly, when Stein receives the intellectual heritage of the Christian tradition and directly engages the thought of Aquinas and the Thomistic tradition, she does so by employing the methodological precision of phenomenology in tandem with her intensive and characteristic attention to the human person, personal subjectivity, and personal individuality.[9]

The Scope of the Present Study

The present study is focused on two of Stein's later works, *Finite and Eternal Being* (*Endliches und ewiges Sein*) and *The Structure of the Human Person* (*Der Aufbau der menschlichen Person*), though it includes supplementary reference to *Potency and Act* (*Potenz und Akt*)—the preparatory work that eventually became *Finite and Eternal Being*—while also drawing on other mature works as relevant to the themes analyzed. These texts are chosen because of their significance during the period of Stein's engagement with Aquinas and the considerable anthropological content contained in each. By analyzing these works, I intend to disclose, on the one hand, (1) how Stein's reception of Aquinas's metaphysical anthropology impacts her mature phenomenological personalism and, on the other hand, (2) how this very engagement leads to a phenomenological confirmation of certain key teachings of Thomistic anthropology. Accordingly, I begin each chapter by exploring how Stein assimilates teachings and principles of Aquinas and the Thomistic tradition to reveal the ways in which her understanding of the human person is strengthened and expanded. I complement this foundational exploration

---

9   Other works not mentioned here include shorter works on phenomenology and ontology, translations of Sts. John Henry Newman and Thomas Aquinas, an autobiographical sketch of life in a Jewish-German family, and various shorter spiritual texts, many of which are found listed in the appended bibliography. For a helpful overview of the characteristic interests, general shape, and progressive development of Stein's philosophy, see Mette Lebech, *The Philosophy of Edith Stein: From Phenomenology to Metaphysics* (Oxford: Peter Lang, 2015).

with an analysis of how Stein both explicates and develops the Thomistic teachings and principles she assimilates, while also noting any divergence from Aquinas and Thomism in her conclusions. Finally, I conclude the study by considering whether Stein can be read as a "Thomist" who presents a "Thomistic anthropology" or a "Thomistic personalism," or whether such identifiers would push her concordance with Aquinas too far while also obscuring the true character of her mature works.[10] Taken as a whole, the principal aim of the study is to manifest the precise range of conceptual agreement between Stein and Aquinas in Stein's mature anthropology, with a view to highlighting Stein's unique contribution to the *philosophia perennis* in the anthropological sphere—a contribution that is accomplished in its most defined form, I suggest, by Stein's focused attention to the human being as a personal subject in tandem with her continued use of the phenomenological method.[11]

Given the general domain of exploration, three areas present themselves as fruitful themes under which to examine Stein's thought—namely, human nature, the human individual, and the human being's relation to God, corresponding to parts I, II, and III, respectively. In these three interconnected spheres, a number of related questions guide the progression of the study, all of which can be grouped under the following more generalized forms:

---

10   This concluding review is important in view of properly assessing Stein's engagement with the Thomistic tradition, in order not to negatively evaluate her understanding of Thomistic anthropology, and in view of assessing the specific contribution she makes to this tradition, in order not to conflate her contribution with plain Thomistic commentary.

11   The term *philosophia perennis*, originating with the Vatican librarian Agostino Steuco and popularized by Gottfried Leibniz, was taken up by Neo-Scholasticism to classify the philosophy of the Western tradition extending from early Greek thought through its progressive synthesis with Christian thought, up to its culmination in the Scholastic period and eventual revitalization in the late modern period with Neo-Scholasticism. Among Neo-Scholastic thinkers the term typically designates the thought of high medieval Scholasticism and most often the thought of Aquinas and subsequent developments of the Thomistic tradition. For a brief history of the term *philosophia perennis* and its development, see Mark Juergensmeyer, *Encyclopedia of Global Religion* (New York: Sage, 2011), 986. Stein herself conceives of the *philosophia perennis* as a dynamic movement of thought that involves a rigorous intellectual investigation of the "meaning of being," an investigation she describes as a "procedure of uncovering the λόγος [*logos*]," and she finds this kind of philosophical procedure exemplified not only in the works of Aquinas and his many prior sources and later commentators but also in that of Husserl and certain other thinkers of the phenomenological movement. WP, 95; see also EES, 522; NFG, 85–87; and NFG, 159–60.

(1) How does Stein understand the teachings of Aquinas that she adopts, and what precisely of their conceptual content does she assimilate into her mature anthropology?

(2) How does Stein resolve problems she finds in the received teachings in order to integrate them into her own developed anthropology and personalism?

(3) Is the resulting conceptual fruit harmonious with or discordant to the Thomistic tradition?

(4) Does Stein provide any significant clarification and development of the teachings of Aquinas and Thomism?

(5) When Stein diverges from Aquinas in some way, what is the precise locus of disagreement that leads to different conclusions?

(6) Are the resulting conclusions squarely opposed to those of Aquinas and Thomism, or are there any openings toward their (at least partial) reconciliation?

(7) Does Stein's mature conception of the human person offer any comparative benefit in accounting for the human being over that of Aquinas and the standard Thomistic presentation?

This manner of "questioning" Stein's mature writings while also assessing their coherence with Thomistic thought represents an effort to think through Stein's engagement with Aquinas in order to reveal the precise range of agreement between their disparate positions, while also attending to outstanding disagreements before finally introducing various avenues toward their reconciliation. In just this way, I show how Stein's phenomenological understanding of the human person undergoes a foundational strengthening through her adoption and assimilation of Aquinas's metaphysical anthropology, and conversely how the Thomistic conception of the human person undergoes a significant deepening through Stein's phenomenological reconsideration of each teaching.

A Note on Method

The analysis of the Thomistic character of Stein's mature thought is rendered somewhat complex because of the immediate and obvious differences between Stein's and Aquinas's presentations of the human person. Both thinkers ascribe to distinct philosophical traditions, Stein to the phenomenological movement and Aquinas to medieval Scholasticism, respectively, with their work marked by this difference of traditions, the distinct languages used by each, coupled with

Introduction

a significant divergence of technical terminology developed and employed, and also by the time-separated historical periods in which each tradition flourished, with all the corresponding variations of culture, politics, and religion.[12] These many differences lead to two distinct ways of doing philosophy and to two characteristically different ways of approaching the question of the human person. Indeed, the distinction of phenomenology and Scholasticism is most evident in the diversity of methods employed, the phenomenological reduction versus Scholastic disputation.[13] Whereas the phenomenological reduction distinguishes itself by exploring the foundations of human knowing while striving to suspend

---

12   Though I here use the term "tradition," according to its general acceptance as a designator of disparate philosophical dispositions, postures, and methods, throughout the remainder of the study I tend to use the term "movement" in contrast to tradition or school, precisely since this term more readily captures the doctrinal fluidity of phenomenology while also appropriately designating the Thomistic school as a living tradition.

13   Stein understands and uses phenomenology in broad accord with the understanding and use of Husserl as it is found in his early thought and works, and particularly as it develops out of the *Logical Investigations*. See Edmund Husserl, *Logical Investigations*, 2 vols., trans. J. N. Findlay (New York: Routledge, 2001, repr. 2008). Though phenomenology can be defined broadly as the study or science of phenomena, its meaning and method is notoriously difficult to settle, both because the interpretation of Husserl and the development of his thought are themselves matters of controversy and because phenomenology is conceived of and practiced in widely different ways by its many interpreters and practitioners—first, as it developed throughout the twentieth century in such thinkers as Max Scheler, Martin Heidegger, Emmanuel Levinas, Jean-Paul Sartre, etc.; then, as it is differently employed in contemporary thought and academia, in philosophy itself and its many subdisciplines (epistemology, logic, ontology, etc.), and in other areas of contemporary teaching and research, from neuroscience to architecture, from literature to religion, etc.; and finally, as it became inextricably interwoven with hermeneutics and existentialism and increasingly began to inform cultural life and artistry. Given the expansive way phenomenology is envisioned, together with corresponding variations in the way its meaning and method are interpreted, I here constrain myself to the understanding and practice of Stein herself. As will become clear in what follows, this means that I take phenomenology to be a method for clarifying the structures of conscious experience (the essence of consciousness and its intentional acts) together with the objects given in conscious experience (the essences of the objects of consciousness given in intentional acts); moreover, in accord with Stein's understanding and practice, I do so with a clearly defined realist disposition, which disposition is well captured by the early phenomenological motto "back to the things themselves [*zurück zu den Sachen selbst*]." More detail regarding Stein's interpretation and use of phenomenology is given below in subsections of the "*Prolegomenon*: A Preparatory Analysis."

all prior philosophical commitments, both theoretical and practical, together with all existential judgements, the medieval Scholastic method was conducted within a well-defined framework of thought and practice, by privileging the debate of alternate philosophical and theological positions while continuing to hold a number of distinct philosophical and theological commitments. Accordingly, throughout the study I strive to take account of these many differences, particularly those related to method and language, while investigating and detailing the anthropological positions taken by each in order to manifest the actual coherence of understanding between the two while remaining respectful of their methodological and linguistic variance. Fortunately, this task is greatly simplified by the fact that Stein herself consciously attends to methodological concerns throughout her works and is consistent in identifying the defined senses of technical terms employed in their native languages. Therefore, in what follows, much of my own work will involve simply flagging these concerns when they arise and treating their consequents appropriately.

Two further methodological considerations deserve mention. In her later writings, Stein directly engages with Aquinas himself, reading many of his texts in their original Latin and performing a number of translations into German, as well as with many Thomistic commentators, reading and citing a number of prominent twentieth century Thomists, including Josef Gredt, Jacques Maritain, Gallus Manser, Étienne Gilson, and Marie-Dominique Roland-Gosselin. This twofold presence of Thomistic teaching in Stein's thought introduces a degree of complexity to examining Stein's engagement with Aquinas, with the consequence that this study necessarily involves parsing the various strands of thought in Stein's mature works, whether "Thomas" or "Thomistic," while being sensitive to Stein's dialogue with the Thomistic tradition.[14] To navigate this complexity, I focus my analysis on Stein's interpretation of Aquinas's teachings according to the particular texts she references and translates and in light of her engagement with the texts of particular Thomistic thinkers, and I will introduce other texts of Aquinas and further Thomistic scholarship only where it helpfully highlights areas of reconciliation when Stein's and Aquinas's positions contrast or conflict. Consideration must then also be made for the theological impact of the Catholic Christian faith on the philosophical investigations of Stein and Aquinas, since both can rightly be identified as "Christian philosophers,"

---

14   For more detail on Stein's recourse to Aquinas and later Thomistic authors, see "Stein's Historical Encounter with Aquinas and Thomism" in the "*Prolegomenon*" below.

Introduction

notwithstanding that this is true only of the mature Stein and that Aquinas identified as a theologian, with both exemplifying a considered synthesis of philosophical and theological reasonings in their works, even while each conceived somewhat differently of this synthesis. This synthesis of distinct disciplines is arguably most apparent in the anthropological sphere, insofar as certain Christian teachings have had and continue to have a profound impact on matters related to philosophical anthropology, most notably that of the doctrine of the Incarnation. Accordingly, throughout subsequent chapters, where appropriate, the theological commitments of Stein and Aquinas will be flagged and addressed, most often in footnotes.[15]

---

15   In her later works, Stein sets forth a philosophy that is positively Christian and specifically Catholic. The rationale behind her understanding rests on three interplaying factors—namely, the nature of philosophy as such, the nature and state of finite being in its relation to Divine Being, and the meaning of being a Christian. Stein argues that the guidance given by Christian Revelation not only secures philosophy from error, thus granting to theology a formal primacy in matters of truth, but also provides material insights that can become authentic sources of knowledge for an expanded reflection on the meaning of being, even to the point of including contents of Revelation naturally inaccessible to human reason. Though Aquinas and the Thomistic tradition more or less sharply delimit the proper spheres of philosophy and theology, committing to philosophy the lone task of elucidating being inasmuch as it is available to natural reason (i.e., reason unaided by the contents of Revelation), following the lead of Jacques Maritain in the ethical sphere, Stein maintains that philosophy in general lies interiorly open for its proper completion through supplementation by the data of Revelation, a completion that, Stein argues, is unavoidably foreshortened if philosophy remains hermetically sealed from Revelation. Stein further argues that such a Christian philosophy, though now no longer pure and independent of the Christian faith, retains its proper character as philosophy inasmuch as it is determined by its mode of investigation—which for her remains foundationally coordinated by the phenomenological method—and the intellectual intention of the thinker coupled with the intentional objects under investigation—that is, the world of experience as experienced, the beings given in experience, and the meaning of being therein encountered. For the purpose of the present study, I take a somewhat narrower stance than Stein on the question of the meaning of Christian philosophy and present it in a more traditionally Thomistic vein. Though I recognize that the Word of God has primacy for the Christian in all spheres of life, and that Revelation provides a guiding hand to philosophy, both through securing it from error and through clarifying its questions and investigations, I maintain that the philosophical fruit of the Christian philosopher should be wholly accessible to reason unaided by Revelation, even while I also recognize that it may well be greatly difficult to attain some such knowledge without the guidance of Revelation. I believe that this narrower stance secures the

Guide to the Present Study

In what immediately follows, I outline the path of analysis as it unfolds in the three subsequent parts—(I) Human Nature, (II) The Human Individual, and (III) The Human Being's Relation to God—and their closely paired chapters—(1) Point of Departure in the "Life of the I" and (2) Human Unity and Bodily Formation; (3) The Material Individual in General and (4) The Human Individual in Particular; and (5) Philosophical Knowledge of God and (6) The Personal Form of the Analogy of Being—in order to provide something of a guiding orientation through the study. Such guidance is needed because Stein's reception and assimilation of Aquinas's teachings proves to be a gradually developing picture, one where the same concepts, sets of concepts, and conceptual interconnections are gradually expanded and refined as the analysis progresses through each chapter. The key to this guide and the study itself, its predominant concept and coordinating principle, is that of the "personal I." This concept is the fruit of Stein's first-person phenomenological mode of approach to the human person, and it provides the guiding line of thought that weaves together the discrete analyses of each section, coordinating them as a unified and ordered whole with one central developing theme. A closely allied concept is that of "bearer," an absolutely crucial concept for Stein, which has its remote roots in her early phenomenological formation with its attention to consciousness, and later attains its fully developed significance in the anthropological sphere when it is forged together with her recourse to the metaphysics of Aquinas. When paired with the concept of personal I, the notion of bearer enables Stein to reveal the unique way the human individual relates to his personal being, both ontologically and actually, and thus also individually, while also grounding the analogical likeness relating all finite being to Eternal Being and the finite personal I to the Divine Personal I.

---

proper purity and autonomy of philosophy as a privileged sphere of common human investigation and communal dialogue, while also not closing the Christian philosopher to the superior light of Revelation and the corresponding guiding hand of grace. Indeed, the Christian submission of faith is perfectly consonant with philosophical investigation, in either the Steinian or Thomistic sense, insofar as the aim of philosophy is knowledge of first truth duly completed, while the virtue of Christian faith is assent to truth received from Truth in Person. For Stein's understanding of Christian philosophy, see esp. EES, 4–6, 31–36; and AMP, 27; and for a lengthier exposition and critique of the same, see Robert McNamara, "The Concept of Christian Philosophy in Edith Stein," in *American Catholic Philosophical Quarterly* 94, no. 2 (2020): 323–46.

In part I I explore Stein's engagement with Aquinas's teachings in the sphere of human nature in general. I here show that Stein begins by phenomenologically confirming the personal nature of the human being together with the composite structure of soul and living-body before seeking recourse to Aquinas's teachings to assist her in detailing the complex structure of this personal nature. The Thomistic teachings Stein adopts and integrates in this sphere are the so-called classical definition of the person as "an individual substance of a rational nature," and the closely interconnected teachings of the substantial unity of the human being and the rational soul's formation of the material body, together with their common hylomorphic foundation. With respect to each, Stein first assimilates crucial conceptual content before developing this same conceptual content through a phenomenological reconsideration of their meaning. This development is most evident in Stein's focus on the personal I as the root principle of personal being, in consequence of which she concludes that the personal I is the bearer of the rational nature and the dominant formal principle in the complex hylomorphic structure of human nature. Then, in some contrast to this fundamentally harmonious reception of Aquinas's teachings in the sphere of human nature, Stein's investigation of the human individual involves a substantial critique of the received teachings of Aquinas, which results in a now famous disagreement with Aquinas over the principle of material individuation. In part II I explore this critique by showing that while Stein's independent investigations lead to conclusions that expressly oppose those of Aquinas and the standard Thomist presentation, her mature understanding of the human individual remains situated against the backdrop of the broader conceptual apparatus of Aquinas and the Thomistic tradition. Indeed, I argue that Stein attains her contrasted conclusions by first arguing against the position of Aquinas on Thomistic grounds and according to Thomistic metaphysical principles before phenomenologically developing an original understanding of the "being-individual" and "qualitative individuality" of the human being—ultimately coming to understand both from the perspective of the personal I as bearer. In part III I proceed to analyze Stein's appropriation of the natural theology of Aquinas, first in terms of her summary acceptance of Aquinas's demonstrations of the existence and attributes of God, then in terms of her assimilation of the Thomistic conception of the analogy of being, here understood as an analogy of proportionality. With regard to each I show that while Stein assimilates the full conceptual content of these interconnected teachings, she simultaneously provides a personalistic reinterpretation of their meaning, one that places the personal in the foreground of our consideration of

God the Creator by unveiling the profound likeness of the human personal "I am" to the Divine Personal "I Am." I conclude this section by arguing that the relational import of this personalistic expansion of Thomistic natural theology is extensive, precisely inasmuch as the human person comes to be understood as the precise location of a profound personal encounter with the personal God.

These three analyses are prefixed by a more general analysis where I perform a preparatory exploration of a number of fundamental questions, which are presupposed to and encompass the subsequent anthropological analyses—namely, those relating to Stein's historical encounter with Aquinas, her subsequent philosophical engagement of Aquinas and Thomism, the relation of phenomenology and metaphysics in her mature thought, and the particular kind of metaphysical realism espoused by Stein in these later works.[16]

In all three areas of investigation—human nature, the human individual, and the human being's relation to God—I show that Stein first receives the teachings of Aquinas and the Thomistic tradition before gradually assimilating these teachings through an independent investigation of the human person in each domain. Though the greater part of Thomistic teachings so assimilated retain their basic conceptual content, notwithstanding certain notable disagreements, Stein also develops and deepens each teaching as they become integral parts of her own mature conception of the human person. This development and deepening is most clear in Stein's reconsideration of all teachings from the perspective of the personal subject. By placing the personal I in the foreground of her investigations, Stein phenomenologically reconsiders the received teachings from the vantage point of personal subjectivity, in such a way that the personal I becomes the coordinating lens through which the anthropological teachings of Aquinas are refocused. Accordingly, throughout the study, in an increasingly more fulsome manner, I propose that Stein's assimilation of the teachings of Aquinas is best understood as a fundamental "personalization" of these teachings. By refocusing all received teachings on the personal I as bearer, and by thereby highlighting the significance of personal subjectivity in human life, Stein significantly develops the meanings of the received teachings of Aquinas and the Thomistic tradition. Yet, she performs this development in a manner that possesses broad continuity with their adopted foundation, with the consequence that her personalization of Thomistic teachings can

---

16   Though these more general analyses are recommended to the reader, the anthropological and personalist focused reader may wish to proceed immediately to the anthropological analyses and use these more general analyses as reference points if needed.

arguably be understood as the fitting phenomenological completion of Aquinas's metaphysical anthropology. Accordingly, the analyses in this study progressively mount the case that Stein's engagement of Thomistic teachings in the area of anthropology should be understood as a successful entry into the broad stream of the *philosophia perennis*, in such a way that Stein can be understood to be someone who provides a significant and original contribution in the sphere of anthropology. In defending this position, I am also suggesting that Stein's phenomenological investigation of the person represents an important contribution to the Christian philosophical tradition, one that respects the philosophical (and theological) prominence of Aquinas and Thomism within this tradition, while also introducing further conceptual depth to its anthropological content.

Accordingly, I conclude the study by proposing that Stein can to a *limited degree* be read as a "Thomist" who presents a "Thomistic anthropology and personalism"; yet, inasmuch as her presentation goes beyond the conceptual content received from Aquinas, and inasmuch as it expressly challenges certain conclusions of the Thomistic tradition, I also recommend it would be better to describe her as a "Thomistically *informed* philosopher" who presents a "Thomistically *informed* anthropology and personalism," precisely so as not to misunderstand the special character of her mature anthropology and metaphysics, while also not misinterpreting the nature of her engagement with and interpretation of Aquinas and Thomism.[17]

---

17 For an overview of the strand of personalist thought identified as "Thomistic Personalism," see Thomas D. Williams, "What Is Thomistic Personalism?," in *Alpha Omega* 7, no. 2 (2004): 163–97; then, for a briefer presentation of its essential character, see Karol Wojtyła, "Thomistic Personalism," in *Person and Community: Selected Essays*, trans. Theresa Sandok (New York: Peter Lang, 1993, repr. 2008), 165–75; and for an example of a lengthier investigation arguably structured according to the same considerations, see Karol Wojtyła, *Person and Act: And Related Essays*, trans. Grzegorz Ignatik (Washington, DC: The Catholic University of America Press, 2021). As indicated in the preface, one can consider Stein's thought to be situated to some degree parallel to that of Wojtyła, first in terms of their shared philosophical formation in the phenomenological and Thomistic traditions of philosophy (and theology), as well as the Carmelite spiritual tradition, then in terms of their common philosophical orientation to the human person with priority, and finally in terms of their often comparable conclusions in anthropological and personalist matters, such that their contribution to the *philosophia perennis*, each in their own way, can be described as introducing conceptual depth of a personalist kind to the Thomistic metaphysical tradition.

PROLEGOMENON:
A Preparatory Analysis

> The reborn philosophy of the Middle Ages and the newly born philosophy of the twentieth century—can they flow together in the one riverbed of the *philosophia perennis*?
>
> —*Edith Stein*[1]

To properly ground Stein's engagement with Thomistic anthropology, it is first necessary to perform an analysis of Stein's engagement with Thomistic thought in general, as well as that of the broader tradition of the *philosophia perennis* as it developed in contact with the Christian faith and its theological doctrines. Indeed, as above intimated, Stein's conversion to Catholic Christianity so impressed her mature thought that one can reasonably divide her philosophical works into two periods, those predating her baptism and fundamentally characterized by her use of the phenomenological method, and those postdating her baptism and fundamentally characterized by the dialogue of Husserlian phenomenology and Thomistic Scholasticism.[2] In this introductory *prolegomenon* I examine the transformation wrought in Stein's philosophy through this transitional period by first briefly exploring the character of her historical encounter with the thought of Aquinas before analyzing the precise manner in which she engages the teachings of the Thomistic tradition. I conclude this section by outlining the relation of phenomenology to metaphysics

---

1   EES, 15.
2   Other scholars differently divide Stein's writings according to chronological and notional markers, and the division here given is not intended to exclude other such divisions; indeed, given the diversity of Stein's works, according to both spheres of investigation and coordinating philosophical methods, as well as the special circumstances of her personal life and religious profession, Stein's writings lend themselves to a number of (I would argue) complementary divisions.

in Stein's mature works, and the particular kind of metaphysical realism espoused by Stein in these same works, since both questions bear close relation to all subsequent anthropological analyses.

Stein's Historical Encounter with Aquinas and Thomism

In the early twentieth century Scholastic thought in general and Thomistic thought in particular experienced a powerful revival in Catholic academia, becoming a sphere of keen research and productive development. This was largely due to the endorsement of Pope Leo XIII in the encyclical *Aeterni patris* (1879) which commends the study of St. Thomas in Catholic educational institutes, together with a number of subsequent ecclesial recommendations in various documents bearing upon the study of philosophy and theology.[3] And so, after finding her initial footing in the simple practice of the Catholic faith, when Stein returns to philosophical investigation she turns her attention to searching out "the intellectual foundations of this world" and "almost as a matter of course [...] first seized on the writings of St. Thomas Aquinas."[4] In and through her encounter with the writings of Aquinas, we find in Stein a distinctively new stage of philosophical interest, development, and productivity. Given her prior formation in phenomenology—a formation that enduringly

---

3   As is clear from references in her later writings, Stein is aware of the ecclesial endorsement of Aquinas in papal documents that stress the foundational and normative character of his teaching and method for Catholic thinkers, both theological and philosophical. Stein explicitly relates familiarity with such ecclesial endorsements (in EES mentioning "decrees of Leo XIII and Pius XI," EES, 13) and not infrequently mentions these and other ecclesial documents in her later works, as well as referring to several Catholic teachings contained in the compendium of doctrinal declarations of Heinrich Denzinger. Given her mature assent to the Catholic faith, as well as her desire to engage in living dialogue with the Neo-Scholastic scholars of her day, this aspect of Stein's recourse to Aquinas is not without significance toward understanding the factors that influenced her mature works. See WIM, 173, 189, 204; BEI, 72–73, 76–78, 84, 141–42, 172; and DF, 130, 138, 143, 171–72, 184–85. See also Heinrich Denzinger et al., *Enchiridion symbolorum definitionum et declarationum de rebus fidei et morum* (1928).

4   EES, 3. Stein initially thought that conversion meant devoting herself entirely to things divine, but eventually came to understand that philosophical investigation could be done in the service of God, precisely inasmuch as the philosopher sets himself at the service of truth via scholarly research and teaching. Interestingly, Stein recounts that this realization "initially arose for [her] as appropriate through St. Thomas." SBB I, nos. 60, 86.

shapes her understanding—Stein's encounter with Aquinas and the Thomistic tradition meant that she experienced "an inner necessity" to bring these two "philosophical worlds" into fruitful "confrontation [*Auseinandersetzung*]."⁵ Stein was not satisfied to leave these philosophical worlds resting side-by-side in her mind and works, more or less compartmentalized and isolated from one another, but rather was motivated to bring them into dialogue so that she might examine the philosophical problems emerging from their encounter, and perhaps attain their suitable resolution. Indeed, as mentioned above, Stein eventually came to understand this confrontation to be the "proper task [*eigentliche Aufgabe*]" of her mature philosophical vocation, her self-described "mission in life [*Lebensaufgabe*]."⁶

Moreover, Stein recognized that a potentially fruitful alliance of phenomenology and Scholasticism was not simply an undertaking of personal interest but "dominated philosophical life and was felt by many as an inner need."⁷ Like a number of her contemporaries, Erich Przywara included, Stein was conscious of a significant rupture running through modern thought with its defined epistemological interests, and the tradition of the *philosophia perennis* with its defined attention to being—and, consequently, between modern philosophy and the revivified instantiation of Scholasticism in twentieth century Neo-Scholasticism.⁸ This sundering of modern thought from its medieval and

---

5 PA, 3–5; EES, 3–4.

6 SBB I, nos. 130, 245, 151–52, 269–72. See also PA, 3–5; and EES, 3–4. The German "*Auseinandersetzung*," here translated as "confrontation," is a somewhat richer term in the German original; while literally meaning "set opposite one another," it encompasses a semantic range that includes examination, argument, and discussion. See also Mary Catherine Baseheart, *The Encounter of Husserl's Phenomenology and the Philosophy of St. Thomas in Selected Writings of Edith Stein* (unpublished doctoral thesis, University of Notre Dame, 1960), ii–v.

7 EES, 4; see also SBB III, nos. 89, 157–559. It is plausible that encouragement for her engagement with Aquinas came from Erich Przywara, a Catholic priest and philosopher with whom she shared a particularly strong desire for the rapprochement of modern and Scholastic philosophies.

8 While on the surface this rupture appears to be related to the different philosophical focal points of modern and medieval thought—that of the question of knowledge versus the question of being—Stein proposes that the divergence of modern philosophy from the *philosophia perennis* has deeper roots in the more or less "complete separation of modern philosophy from revealed truth," coupled with a disregard for the philosophical concept of God as Creator, all of which means, for Stein, that modern philosophy has become "to a large extent a godless discipline" (EES, 13).

ancient roots presented a serious difficulty for Stein, since she sensed that such an unmooring of "the living thought of the present" unnecessarily foreshortened philosophical investigation and narrowed the horizons of human knowledge. Her response was to attempt to bridge the gap between the "the reborn philosophy of the middle ages and the newly born philosophy of the twentieth century," all the while motivated by the question of how they might run together in the "one riverbed of the *philosophia perennis*," and she described this task as an "endeavor to achieve a consolidation of medieval thought with the living thought of the present."[9] As a result, all major philosophical works penned after her conversion are conditioned by the encounter of phenomenology and Scholasticism, and they represent a living expression of this same encounter. Though Stein certainly recognized that Aquinas and Scholasticism could not simply be equated, and neither could Thomas and Thomism, she gave pride of place to the thought of Aquinas within the Scholastic philosophical tradition, as did the Neo-Scholastic philosophers with whom she entered into dialogue.[10] Indeed, Stein discovered in Aquinas's writings ready access to "the three great intellectual currents" that "shaped occidental thought in the Middle Ages"—namely, those of Aristotle, St. Augustine, and Pseudo-Dionysius—and claimed that in "the life's work of St. Thomas Aquinas, the effects of these three currents are clearly visible and perhaps have not exercised a greater influence on later times in any other way [than through the synthesis of Aquinas]."[11]

---

9   EES, 4, 15.
10 See GT I, 204; and NFG, 119n1. The Neo-Scholastic scholars of Stein's day also privileged the thought of Francisco Suárez (Suarezism) and Bl. John Duns Scotus (Scotism), and Stein's engagement with Aquinas was not in isolation from these and other thinkers of the Christian philosophical tradition. Among others, Stein most frequently engages St. Augustine and Pseudo-Dionysius, while also referring to the ancients presupposed of this tradition, Plato and Aristotle, as well as their medieval Muslim commentators, Avicenna (Ibn Sīnā) and Averroes (Ibn Rushd). The predominance of the thought of Aquinas in Stein's mature works is (at least partially) confirmed by her frequent citation of Aquinas; in EES, PA, and AMP, as listed in the indices of each work in their Herder critical edition, Aquinas is cited a total of 109 times, and according to an electronic word search is referred to a total of 334 times; whereas the same tallies for other frequently cited authors are the following (in order of quantity): Aristotle: 80, 227; Augustine: 33, 53; Conrad-Martius: 28, 38; Husserl: 55, 49; and Scotus: 10, 11.
11 WGE, 22. For the mature Stein, this ready access to the intellectual tradition of Western thought, carefully sifted and synthesized by Aquinas, represents a valuable resource for her engagement with Christian philosophy (and theology) in general, precisely

Prolegomenon: A Preparatory Analysis   xliii

As is evident from her later writings, Stein has profound respect for Aquinas, describing him as "a man who had received an extraordinary faculty of understanding as his pound from God," so as "to become one of the greatest guides" in the life of the mind, with the result that she gave herself over to his masterly guidance as "a reverent and willing pupil."[12] In an illuminating excerpt of *Potency and Act* (*Potenz und Akt*), Stein says, "One feels oneself at the hands of a guide who is very sure of his way. Credibility is guaranteed by the abundance of results that are obtained in following this way, solutions to problems that upfront bear the stamp of truth, and which then prove fruitful by casting light on whole areas—theoretical and practical—that initially lay in darkness."[13] But, having no prior formal education in Thomistic philosophy, or indeed in Scholasticism more broadly, Stein acknowledged that she was at a disadvantage in her attempt to accomplish this weighty undertaking.[14] Notwithstanding this insufficiency, Stein immersed herself in Thomistic philosophy and progressively assumed the burden of its resolution with phenomenology, all in the modest hope that her effort might provide incentive to others to engage more expansively in this same undertaking.[15] And so, in the later part of the 1920s, Stein began her direct and thorough study of the thought of Aquinas, first with the more properly philosophical genre of his works, the *Quaestiones disputatae*, and initially through the provision of an annotated translation cum philosophical transposition of the *Quaestiones disputatae de veritate*, published in two volumes as *Des Hl. Thomas von Aquino Untersuchungen über die Wahrheit* (1932), and through a similarly interpretive translation of *De ente et essentia*, published as *Über das Seiende und das Wesen* (1932).[16] Together with these substantial translation tasks,

---

      inasmuch as it provides her with a well-prepared and systematic means to access the wide riverbed of the *philosophia perennis*.

12   BEI, 156; and EES, 3.

13   PA, 3.

14   In a letter to the Dominican Provincial, Fr. Laurentius Siemer, after receiving his critique of her translation of QDV, Stein humbly admits, "How little I know Thomism, no one knows better than I" (SBB II, nos. 345, 366), and she elsewhere explains that were she twenty years younger she "would start from the bottom up with the study of philosophy and theology" (SBB I, nos. 206, 224).

15   Stein describes EES as a work "written by a learner for fellow learners." EES, 3.

16   Stein's "translations" of QDV and DEE are more like interpretive commentaries in a contemporary philosophical key than faithful translations of the plain meaning of the texts, and she renders QDV in a contemporary style of straight prose rather than as

both of which involved transposing Aquinas's medieval mode of proceeding into the mode of discourse of modern philosophy, Stein produced a number of major philosophical works directly engaging the thought of Aquinas and the Thomistic tradition—namely, the short but significant fictional dialogue, *Was ist Philosophie? Ein Gespräch zwischen Edmund Husserl und Thomas von Aquino* (1929), followed by the treatises, *Potenz und Akt* (1931), *Der Aufbau der menschlichen Person* (1932), and, her magnum opus, *Endliches und ewiges Sein* (1936–37). Stein closely studied many other works of Aquinas, including the following, *Quaestiones disputatae de anima*, *Super Boetium De Trinitate*, *In librum Beati Dionysii De divinus nominibus expositio*, *Quaestiones disputatae de potentia*, *Quaestio disputata de spiritualibus creaturis*, *Summa contra gentiles*, and *Summa theologiae*.[17] She was also familiar with the works of a number of significant twentieth-century Thomistic scholars—namely, Josef Gredt, *Die aristotelisch-thomistische Philosophie*, volumes 1 and 2, also in the Latin original, *Elementa philosophiae Aristotelico-Thomistiscae*, Martin Grabmann, *Die Kulturphilosophie des hl. Thomas von Aquin* and *Die Werke des hl. Thomas von Aquin*, Gallus Manser, *Das Wesen des Thomismus*, Marie-Dominique Roland-Gosselin, *Le "De ente et essentia" de saint Thomas d'Aquin*, as well as those of Jacques Maritain, *De la philosophie chrétienne*, and Étienne Gilson, *Le Thomisme. Introduction au Système de Saint Thomas d'Aquin*.[18]

---

a series of disputed questions with objections and responses. This has perfect accord with Stein's manner of engaging the thought of Aquinas as a living tradition and her attempt to understand him from the perspective of contemporary philosophy rather than simply recounting his thought according to the mode of historical philosophy and philosophical exegesis.

17 See Thomas Aquinas, *In librum Beati Dionysii De divinus nominibus expositio* (Rome: Marietta, 1950); QDA; QDP; QDSC; SCG; and ST.

18 See Josef Gredt, *Die aristotelische-thomistische Philosophie*, 2 vols. (Freiburg i. Br.: Herder, 1935); Latin original: *Elementa philosophiae Aristotelico-Thomisticae* (Freiburg i. Br.: Herder, 1929); Martin Grabmann, *Die Kulturphilosophie des hl. Thomas von Aquin* (Augsburg: B. Filsner, 1925); *Die Werke des hl. Thomas von Aquin* (Münster, Westfalen: Aschendorffsche, 1931); Gallus M. Manser, *Das Wesen des Thomismus* (Fribourg: Divus Thomas Jahrbuch für Philosophie und spekulative Theologie, 1924); Marie-Dominique Roland-Gosselin, *Le "De ente et essentia" de saint Thomas d'Aquin* (Paris: Librairie philosophique J. Vrin, 1948); Jacques Maritain, *De la philosophie chrétienne* (Louvain: Revue Philosophique de Louvain, 1932); and Étienne Gilson, *Le Thomisme. Introduction au Système de Saint Thomas d'Aquin* (Paris: Nouvelle édition revue et augmentée, 1922).

Stein's Philosophical Engagement with Aquinas and Thomism

Stein sees in medieval Scholasticism "not a rigid and immutable doctrinal system, but a highly mobile, intellectual life, with tensions, contradictions, and struggles," something regarded as true by Stein both with respect to its objective reality as a developed system of thought and with respect to its actual practice by her Neo-Scholastic contemporaries.[19] Consequently, when she engages the thought of Aquinas and Thomism, she does not do so as if it were "a finished conceptual system" but rather as it really is, "a living intellectual structure," which must be "inwardly appropriated and gain new life within" if it is to be appropriated in a properly philosophical way.[20] In terms of accomplishing this task, Stein recognizes that *the question of being* stands at the center, stating, "The confrontation between Thomistic and phenomenological thought takes place in the objective treatment of *this* question," the question of "the *meaning* of being."[21] Stein also recognizes the centrality of being in the philosophy of Aquinas, saying, "As a core inventory of the Thomistic organon, we may well regard the idea of being [*Sein* (Latin: *esse*)] and the basic forms according to which it is determined."[22] And in the earlier mentioned fictional dialogue between Aquinas and Husserl, "*Was ist Philosophie?*," Stein has Aquinas say, "Foundationally, all questions are reduced to questions of being [*Seinsfragen*], and all philosophical disciplines become parts of a great ontology or metaphysics."[23] Given this recognized centrality of being, and notwithstanding its controversial character in phenomenology and its practitioners, in addition to her repeated disagreements with Husserl over this very question, Stein places being at the center of her mature investigations and inward appropriation of Thomistic thought.

However, as a result of her characteristic intellectual integrity, coupled with her understanding of the nature of philosophy, Stein is not content with a naïve assumption and transmission of the thought of Aquinas, nor is she satisfied

---

19   DF, 226, referring to the systems of both St. Thomas Aquinas and St. Albert the Great. See also EES, 3–8; WGE, 22; and SBB III, nos. 89, 157–59.
20   EES, 14.
21   EES, 4, emphasis added; and EES, 490. See also Baseheart, *Phenomenology and the Philosophy of St. Thomas*, 117–20, 123–26, esp. 138–39.
22   PA, 7.
23   WP, 104.

to simply compare and contrast the philosophical positions of Aquinas and Thomism with those of contemporary philosophers, as may be adequate for an historian of philosophy. Rather, she is determined to inwardly appropriate the received philosophical heritage by performing an *objective treatment* of being while intellectually grappling with the received tradition of Aquinas.[24] In *Potency and Act* Stein clarifies the rationale behind the need for such a treatment, there saying,

> The philosopher must not only be able to see and show *that* another has proceeded in such and such a way; he must not only have insight into the connections from the grounds to the conclusions; rather, he must *grasp why* it is so. He must go down to the grounds themselves and grasp *them*; this is to be seized and overcome by the grounds, to decide for them and inwardly retrace the path from grounds to conclusions, and possibly go even further than his predecessor; or, to overcome them, that is to break through to freedom from [the grounds and conclusions] and choose another way.[25]

This quotation indicates something of the core meaning of philosophical investigation for Stein and the fundamental orientation required of the philosopher when attempting to appropriate any inherited intellectual tradition. The philosopher must seek a living encounter with the matters under investigation so as to achieve a comprehensive and penetrating grasp of the *why* of the field of investigation, even when this encounter is conceptually mediated by insights received from other philosophers and other philosophical traditions. Such is the proper mode of approach for the philosopher *qua* philosopher, and such is the proper mode of approach for an *objective* investigation, with the consequence that Stein consistently follows this process in her engagement with Aquinas and Thomism. This is the path "toward a living encounter with the minds [*Geister*] of the past, and to the insight that beyond all times and barriers that separate peoples and schools, there is something common shared

---

24 Angela Ales Bello presents a similar picture of the way Stein engages with the thought of Aquinas while also noting the respect Stein has for Aquinas's thought. See Angela Ales Bello, "Thomas von Aquino in Edith Steins Interpretation," in *The Hat and the Veil: The Phenomenology of Edith Stein*, Ad Fontes: Studien zur frühen Phänomenologie, 3, ed. Jerzy Machnacz et al. (Nordhausen: Traugott Bautz, 2016), 15–25: 15–17, 24–25.

25 PA, 4.

by all those who sincerely seek the truth."²⁶ Stein concludes the above indented paragraph saying, "To be overcome by the 'grounds' of St. Thomas would mean to capture or seize him philosophically for ourselves. To overcome the grounds [of St. Thomas] would mean to 'be finished' with him philosophically." As will become clear, Stein both "overcomes" and "is overcome" by Aquinas, she is both "conqueror" and "conquered," so that she never simply "finishes" with his thought and that of the Thomistic tradition. Rather, she enters into an ongoing transhistorical dialogue of give-and-take with Aquinas's teachings and those of the Thomistic tradition, even while eventually coming to disagree with him and the standard Thomistic position on certain decisive points.

To achieve the appropriate philosophical clarity required for such an objective treatment, Stein continues to employ the phenomenological method introduced by Husserl and describes the "elementary principle of the phenomenological method" as the "unmediated intuition" of the objects of experience so as "to grasp in one's gaze *the things themselves* [die Sachen selbst *ins Auge fassen*]."²⁷ Stein chooses phenomenology because attending to things as they are given in experience provides the requisite focus on objects that makes possible an objective treatment. Since phenomenology attends to phenomena as the primary given of experience—that feature of experience in which things appear for consciousness and thereby become objects available for cognition, volition, etc.—it enables the practitioner to remain deeply oriented toward the world of objects precisely as they are given in experience. When used in a phenomenological context, experience simply means *undergoing* (*erfahren*) or *living through* (*erleben*) something or other, and when further qualified by consciousness this undergoing and living through includes spiritual or intellectual (*geistige*) life, irrespective of whether this be cognitive, volitional, or affective.²⁸ Typically, both dimensions, the undergoing and the living through, are significant for consciousness, since both are ordinarily

---

26 EES, 4.
27 AMP, 28; see also PA, 4–5; EES, 19–20; and compare Husserl, *Investigations*, 1:168, and also his "Foreword to the Second Edition," 4. For more on a phenomenological understanding of intuition, and indications of its closeness to a Thomistic understanding of abstraction, see below, liin41, livn44, and for more on the phenomenological method itself and its relation to Scholasticism, see the immediately next section, "The Relation of Phenomenology and Metaphysics."
28 The English "experience" translates the German "*Erfahrung*" (noun) or "*erfahren*" (verb)—literally "undergoing" or "to undergo"—and "*Erlebnis*" (noun) or "*erleben*" (verb)—literally "living through" or "to live through."

included in experience, even while some bodily and psychic experiences (i.e., bodily and psychic states) are undergone by the subject without having any lived-through aspect. In tandem with Aquinas, Stein recognizes that conscious experience has its foundation in the senses and sense experience, where the senses are understood to provide the foundational data of conscious experience even while not all succeeding contents of knowledge take the warrant for their validity from the senses and sense experience.[29] And since consciousness is found *to tend toward* the objective world in sense experience, an essential feature of experience is its intentionality, where intentionality is understood to be the defining feature of consciousness, which "picks out" particular objects, in determinate ways, with determinate senses—corresponding to the objects consciously intended, the intending acts of consciousness, together with the intentional significance of such objects for the conscious subject.[30]

Yet notwithstanding this ongoing recourse to phenomenology, Stein does not continue with the phenomenological method without introducing certain significant adjustments, and she comes to characterize her use of the method as "phenomenology (in my modification)."[31] This modification bears reference first, I suggest, to Stein's recognition of the independent actuality of the world of experience, as a natural or real world, since "genuine analysis of the givenness of reality leads to the suspension of the transcendental reduction and to a return to the attitude of the believing acceptance of the natural

---

29 See below, lxvi–lxvii.
30 Intentionality is absolutely central to Husserlian phenomenology and can be broadly understood as the object directedness of conscious experience, where consciousness is understood to intend an object (thing, person, event, state of affairs, etc.) in a determinate kind of conscious act (perceiving, imagining, judging, believing, etc.) with a determinate sense (as Venus, Morning Star, Evening Star, etc.). The phenomenological use of intentionality comes to Husserl remotely from Scholasticism—though not without significant modification—via Franz Brentano, who conceived of intentionality as the demarcating feature of the mental through the inexistence (*Inexistenz*) of objects in the mental subject. For a history of Husserl's reception of intentionality from Brentano, see James C. Morrison, "Husserl and Brentano on Intentionality," in *Philosophy and Phenomenological Research* 31, no. 1 (1970): 27–46.
31 SBB I, nos. 163, 181. Stein recognizes that it was also providentially helpful to take a break from the practice of phenomenology before setting out on this task, so as "to win the necessary distance […] in order to consider the phenomenological method with critical eyes," and remarks that she "earlier handled [the method] far too naively." SBB III, nos. 89, 158.

world."[32] The just-mentioned "transcendental reduction" (interchangeable with "phenomenological reduction") is a methodological device employed by phenomenology to effect a withdrawal from the "natural attitude," understood as that attitude maintained in everyday life and experience (as well as in the practice of the natural sciences), with a corresponding entry into the "phenomenological attitude," understood as that attitude deemed appropriate for the philosopher as such. This latter attitude draws the philosopher back from his natural immersion in the world so that he can reflectively attend to what is immediately given in experience, just as it is given—that is, to what is *immanent* in consciousness as such—and thus disclose the essential structures of consciousness together with the essences of the objects given in experience.[33] Accordingly, the phenomenological attitude involves applying the phenomenological *epoché* (ἐποχή), which involves *bracketing* and *suspending* prior knowledge judgments, including existential judgments, so that nothing inhibits, overlays, or obscures the philosopher's immediate first-person engagement with the phenomena. However, as the quotation above implies, Stein applies the *epoché* and enters the phenomenological attitude via the reduction only to furnish the focused and unbiased objectivity required for an objective investigation, before then opening the brackets that suspend judgement in a return to the experienced world as existentially announced—together with all other reasonably held prior knowledge commitments.[34]

With respect to Stein's engagement with the thought of Aquinas and Thomism in particular, Stein's modification bears reference to her understanding that the phenomenologist can have recourse to insights received from thinkers

---

32 NFG, 108. See also, PA, 16–18; and Baseheart, *Phenomenology and the Philosophy of St. Thomas*, 117–20.

33 For the sake of simplicity and consonant with traditional English usage, I use the masculine form of pronouns in their general human reference (to all human individuals regardless of sex determination) throughout the book.

34 Though the *epoché* involves the suspension of all kinds of knowledge judgments, those theoretical, practical, causal, historical, etc., I attend at first only to the question of existential judgments since I regard this as Stein's most important modification of the phenomenological method, whereas below I proceed to show that Stein applies the suspension of other knowledge judgments only in a qualified way while they undergo their testing via the phenomenological method before returning to their acceptance, even if now appropriately adjusted or corrected. The question of Stein's embrace of philosophical realism and its relation to her practice of phenomenology is treated in greater detail immediately below. See lxvi ff.

outside the phenomenological tradition in order to supplement his own investigations. This openness to extra-phenomenological thinkers is grounded in the nature of philosophy, coupled with the way philosophy has been practiced throughout the ages in the *philosophia perennis*, both of which Stein argues have a distinctively phenomenological character. Indeed, she maintains that the phenomenological method is basic to philosophy itself and methodologically determinative of philosophical investigation, precisely insofar as philosophy is grounded in conscious experience and seeks comprehensive knowledge of what is given in experience. Consequently, Stein contends that phenomenology has been practiced by all "great philosophers" throughout the ages, even if its practitioners did not have explicit awareness of the precise nature of the method, or indeed to the exclusion of other appropriate methods of investigation.[35] Such engagement with other thinkers and their philosophical produce is also consistent with Stein's understanding of the intersubjective constitution of objects, where constitution is understood by phenomenology to be the way in which objects are disclosed for conscious subjects in and through the synthesizing activity of consciousness. In acts of constitution the conscious subject, so to speak, "unpacks" the contents of experience by disclosing the experiential unities of meaning contained in experience, thereby rendering the various objects of experience from the most basic contents of the stream of experience. However, though consciousness is thus involved in rendering its own intentional objects, constitution should not be understood as something constructive, where objects would be taken to conform to consciousness and its constitutive activities, but rather as something fundamentally *disclosive* and *receptive*, where consciousness is taken to receptively conform to its objects even while actively engaged in disclosing their meaning.

And since the activity of constitution is not performed in isolation from other conscious subjects or from the common life of society, Stein argues that the objective world is constituted, at least partially, through the common

---

35 See AMP, 28. See also, Christof Betschart, *Unwiederholbares Gottessiegel: Personale Individualität nach Edith Stein* (Basel: Reinhardt, 2013), 201–2. Presenting phenomenology in this way is simply highlighting the unencumbered precision and focused objectivity of the phenomenological method, as that methodical apparatus that makes it possible to detail the objective content of experience, fully and comprehensively, without prior and presupposed judgments, and/or without any related conceptual prejudices.

orientation of multiple subjects to what is experienced.[36] This collective effort of intersubjective constitution enables a plurality of subjects to understand the world together with one another through their common orientation to the experienced world alongside one another. Such an understanding of the intersubjectivity of constitution (together with her just-mentioned understanding of the universality of the phenomenological method) naturally impacts Stein's practice of philosophy as an objective science and undergirds her interest in "working together" with the insights and teachings of other philosophers and their philosophical traditions—including those of Aquinas and the Thomistic tradition.[37] And so, upon the foundation of these three interconnected modifications of the phenomenological method— the recognized actuality of the natural world, the (essential) relation of the phenomenological method to philosophy, and the corresponding intersubjective constitution of objects—Stein allows herself to be guided by Aquinas and Thomism in her mature philosophical investigations without thereby divesting these investigations of their focused objectivity, and without depriving the phenomenological method of its proper rigor and thoroughness.

The philosophical insights and teachings of Aquinas and Thomism Stein engages can be generically captured under the terminology of conceptual

---

36   See Lebech, *Phenomenology to Metaphysics*, 19–21, 134–38. I note here that this insight of the role of intersubjectivity in the constitution of the objective is found already in the thought of Husserl, and becomes especially apparent in his later writings.

37   Of the kind of collective philosophical enterprise in which Stein was engaged, Francesco Alfieri notes: "[Husserl's] pupils, which included Hedwig Conrad-Martius, Alexander Pfänder, Max Scheler, Jean Hering, Alexandre Koyré, Gerda Walther etc., were forged in this collective spirit, which shaped their way of working to the point that it enabled them—particularly Stein and Conrad-Martius—to follow the principle of *epoché* and phenomenological reduction with regard to 'archaeological excavations' that were not directed, as in Husserl, purely and exclusively toward the vastness of the Transcendental Ego, but also toward the contributions of the medieval tradition." Francesco Alfieri, "The Presence of Duns Scotus in the Thought of Edith Stein: The Question of Individuality," trans. George Metcalf, in *Analecta Husserliana*, 120 (Cham: Springer, 2015), eBook, 3. Though the intersubjective constitution of objects here detailed is understood by Stein as something primordial to conscious experience and cannot simply be equated with the higher-order intellectual activity involved in sharing philosophical concepts, propositions, and arguments, Stein's understanding of intersubjectivity evidently shapes her understanding of the whole philosophical enterprise, naturally leading to a complementary understanding of the intersubjectivity of human knowing and knowledge itself. I am thankful to Josef Seifert for pointing out this important distinction.

apparatus (*Begriffsapparat*) or conceptual-methodological apparatus (*begrifflich-methodischen Apparat*).[38] Stein uses these and coordinate terms to designate the particular conceptual toolset of basic concepts, sets of concepts, and conceptual interconnections produced by a philosopher or philosophical tradition to identify and define a particular sphere of investigation. With this terminology Stein expressly describes the conceptual content of the philosophy of Aquinas and Thomism, as well as that of Aristotle inasmuch as his thought was adopted by Aquinas and other Christian thinkers in the thirteenth century. Stein understands concepts and conceptual interconnections to be products of the human mind and a medium through which the things themselves and their interrelations are grasped by the knowing subject. The concept, she says, "is a purely theoretical structure, i.e., its task is to grasp objects with understanding."[39] Through concept formation the act of intellectual apprehension through which an object is experienced is completed in the intellectual "taking hold" of the object, where the object already apprehended comes to be understood in some or other determinate way without thereby annulling the possibly ongoing apprehension of the experienced object. And since concept formation is possible not only with respect to discrete objects but also with respect to the objective order of an interconnected complex of objects, the conceptual fruit of such a grasp lies open to its own arrangement in correspondence to the objective order of being.[40] The interconnected set of concepts with their manifold of conceptual interconnections is then identified as a conceptual apparatus (or conceptual-methodological apparatus), understood as the intellectual toolkit through which a sphere of philosophical investigation is coherently identified, disclosed, and explicated. Such apparatuses can then be signified in words and become the common intellectual medium of a plurality of conscious subjects and the basis of a shared conceptual grasp of the experienced world, thereby forming an intellectual community with its own intellectual heritage.[41]

---

38 AMP, 27; SBB III, nos. 81, 147–48; DF, 206–7; KDS, 18–19; and WIM, 10. Stein also uses this terminology to designate the conceptual toolsets of other philosophers. See LJF, 140–41.
39 PA, 95.
40 See PA, 21–22, 95, 98–99; and AMP, 21–22.
41 Stein's understanding of concept formation largely corresponds to that of Aquinas. For Aquinas, the foundation of all intellectual operation is the reception of the intelligible species (*species intelligibilis*) of the actual or imagined object. The intellect first receives the intelligible impress of the cognized object—called the impressed species (*species impressa*) by later Scholastics—before this intelligible impress becomes the formal

Yet, since concepts are products of the human intellect that approximate the objective world more or less accurately, every conceptual apparatus takes greater or lesser hold of the objects it identifies and seeks to disclose and explicate. Stein says, "The concept which the human individual forms is aimed at the ideal concept [...] but remains more or less behind it through incompleteness and perhaps also through falsehood"; and again, "Everyone has his 'conceptual

---

principle of the further intellectual operation of concept formation—producing the corresponding expressed species (*species expressa*). Both impressed and expressed species are identified with the intelligible species since both are that whereby the intellect apprehends the actual or imagined object, even though both play different and complementary roles in the act of understanding, with the former revealing the intellect's receptivity to the object, and the latter manifesting the intellect's productivity according to which the object is finally grasped in understanding (either as an individual whole, or according to various formal aspects or notions found in the thing, such as those of genera of various degrees of generality or proximity, etc.). Aquinas variously identifies the produced concept as the mental word (*verbum mentis*), interior word (*verbum interius*), or word of the heart (*verbum cordis*), since the concept as inner word is precisely that through which understanding is attained and intellectual operation duly completed in the expression of understanding. Concepts can then be joined or divided through intellectual acts of judgment and expressed in propositions that either simply posit the actuality of objects known via their concepts, or represent conceptual interconnections patterned after the objects cognized. Finally, the interior word can become the exemplar formal cause of the exterior word (*verbum exterius*) of human speech, also called the voiced word (*verbum vocis*), and it is through the voiced word that concepts and conceptual interconnections, with all their undergirding judgments, including existential judgments, are ordinarily communicated by the knowing subject to other knowing subjects (and, of course, via other forms of bodily expression, such as sign language and written script). Interestingly, like Stein, Aquinas describes the concept or interior word as "like an instrument [*sicut instrumento*]" of the intellect in the act of understanding—and so, something like an apparatus—though he is at pains to clarify that the concept is a formal rather than instrumental sign, precisely since the concept has an essentially signifying character with respect to the known object according to its intentional mode of being and intelligible content. For Aquinas's understanding of concept formation, see esp. QDV, 1.3; 1.12, co; 4.1; ST, I, 34.1, ad 1; I, 107.1, co; SCG, 4.11, nos. 8–19; and Quodl, 5.5.2; and for a Thomistic presentation of the same, see Joseph Owens, *An Elementary Christian Metaphysics* (Milwaukee, WI: Bruce, 1963; repr. Houston: Center for Thomistic Studies, 1986, repr. 2013), 234–59; Jacques Maritain, *Degrees of Knowledge*, trans. Gerald B. Phelan (Notre Dame, IN: University of Notre Dame Press, 1998, repr. 2014), 122–36; and William W. Meissner, "Some Aspects of the *Verbum* in the Texts of St. Thomas," in *The Modern Schoolman* 36 (1958): 1–30.

world' that can be more or less congruent with the actual [world], but also with the 'world of ideal concepts' and with the conceptual worlds of others."[42] Accordingly, Stein reasons that any given conceptual apparatus admits of further degrees of clarification and development—or indeed, adjustment and amendation—in view of providing a more fitting conceptual grasp of the experienced world. Such clarification and development is realized when concepts are reformulated so they possess greater precision and depth, which precision and depth is evident in the greater intellectual "illumination" of the object domain grasped by the given apparatus. Hence, when Stein receives the conceptual apparatuses of Aquinas and Thomism—as well as that of other philosophers and thinkers, Christian and non-Christian alike—they remain for her "always only a starting point for an objective consideration [*sachliche Erörterung*]."[43] She reasons that the adoption of a given conceptual inheritance, even that of a trusted and endorsed source like Aquinas, requires an objective investigation if it is to be appropriated in a properly philosophical manner and remain fitting philosophical heritage for transmission to future generations. Thus, for Stein, as explained above, the philosophically appropriate mode of adoption is achieved by objective investigation performed in tandem with the received apparatus. If through such an investigation the reformulation of a particular concept or conceptual interconnection proves necessary, the conceptual apparatus is not left undisturbed but is rather reconfigured and/or revised accordingly.[44]

---

42   EES, 96.
43   EES, 4. Stein also indicates that a particular conceptual apparatus can hamper the absorption of something new, and thus limit and obscure one's understanding of the experienced world. See SBB III, nos. 81, 147–48.
44   Like Stein, Aquinas recognizes that concept formation is fallible. Although he considers the foundation of concept formation in the impressed species to be something reliable or trustworthy (meaning a faithful reception of the object experienced inasmuch as the senses have faithfully given the object, which senses have their own inbuilt faithfulness with respect to their proper objects), since the formation of concepts and their related judgments are productive acts of the intellect, the intellect can err in its conceptualization and formulation of propositions, especially as it advances further in knowledge beyond the immediate content given in and through the impressed species. The Scholastic distinction between the formal concept—the conceptual content of the act of the intellect intending the object—and the objective concept—the comprehensive conceptual content of the actual object represented by the formal concept—can then be understood to parallel Stein's recognition of the actual (and, by

One can understand this as a process of phenomenologically "testing" the received apparatus in view of its validation or falsification, whether this validation or falsification be complete or only partial. Such testing is performed by returning to the things themselves as they are given in experience according to what phenomenology calls *eidetic intuition* and *variation*.[45] Eidetic intuition or essence-viewing (*Wesensschauen*) is the intellectual "beholding" of the object given in perception or imaginative presentation with a view to gaining insight into its essential structure by attending only to what is necessary in the intuited object.[46] Eidetic intuition is advanced by eidetic variation when the intellect systematically places before itself a number of varied exemplars of the object under consideration, most often through variation of the features of the object. This process gradually bears fruit by bringing greater intuitive clarity to the necessary features of the essence while simultaneously leaving aside all nonnecessary features, thus furnishing eidetic intuition with its appropriately clarified essential structure. As a result of insight gained through such focused attention to what is essential while simultaneously ignoring what is incidental, the conceptual apparatus by which certain objects are grasped can be measured against its foundation in the essential determination of the things given in experience. This measuring "tests" the fittingness of the apparatus to identify the intended objects through the coincidence or lack thereof of what is subjectively conceptual to what is objectively essential. To the degree that the apparatus coincides with the essential structures of the objects given in experience, to that same degree the object domain is illuminated and the conceptual apparatus validated; conversely, to the degree that the apparatus fails to coincide with the objects of experience, to that same degree the object domain is obscured and the conceptual apparatus

---

degree, usual) imperfection of conceptualization relative to the essential content of the objects given in experience. See immediately above, liin41.

45 The nature of eidetic intuition and variation can be found summarized in the first part of Edmund Husserl, *Ideas Pertaining to a Pure Phenomenology and to a Phenomenological Philosophy*, 2 vols., trans. W. E. Pohl, T. E. Klein, and F. Kersten (The Hague: Martinus Nijhoff, 1983, 1989), 1:5–48.

46 For an analysis of Stein's understanding of the closeness of a phenomenological understanding of eidetic intuition to a Thomistic understanding of abstraction, see WP, 91–118; 108–81; and also Robert McNamara, "Essence in Edith Stein's Festschrift Dialogue," in *"Alles Wesentliche lasst sich nicht schreiben,"* ed. Andreas Speer and Stephen Regh (Freiburg i. Br.: Herder, 2016), 175–94: 179–83.

falsified. If the apparatus be entirely falsified, it can be discarded; if partially falsified, as would be more usual, the apparatus can be adjusted and refined, either superficially or substantially, where appropriate.

As a consequence of this fallibility of concept formation, and the above detailed Steinian understanding of philosophical investigation, when Stein receives the "conceptual world" of Aquinas and Thomism, she performs the work of assimilating its conceptual apparatuses according to this process of returning to the things themselves and testing the received apparatuses. The focused objectivity in the process ensures that the received teachings of Aquinas and Thomism are assimilated only inasmuch as they pass the rigor of her testing, while being appropriately clarified and deepened inasmuch as they do not yet sufficiently align with the object domain under investigation—at least according to the results of her own investigations. The beneficial outcome of this testing is twofold and works favorably in both directions. On the one hand, Stein's mature thought can be foundationally expanded and augmented by assimilation of significant conceptual apparatuses received from Aquinas and the Thomistic tradition; on the other, the received teachings of Aquinas and Thomism can be refined and developed or adjusted and amended as they are integrated into Stein's mature conceptual worldview.[47] In this way Stein can remain faithful to the vocation of a philosopher—as one borne toward wisdom in a first-person engagement with the world—while also entering into the broad stream of the *philosophia perennis* by gradually assimilating the Scholastic tradition of Aquinas and progressively providing her own contribution. So understood, Stein first receives the intellectual "nourishment" of the teachings of Aquinas as fitting intellectual "matter" for her own grasp of the world, before transforming that same received matter into an integrated and functional component of her own intellectual *corpus* with its corresponding organization and articulation. Through such living assimilation of Thomistic teachings, the thought of Aquinas comes to life again in the thought of Stein and in the new environment of modern philosophy, just as the thought of Aristotle had once come to life again in the thought of Aquinas and in the new environment of medieval Christianity. One can understand this assimilation

---

47   On the other hand, René Raschke notes that Stein sees in this proficiency of phenomenology to clarify Scholastic concepts a special service rendered to the history of philosophy. See René Raschke, "*Begriff*," in *Edith Stein-Lexikon*, ed. Marcus Knaup and Harald Seubert (Freiburg i. Br.: Herder, 2017), 57–59. In an insightful turn of phrase, Donald Wallenfang speaks of Stein utilizing "the grammar of metaphysics." See Donald Wallenfang, *Human and Divine Being: A Study on the Theological Anthropology of Edith Stein* (Eugene, OR: Cascade Books, 2017), xxvi.

according to the oft-repeated maxim of Aquinas, that "whatever is received in anything is received through the mode of the recipient."[48] Hence, I propose that Stein's engagement with the thought of Aquinas represents a "progressive incorporation" of the inherited conceptual apparatuses into a phenomenologically developed conceptual articulation of the meaning of being.

In *Potency and Act*, Stein indicates that "the investigation itself gives an account of the method of analysis," insofar as the clarity achieved through her objective treatment of the question of being in tandem with the conceptual apparatuses of Aquinas "justifies" her method and the conclusions she reaches.[49] In the present study, I strive to unearth this justification in the domain of anthropology in particular, by manifesting the precise range of conceptual agreement in Stein's mature thought with the foundational anthropology of Aquinas and Thomism, while simultaneously disclosing the way Stein further refines and develops the received teachings of Aquinas and the broader Thomistic tradition. By attending to what is common in their differing presentations of the human person, while also delineating the conceptual development introduced by Stein, my overall aim is to emphasize the substantial crossover of conceptualization between Stein and Aquinas, while simultaneously identifying the original and significant contributions Stein introduces into this anthropology. Such an emphasis is important given Stein's stated philosophical "mission in life," that of entering the *philosophia perennis* as an active contributor through phenomenologically engaging the teachings of Thomistic Scholasticism. Of course, such emphasis of commonality and development does not mean ignoring the express disagreements to be found between Stein and Aquinas, or indeed overlooking the less serious shadings of contrast between their anthropological presentations. It merely indicates deliberately drawing attention to the considerable agreement undergirding the more famous disagreement, while also identifying and detailing the several significant contributions Stein makes to the anthropological tradition of the *philosophia perennis*. By so highlighting how deeply the thought of Stein and Aquinas "runs together" in the broad stream of the *philosophia perennis*, with particular focus on the question of the human person, while also attending to the important original contributions Stein makes in this sphere, the fruit of Stein's mature philosophical calling is brought to light and given due clarification.

---

48   Among others, see ST, I, 75.5, co.
49   PA, 4.

The Relation of Phenomenology and Metaphysics

At a general level of analysis Stein's encounter with the thought of Aquinas can be characterized as a confrontation of phenomenology and metaphysics. Accordingly, the question of the relation of phenomenology to metaphysics deserves a separate analysis in order to properly ground all subsequent analyses, which further analyses unfold and develop in the anthropological sphere what is here set forth all too briefly.[50]

First, for Stein, what is metaphysics? In *Finite and Eternal Being* Stein summarizes her understanding of metaphysics, there saying, "*Metaphysics concerns the meaning of being* [den Sinn des Seins] *as such* [...] the fundamental question for the foundation of metaphysics is the question of the meaning of being."[51] This summary description should be understood as Stein's reformulation of the perennially valid question first posed by Aristotle: "τί

---

50 In outlining the relation of phenomenology and metaphysics so briefly, I keep in mind Stein's injunction in WP, "The relationship between scholastic and phenomenological methods cannot be dismissed with a few clichés. On both sides one must not shy away from the effort to pursue 'subtle' individual analyses in order to reach a real understanding of this or that issue, which is the primary prerequisite for the discovery of their mutual relations" (WP, 117).

51 EES, 489–90; and see above, xlvn21. I note here that Stein's particular formulation of the concern of metaphysics attends to "the meaning of being," where being is formulated in the infinitive—"*sein*" in German, "*esse*" in Latin, and "to be" in English. This stands in some contrast to the frequent charge against Stein that she ignores the existential significance of beings (*Seienden, entia*) and the corresponding actuality of being (*Sein, esse*)—particularly by those sympathetic to the Thomist metaphysical approach that takes being (*esse*) to be the ultimate metaphysical principle. I take up this question of being (*Seiend, ens*) and being (*Sein, esse*) again below when treating the analogy of being in chapter 6. Of further interest here is the context wherein Stein provides this formulation of the primary question of metaphysics—namely, in an appendix to EES where she critically analyzes Martin Heidegger's *Sein und Zeit* (Being and Time) and argues that metaphysics is "not only about the human being"— and just a few lines later continues, "Whoever skips over the question of the meaning of being [*Sein*], which lies in the very understanding of being [*Seinsverständnis*] itself, and carelessly 'projects' the 'understanding of being [*Seinsverständnis*]' of the human being, is in danger of cutting himself off from the meaning of being, and as far as I can see Heidegger has succumbed to this danger" (EES, 489–90). See Martin Heidegger, *Sein und Zeit* (Halle: M. Niemeyer, 1927); English translation, *Being and Time*, trans. J. Stambaugh, rev. by Dennis J. Schmidt (Albany, NY: State University of New York Press, 2010).

τὸ ὄν [...] τίς ἡ οὐσία"—What is being and what is essence (or substance)?—a questioning Stein describes as the perennial *leitmotif* of metaphysics.[52] Stein's reformulation places explicit emphasis on the *meaning* of being *and* on the *actuality* of being—that is, on the λόγος (*logos*) of being and on the "to be" of being.[53] Metaphysics then has the goal of attaining a comprehensive grasp of being, both with regard to the essential structures (German *Wesen*, Latin *essentia*) of all actual and possible beings (German *Seienden*, Latin *entia*), the principle whereby beings are determined as what they are, and with regard to the very actuality of being itself (German *Sein*, Latin *esse*), the principle whereby beings stand in existence with their very own actuality. This means that metaphysics includes ontological considerations, where ontology is understood as the "theory or philosophy of essence" and phenomena are taken to be the exemplary basis for such ontological considerations—with ontology then divided into formal and material ontologies. Whereas formal ontology is the science of the essential structures of objects universally applicable across all regions of being and is closely correlated with formal logic, material ontology is concerned with the essential structures of determinate objects in determinate object domains, and seeks to unveil what is invariant in these objects and object domains while leaving aside all that is variant and transitory.

---

52   Meta, 5.1, 1028^{b}4.
53   EES, 11. For Stein, the Greek λόγος (*logos*) identifies the meaningfulness of being, precisely since all being, whether actual or possible, all intuition and conceptualization, and all voiced expression of understanding is embraced and permeated by λόγος. Moreover, she recognizes that the λόγοι (*logoi*) of finite beings are ultimately rooted in the primordial divine Λόγος (*Logos*), understood both philosophically and theologically, the eternal and completed fullness of being and final coherence of all meaning, both finite and Infinite. See esp. EES, 107–8; AMP, 2–3, 9–10; WGE, 122, 129–31; and NFG, 75–76. An understanding of the Divine Λόγος, creaturely λόγοι, and their relation finds its primary historical proponent in St. Maximus the Confessor (ca. 580–662), though Stein's understanding seems to have been formed primarily through her study of Pseudo-Dionysius (ca. 5th–6th centuries) and secondarily through the interpretive tradition that includes St. Maximus the Confessor. In his *Ambigua* (book of difficulties), esp. *Ambiguum* 7, St. Maximus discusses the one Uncreated Λόγος in which the many creaturely λόγοι have their ultimate ground and meaningful coherence, and identifies the many λόγοι as both ideal and actual, both universal and particular. See Maximos the Confessor, *On Difficulties in the Church Fathers: The Ambigua*, 2 vols., ed. and trans. Nicholas Constas (London: Harvard University Press, 2014); and Pseudo-Dionysius, *The Divine Names*, in *The Complete Works*, trans. Colm Luibheid (New York: Paulist Press, 1987), 47–132.

Together with this general ontological aim, and in some contrast to the predominating interests of Husserl, Stein is particularly interested in detailing the various material ontologies of the *actual* or *real* world, which interest foundationally coordinates her ontological considerations by situating them with respect to a clearly defined metaphysics.[54] As a result, Stein presents her mature philosophy in distinctly metaphysical terms and understands metaphysics as a "science of the things in themselves" and a comprehensive "science of *this* world," which science though inclusive of ontological considerations is not restricted to pure ontology but rather focuses on the actuality of beings.[55] Hence, Stein's understanding of metaphysics is distinguished from ontology as the pure science of the categories of objects of understanding—even while still inclusive of ontological considerations, both formal and material, both actual and possible—and from a traditional Thomistic conception of metaphysics with its concerted attention to actual beings—even while Aquinas himself was not averse to purely formal considerations.[56] Philosophical anthropology then represents one particular object domain of a broader material ontology falling under a more general metaphysics with a kind of ontological priority, given the all-encompassing essential structure of human nature.[57]

What is phenomenology for Stein? As indicated above, Stein's understanding of phenomenology largely correlates with the presentation of phenomenology first given by Husserl in his *Logical Investigations*, while also tracking refinements given in her later works, particularly *Ideas* I and II. She considers the phenomenological method to be the philosophical method *par excellence* and understands it to have the foundational role of clarifying and justifying human knowledge, since the method provides privileged access to "the solution of all fundamental philosophical problems."[58] Following Husserl, Stein understands phenomenology to be the science

---

54 See PA, 20ff., 54ff.; EES, 182–84.
55 NFG, 131; EPh, 70; emphasis added.
56 As noted above (xxxiiin15), Stein's understanding of metaphysics diverges from Aquinas also in her claim that metaphysics can attain its sufficient completion only through recourse to the data of Revelation in "a metaphysics oriented to the faith." DF, 183; see also SBB I, nos. 230, 255; NFG, 184.
57 See AMP, 25–29. Lebech describes the content of AMP as a "confluence of phenomenology and metaphysics." Lebech, *Phenomenology to Metaphysics*, 98.
58 EPh, 22; see also, PE, 11. As noted above (xxxin13), the meaning and method of phenomenology is difficult to settle without controversy, both because the interpretation of Husserl's thought and its development is controversial, and because phenomenology is conceived of in numerous different ways by its many practitioners. Given this problem,

Prolegomenon: A Preparatory Analysis

of consciousness and conscious experience, which has the phenomenal world as its object of study—that is, the world as it is given in experience to the conscious subject—and the task of disclosing the essential structures of consciousness and the objects of consciousness. That which unites the conscious subject to the experienced world is the intentional relation, understood as the directedness of consciousness to the experienced world, its persons, things, events, and states of affairs. The phenomenological method is employed to clarify, on the side of the subject, the fundamental structures of consciousness, thus furnishing the *noetic* aspect of experience, and on the side of the object, the essential structures of the objects given in experience, thus furnishing the *noematic* aspect of experience.[59] The structures of consciousness are disclosed in the phenomenological reduction, which lays bare the noetic aspect, and the structures of objects are disclosed in the related activities of eidetic intuition and variation, which lay bare the noematic.[60] The bracketing that takes place via the phenomenological reduction enables focus on the synthetic activity of consciousness in the act of constitution, according to which objects of experience are disclosed for consciousness in determinate ways with determinate senses.[61] The rigorous and faithful detailing of these two dimensions of experience in intentional acts, the subjective and the objective, having focused on the immediate content of experience and bracketed all else via the phenomenological reduction, first clarifies all knowledge gained via what is immediately present in consciousness, and then justifies higher-order knowledge by providing the appropriately clarified ground of such further knowledge in that which is immediately given.[62]

Given this clarifying and grounding role with respect to knowledge, as well as the inner potential of phenomenology to justify its own method in addition to its findings, phenomenology claims for itself the title of first and universal philosophy, as that philosophical discipline through which all other disciplines

---

I here restrict my analysis to the understanding and practice of Stein.

59 Put simply, the noetic content of experience identifies the nature/structure of intentional acts, whatever kind they be, whereas noematic content identifies the object held in the intentional act—e.g., the noetic is the thinking act, the noematic is what is thought about.

60 See PA, 11; and also EPh, 12.

61 As indicated above (xxivn2; lxvi–lxviii), though Stein presents constitution as an activity of cognition conditioned by the nature of the intellect and intellectual activity, she certainly does not present constitution as something constructive but rather as disclosive—i.e., constitution uncovers the meaning of the objects given in cognition, etc.

62 See EPh, 19.

can be adequately grounded.[63] Yet this claim is true for Stein only in a limited sense, since it is clear for her that phenomenology does not exclude metaphysical reasoning, and neither does it negate the claim of metaphysics to the title of *first philosophy*, a title originally proposed by Aristotle and later defended by Aquinas.[64] Since the term first has many meanings, and since metaphysics denotes philosophical wisdom achieved by attaining knowledge of the first principles of reality duly completed, metaphysics legitimately lays claim to the title of first philosophy. Moreover, since metaphysics provides the possibility of achieving knowledge of the absolutely first principle of being, God, at least in terms of his existence and basic attributes, metaphysics evidently furnishes the knowing subject with the greatest possible object of natural knowledge.[65] Accordingly, though phenomenology continues to claim primacy in the order of *knowing* for Stein, metaphysics enters her mature thought holding primacy in the orders of *knowledge* and *being*. Notwithstanding the privileged ability of phenomenology to disclose the structures of consciousness and knowing, metaphysics comes to represent the proper completion of human knowledge, representing "a self-enclosed worldview" and "overall picture of the world."[66] This means that while the mature Stein continues to employ the phenomenological method to ground her philosophical reasoning, she simultaneously holds that phenomenology requires further metaphysical reasoning to complete its investigations, and indeed that phenomenology can be completed *only* through such inferential reasoning and judgment. Otherwise stated, though phenomenology is understood by Stein to be methodologically foundational, it is only through achieving a well-rounded and coherent metaphysics that the ultimate goal of philosophy is attained.

Such complementarity of phenomenology and metaphysics is possible for Stein because of the metaphysical openness she recognizes in phenomenology—

---

63 See NFG, 160, 210–11, 292–94; and PA, 18–20.
64 Meta, 4.2, 1004^{a}1; 6.2, 1026^{a}30; and 11.4, 1061^{b}15.
65 See EES, 27–28. Stein regards the ultimate object of philosophy as knowledge of God, and when comparing Husserlian phenomenology and Thomistic Scholasticism positively evaluates the "theocentric" philosophical orientation of Scholasticism in contrast to what she calls the "egocentric" orientation of phenomenology. Obviously, according to her modified use of the method, phenomenology at her hands can no longer be understood as reductively egocentric. See WP, 91–118; and also McNamara, "Festschrift Dialogue," 175–94: 178–79, 192–94. See part III below for Stein's fully developed natural theology.
66 AMP, 2; and SBB III, nos. 102, 176.

that is, the fact that the phenomenological method leaves metaphysical questions without *a priori* resolution and susceptible to their completion in further reasoning of a metaphysical kind. As noted above, according to Stein's method, metaphysical judgment regarding the actuality of the world is at first suspended only to secure the focus that enables consciousness to attend to what is immediately given, thus allowing for the objects of consciousness to manifest most fully.[67] Yet, as also noted, Stein reasons that any bracketing applied in achieving the reduction must itself be dropped if one is to properly comprehend what is given in experience. She says, "We will be able to say something about the relation of the I to the worlds beyond only if we remove the restriction of the consideration of the region of being that is immediately and inseparably belonging to us."[68] That is, if one is to grasp what is immanent to conscious experience, if one is to be truly faithful to the *givenness* of objects, the methodological device of the reduction must itself be suspended in a return to acceptance of the actuality of the world. Only then does the givenness of objects have adequate account.[69] Consequently, when phenomenologically investigating any particular object domain, Stein finally sets aside the phenomenological reduction in order to attend to the actuality of the objects given in experience and recognizes for these objects a clearly defined existential valence. Hence, contrary to the implications of Husserl's later writings, the practice of phenomenology does not imply transcendental idealism, but rather stimulates further reasoning of an inferential kind and readily supports metaphysical realism.

At Stein's hands, then, phenomenology can render valuable service to metaphysics by grounding metaphysical knowledge in what is immediately given in experience, and this service is especially clear when considering the essences of actual things. Given the significance of essence (*essentia*) in the metaphysics of Aquinas, and the further closeness Stein recognizes between the

---

67 Ales Bello helpfully describes phenomenology as something that never exhausts the givenness of experience but is rather something that must be "begun ever anew." See Angela Ales Bello, "Edmund Husserl and Edith Stein: The Question of the Human Subject," trans. Antonio Calcagno, *American Catholic Philosophical Quarterly* 82, no. 1 (2008): 143–59: 148.

68 EES, 57.

69 The enduring identity of the objects of consciousness should be considered a special aspect of this givenness—that is, that the objects of experience typically remain before consciousness with stability of presentation that endures throughout a defined temporal span, while also possessing the inherent potential to be turned toward again and again, all of which bespeaks the independent actuality of such objects.

Thomistic understanding of intellectual abstraction and the phenomenological understanding of eidetic intuition, the service phenomenology can render Thomistic metaphysics is most apparent, as above argued, in the ability of phenomenology to substantiate and further clarify the conceptual apparatuses of Thomistic philosophy with their referent in the essences of the actual world.[70] Through keeping the things themselves always in view whenever undertaking any conceptualization whatsoever, and thus anchoring received apparatuses in their natural reference to the objects of experience, Stein's modified use of the phenomenological method provides an ongoing potential for a critical stance-taking with reference to inherited teachings. Any possible encrustation that encumbers the received teachings can be cleared away in view of attaining a more refined and subtle grasp of the particular object or object domain. This mode of engaging metaphysical teachings corresponds to the earlier identified "testing" of received conceptual apparatuses, a process by which the inherited concepts and conceptual interconnections are "measured" against the objects given in experience in view of adjusting or developing where appropriate. It is in precisely this way, as argued above, that Stein engages the received metaphysics of Aquinas, and while she grants to his metaphysics a privileged position in her mature thought, she does not incorporate it into her own worldview without such testing.[71]

---

70   See above, li–lvii; see also NFG, 89, 165; and McNamara, "Festschrift Dialogue," 175–94: 179–81.

71   In contrast to this position of Stein regarding the compatibility of phenomenology and metaphysics, and basing his reasoning on Husserl's *Cartesian Meditations*, Maritain argues against the possibility of phenomenology rendering this service to metaphysics. He identifies what appears to be fundamental methodological problems with phenomenology, first in terms of the appropriation to the intellect of "a constitutive and constructive role," then in terms of the phenomenological bracketing of actual being and the uncritical admission of "the *possibility of thinking of being while refusing to think of it as being*." In contrast, I have shown that Stein would argue that while phenomenology is constitutive it is not constructive but rather is disclosive, and that the methodological bracketing of phenomenology simply allows the investigator to focus on the inherent structure of consciousness and on the necessary structures of essences only to open the bracketing in a return to the existential givenness of the actual world. Gilson similarly critiques the first-person starting point by arguing that the givenness of extramental reality together with the givenness of the *cogito* indicates that the *cogito* cannot be understood as an isolated starting point separated from the cognitive experience of extramental reality. I suggest that Stein would agree with Gilson that the *cogito* is not so isolatable from the objects of the experienced world, but that

The Metaphysical Realism of Stein's Phenomenology

With Stein's above-detailed introduction of phenomenology into the organon of the *philosophia perennis*, with an eye turned toward the metaphysical realism of Aquinas and the Thomistic tradition, the question of the kind of philosophical realism espoused by Stein deserves initial clarification.[72]

The English "real," as well as the German "*der Real*," including its derivatives, realism, realist, etc., takes its meaning from the Latin *res*, meaning thing, matter, fact, etc.[73] Accordingly, the real is the thing identified by the knower, realism is the claim that the thing identified has being independent of the knowing mind, and a realist is one who holds such a claim. Realism is then a metaphysical assertion about the objects of conscious experience, that such objects exist in some way independently of the knowing subject, having a mode of being that does not depend on the knowing subject. Realism is differently determined according to the kind of object or class of objects held to have this independent mode of being. It is first most often specified in contrast to idealism, which posits a more or less radical dependence of known objects on the knowing mind, though differently determined in different philosophical systems, whereas realism holds that such known objects have being independent of the knowing mind, in an actual, real, or natural world. It is then also specified with reference to universals, identifying such objects

---

       she would also leave room for investigating the *cogito* together with the structures of consciousness in tandem with the given world via the phenomenological reduction. See Jacques Maritain, *Degrees of Knowledge*, 107–14: 107–8; and Étienne Gilson, *Thomist Realism and the Critique of Knowledge*, trans. Mark A. Wauck (San Francisco: Ignatius Press, 1986, repr. 2012), esp. 55–85.

72 As with the above-outlined problem of the relation of metaphysics and phenomenology, this question deserves lengthier treatment not possible within the confines of this study. In particular I don't treat the progressive development of Stein's realist commitments, but here only briefly note that Stein espoused some form of metaphysical realism throughout her philosophical career, and is therefore often rightly classified together with other realist phenomenologists of the early part of the twentieth century, including Max Scheler, Adolph Reinach, and Dietrich von Hildebrand. Indeed, Stein's realism is apparent in her earliest philosophical works, was frequently voiced by her to Husserl in disagreement with his developing transcendental idealism, and gains clarity and definition throughout her later philosophical writings during the period of her engagement with Aquinas and Thomism, and the Christian tradition more broadly.

73 See entry for "*res*" in Charlton T. Lewis and Charles Short, *An Elementary Latin Dictionary* (Oxford: Oxford University Press, 1963).

as in some way independent of the knowing mind, whether founded in the actual things of the natural world, or founded in some way "beyond" the things of the actual world, in addition to their being "beyond" the knowing subject. Evidently, these two applications of realism are inherently related, even if distinct from one another, and even while the latter specification is narrower in extension.[74]

With consideration for the mind-independent reality of the world, is Stein a realist? Yes, in this respect, Stein is a realist, since she "sees in natural experience the point of departure for all thinking that leads beyond [natural experience]" and considers the world of experience to be an "actual or real" world.[75] As seen above, this acknowledgment of the reality of the experienced world is a function of her recognition that known objects are announced in experience as having a mind-independent mode of being. Since such objects are *given* to the knowing mind as coming from beyond what is immanent to consciousness, Stein reasons that the independent actuality of such objects is co-given together with their immanent presence in conscious experience. This givenness of objects is further substantiated by the intersubjective constitution of objects—as something foundationally mediated by acts of empathy, but which also includes other forms of communal experiencing and interpersonal communication—so that the world is given for the conscious subject as something that evidently stands over against the subject and a plurality of subjects.[76] The upshot of this givenness of the experienced world is the potential for the mind to truly "rest" on the independent actuality of the world, before it proceeds to deepen its conceptual grasp of its objects by making manifold further inferences about the world and

---

74 Of course, this broad outline of positions is not intended to be exhaustive, since realism and idealism admit of various shades and qualifications, especially inasmuch as realism is typically applied with a selective scope and idealism is often determined together with wider epistemological positions.

75 EES, 262; and NFG, 188. See also, EES, 282: "We have grasped 'existence' as being [*Sein*] independent of the cognizing (finite) spirit, as the being [*Sein*] of objects set out for themselves [...]. All thinking is thinking of or about something, or also the forms of something."

76 In her earliest work on empathy, Stein details the importance of acts of empathy for the constitution of the outer world, even to the point of arguing that the objective world is given in an essentially intersubjective way, inasmuch as the comprehensive constitution of objects can attain its proper completion only together with acts of empathy. See PE, 81–83, where she states: "Thus, empathy, as the basis of intersubjective experience, becomes a condition of the possibility of a recognition of the existing outer world."

its things. And even while Stein allows that not all knowledge "takes its *warrant* from experience," here understood as sense experience, but can have a basis of validity in pure reason, somewhat like the *intellectus principiorum* of Aquinas, nonetheless she firmly maintains that all thinking must have its basis in sense experience and remain rationally coherent with what is sensorily given, since "a thinking of which the result is not the justification but rather the annulment of experience [...], is groundless and does not deserve our trust."[77] Thus, Stein argues that the naturally experienced world is the foundation for all further thinking according to which the knowing subject advances in knowledge and progressively develops a structured conceptual grasp of the world.

Yet, despite this foundationally realistic stance, Stein also recognizes that conscious experience is something essentially complex, inasmuch as cognition is at least partially conditioned by the knowing subject and its particular cognitive constitution. Since conscious experience necessarily involves the relativity of knowing subject and known object, not only does the known object determine the content of experience, but so too does the knowing subject. That is, inasmuch as conscious experience is mediated by the cognitive structure of the knowing subject, which in the human person includes the senses together with the structure of the living-body, Stein reasons that the specific cognitive structure of the subject is significant for the way the individual comes to know the world, and also for his ensuing knowledge of the world. And so, even while the natural world is certainly real for Stein, having an actuality of being independent of the human subject, since it is also a world given to the human subject in and through sense experience, it is very much an *experienced* world.[78] In a short work on the significance of phenomenology contrasting realism and idealism, Stein puts her position in the following way:

> Naive realism takes things as they appear before the eyes of the human being and posits them as absolute without realizing how much of what stands before him is conditioned by the interrelation between the human being and his world; he forgets himself as a factor in

---

[77] EES, 287; emphasis added. Stein elsewhere notes, "As a philosopher, you may say you lacked compelling motives to decide between idealism and realism. But in practical life you will not wait for this decision but will deal with the world as a reality—as all idealists do when they have their senses intact. Whoever does otherwise will be called a fool." SBB III, nos. 117, 191.

[78] See EES, 50–51, 254–59, 285, 321, 333, 390, 421.

the constitution of his world. The idealist is so captivated by the discovery of the subject's part in the constitution of the world that he posits it as absolute and loses sight of the dependencies in which he finds himself.[79]

Stein wishes to overcome the false dichotomy that threatens to reduce the subject-object polarity of knowledge to a plain subjectivism (= radical idealism) or a plain objectivism (= naïve realism), by recognizing that knowing involves a complex intentional relation of human subject and known object with contributing factors on both sides.[80] So considered, Stein is evidently not an idealist or constructivist when it comes to knowledge, but neither is she a so-called naïve realist.[81]

With consideration for the mind-independent reality of universals, is Stein a realist? Yes, again here Stein is a realist. In contradistinction to the doctrines of exaggerated realism, nominalism, and conceptualism, and in like manner to Aquinas, Stein adheres to what has come to be called moderate realism. In Stein's words, the moderate realism of Aquinas and Thomism "distinguishes between the matter, or that which is contained in the universal concept [...], and the form of universality," and ascribes "to the matter being in the individual thing and to the form being only in the mind."[82] Stein largely aligns herself with this standard reading of Aquinas and maintains that the universal is no mere concept or name (as in conceptualism or nominalism, respectively) but rather is something objective, having being in actual individual things where the matter of universality is found, and in individual knowing minds where the

---

79 NFG, 156.
80 Indeed, this false dichotomy is indicated by the mutually interdependent concepts of subject and object. Since to be a subject is to be the kind of thing (or power) that has the capacity to direct itself (or be directed) toward some other thing, and correlatively, to be an object is to be the thing toward which the subject is directed, subject and object are mutually implied by definition. In the most exalted case, persons are the kinds of thing that are eminently able to direct themselves (and their intentional powers) toward other things (whether mere things, events, or persons), which things then become their objects (the objects of their intentional powers).
81 Consequently, we can say that Stein is both a metaphysical and epistemological realist, even while her epistemological realism involves certain limited qualifications (over against that of Thomism), which then go on to impact the developed character of her metaphysical realism.
82 EES, 93.

form of universality is found. However, in accord with her own ontology and metaphysics, Stein distinguishes her position from that of Aquinas and argues that the universal also has its own mode of being independent of known things and knowing minds, a mode of being she calls *essential being* (*wesenhaftes Sein*).[83] Thus, Stein maintains that the meaningful determination of the universal has being not only in the actual individual, whether formally determining individual things or intentionally determining knowing minds, but also in itself, inasmuch as it possesses an independent mode of being as an enclosed meaning structure.[84] Indeed, Stein argues that it is precisely this mode of being that provides the ultimate ground of the meaningful determination of any and all actual individual things, while also securing the distinct objectivity she maintains is necessary for universals with respect to any and all knowing minds.[85]

---

83   EES, 93. Though Stein herself indicates that her distinctive subspecies of moderate realism may lie closer to that of Scotus than Aquinas, Victor M. Salas argues that Stein's position has close kinship to Henry of Ghent's doctrine of essential being (*esse essentiae*) and questions whether Stein could meet the objections in the later medieval reception of this doctrine. See Victor M. Salas, "Edith Stein and Medieval Metaphysics," in *American Catholic Philosophical Quarterly* 85, no. 2 (2011): 323–40.

84   By my use of "determination" (here and below) I am identifying the boundary or limit of the designated object, whether that object be a unit of meaning or an actual thing; so considered, the determination of any given thing is the intelligible *terminus* of the object establishing it as *what* it is. In the context of the anthropology that follows (see below, esp. 47ff.), my use corresponds to Stein's use of "*Bestimmung*" and Aquinas's use of "*determinatio*."

85   See EES, 62–112. Despite the apparently elusive nature of essential being, Stein argues that we approach essential being in all encounters with meaning, in our immediate encounter with the meaningful things of the natural world and our intuition of meaning in these things, in our formulation of meaningful concepts and propositions that significantly pattern the objects of the natural world, in our reflection upon the meaningful contents of consciousness itself and its activities, and in our communication of meaning via linguistic expression and our corresponding comprehension of these same expressions. In all these areas wherein meaning is found, Stein maintains that the meaning so encountered has its ultimate finite ground and coordinating basis in the essential structures to which she grants the mode of essential being, even while its proximate basis can be manifold, i.e., thing, thought, or word. Consequently, for Stein, we can strongly state that without essential being there is no finite meaning. For an informative presentation of essential being, see Thomas Gricoski, *Being Unfolded: Edith Stein on the Meaning of Being* (Washington, DC: The Catholic University of America Press, 2020), esp. the chapter "The Mode of Essential Being," 60–80.

With this extension of the moderate realism of Aquinas and Thomism to grant a distinct kind of being to universals, Stein understands herself to be uniting the disparate ontological positions of Plato and Aristotle.[86] Moreover, in making this claim she appears to be making the case that her presentation is consistent with the metaphysical framework of Aquinas and Thomism. After an extended quotation taken from Aquinas's commentary on Aristotle's *Metaphysics*, concluding with the following decisive line, "*What the intellect knows must be the same in the thing yet not in the same way*," Stein argues that since the self-same meaningful determination is to be found in the known thing *and* in the knowing mind, this meaningful determination must really be something in itself.[87] With Aquinas, Stein identifies this meaningful determination as the *whatness* (German *Washeit*, Latin *quidditas*) and argues that the meaning of the whatness can be found instantiated in actual things—as that which meaningfully determines the essence as the *what of the essence* (*Wesenswas*)— and in individual minds knowing actual things—as that which meaningfully determines the mind through its intentional relation to known objects. This means that two ontologically distinct modes of being can be granted to the self-same meaningful determination—namely, actual being *in rerum natura* (in the things of nature) and intentional being *in intellectu* (in the intellect).[88] Yet, whether this same meaningful determination is actualized in individual things or intellectualized in knowing minds, the meaning structure remains identically itself throughout its distinct actualization and intellectualization, and indeed, regardless of whether or not it is ever actualized or intellectualized. Consequently, Stein concludes that the meaningful determination of the universal must indeed be something in itself and have a mode of being distinctly its own as an enclosed meaning structure, a mode of being she calls essential being, precisely inasmuch as it is the ultimate finite ground of the meaning of essences and what is essential.

---

86 Though Stein's position evidently goes beyond the moderate realism of Aquinas and Thomism, her position cannot simply be equated with "platonic realism" as it is ordinarily understood, precisely since Stein argues that the universal having essential being should not be understood as something with subsistent being after the manner of the things of the actual world. Indeed, Stein questions the identification "platonic realism" as "exaggerated realism" and footnotes the following indicative musing in EES (96n84): "Admittedly, I have never been able to convince myself that Plato actually held the theory of ideas that Aristotle fought against in his Metaphysics."

87 EES, 95; emphasis original.

88 EES, 95.

Prolegomenon: A Preparatory Analysis

There is another basis in Aquinas's texts revealing further possible partial alignment with Stein's position on essential being, even while this basis remains brief and undeveloped. In DEE, when discussing the being of essences, Aquinas speaks of a way to think about essences that he calls an absolute consideration (*absoluta consideratio*), saying,

> Now the nature or essence thus accepted can be considered in two ways: in the first way, according to its proper meaning [*rationem propriam*], and this is an absolute consideration of it. In this way nothing is true of it except what comes together with it as such. And whatever else is attributed to it is attributed falsely. [...] In another way, nature or essence can be considered according to the being it has in this or that. [...] Now this nature has a twofold being, one in the singular and another in the soul, and according to both accidents follow upon the nature.[89]

Aquinas here recognizes that an essence can be considered not only according to the being it has in actual individuals, whether in known things or knowing minds, but also according to the meaning it has *in itself*, "according to its proper meaning." In this latter sense nothing is true of the essence except what is proper to it—neither unity nor multiplicity, neither actual nor intentional being, nor any inhering accident—and it is precisely this "openness" of the essence absolutely considered that enables the self-same meaning to be found in actual individuals—in one *and* in many, in actual things *and* in knowing minds, together *with* all its inhering accidents. Such absolute consideration evidently parallels certain decisive features in Stein's consideration of essences, but it remains undeveloped in Aquinas's writings and he certainly does not hold to or argue for essential being, even while such a mode of being was maintained by other Scholastics of his era—most famously, Henry of Ghent (ca. 1217–93).[90]

---

89 DEE, 3, 26–56.
90 See above, lxixn83. This absolute consideration of essence (or any intelligible aspect of being) considers the meaningfulness of the essence without associating any mode of being with the essence so considered, whether actual or intentional. Therefore, an essence absolutely considered is both the intelligible content of the actual being and the intelligible content of the thought about the actual being (brought about via the act of intellectual abstraction), but without possessing any mode of being, neither actual nor

In summary we can conclude by saying that Stein certainly recognizes the independent actuality of the experienced world as a natural, actual, or real world, while simultaneously granting to this world a qualified priority in the order of knowing—that is, as the grounding basis of human knowledge—and further recognizes three distinct and coordinate modes of being for the universal (and indeed, for any meaning structure), those of actual being (*wirkliches Sein*), intentional being (*gedankliches Sein*), and essential being (*wesenhaftes Sein*). This represents a novel extension of what can broadly be identified as Stein's espousal of moderate realism.[91]

Conclusion:
Stein's Progressive Incorporation of Aquinas's Teachings

When Stein returns to direct philosophical investigation after her conversion to Christianity and enters the broad stream of the *philosophia perennis* with her unique philosophical skillset, that of phenomenology, she deliberately turns to the Christian philosophy of Aquinas and the Thomistic tradition to guide her investigative efforts. In this *prolegomenon*, I examined the process Stein employs to set about engaging the thought of Aquinas and Thomism and have shown that her modified use of phenomenology enables her to perform an objective investigation of the meaning of being while simultaneously engaging

---

intellectual; rather, the essence so considered has all the purity of its own meaning and nothing else. See also ST, I, 85.1, ad. 1.

91 It should be noted that Stein's stance on the mind-independent reality of the objects of cognition, both in terms of the actual things of the natural world and in terms of the essential being of universals, is contextualized within a person-centered metaphysics, where all objects of any kind are understood to bear final reference to persons, whether they be the finite persons of the created order or the infinite and uncreated personal God. Yet, whereas the objects of cognition are prior to and independent of the intentional relation of finite persons to these same objects—since the finite intellect is measured by the actuality and essential structure of the objects cognized—when considering the infinite personal God the cognitive relation is reversed—since divine knowledge is both prior to and the source of the actuality and intelligibility of created things. I further note that while this person-centered realism is more apparent in Stein than in Aquinas, her thought in this area presents no contradiction to the thought of Aquinas—or indeed the Christian philosophical and theological traditions more broadly—who understands divine ideas as the formal exemplar cause of all actual things, and created persons as having a preeminent mode of being within the natural order.

teachings received from Aquinas and the Thomistic tradition. In this way, Stein intellectually grapples with the Thomistic metaphysical framework and gradually appropriates the many fruitful insights she discovers through her independent investigations. She thereby receives the metaphysical inheritance of Aquinas and Thomism as a reverent and willing pupil, yet without at all standing passively before this conceptual inheritance, but rather engages in the painstaking task of actively assimilating key teachings into her mature worldview. I have identified this process of assimilation as Stein's "progressive incorporation" of the received conceptual apparatuses of Thomism into her Christian metaphysics in her gradual ascent to the meaning of being. Thus, Stein assimilates the intellectual "matter" she receives from Aquinas and Thomism by first transforming this "nourishment" before giving new life to Thomistic thought in the context of contemporary philosophy. From this we see that Stein's engagement with Thomistic metaphysics has beneficial outcomes in two directions. On the one hand, Stein can receive a coherent metaphysical schema that enables her to deal effectively with the natural world as an actual or real world; on the other, she can refine and develop these same Thomistic teachings by measuring all received concepts against the things themselves as they are given in experience. Since, in Stein's words, "no system of human thought is so perfect that we have no further need of objective clarity," such investigative work is necessary for the philosopher *qua* philosopher, or indeed, for the human being *qua* truth seeker.[92] In this way, Stein's thought is foundationally strengthened by her incorporation of significant metaphysical apparatuses received from Aquinas and Thomism, while Thomistic metaphysics is simultaneously confirmed, substantiated, and further developed by Stein's phenomenological reconsideration.

---

92   EES, 4.

Part I

Human Nature

> Individuals of a rational nature have a special name;
> and this name is person.
>
> —*Thomas Aquinas*[1]

Beginning with the most original knowledge of the certainty of one's own being as it is given in conscious experience, Stein unfolds a whole series of further dimensions to the being of the self, inasmuch as first-person experience reveals the self to be given as a personal being structured as a composite unity of soul and living-body. To adequately clarify the nature and character of this personal being, as well as the composite structure of soul and living-body, Stein adopts certain anthropological teachings of Aquinas and employs these teachings to account for the structure of human nature. In part I I analyze Stein's adoption, first toward revealing the *rationale* behind her recourse to Aquinas in this particular area, then toward manifesting *what* precisely of his teachings she adopts and incorporates, and finally toward clarifying *how* she understands and develops the conceptual content of each. The analysis is divided into two chapters. In chapter 1 I detail the phenomenological starting point of Stein's investigation before analyzing her adoption and progressive assimilation of the classical Boëthian definition of the person according Aquinas's interpretation. In chapter 2 I analyze Stein's engagement with two further anthropological teachings of Aquinas, those of the substantial unity of the human being and soul's formation of the body, together with their shared hylomorphic

---

1 ST, I, 29.1, co.

foundation. In both chapters I show how Stein reconsiders the meaning of each teaching through an objective investigation of the human person while also deepening their conceptual content by attending to the significance of personal subjectivity in the being and life of the human individual. In the end, Stein comes to present the whole of human nature as meaningfully determined and teleologically ordered in a complex of interconnected ways, with all ultimately subordinated to a thoroughgoing personal formation of this nature. In this way, Stein develops the received teachings of Aquinas beyond their adopted foundation in distinctively personalist ways while simultaneously remaining rooted in a Thomistic anthropological presentation.

Aside on the Meaning of "Human Nature"

Stein does not extensively thematize the concept nature (*Natur*) in her mature works, even while she uses the term liberally throughout these works.[2] Nevertheless, her conception of its meaning is clearly discernible from the way she uses the term, and from her summary interpretation of Aristotle's use of *phusis* (φύσις), usually translated as nature. The interrelated meanings Stein attributes to nature can be classified under the following two headings, the first of which has its origin in the second: (1) as a denominator of the created cosmos as one whole, where nature is defined in reference to its origin in and distinction from God, and also its distinction from the spheres of human artifice and extraordinary divine activity; and (2) as a denominator of the meaningful determination of finite beings, in view of their proper activity (and passivity), and according to their corresponding teleological ordination, both of which are found exemplified in living beings as generative and active.[3] Thus, in some contrast to Husserl, Stein does not hold to a simple opposition of nature and spirit or mind (*Geist*), and this is most clear in her adoption of the so-called classical definition of the person as "an individual substance of a rational *nature*."[4]

In contrast to Stein's relatively sparse use of nature, the closely related term essence (*Wesen*), as well as its derivatives, receives lengthy examination and is clearly her preferred term when designating the meaningful determination of

---

2   For this and following, see esp. EES, 160–64, 113–238, 307–10, 338–39; AMP, 14, 17, 161–62; and PA, 201–7.
3   For the meaning given for "determination," see above, lxixn84.
4   See EES, 307–9.

things. The close relationship of the concepts is found in Stein's understanding of the unfolding (*Entfaltung*) of essences in living natures via what she calls the essential-form (*Wesensform*).[5] Whereas essence designates the meaningful determination of any given thing, the essential-form designates that same meaningful determination but now with reference to its formal part alone and its corresponding power to unfold in teleologically ordered activity (as exemplified in living beings). So considered, the essential-form represents the core of the crossover between the allied concepts of nature and essence since it shows the grounding of teleological activity in the formal determination of the essence. Stein herself indicates this when she associates the Aristotelian notion of *phusis* with her own concept of the essential-form and further identifies the essential-form with the Aristotelian *morphe* (μορφή) and the Scholastic substantial form (*forma substantialis*). Through its power to unfold, the essential-form works toward attaining the completion of what Stein calls the pure form (*reine Form*) of the individual and its associated species, identifying this with the Aristotelian *eidos* (εἶδος) and understanding it as the ideal formal terminus toward which the essential-form actively unfolds.

From this brief overview, we can see that Stein's mature understanding of nature is closely aligned with that of Aquinas, who often uses the terms essence (*essentia*) and nature (*natura*) as synonyms for the meaningful determination of things, even while there remain the same subtleties of signification in Aquinas, who understands the substantial form to be the inner principle of determination and any associated teleological activity.[6] For the purposes of the present study, I use the term nature in the above-detailed Steinian and Thomistic senses, where nature is understood to denominate the meaningful determination of individual things (especially living things) in view of their teleological activity through the powerful dynamism of the essential-form (= substantial form). Moreover, I take human nature to be one kind of nature among a plurality of natures in a created natural world, and I understand all human individuals to include in their full essential determination their being-human, so that all

---

5   In *Being Unfolded*, Thomas Gricoski examines Stein's metaphysics of unfolding, arguing that it is a concept of central significance in Stein's mature thought and provides an interpretive development of it as the point of departure for a fundamentally relational ontology. See Thomas Gricoski, *Being Unfolded: Edith Stein on the Meaning of Being* (Washington, DC: The Catholic University of America Press, 2020).

6   For a brief, but pointed outline presentation of these concepts in Aquinas, see DEE, 1:27–52.

human individuals can be understood to be members of one and the same human species. Finally, I take human nature to include the fact that the human being is a person, since, for Stein, as for Aquinas, "When we speak of the 'nature' of the human being, we mean the essence of the human being as such, and therein included is the fact that he is a person."[7] Moreover, alongside both thinkers, I recognize the distinction but not separation of person and nature, something carefully worked out in the early Christological controversies, since the person is not reducible to his nature even while the person possesses his nature as the meaningful determination of his being and life.[8]

---

7   EES, 310.
8   The distinction and relation of person and nature is (partially) unpacked below alongside the analysis of human nature and the human individual.

Chapter One

Point of Departure in the "Life of the I"

> Whenever the human spirit in its search for truth has sought after an undeniably certain starting point, it has come upon something inescapably close: the fact of its own being.
>
> —*Edith Stein*[1]

Stein begins her objective investigation in *Finite and Eternal Being* with the self-evidence of one's own being as it is given in conscious experience, the always present "I am" that is found in first-person inner awareness in any and all experiences whatsoever.[2] In turning to this immediate datum of experience, Stein is consciously following the path of Edmund Husserl (and René Descartes before him), though not exclusively, and rather traces her understanding to that of St. Augustine, in his recognition of this certainty against radical skepticism, and notes that Aquinas also acknowledges this fact as a self-evident truth of the knowing subject.[3] Stein calls this given of experience our "most

---

1 EES, 40.
2 See EES, 40–42; PA, 9–10; and also AMP, 12–13; and WP, 114. Some of the following can be found in an earlier version in Robert McNamara, "The Cognition of the Human Individual in the Mature Thought of Edith Stein," in *Philosophical News: Dietrich von Hildebrand and Christian Personalism*, ed. Elisa Grimi, 16 (2018): 131–43: 131–36.
3 See PA, 18n1, where Stein references QDV, 10.8. Therese Scarpelli Cory shows that Aquinas holds a complex theory of human self-knowledge, inclusive of what she calls "habitual" and "actual self-awareness," the latter of which can include both "implicit" and "explicit self-awareness," as well as the further possibility of attaining "scientific

original knowledge," since it is "what is closest to me, inseparable from me, and therefore a starting point behind which I can go no further back."[4] In this respect, the "I am" of conscious experience is an undeniable first truth for Stein, a primordial given that furnishes a sure point of departure for all further thinking, and an equally incontrovertible starting point from which philosophical investigation can begin.[5] Accordingly, even while she recognizes other starting points of investigation, Stein takes this first truth as the point of departure for her investigations in *Finite and Eternal Being* and from here begins to unfold a whole series of further truths. Importantly, this first truth is not understood by Stein to be the mere fact of the *existence* of the conscious I, a simple binary in answer to the question of existence that concludes to the proposition "I am" as a bare affirmation. Rather, in similarity to Augustine,

---

knowledge" of the self through inferential reasoning on the prior foundation of habitual and actual self-awareness. See Therese Scarpelli Cory, *Aquinas on Human Self-Knowledge* (Cambridge: Cambridge University Press, 2015), esp. 63–65, 215–20. As becomes clear in what follows, this presentation has clear parallels to Stein's phenomenological exploration.

4   EES, 41. By most original knowledge (*ursprünglichste Erkenntnis*) Stein does not mean that such knowledge is the first item of knowledge (by way of content) possessed by the knowing subject in the order of time, but rather that such knowledge is found together with any and all knowledge whatsoever, even if it is not reflexively attended and made the direct object of cognition in a particular knowing act. Ian Leask highlights that for Stein this primordial knowing is established immediately for the knowing subject, in such a way that it is found to be ontologically and logically prior to any intentional act or, indeed, to any act of reflection. Ian Leask, *Being Reconfigured* (Newcastle upon Tyne: Cambridge Scholars, 2011), 82–83, 114.

5   The grammatical function of the "I" as personal pronoun indicates the special character of this awareness and any corresponding knowledge. The "I" is a pronoun that can only be explained in light of first-person experience, when the person experiences itself as the inner subject of conscious experience in a way that yields the self precisely as an *I*. Moreover, on the basis of this inward subjective self-awareness, the person can then intend the self in a reflexive intention that objectifies the self, in such a way that the I is then in the intention in two ways, both as the subject intending and as the object intended; yet, despite the subject-object complexity of the intention, the I is given in the act of knowing in the unified simplicity of knower and known, all of which is captured and signified by the direct reflexive form of the pronoun. One could perhaps call this a special kind of *self*-evident knowledge, inasmuch as it is an evident knowing of the self as a self to the self, even while it differs greatly from a propositional form of self-evident knowledge. The precise character of this knowledge will be become apparent as the analysis proceeds, and esp. in chapter 4 on the human individual.

Stein reasons that this truth includes awareness of one's own being as a living and understanding being. Since the conscious I is found present in all of what Stein calls the "spiritual stirrings" of consciousness—a general category of intentional acts that includes all thinking, willing, and spiritual feeling—the conscious I is concomitantly given as a living being with a spiritual mode of life, and so is equally a *living and spiritual I*.[6]

Indeed, spiritual stirrings are the very life of the conscious I since the I lives its distinctive mode of being in and through all spiritual stirrings, whether they be acts of thinking, willing, or spiritual feeling. The conscious I is also inwardly aware of its being in and through these same spiritual stirrings, yet such awareness culminates in appropriately clarified knowledge only through further rational reflection. Though awareness of the being of the conscious I requires no such rational reflection, all rational reflection has its foundation in the conscious I since it is discovered as the ever-present basis of rational activity.[7] For Stein, rational reflection discloses the presence of three transcendent (in the phenomenological sense) worlds beyond what is immediately given in conscious experience, the "inner world" of the self undergirding the life of consciousness, the "outer world" of sensible things within which consciousness is situated and which fills consciousness with its intentional contents, and the "world above" that is announced together with the characteristic finitude of consciousness, the world of the absolutely transcendent other.[8] These three transcendent "worlds" are always already disclosed in conscious experience

---

6   See EES, 41, 42n11; PA, 9–12, 83–84. Stein uses the phrase spiritual stirring (*geistige Regung*) to denote intentional acts in order to avoid confusion with the diverse uses of the term "act" in phenomenological and Scholastic thought. I typically translate "*Geist/geistige*" as "spirit/spiritual" rather than as "mind/mental" as I believe this most accurately represents Stein's intended meaning when using these terms, though their translation as mind/mental should be kept in mind throughout. In some contrast to Aquinas, Stein deliberately attends to the affectivity of spirit and the intentionality of this affectivity, though I will not here closely compare and critique Stein and Aquinas on this significant theme.

7   See PA, 14; EES, 51–52; AMP, 85.

8   See EES, 56–58, 239, 311; and PA, 16–18. By her use of world (*Welt*) in this context, whether qualified as inner, outer, or above, Stein intends to designate all that lies beyond the immediately given conscious I—and thus all that lies "transcendent" to the I—but which nonetheless conditions the life of the I in various ways depending on whether it is qualified as inner, outer, or above. Leask pithily captures all this transcendent orientation of consciousness when he says, "The immediacy of the 'self' entails what necessarily exceeds the self itself." Leask, *Being Reconfigured*, 86.

together with the originally given I, yet they await the rational engagement of the I so that their conceptual character can be appropriately clarified. Such rational engagement takes place when the I follows through on what is immediately present in conscious experience and reflects on the way the immanent contents of consciousness point beyond themselves in manifold interrelated ways. In just this way, the I moves beyond the sphere of immanence towards unveiling the truth of what is co-given together with the truth of its own being, in opening outward toward the being of the "inner and outer worlds" as well as that of the "world above."

Rational reflection on the "inner world" begins when the I turns back upon itself and reflects on the givenness of its own being and life, out of which there arise three questions: "What is this being of which I am aware? What is the I that is aware of its being? And what is the spiritual stirring in which I am, and in which I am conscious of myself and of the stirring?"[9] Reflection on the "outer world" begins when the I attends to the way the outer world fills the life of consciousness with the sensibly given contents of experience, the most basic intentional correlates of its spiritual stirrings. And reflection on the "world above" begins when the I attends to the fleeting character of conscious life and the co-given finitude of the being of the I, through which the conscious I alights on the idea of an enduring and completed fullness of being. To come to foundational knowledge of the being of the conscious self, Stein takes the "inner" and "outer worlds" as the primary spheres of investigation, and she follows two ways of philosophizing she calls Augustinian and Aristotelian, respectively, only later attending to the "world above" by employing the conceptual aid of the analogy of being. According to the "Augustinian way," Stein looks to "the *life of the I* [*dem* Ichleben]" to provide an understanding of the self as it is inwardly disclosed, and according to the "Aristotelian way," she looks to "the world of *sensible things* [*der Welt der* sinnenfälligen Dinge]" to provide an understanding of the self as it is outwardly perceived in sensible experience

---

9   EES, 42. Compare PA, 10. I am grateful to Walter Redmond for his felicitous translation of these questions which I have here only slightly adjusted. Angela Ales Bello helpfully describes Stein's investigative procedure as follows: "to mine the interiority of the human being and to examine its external manifestations." Angela Ales Bello, "Edmund Husserl and Edith Stein: The Question of the Human Subject," trans. Antonio Calcagno, *American Catholic Philosophical Quarterly* 82, no. 1 (2008): 143–59: 146. Compare Scarpelli Cory, *Human Self-Knowledge*, esp. 77, 87.

as a body among bodies.[10] Both ways give access to knowledge of the being of the self, and only by attending to both ways is it possible to attain conceptual knowledge of the kind and mode of being of the conscious self.[11]

So considered, these two ways of philosophizing are not to be understood as radically divergent approaches to philosophy, somehow standing side-by-side without any inherent relation, and perhaps even opposed to one another. Rather, Stein regards these ways as reciprocally complementary, since only by attending to both is a fully comprehensive knowledge of the self and what it means to be human made possible. While Stein grants foundational and coordinating priority to the Augustinian way of proceeding, at least as she presents her investigation in *Finite and Eternal Being*, she recognizes a complementary priority for the Aristotelian way, precisely inasmuch as she recognizes that inner certainty of the self is not ordinarily first in the order of knowing, and, more importantly, it is only according to an Aristotelian mode that knowledge of the self inhabiting a real outer world together with other selves is attained.

In accord with Aquinas's presentation of the order of knowing, Stein reasons that knowledge ordinarily begins with the persons, things, events, and states of affairs of the outer world, and only later comes to rational clarity over the being of the immediately given self. Moreover, and again in accord with Aquinas, Stein reasons that knowledge of the self and its inner world is not given in isolation from knowledge of the outer world, but rather is co-given together with knowledge of the outer world, and with ever-growing degrees of clarity as one progresses in knowledge of the outer world. Indeed, according

---

10   EES, 239; see also EES, 29–31, 60–61. The decision of Stein to have recourse to the Aristotelian way in tandem to the Augustinian is an important methodological choice for Stein, one that positions her as an epistemological realist and enables her to align more closely with the thought of Aquinas. Moreover, Stein's practice of the Augustinian way cannot be understood as a pure philosophy of consciousness but must be understood as one aspect of an overarching philosophy of being within which a philosophy of consciousness is situated. As indicated above, this methodological choice follows upon Stein's recognition of the way objects of consciousness are *given* to and for consciousness, and since consciousness is always consciousness *of* something, the conscious subject is only ever given together with its objects.

11   Evidently then, for Stein, the "I" and the "self" cannot simply be equated, even while they can be identified with each other as inherently overlapping realities; one can then also say that the I is, in a certain respect, the most inward dimension of the self. See immediately below, "Exploring the Inner Depth of the 'Life of the I.'"

to the intentional correlation uniting consciousness and the experienced world, Stein recognizes that the natural orientation of the I is to the sensibly given outer world, even while it is always inwardly aware of itself in and through this intentional presence to the outer world. Therefore, though Stein begins her investigation with the certainty of the consciously given self, she does not endorse this starting point as the *only* place from which to begin philosophical investigation, and rather moves toward immediately completing this inner starting point with philosophical investigation of the outer world in an Aristotelian mode—and one could also say Thomistic.[12]

Exploring the Inner Depth of the "Life of the I"

To disclose the nature of the "inner world," Stein reflects on the "life of the I" by beginning with what she, following Husserl, calls "units of experience [*Erlebniseinheiten*]."[13] A unit of experience is defined as anything that is

---

12   As mentioned above (5n3), Stein's understanding here clearly parallels that of Aquinas, as shown in Scarpelli Cory's study, where she shows that the subject of the self and the object intellectually grasped "are co-manifested in the act of cognition," for Aquinas, so that "I only ever encounter myself *in the mode of thinking about something.*" Scarpelli Cory, *Human Self-Knowledge*, 160, 171. At this stage of analysis, it is worth noting that Stein's presentation stands in stark contrast to the position of Jean Paul Sartre, whose early philosophical article arguing against Husserl, *The Transcendence of the Ego* (*La Transcendance de l'ego*, 1937), completely undoes the significance of the "I [ego]" in the structure of experience and the experiencing subject. By removing the I from the domain of immanence and placing it in the domain of transcendence, Sartre ignores the evidently given unifying pole of consciousness and thus destroys the unity of consciousness and conscious experience. See Jean Paul Sartre, *The Transcendence of the Ego*, trans. Andrew Brown (London: Routledge, 2004). I further note that in this area Stein's presentation resonates deeply with certain aspects of the position of Emmanuel Levinas, whose early work inspired by Husserl and Heidegger, *The Theory of Intuition in Husserl's Phenomenology* (*La théorie de l'intuition dans la phénoménologie de Husserl*, 1930), reveals the absolute centrality of consciousness and the being of consciousness, *le soi et l'autre*, the self and the other. By ratifying Husserl's recognition of the centrality of consciousness and by further arguing that this centrality is grounded in the eminent mode of being of consciousness, Levinas confirms Stein's insight that the conscious I is given in experience as a reality possessing existential valence with immediate self-evidence. See Emmanuel Levinas, "The Phenomenological Theory of Being: The Absolute Existence of Consciousness," in *The Theory of Intuition in Husserl's Phenomenology*, trans. Andre Orianne (Evanston, IL: Northwestern University Press, 1995), 17–36.

13   EES, 47n29, where she references the phenomenological provenance of the phrase. See

built up and structured as a whole in the life of the I and then endures for a definite period of time. Units are that *in which* and *by which* the conscious I lives its life, since, on the one hand, each unit depends on the being of the I for its own being, and, on the other hand, each unit fills and structures the life of the I with its particular experiential contents. Each unit has an evidently complex character, involving the conscious I, an intentional act by which the object is seized, and the object so intended in the act. Whereas the object is the determining focal point of the experience, as that toward which the I is directed in its act, the act is that which determines the unity and character of the experience, so that it is an experience of a particular object in a determinate way with a determinate sense. A typical example of a unit of experience repeatedly used by Stein is "joy." Joy is an experience that includes the conscious I as its subject, the object about which the I is joyful, and the joyous act of the subject. The joyful object, an object motivating joy for some or other reason, lies at the heart of the experience, as that toward which the I is oriented in the experience, and the act of joy, an intentional act enacted by the I, governs the structure, unity, and course of the experience, determining it as this very experience with its own discrete character.

Each unit of experience is fleeting in being, coming to be and passing away as the conscious I transitions from one unit to the next via the motivational structure of consciousness, yet the *being* of the I with its own experiential life welling up from within remains the ever-present foundation of experience.[14] Accordingly, Stein argues that experience evinces a dimension of being that is both "transcendent [*jenseitig*]" and "hidden [*verborgen*],"[15] transcendent inasmuch as it is not immediately present in experience, even while it *underlies* and *upholds* experience, and hidden inasmuch as it remains partially veiled to the reflective look of the I, even while it *conditions* the meaningful contents of experience. Thus, Stein reasons, the "whole of conscious life is not synonymous with 'my being'—[conscious life] is like an illumined surface over a dark depth,

---

Husserl, *Investigations*, 1:193–94. Stein does not use this particular phrase in either PA or AMP, though she does frame the life of the I in the same manner in both texts.

14 As mentioned above (see 5n2), in tandem with Husserl, Stein understands the intentional life of the I to follow a rational lawfulness she designates as motivation, where motivation is understood to be that which determines the path of acts of constitution and thus connects successive intentional acts.

15 See EES, 51–52, 56, 311; and PA, 14.

which [depth] announces itself through this surface."[16] Rationally illuminating this "inner world" involves attending to the determining and conditioning influence of the depth upon what is immediately present on the surface of conscious life. When we attend to this influence, Stein argues we come to recognize the "thing-like" character of the depth, and she further identifies this depth as something substantial, precisely since it both underlies *and* upholds the living current of consciousness as that upon which the illumined surface of consciousness depends, while simultaneously conditioning experience by qualifying its meaningful contents.[17]

For Stein, the necessity to conclude to a substantial self rests on three interplaying givens of experience, givens that while immanent in consciousness evince truths of a properly transcendent character, making recognition of such substantiality a necessary conclusion in order to account for experience.[18] First, the conscious I is an ever-present constant of experience despite the flowing character of experience, both with regard to the various acts of the I and with regard to the various objects intended, indicating that the being of the I endures throughout the entire temporal span of conscious life. Again, the I is able to traverse the temporal range of experience, recalling past and anticipating future experiences, while itself remaining present in the dimensionless "now," further indicating that the I possesses enduring identity through the whole span of experience. Finally, the flow of conscious life is qualitatively conditioned in various ways on the side of the I, with a conditioning that is both persistent and transient, indicating that the being underlying conscious experience must have its own qualitative determinations that variously affect its experiential contents. As a result of these three interwoven givens, Stein maintains that the life of the I can be adequately explained *only* through recourse to a substantial basis underlying experience. Moreover, she reasons that this substantial basis cannot be a bare substrate underlying experience, but rather must be something that can uphold the stirrings of consciousness, and so must have an independent mode

---

16   EES, 311. The inner depth is "dark [*dunklen*]" in the sense of hidden, not in the sense of morally corrupt or psychologically chaotic, even while these two further kinds of darkness can (and often are) also be present in the inner depth.

17   PA, 14; see EES, 312, 319–20; PA, 168–69. See also Peter J. Schulz, "Toward the Subjectivity of the Human Person: Edith Stein's Contribution to the Theory of Identity," trans. Christina M. Gschwandtner, in *American Catholic Philosophical Quarterly* 8, no. 1 (2008): 161–76: 167–68.

18   See EES, 50–56; and PA, 14, where Stein mentions only the first and last.

of being together with a range of spiritual powers at its disposal. That is, if the inner depth not only underlies but also upholds the contents of experience, it must have being in itself and this being must endure with identity through time, while also having the potential to bear various qualitative determinations, and must have a range of spiritual powers arrayed in correspondence to its varied spiritual doings.

As a result, Stein concludes that a *subsistent spiritual substance* must underlie the life of consciousness, and that this spiritual substance must have a range of *properties* and *qualities*, both persistent and transient, as well as inherent *spiritual faculties* and a corresponding ability to wield these faculties in various kinds of *spiritual acts*.[19] All this, Stein reasons, becomes manifest in consciousness through the underlying, upholding, and conditioning of units of experience, even while what becomes apparent in this way in the life of the I remains transcendent to the immanence of consciousness. Yet, consciousness should not here be understood in any way that implies its hypostatization. Rather, it must be understood as that feature of the life of the I that emerges as an illumined surface over the underlying depth of the being and life of the I.[20] The mode of being of the I simply cannot be reduced to consciousness and the exercise of spiritual powers, and the "self" of first-person experience cannot simply be equated with the conscious subject, but rather must be understood to include a substantial basis that grounds the I and the life of consciousness.

19 See PA, 168–69; and EES, 312, 319–20. In EES, Stein translates Aquinas's "*subsistentia*" as "*subsistierendes*" rather than "*subsistenz*," which Redmond theorizes Stein does to indicate the parallel with "*seiendes*." Unless otherwise indicated, all uses of the term "substance" in what follows should be taken in the sense of "first substance," that which has being in itself and not in another, and that which is not itself predicated of any other, in contrast to accidents, which the substance underlies and in which they have their being, and which are then predicated of substance. Hence, my use of the phrase "subsistent substance," since "subsistence" directly signifies this primary mode of being, in contrast to "substance" which directly signifies only the underlying feature of primary being and/or predication.

20 In "Thomistic Personalism" Wojtyła argues that it is precisely this kind of hypostatization that has caused many of the difficulties associated with modern philosophy and its reception, which he describes broadly as a "philosophy of consciousness" with a primary interest in epistemology, in contrast to ancient and medieval philosophy, which he describes as a "philosophy of being" with a primary interest in metaphysics. See Karol Wojtyła, "Thomistic Personalism," in *Person and Community: Selected Essays*, trans. Theresa Sandok (New York: Peter Lang, 1993, repr. 2008), 169.

Accordingly, Stein forcefully concludes, "Spiritual being *requires* a spiritual substance," and more pointedly still, "the being of the I is *unthinkable* without this being possessing substance."[21]

Reframing all this in ordinary terms, one can say that the life of consciousness is that which is closest to each and every subject, an innermost given of experience, irrevocably found together with any and all experiences whatsoever. Yet, the life of consciousness does not hover in the void without any inner ground, but rather rises from an inner depth that becomes manifest in and through its bright illumination. Though this inner depth is never present in conscious experience as such, its presence is perpetually announced as the inner condition of its actuality, determinate character, and qualitative conditioning. The nature of this "inner world" can then become ever more accessible to the conscious subject through the ever-flowing stream of its experiential life and can be brought to a more fulsome givenness through the course of life rationally engaged and reflectively clarified via the intentional life of consciousness.

A Personal Substance Composed of Soul and Living-Body

To identify the nature of the substance underlying consciousness, Stein uses the term "person," precisely since, as we have seen, the substance evinced in experience possesses a spiritual mode of life.[22] Evident in Stein's analysis up to this point is the spiritual life of consciousness, as is clear in her identification of the characteristic life of the I as *spiritual* stirring. Spiritual stirring is that which is closest to consciousness; in all spiritual activity the I tends toward the world in an intentional way and thereby enters into living engagement with the world, its persons, things, events, and states of affairs. Yet, in being so aware of the objective world in intentional acts, the conscious I does not lose awareness of itself, but rather remains inwardly aware of its own life in and through this outward orientation. The conscious I is thus given as possessing a direct mode of presence to the outer world in all intentional acts while simultaneously possessing an intimate mode of self-presence. These are two distinct moments

---

21 PA, 86; emphasis added.
22 Already in her early works, Stein utilizes the concept "person" to designate the being of the self given in conscious experience, and primarily in terms of the "core of the person [*Kern der Person*]," taken together with personal value response as revelatory of the person, but she there does so without involving the classical metaphysical apparatus employed in these later works. See PE, 114–31; IG, 189–99; and EPh, 101–4, 134–36.

of awareness that, though distinct, are *always* given together: an awareness of and corresponding presence to the objective world, together with an awareness of and corresponding presence to the subjective self. Yet, for Stein it is precisely these features—awareness and presence, the objective and the subjective—that represent the distinctive marks of spiritual life, inasmuch as this dual polarity exhibits the outward openness and inward transparency that is essential to spiritual being.[23] In contrast to material being, which is naturally self-enclosed and opaque, spiritual being tends toward the objective world while remaining inwardly present to the subjective self, and can therefore be *with* the objectively other while remaining perpetually *with* the subjective self. Simply put, spiritual being is simultaneously self-aware and self-present *while* being other-aware and other-present, with both moments interpenetrating in the experiential life of the subject. Moreover, together with this polarity, spiritual being remains in transcendent possession of itself, not losing itself in experience through its intentional presence to the other, but rather fulfilling itself in and through this very outward orientation.

This twofold radicality—the radicality of self-possession and alterity—exhibits that the being of the substance underlying experience must be spiritual being, and since "what is self-dependent insofar as it is spiritual is called *person*," the being underlying conscious experience must also be a person.[24] This means that the conscious I is never given in experience as an abstract point, so to speak—whether the pure I (*das reine Ich*) of Husserlian phenomenology or the I think (*cogito*) of Cartesian doubt—but is always given

---

23 See EES, 50, 192–93; and AMP, 78–81, 99–100. Such outward openness and inward transparency is simply not found in material being, nor is it possible for material being, which is both enclosed in itself and inwardly opaque. Moreover, the transcendence of spirit is possible precisely because of this simultaneity of presence, where spirit passes beyond the confines of its own being through its inherent openness to the other. In addition to these essential marks of spiritual being, for Stein, we can also add that unlike matter spirit does not have parts outside parts but rather is always itself through and through, even while spirit can have a virtual complexity through its arrayed powers.

24 PA, 85; see also PA, 84–87; and EES, 303–7. Though Stein recognizes and notes a subtle difference of meaning between "subsistence" and "self-dependence," by identifying self-dependence as that perfection of an essence that completes its structure and renders it capable of the perfection of existence, she also recognizes their closeness in meaning as well as their actual coincidence in being, since only self-dependent essences are capable of the further perfection of existence by which they subsist.

as a "living-spiritual-personal I [*lebendig-geistig-persönliche Ich*]."²⁵ Even while the I can be considered in abstraction from the spiritual and personal structure—as the pure I or the *cogito*—where the empty formality of the I provides the possibility of the punctual kind of being of consciousness, precisely as such an abstraction the I has no actual independence from the transcendent depth and no separation from its substantial spiritual basis. Accordingly, we can see that the emphasis Stein places on consciousness rising from the depth is a decisive feature of her understanding of experience. In consistently recognizing the inner dependence of the I in her phenomenologically coordinated investigations, Stein is careful to attend to the "more" of conscious subjectivity in a manner that is metaphysically pregnant from the outset, and she can readily move toward metaphysical conclusions without in any way disregarding the rigor required to phenomenologically detail what is immanently given in experience. It is an investigative stance that pursues the precision of phenomenology while at one and the same time attending to all that is announced in the immanence of consciousness. This clearly exhibits the Augustinian, rather than Husserlian or Cartesian character of Stein's investigative starting point, and it subsequently enables her to align more closely with Aquinas's presentation of the human being as a spiritual and personal substance.²⁶

---

25   See EES, 320. According to a similar reading of Stein, Christof Betschart indicates that Stein's mature understanding of self-dependence allows her to bridge the gap between the phenomenological conception of the pure I and the Scholastic understanding of the person by conceiving of the self-dependent person as a necessary condition of the possibility of conscious life. See Christof Betschart, *Unwiederholbares Gottessiegel: Personale Individualität nach Edith Stein* (Basel: Reinhardt, 2013), 230–31; and *"Person,"* in *Edith Stein-Lexikon*, ed. Marcus Knaup and Harald Seubert (Freiburg i. Br.: Herder, 2017), 278–81; and also Claudia Mariéle Wulf, "Ich," in *Stein-Lexikon*, 185–88; Marian Maskulak, *Edith Stein and the Body-Soul-Spirit at the Center of Holistic Formation* (New York: Peter Lang, 2007), 59–60; and Schulz, "Theory of Identity," 161–76: 172–73.

26   By here detailing and highlighting Stein's attention to the substantial depth of the personal self, I do not intend to imply that Husserl did not recognize more to human subjectivity than the pure I (*reine Ich*), or that Descartes did not eventually present a fuller picture of human subjectivity than the bare I think (*cogito*); rather, I simply wish to show that Stein expressly attends to this depth throughout her investigations. Moreover, even while Husserl speaks of the transcendent I, the psyche, and the body, there is little indication he considered these substantive in the decidedly metaphysical way understood by Stein, and even while Descartes identified the *cogito* with the mind and soul, and at length returned to the reality of the body, the soul is now left impoverished in its conflation with mind, and the body is reduced to a mere extended thing (*res extensa*) with mechanical

To further explicate the nature of the personal substance in view of providing a greater degree of conceptual clarity over the structure of the transcendent depth, Stein proceeds to describe it as a structural complex of "soul" and "living-body."[27] For Stein, knowledge of the complex structure of the person is first given in experience through the conditioning of the contents of experience that occurs on the side of the subject. As seen above, units of experience are not only upheld in being by the personal subject but are also conditioned in their content from hidden depths of the self. This conditioning is manifest in all conscious experience but is most evident when there is a disjoint between the object experienced and the contents of the experience. Something that could, or indeed should, motivate an intentional act of this or that kind may not be experienced by the personal subject as subjectively motivating. A particular object that is an objective motive for joy, for example, may not motivate joy in the personal subject or the kind or degree of joy claimed by the object in its integral meaningfulness. But since the reason for this cannot lie on the side of the object, since the particular object is recognizably a motive for joy, the reason must lie on the side of the subject. The personal subject is not awakened to joy by the joyous object because of some indisposition on the part of the subject, whether transient or enduring, with the consequence that the subject cannot tend toward the object with befitting experiential content—that is, with a proportionate act of joy. This kind of conditioning, Stein argues, indicates that the subject must have a complex structure that admits of various qualifications that foundationally determine the subject and thereby condition its experiential life.

The precise nature of this complex is made available for consciousness in what Stein, following Husserl, calls self-perception and inner perception.[28]

---

operation and a loosely defined and intellectually incomprehensible relationship to the thinking thing (*res cogitans*). Compare Edmund Husserl, *Logical Investigations*, 2 vols., trans. J. N. Findlay (New York: Routledge, 2001, repr. 2008), 2:103–69; and René Descartes, *Meditations on First Philosophy*, in *Descartes Philosophical Writings*, ed. and trans. Elizabeth Anscombe and Peter T. Geach, intro. by Alexander Koyré (Indianapolis: Bobbs-Merrill Educational Publishing, 1971, repr. 1983), esp. *Meditations* 2, 6.

27 See EES, 51, 310–15; AMP, 83–92; and PA, 168–78. Compare PE, 55–74.

28 EES, 312, 319. Though Stein distinguishes self-perception (*Selbstwahrnehmung*) from inner perception (*innere Wahrnehmung*), indicating that the former involves the whole of the self, whereas the latter primarily involves the living-body, she uses self-perception only once in EES (319) and refers to both kinds of perception as inner perception in all further investigations.

Joy and sadness, and all comparable experiences, are not only immediate experiences of the living-spiritual-personal I, nor are they simply found present in their conditioning of the contents of experience, but rather are also experienced through inward perception of one's own inner being and life. First, in "self-perception" they are experienced as inwardly pervading an expanse of the life of the subject with their particular experiential character, thereby disclosing an interior expanse Stein identifies with the traditional term "soul."[29] Then, in "inner perception" the very same contents are experienced through their manifestation in a materially extended dimension of the self Stein identifies with "living-body."[30] Thus, in self-perception of the inwardly expansive soul, and in inner perception of the outwardly extended body, each taken individually and both taken together, the nature of the inner depth of the personal subject is disclosed as a structural complex of soul and living-body.[31] Moreover, Stein argues that the soul and living-body are thereby also given together in a profound unity of being with one another and with the personal I, inasmuch as one and the same experience is simultaneously a direct experience of consciousness and an inwardly perceived experience that pervades the expansive soul and materially extended body.

Supplementing these introspective givens, Stein further argues that the extended living-body is also given in outer perception as the body of the personal self in a way that complements these inward experiences.[32] First, *this* very material body is given as the locus of sensory interaction with the outer world via the exterior senses, and the instrument of active engagement with the same sensed outer world via all living activity manifest in the body. Moreover, both outer perception *via* this material body and *of* this material body have a unique correspondence with inner perception of the same spatially extended body. Finally, unlike all other material bodies of the sensibly given outer world, outer perception of *this* material body

---

29   See AMP, 85–86, 104, 113; and EES, 50–51, 56. When said of the soul, "expanse" is used in both literal and metaphorical senses, literal inasmuch as the soul animates the extended body, and metaphorical inasmuch as the soul has an interiority that is without material extension, but which is nonetheless best understood as "spatial" and "expansive."

30   See AMP, 52, 105–6, 113; and EES, 312–14. In German, the distinction between *Leib* (living-body) and *Körper* (body) captures well the difference between the ensouled body and the physical body.

31   See Betschart, "Seele," and "*Person*," in *Stein-Lexikon*, 334–38, 278–81; Maskulak, *Body-Soul-Spirit*, 60–61; and Schulz, "Theory of Identity," 161–76: 165–66.

32   See EES, 312–13, 317–20, 364; PA, 168–69.

has certain limitations that cannot be overcome by local movement and/or postural changes—I cannot leave *my* body behind and encounter the outer world from an entirely different location in place and time; *my* actual perspective is ineradicably tied to *my* body.[33]

In all these ways—through the underlying conditioning of conscious experience; through self-perception of the expansive soul and inner perception of the material body; through outer perception via the material body and outer perception of the material body; through active engagement with the things of the outer world via the material living-body; and through the close correlation of all these consciously given experiences—the subsistent spiritual substance upholding conscious experience is not only given as a personal substance, but is also given as a structural complex that is at once soul and living-body. Consequently, Stein reasons that soul and living-body are joined in a profound unity that is best described as a living unity of animating-soul and animated-body, since inner perception reveals one and the same experience to be jointly manifest in the soul and living-body, and since the correlation of inner and outer perception reveals the soul to be the animating principle of sensation and motility; and, conversely, since the living-body is given as the locus of expression for the soul and its living activities.[34]

Thus, Stein concludes that the conscious I immediately given in experience is not identifiable merely as a *living, spiritual, and personal I*, but rather must also be identified as a *soulish and bodily I*, where the whole of soul and living-body are as much "my life" as "my thinking" and "my joy" are my life.[35]

---

33 Mette Lebech provides a detailed treatment of Stein's understanding of the constitution of the living-body (which Stein treats more fully in her early works), especially as regards the intersubjectivity of such constitution. See Mette Lebech, *The Philosophy of Edith Stein: From Phenomenology to Metaphysics* (Oxford: Peter Lang, 2015), 55–57. Donald Wallenfang highlights the correlation of inner perception of the embodied soul with outer perception of the ensouled body. See Donald Wallenfang, "The Heart of the Matter: Edith Stein on the Substance of the Soul," *Logos: A Journal of Catholic Thought and Culture* 17, no. 3 (2014): 118–42: 119–21.

34 Alice Togni shows that Stein is working with an understanding of human unity from the very beginning of her philosophical career and sets Stein's understanding into relief against that background of Husserl's conception of transcendental subjectivity. See Alice Togni, "Edith Stein in Dialogue with Husserl: The Person as a Psycho-physical Unity," in *The Hat and the Veil: The Phenomenology of Edith Stein*, Ad Fontes: Studien zur frühen Phänomenologie, 3, ed. Jerzy Machnacz et al. (Nordhausen: Traugott Bautz, 2016), 39–64. See also Knaup, "*Leib*," in *Stein-Lexikon*, 228–31.

35 EES, 313. Since there is no easy translation of the German "*seelisch*" (the adjectival

Stein's Recourse to the Anthropology of Aquinas

With her identification of that which underlies conscious experience as a personal substance structured as spirit, soul, and living-body, Stein has passed beyond the confines of what is immanent to consciousness and into the sphere of what is transcendent (in the phenomenological sense). In concluding to the reality of "substance," "person," "soul," and "living-body," and in providing summary conclusions regarding their interrelation, Stein has made metaphysical claims, claims that require further inferential reasoning to appropriately unpack their content.[36] Such metaphysical claims are necessary, Stein argues, if one is to understand the nature of conscious experience and its immanent contents, because consciousness together with its units of experience cannot be accounted for from the pure immanence of consciousness. Since the immanent contents of consciousness evince a range of being that lies beyond the restricted domain of consciousness, the immediately given contents of experience cannot be understood without concluding to the reality of such transcendent entities. Therefore, upon the foundation of experience phenomenologically investigated, having already achieved a preliminary outline of the meaning of "substance," "person," 'soul," and "living-body," Stein moves to a metaphysical mode of reasoning in order to attain a more comprehensive grasp of the personal substance and its complex soul-body structure.[37]

---

form of *Seele* (soul)), and since "psychic" translates the German "*psychische*," which has a subtly different meaning for Stein, and which also has unfortunate connotations in English, I am constrained here to use the somewhat strained English form "soulish." I note here that Stein's treatment of the body and its significance has clear parallels with the comparable reflections of Maurice Merleau-Ponty in his *Phenomenology of Perception* (*Phénoménologie de la perception*, 1945). See Maurice Merleau-Ponty, "Part I: The Body," in *Phenomenology of Perception*, trans. Colin Smith (London: Routledge, 2012), 77–205.

36 Though Stein most often uses neuter pronouns when considering the I in abstraction, when she speaks of the personal I, person, human being, etc., she usually transitions to the use of gendered pronouns, presumably because such use more adequately captures the sense of some*one* rather than some*thing*; and presumably also because the embodied person is given as sex-determined rather than neuter. Accordingly, from this point forward, except when speaking of the abstract or pure I, I use the gendered form of the pronoun to identify the I, personal I, person, human being, soul, etc.; and for the sake of simplicity and consonant with traditional English usage, I use the masculine form throughout in its general reference to all human individuals regardless of sex.

37 I note here that already in her earliest philosophical investigation on empathy (PE),

To perform this further metaphysical investigation, Stein seeks assistance from the anthropological tradition of the *philosophia perennis* in order to detail the nature of the "person," "soul," and "living-body." As noted above, the teachings Stein relies upon are the classical definition of the person and the closely related teachings of the substantial unity of the human being and the soul's formation of the material body.[38] With regard to the person, Stein seeks assistance primarily from Aquinas while supplementing her investigation with insights received from Augustine; with regard to substantial unity and the formation of the body, Stein again seeks assistance primarily from Aquinas while also engaging the writings of Aristotle and Hedwig Conrad-Martius.[39]

> Stein treats of the constitution of the person together with that of the soul and living-body when she treats of empathy "as a problem of constitution," and seeks "the solution to the question of how [...] the psychophysical individual, the personality, and the like are built-up within consciousness." Stein there shows that the I is given as "'it itself' and no other," together with an undergirding structure, possessing "substantial unity" and "persistent properties," which she identifies as the "substantial soul," before providing a proportionally lengthier exposition of how the living-body is given together with the soul in the unity of lived experience. Over the course of her phenomenological analysis, and in a manner patently consistent with her later works, it is clear that Stein both firmly establishes the unity of the conscious I, soul, and living-body, and recognizes the significance of this unity for constituting the fully completed structure of the conscious self as a human self. Indeed, though the emphasis is sometimes different in PE (and other early works) than in her later works, I can find no definitive contrast, and certainly not a contradiction, between the earlier and later works. See PE, 53–74, esp. 57–65.

38   This definition was first introduced by Boëthius and later commented on by many philosophers and theologians of the medieval era, such as Richard of St. Victor, St. Albert the Great, and, of course, St. Thomas Aquinas. See Anicius Boëthius, *Liber de persona et duabus naturis contra Eutychen et Nestorium*, trans. H. F. Stewart, and E. K. Rand (London: Heinemann, 1958), chap. 3. I regard the Boëthian definition as classical, even though it did not garner the universal endorsement of patristic and medieval thinkers (or indeed the unqualified endorsement of Aquinas), since it certainly became a coordinating point of reference for discussion regarding the nature of the person throughout the medieval era and into the modern and contemporary eras, and accordingly was taken up by Neo-Scholastic thinkers in their interpretation of the *philosophia perennis*. For more detail regarding these qualifications, see Scott M. Williams, "Persons in Patristic and Medieval Theology," in *Persons: A History*, ed. Antonio Lolordo (Oxford: Oxford University Press, 2019), 52–86.

39   Notwithstanding the significance of these other thinkers for Stein's fully developed position, in accord with the purposes of my investigation, I here only analyze Stein's engagement with the teachings of Aquinas.

Stein turns to Aquinas in a primary way in both these areas because of the basic coherence of her phenomenological conclusions with his in these same areas. In light of this basic coherence, Stein can engage the conceptual apparatuses of Aquinas to provide the outline metaphysical structure required to sufficiently account for what has been given in experience, while continuing to employ phenomenology to investigate the fittingness of these apparatuses to grasp the nature of the beings in question, thus "testing" the apparatuses against the things themselves given in experience. In this way, Stein can situate her investigation of human nature in direct relation to the anthropology of Aquinas while concomitantly encountering the thing itself via an objective investigation of the person, soul, and living-body, as also their interrelation. This deliberate positioning against the backdrop of Aquinas's anthropology leads to a positive development in two directions. On the one hand, Stein attains valuable assistance from Aquinas toward comprehensively detailing the completed structure of human nature as a personal nature; on the other hand, Stein achieves basic confirmation and corroboration of Aquinas's anthropology in its broad conceptual outline, before further expanding and deepening its conceptual content.

In relation to the former, Stein indicates her need for Aquinas for two closely related reasons.[40] First, since the transcendent dimension disclosed in experience is to some degree a "hidden" and "dark" depth that requires inferential reasoning, she can receive valuable assistance from Aquinas toward illuminating the path of her investigation, in view of attaining a more adequate description of the substantial structure of the person. Then, since attaining detailed knowledge of the exact relation of soul and living-body is possible only "in a very complicated and mediated way," Stein can use the apparatuses of Aquinas to aid her resolution of various difficulties surrounding this important problem.[41] In so seeking Aquinas's help, Stein maintains that her anthropology is thereby capable of being more comprehensive, while receiving a degree of protection from any inadvertent one-sidedness, inasmuch as she holds her independent investigations in inner tension with the time-tested teachings of Aquinas and Thomism. *In relation to the latter*, the confirmation and

---

40 For this and what follows, see EES, 51, 56, 63, 311; PA, 14–15; and AMP, 281.
41 PA, 169. I note here that Descartes took this problem to be insoluble since the union of soul and body, though perceptible, could be known only obscurely with the result that a clear and distinct idea of the character of this unity could not be achieved. See Descartes, *Descartes Philosophical Writings*, esp. *Meditations* 2, 6.

corroboration of Aquinas's anthropology is again twofold. First, by having already concluded to the same realities set forth in Aquinas—the person, soul, and living-body, together with their unity—and achieving conceptual outline of these realities that basically accords with Aquinas's position, Stein confirms the cogency of these apparatuses from a phenomenological perspective, and thereby attains initial affirmation of the nature of the *compositum humanum* as traditionally understood. By following this initial confirmation with further phenomenological investigation in consort with Aquinas's teachings, while consistently referring to the thing itself—the human being—as attended to in eidetic intuition and variation, Stein provides further corroboration of the depth of truth to be found in these teachings. This confirmation and corroboration stands true, as will be shown below, even while Stein reinterprets their meaning while integrating their conceptual content into her mature understanding of the human person.

* * * * * *

For the remainder of this chapter, I analyze only Stein's incorporation of the classical definition of the person and reserve my exploration of Stein's assimilation of Aquinas's teachings regarding human unity and bodily formation for the next chapter. In this way, the analysis of the present chapter grounds these later analyses in the personal character of human nature, while these later analyses suitably complete the exploration of the person here undertaken. Yet, before moving directly to a consideration of the definition of the person, I note that while I have thus far focused on understanding the personal subject almost entirely from a first-person perspective according to her Augustinian way, as noted above Stein's conception of the being and life of the subject is developed in completion only through recourse to the "outer world" (as well as to the "world above"). Though phenomenological investigation of the inner world is all that is necessary to bring us to the threshold of Stein's metaphysical investigations and adoption of the teachings of Aquinas, reflection on what is sensibly given in outer perception, both of the self and of the other, is necessary if one is to substantiate and universalize the results garnered from this first-person perspective. Therefore, from here forward, and in all subsequent chapters, I consistently appeal to Stein's Aristotelian way of philosophizing, as did Stein herself in her investigation of human nature. Indeed, it is only through such outward-oriented exploration that we can come to understand the nature of the personal subject as a human individual possessing a *common* human nature, numbered as one of the human species and an integrated member of various overlapping communities, oriented toward the world together with other conscious subjects.

The Person: A Subsistent Rational Individual

In *Finite and Eternal Being*, Stein begins her exposition of the meaning of being a person by citing the Boëthian definition of the person, "*rationalis naturae individua substantia*, an individual substance of a rational nature," and proceeds by citing sizeable excerpts of Aquinas's texts while reflecting on the meaning of the definition as understood by Aquinas.[42] In this way, Stein progressively appropriates the meaning of the classical definition in continuity with Aquinas, while simultaneously unfolding her own understanding through an independent phenomenological investigation. Stein's consequent development and deepening of the definition is seen in a number of closely related areas, but is no more evident than in her introduction of the concept bearer (*Träger*) to designate the person, and her corresponding identification of the personal I (*persönliche Ich*) as the bearer of the rational nature. By introducing these new concepts and reconsidering the content of the classical definition from their coordinating perspective, Stein provides a new organizing principle of the definition and sets into relief all of its essential elements. Stein's use of the concept bearer harks back to her phenomenological formation and appears in her early writings as a concept designating the transcendent depth underlying experience.[43] In her mature works, the term retains this basic significance in

---

42 EES, 304, citing ST, I, 29.1, arg 1. As with Aquinas, Stein reflects on the definition of "person" first and primarily with respect to its divine attribution; yet, in contrast to Aquinas, her reflections quickly turn to a consideration of its human attribution (see esp. EES, 307–11); and again, as will be shown below, following Aquinas, Stein accepts the Boëthian definition—formulated by him as "*naturae rationabilis individua substantia*"—by interpreting and clarifying its meaning in tandem with Aquinas's interpretation and recasting as "*subsistens in rationali natura*." I would like to thank Jadwiga Guerrero van der Meijden for bringing to my attention the subtle difference in Boëthius's formulation of the definition from that taken up by later commentators, including Aquinas, and for indicating the "potential" or "modal" character of the differentiated adjectival suffix—*rationabilis* versus *rationalis*—in Boëthius's formulation. See Jadwiga Guerrero van der Meijden, *Person and Dignity in Edith Stein's Writings* (Berlin: De Gruyter, 2019), 2n7.

43 See esp. PE, 55–56, 56–74; and PK, 21–24. As noted above, in these works Stein also

relation to consciousness but is also extended to encompass various foundational features of being in general, having an eventual reach of meaning that traverses all regions of being and is applied in the wholly different contexts of actual, essential, and intentional modes of being.

The core meaning that remains the same can be captured by the phrase "that which underlies and upholds," since the bearer underlies and upholds that which is borne. When further specified, this core meaning takes the following range of particular significations. First and foundationally, (1) bearer identifies the individual thing (*Einzelding*), the completed whole with all its structural parts, since the individual thing bears itself and bears its own being and essence within itself.[44] According to a closely related sense, (2) bearer identifies the subsistent substance (*subsistierende Substanz*) or hypostasis (ὑπόστασις), the self-dependent whole relative to its structural parts, since the subsistent substance bears all substantial parts as one unified whole.[45] Then also, (3) bearer identifies the essential-form (*Wesensform*), the (living) inner form that powerfully shapes the (living) individual as one whole, since the essential-form bears the being (and life) of the (living) thing through its formative efficacy.[46] Finally, (4) bearer identifies the empty-form of the thing (*Leerform des Dinges*), the final formal determination of the individual thing relative to its partial formal (and material) subdeterminations, since the empty-form bears its correlative formal (and material) fullness.[47] As evident from these varied uses, Stein is indicating that the reality identified as bearer has a certain preeminence relative to what is borne, since (1) the individual thing bears itself and its own being and essence; (2) the subsistent substance

---

uses the terms "transcendent I" and "substantial soul" to identify the reality bearing consciousness.

44 See EES, 187–88, 338–39.
45 EES, 187–88, 338–39.
46 See EES, 206, 216, 223–24, 228–30.
47 EES, 206, 216, 223–24, 228–30; and also EES, 399–403, 412–14. In this last respect, the empty form of the thing, or simply the empty-form "thing," can also be identified as the empty-form "object," when "object" is understood in a narrow sense with the same semantic range as "thing," rather than what can be objectified—that is, anything formally identifiable by consciousness/reason, whether singular or collective, whether of the same or different kinds. With her use of "form" here, Stein is not using it in an Aristotelian-Thomistic sense, but in a sense closer to that of phenomenology, formal ontology, and formal logic. See EES, 194, 247–49, and 314n28.

bears its substantial parts; (3) the essential-form inwardly bears the being (and life) of the (living) thing; and (4) the empty-form bears its correlative formal (and material) fullness. The bearer has this preeminence because it has a certain limited self-dependence relative to what is borne, even while it is not independent of what is borne, precisely inasmuch as the bearer is inherently correlated to what is borne. Consequently, we can see that for Stein "bearer" is a term and concept of general use that identifies an absolutely fundamental feature of reality applicable in correlated ways at all dimensions of analysis, actual, essential, and intentional.

Stein then employs this already developed concept in her interpretation of Aquinas's understanding of the person, using it first simply as a translation of various Latin terms Aquinas uses to designate the personal substance from this or that notional aspect, and thereby as a fitting interpretive key for the meaning of these same terms and related others. Thus, the bearer comes to be identified with the supposit (*suppositum*) and the subsistent (*subsistentia*), as a translation and interpretive key to their meanings, since the supposit bears its predications and the subsistent bears its being, and with hypostasis (ὑπόστασις), as a suitable interpretive key to its meaning, since the hypostasis bears its accidents.[48] But since what these names signify in general, as Aquinas says, "this name 'person' signifies in the genus of rational substances," Stein introduces the term bearer to identify the person with respect to these same notional aspects, while also respecting the subtle differences of meaning signified by each term and its corresponding concept.[49]

What is the rationale behind Stein's introduction of this concept? A foundational reason is found in Aquinas's own texts. When Aquinas is making the case for the manifold meaningfulness of the term "person," as supposit, subsistent, and hypostasis, he repeatedly uses the Latin "*supponitur*" as a descriptive term to elucidate different shades of meaning.[50] "*Supponitur*," which

---

48 See EES, 291, 304–6, translating ST, I, 29.2, co.; I, 29.3, ad 2: "It is a great dignity to be a bearer [Latin original, *subsistere*] of a nature endowed with reason"; "According as [that which subsists in the genus of substance] is bearer [Latin, *supponitur*] of a general nature (*supponitur*), it is called a thing (*res naturae*) [...] According as it is bearer [Latin, *supponitur*] of properties (accidents) it is called a 'hypostasis.'"

49 ST, I, 29.2, co.

50 Aquinas explains the relation of these terms to the term "person" by showing the way they variously identify substance when its meaning is not equated with essence, quiddity, *ousia*: "In another sense substance means the subject or suppositum that subsists in the genus of substance. To this, taken generally, can be applied a name

has the same root as "*suppositum*," is derived from the verb "*supponere*," meaning "to put, place, or set under," and in translations of ST is often rendered as "underlies" in English or as "*trägt*" in German.⁵¹ Consequently, when Stein is interpreting Aquinas's texts and applying the term bearer (*Träger*) to the person as supposit, subsistent, and hypostasis, she is at first simply making explicit a depth of meaning already contained in the texts of Aquinas, inasmuch as these terms variously signify that which underlies and upholds. So considered, Stein's introduction can also be taken as a further clarification of Aristotle's use of *hupokeimenon* (ὑποκείμενον)—that which underlies—as he searches for the primary object of metaphysics, since *hupokeimenon* signifies the ultimate subject of being and predication, something not found in another nor said of another (and in the many respects enumerated by Aristotle). What signification bearer adds to *hupokeimenon* beyond that of underlying is the further meaning of upholding, a signification already implicit in the Aristotelian concept and taken over by Aquinas in his understanding of substance, as is evident by the way both thinkers use their terms. Stein then simply locates and highlights this significance by drawing out its meaning in her use of bearer as an identifier of substance in general and person in particular.

Two further reasons indicating the rationale behind Stein's terminological transposition are discernible from the way she uses the concept throughout her later works. First, as noted above, the term has already been usefully applied in the sphere of being in general and is an indispensable concept in her comprehensive ontology of actual and essential modes of being. Then,

---

signifying intention, and so it is called suppositum. It is also called by three names signifying a reality, those are natural thing, subsistence, and hypostasis, according to a threefold consideration of the substance so named. For, as it exists in itself and not in another, it is called subsistence, since we say that those things subsist which exist not in another but in themselves. On the other hand, as it underlies some common nature, it is called a natural thing; as this man is a human natural thing. As it underlies the accidents, it is called hypostasis or substance. What these three names signify in common in the whole genus of substances, this name person signifies in the genus of rational substances." ST, I, 29.2, co.

51 See entry for "*suppono*" in Charlton T. Lewis and Charles Short, *An Elementary Latin Dictionary* (Oxford: Oxford University Press, 1963). The term "*Träger*" also appears repeatedly in the Thomistic commentary of Josef Gredt and is then also found in Stein's frequent citations of Gredt's commentary in her investigation of the individual. See EES, 395ff.; and Josef Gredt, *Die aristotelische-thomistische Philosophie*, 2 vols. (Freiburg i. Br.: Herder, 1935).

more specifically, the term has a semantic range that can encompass not only being in general but also the unique kind of being of consciousness, rationality, and freedom, which means that the term can have an additional range of meaning when applied to personal being in particular. This twofold usefulness means that Stein can attribute "bearer" to all kinds of personal beings in like manner to the way she uses the term in the sphere of being in general, as signifying the individual thing and subsistent substance, differently determined by an essential-form and empty-form, while also attributing the term in a way specific to personal being, as signifying the intentional mode of life of consciousness, rationality, and freedom.[52] In this latter more restricted use, Stein attributes the term according to a twofold basic sense, namely: (1) the person as bearer of conscious experience and spiritual stirring; and (2) the person as bearer of the rational nature. Each of these uses includes and respects the general ontological meaning of bearer—an objective signification—while also including the meaningful way the personal substance bears that which is specifically personal—a corresponding subjective signification. Thus, in one and the same term, both the objective and the subjective aspect of being a person are conceptually embraced and revealed to be reciprocally explanatory.

In relation to the former, (1), the person is evidently the bearer of conscious experience, since the person stands behind the entire flow of conscious life as its enduring substrate, underlying and upholding the ever-present flowing manifold of experience. Together with consciousness we discover the personal subject to be a being spiritually awake in the world, aware of the objective outer world and aware of himself as the subject experiencing the outer world. Moreover, the personal subject is evidently not merely awake and aware in a passive or inert manner, but is clearly engaged in and with the world through his spiritual stirrings. Spiritual acts have their basis in the being and life of the subject, receiving their own being from the interior depth of the person, yet these same spiritual acts are at the disposal of the person in a unique way,

---

52 Betschart and Schulz similarly highlight the significance of Stein's identification of the person as "bearer." See Betschart, *Unwiederholbares Gottessiegel*, 227–29, 234–35, 246–51, 288–89, 340; "Edith Steins Vermittlung zwischen einem klassischen und einem modernen Personbegriff," in *The Hat and the Veil: The Phenomenology of Edith Stein*, Ad Fontes: Studien zur frühen Phänomenologie, 3, ed. Jerzy Machnacz et al. (Nordhausen: Traugott Bautz, 2016), 91–101; and Schulz, "Theory of Identity," 161–76: 173–75.

since the personal I can direct and order all spiritual acts and everything that naturally follows upon these acts. Thus, the person is bearer of experience in two closely related senses, as the personal subject underlying experience as its enduring conscious substrate, and as one who lives a distinctively personal life in all spiritual stirring. According to this first sense, then, the personal subject is bearer not only as an "individual thing" and "subsistent substance," like any and all other things and substances, bearing themselves and their substantial parts, but precisely as a *personal* subsistent individual, the person bears his personal being with its substantial composition in a personal manner—that is, as its conscious, rational, and free bearer. Hence, we see that the person has himself in hand in conscious experience and spiritual living, undergoing and living through that which is given—and thus bears his personal being in a personal way as its personal subject.[53]

Yet, the person is bearer in a still more fundamental sense, (2), since the person is "the bearer of a nature endowed with reason [*als Träger einer vernunftbegabten Natur*]," a nature implying both rationality and freedom.[54] As seen above, Stein makes a distinction in all individual things between the bearer of the essence—the empty-form "thing" as its final formal determination—and the fullness of the essence that is borne by the empty-form—the formal (and material) subdeterminations of the essence. The empty-form "thing" sets the individual apart and encompasses the formal (and material) fullness of the thing, so that it is essentially determined in this or that way, having its own being and action in the world together with other things. Thus the empty-form bears the essential fullness of the thing, and conversely, the essential fullness of the thing is borne by the empty-form, with both together constituting the completed essence of the thing.[55] Yet, since the bearer of the essence for personal

---

53 Here we see the close relation between bearer and conscious experience, precisely inasmuch as both include the sense of "undergoing" and "living through."
54 See EES, 308.
55 The "emptiness" of the empty-form does not imply that this form is without its own formal determination, or that it can ever be found in actual being without its accompanying formal (and material) fullness. Rather, Stein (and phenomenology more generally) identifies the empty-form as empty only because its nature is to be filled with further formal and material content so that the individual can attain its full formal (and material) determination as the specific kind of thing it is. Therefore, the empty-form and its formal (and material) fullness are mutually implied and reciprocally interdependent in the formal structure of the (material) individual, such that one never finds an empty-form without further formal (and material) content, and one never

being cannot simply be identified with the empty-form "thing," since persons are not mere things and cannot be equated with mere things, Stein argues that the ontological role of the empty-form "thing" in all non-personal individuals is replaced by the empty-form "personal I" in all personal individuals.[56] This means that the personal I takes a position of ontological preeminence in the formal (and material) structure of the personal individual, bearing the formal (and material) fullness as its empty-formal bearer. Thus, the "personal I" is that particular formal determination of the personal substance that formally encompasses the whole of the personal essence, encompassing all formal (and material) subdeterminations as their bearer, with the natural consequence that the personal I also encompasses and bears the essential determination of the rational nature itself. And so, for Stein, not only is the rational nature of great significance for the personal subject, but so too is the personal I that bears that rational nature as the inner "pole" of the personal individual. Simply, because the rational nature is the kind of nature that is borne by a personal I, the fact of its being borne by this very personal I is of paramount significance.

Indeed, this kind of bearing of the rational nature is of primary significance, since it is the bearing to which all other kinds of bearing in the personal substance return as to their ontological root. This rooting is seen especially in the dynamism of personal life that follows upon the essential structure of the person. Since the life of the personal I wells up from within the person as a life properly his own, the personal I is capacitated to enter into conscious, rational, and free engagement with the world. The personal I rises to the radiance of consciousness from the transcendent depth of the personal substance and expresses his own being and life in and through his free spiritual stirrings—all thinking, willing, and spiritual feeling. The personal I is the source of a special kind of life, a life that not only faces the world as its spectator, but rather enters into meaningful engagement with the world, its persons, things, events, and states of affairs.[57] This engagement is both that through which the

---

finds formal (and material) content without an encompassing empty-form enclosing it as a fully determined essential structure.

56 EES, 320.

57 For this and following, compare Wojtyła, "Thomistic Personalism," in *Person and Community*, 165–75; and "The Personal Structure of Self-Determination," and "Subjectivity and 'the Irreducible' in Man," in *Person and Act: And Related Essays*, trans. Grzegorz Ignatik (Washington, DC: The Catholic University of America Press, 2021), 457–66, 536–45, respectively.

personal I manifests himself in the world as a person, and that through which he progressively shapes his own personal being via this same manifestation. As a result, the personal I who already bears his rational nature essentially is further capacitated to bear that same nature in the actual dynamism of life. In so doing, the personal I takes his nature in hand, so to speak, and determines the course of his personal unfolding in the world, ideally attaining a dynamic possession of himself in a manner that matches his already given ontological possession. This dynamic possession of the rational nature reveals that the already established ontological possession of the subject is given over to the individual as a personal and ethical task to be completed over the course of life via his self-manifestation in the world. This, for Stein, seems to be a fundamental meaning of *being a person.*

So understood, it is clear why Stein attributes relative priority to the personal I over against the rational nature. Though the personal I is personal only because of its bearing a nature that is rational, as is clearly indicated in Stein's adoption and assimilation of the classical definition, the personal I possesses ontological predominance relative to the rational nature, as is clearly evident in the experiential dominance of the I. Notwithstanding the notional distinction of "rational nature" and "I," the conscious I is never found in *actual* being without the corresponding essential fullness of the rational nature that it bears—thus constituting it as a *personal* I. Indeed, since the I requires the spiritual stirrings of the rational nature for its mode of life as an I, the I as empty-form is evidently needful of the essential fullness of the rational nature for its ontological completion. On the other hand, since the rational nature requires an inner pole that orients and directs its spiritual stirrings, the essential fullness of the rational nature is needful of the empty formality of the I. And so, even while "I" and "rational nature" can be abstractly considered in distinction from each other, I and rational nature are mutually implied and reciprocally necessary if they are to fulfill their proper formal character, and so are inseparably united in the self-dependent essence that attains the actuality of being. Indeed, these latter requirements of self-dependence and actuality are already implied in Stein's starting point, precisely inasmuch as she discovers the conscious I as living and actual—as the "I am" of first-person experience—and never merely as an abstract pole of consciousness separated from the actuality of spiritual living, a life awake and aware.[58]

---

58 See EES, 304–7, 309, esp. 320–21. Betschart also closely attends to such abstract (pure I)

This is an important dimension of Stein's understanding, especially given the order of her investigations, as they are carried out from the perspective of the *actual* being given in experience, the kind of experience that reveals the ontological unity of the person as a *subsistent substance* with a range of spiritual powers at his disposal. In experience, appropriately analyzed, the personal I is manifest as the luminous apex of personal life wherein the personal substance rises to the bright light of consciousness, with an ability to be present to the self while being intentionally present to the other. As a result, every person (suitably developed) can address himself as "I," where this "I" is revealed to be the pivotal origin of all personally determined spiritual acts—all acts of "I think," "I will," "I feel," etc., or simply, the most primitive act, "I am." And though, as personal pronoun, this "I" can be understood to denominate the whole of the personal nature and substance, as is often the case in ordinary usage, Stein reveals that the "I" not only designates the "self" as one substantial whole, but also identifies a distinct structural dimension of the personal subject, a part of the complex formal whole of the person, the inner pole of the personal nature and the dynamic center of personal life. Moreover, Stein shows that this dimension is preeminent, since it grounds the whole of the personal nature as its ultimate principle, bearing all that lies in the personal subject—actually-dynamically, essentially-ontologically.

Assessing Stein's Introduction of the "Personal I" as "Bearer"

Even though Stein's mature conception of the person is framed by Aquinas's presentation of the Boëthian definition, and even while her reflections remain rooted in his interpretation of the definition, Stein's reconsideration of the conception of the person from the perspective of the "personal I" as "bearer" represents a significant departure from the presentation of Aquinas. Since the primordial given of the conscious I is the starting point to which Stein's investigations bear ongoing reference, her reflections naturally come to bear the peculiar imprint of this starting point, with the result that the personal I becomes the new coordinating lens according to which the classical conception is reconsidered. This stands in evident contrast to Aquinas for whom there is no express consideration of the person from the perspective of the I as bearer.

---

and concrete (subsistent) considerations when considering the being-individual of the human being. See Betschart, *Unwiederholbares Gottessiegel*, 233–34, 246–51, 257–58, esp. 287–89, 340.

However, I think it would be a mistake to understand Stein's reinterpretation as a contradiction of Aquinas's thought. Indeed, I suggest that Stein's attention to the personal I as bearer readily complements Aquinas's understanding of the person and further deepens our understanding of being a person to the defined benefit of Thomism and the *philosophia perennis*. Moreover, I suggest that this deepening is wrought by Stein's attention to the subjectivity of the person as a complement to Aquinas's attention to the objectivity of person. In what follows, I delineate this deepening by analyzing Stein's understanding with reference to its adopted foundation in Aquinas's thought.

However, before moving directly to the question of Stein's reinterpretation of the classical conception, it is worth attending briefly to Stein's analysis of the personal character of human nature. For Stein, the human being is first and foremost a personal being, where the essentially personal nature distinguishes the human being from all other beings of the natural world. This means that when Stein investigates the structure of human nature, she never does so without attending to personal subjectivity and all that is essentially personal.[59] This is clearly apparent in her repeated investigation of the human being as a person and, as will be shown below, in her recognition of the personal character of human individuation, as well as in her corresponding understanding of the human person's unparalleled relation to the personal God. The preponderance of investigations, both early and late, reveal that Stein considers the distinction between persons and non-persons to be the fundamental dividing line of created being and the corresponding cosmic hierarchy of natural kinds. This means

---

59 See esp. EES, 310–21; and AMP, 78–92. Marian Maskulak maintains that according to Stein's strict use of the term, "person" would not apply to a human being who has not yet developed a spiritual and personal mode of life and begun a path of personal formation, though she still finds room in Stein's thought for recognizing the equal dignity of the undeveloped human being, through the presence of the spiritual soul from conception, and the spiritual soul's ability to receive the indwelling presence of God. In contrast I argue that Stein maintains a strict relationship between human nature and personhood—given her attention to the person as the subsistent substance underlying and upholding conscious life, her identification of human nature as a personal nature, and her argument for the presence of human nature in completion from fertilization—and thus holds that the existence of a human individual necessarily implies the presence of a person. Accordingly, there is every reason to believe that Stein holds to the personhood of the undeveloped, underdeveloped, or impaired human individual. See Maskulak, *Body-Soul-Spirit*, 95–96; see AMP, 132; and compare EES, 310–13.

that the personal nature of the human being provides the pivotal criterion for Stein for classifying the human over against other species of the natural world.[60] Yet, we do not find such attention to the essentially personal and personal subjectivity in the anthropological writings of Aquinas, and nowhere does Aquinas perform a separate thematized analysis of the human being as a person. Though he certainly understands human nature to be a personal nature, as evinced in his frequent reference to the human being as a person, he touches upon the personal in human nature only within the larger context of theological reflections on its attribution to God.[61] And though philosophical access to God as personal is given for Aquinas via the natural perfection of personhood, this does not prompt him to perform an in-depth analysis of the personal character of human nature or an extended analysis of the concept in its applicability to the human being. In Stein's doing so, we find valuable service performed for the tradition of the *philosophia perennis*, one that expresses what is implicit yet unattended to in the writings of Aquinas and many subsequent Thomistic thinkers, with some notable exceptions, including Wojtyła. Indeed, in many ways Stein's writings run parallel to the writings of Wojtyła, both in terms of their common attention to the personal in human nature, and in terms of their presentation of Thomistically inspired personalisms.[62]

---

60   In following Stein's manner of investigating, one discerns a subtle contrast in her thought with the traditional Aristotelian classification of the human being as a "rational animal," which situates the human individual within the human species with primary reference to the animal genus, as one natural species within a greater natural whole. In contrast to this horizontal manner of classifying the human individual, Stein stresses the vast ontological difference introduced by rationality and attends to the ensuing significance of the individual as such, with the consequence that Stein primarily "classifies" the human being in a vertical manner as a personal kind of being among other personal beings with analogical likeness to angelic and Divine Being. Of course, this does *not* mean that Stein disagrees with or disregards the Aristotelian manner of classifying the human individual— she certainly recognizes the cogency and correctness of this classification—rather, she simply considers the human being primarily from the perspective of the personal and in light of the unparalleled importance of the individual.

61   For a sample of Aquinas's references to the human being as personal, see, ST, I, 29.4; SCG, 4.35, 43; DP, 9.4, co. And, since, for Aquinas, "person signifies what is most perfect in all nature" (ST, I, 29.3, co.), and all true perfections can be attributed to their divine exemplar in a preeminent way, the analogous attribution of "person" to Divine Being is its primary and most proper attribution, even while it is theologically attributed with reference primarily to the distinct Persons of the triune God.

62   Among others, see Wojtyła, *Person and Act*; *Person and Community*; *Love and*

Yet, this deliberate "personalization" of our understanding of human nature does not require attending to the significance of the "personal I" within the structure of human nature, nor does it require adverting to the concept "bearer" as that which clarifies the position of the personal I within this structure. We then find the full depth of Stein's reinterpretation of the classical conception only by attending to these further insights provided by Stein's ontology of the person. Indeed, Stein's innovation is best highlighted by focusing on the way the personal I is bearer of the rational nature and the consequent experiential life of the personal subject as a subsistent spiritual substance. Attending to the personal I as bearer not only highlights the originality of Stein's position with respect to the adopted teachings of Aquinas, but also positions her phenomenological insights alongside the comparable personalism of Wojtyła. As seen above, the term "bearer" has manifold meaningfulness when applied to personal being, and each fold of meaning must be examined separately. A first division is found in (1) the person as bearer of conscious experience and spiritual stirring, and (2) the person as bearer of the rational nature. The former spur then has the further subdivision: (1a) the person as spiritual substance evinced in bearing conscious experience; and (1b) the person as spiritual subject manifesting self in bearing spiritual stirring.

Beginning with the first spur, (1), according to the two senses of its subdivision, (1a) and (1b), we find a close alignment with Aquinas's presentation of the person. With regard to (1a), the person as spiritual substance evinced in bearing conscious experience, the alignment is seen in Stein's use of "bearer" simply as a translation and interpretation of Thomistic terms identifying the person—namely, those of supposit, subsistent, and hypostasis. In this sense bearer is a denominator of the person as a rational substance, which like all other substances has an independent mode of being relative to what is dependent in its being and predicated of its being. The person as bearer has being *in* himself, while *underlying* and *upholding* all properties and accidents that inhere in

---

Responsibility, trans. Grzegorz Ignatik (Boston: Pauline Books and Media, 2013). I note here that though the question of the precise Thomistic character of Wojtyła's personalist philosophy is somewhat controverted, it is at least clear that he presents a personalism that is self-consciously Thomistic, as is manifest most clearly in his paper of the same name, "Thomistic Personalism," where he traces in broad outline a personalism that has its point of departure in Thomistic anthropology, and there presents the structure and powers of the human soul in a manner that is entirely Thomistic.

his being, including conscious experience, and is consequently the ultimate subject of predication while himself being unpredictable of anything else. So understood, "bearer" is attributed to the person merely as a further unfolding of the meaning of the Boëthian definition according to Aquinas's use of the verb "*supponitur*" to describe the person, but now with express attention to the upholding involved in being a substance and to the consequent upholding of conscious experience. With regard to (1b), the person as spiritual subject manifesting self in bearing spiritual stirring, the alignment is seen in Aquinas's presentation of the way the person is the substantial subject of rational acts. For Aquinas it is not powers that act but substances that act through powers. With respect to the personal nature, then, it is not the rational power that reasons, nor the volitional power that wills, but the person that reasons and wills via the rational and volitional powers. Thus, the person is the principle of his acts even while acting through the powers that make these acts possible. And indeed, this substantial origin of action is most apparent in the rational powers and all subordinate powers subject to rational freedom, inasmuch as these powers lie under the dominion of the individual himself. Thus, for Aquinas, like Stein, the person "underlies" his rational acts as their foundation and source, even while "upholding" these same personal acts whereby he manifests his being in the world.[63] Therefore, in these first two senses—(1a) the person as spiritual substance, and (1b) the person as spiritual subject—I submit that Stein's presentation of the person has basic accord with that of Aquinas. Yet, Stein also moves beyond the understanding of Aquinas when she locates the origin of personal acts in the personal I as a distinct dimension of person life. Since the personal I rises to the awareness of consciousness and wields the spiritual powers of thinking, willing, and feeling, Stein argues convincingly that the personal I is the originating principle of personal acts and the directing source of personal life.

With regard to the second division (2), the person as bearer of the rational nature, we certainly find development beyond Aquinas which substantially adjusts our understanding of the classical conception. In distinguishing the personal I from the rational nature and identifying the personal I as the bearer of the nature, Stein establishes the personal I as the ultimate ground of personal being.[64] According to the classical conception, the rational nature specifies the

---

63 See ST, I, 75.2, ad 2.
64 Citing Gredt, Betschart notes that the distinction of person and the rational nature was already taken up by Aquinas in the theological debate surrounding *subsistentia*,

substance as a person, and is that whereby personal being is distinguished from all non-personal kinds of being. With the newly introduced concept of personal I as bearer, we find the personal I placed in a position of ontological preeminence relative to the rational nature. Though the personal I is personal precisely because of the bearing of a nature that is rational, nevertheless the personal I now stands at the center of the complex whole as its ontological linchpin. By so centering the conceptual content on the personal I, Stein introduces new depth to our understanding of the person as it has been classically conceived, inasmuch as the personal I becomes the new coordinating lens of the classical conception. The personal I is thus brought into the foreground and highlighted in its ontological significance. Yet, this new focus does not undermine the significance of the rational nature, nor indeed the actuality of subsisting in a rational nature, both of which remain significant for Stein, as they were for Aquinas. Rather, Stein's adjusted focus simply augments our understanding of the meaning of being a person by explicitly attending to the *personal kind of bearing* of the rational nature via the *ontological* bearing of the personal I, and the corresponding *personal mode of bearing* that same rational nature via the *actual* bearing of the personal I.[65] Therefore, I submit that Stein does not stand in contradiction to Aquinas even while she develops beyond his presentation through her Augustinian way of philosophizing and corresponding use of the phenomenological method—both of which are clearly evident in the allied concepts of personal I and bearer.[66]

---

and the particular kind of subsistence of persons by virtue of the special mode of being possessed by persons. Yet, Stein goes further by not only distinguishing the subsistent person and the rational nature, but also the personal I and the rational nature, and according to the particular sense of bearing that correlates with the empty-form (phenomenologically understood). See Betschart, *Unwiederholbares Gottessiegel*, 227–29, 234–35, 246–51; and Gredt, *Philosophie*, 2, 115.

65 The idea of the personal *kind* and *mode* of bearing is taken up repeatedly below and given further conceptual depth. In brief: The personal *kind* of bearing relates to the personal I formally encompassing the personal nature, and so is an *essential* or *ontological* kind of bearing, whereas the personal *mode* of bearing relates to the personal I embracing the actuality of being of the subsistent person, and so is an *actual* or *real* mode of bearing. See esp. chap. 4, 126–170, and chap. 6, 204–245, in this work.

66 The absence of contradiction between Stein and Aquinas in this area is briefly signaled in ST, I, 2.3, when Aquinas argues for the existence of God and introduces his demonstrations with the authoritative statement, "It is said [...] by the Person of God, I Am Who Am [*ego sum qui sum*]." ST, I, 2.3, sc. Though Aquinas is here evidently focused on the "Am" as indicative of the existence of God rather than on

This notion of personal I as bearer has further import in the axiological sphere when it comes to recognizing the dignity of the human person. Whereas Aquinas places the emphasis of personal dignity on subsisting in a rational nature, saying, "It is of great dignity to subsist in a rational nature [*magnae dignitatis est in rationali natura subsistere*],"[67] Stein indicates that personal dignity should now be centered on the personal I, saying, "It is a great dignity to be the *bearer* of a nature endowed with reason [*es eine große Würde ist, Träger einer vernunftbegabten Natur zu sein*]."[68] Stein is at first sight here

---

the "I" as indicative of the personal with reference to God (compare SCG, 1.22, no. 10), he explicitly states that it is a *personal* God (*"ex persona dei"*) that is shown to exist in this way and thus implies the significance of the *ego* part of the enunciation (which pronoun, it should be noted, is not grammatically necessary in Latin; the *sum* is sufficient). For further support of this reading of Stein's compatibility with Aquinas, one could turn to the writings of Wojtyła where he brings together a Thomistic presentation of the human being with a phenomenological presentation of personal subjectivity—even though Wojtyła typically presents the "I" as synonymous with the "self" (with both understood as the entirety of the acting personal subject) when he harmonizes the phenomenological and metaphysical. See esp. Wojtyła, "Participation or Alienation," and "Subjectivity and 'the Irreducible' in Man," in *Person and Act*, 514–31, 536–45; and Wojtyła, *Love and Responsibility*, 67–71. Further supporting this assessment, Scarpelli Cory argues that while there is "no encounter with or observation of a bare 'I' or bare 'I think' in Aquinas's writings, this should not be understood to preclude abstract considerations of the 'I,' and presents a plausible reading of Aquinas's understanding of the 'I' as the pronoun that identifies the enduring *subject* of the life of the person." See Scarpelli Cory, *Human Self-Knowledge*, 170–73, 199–214. And yet, Aquinas's understanding of the I certainly does not equate with Stein's understanding of the conscious I as a distinct structural dimension with formal dominance within the personal whole (nor would Wojtyła's conception).

67   ST, I, 29.3, ad 2. See also Gilles Emery, "The Dignity of Being a Substance: Person, Subsistence, and Nature," in *Nova et Vetera* 9, no. 4 (2011): 991–1001. For an appreciation of the manifold aspects of Aquinas's understanding of the dignity of the human person, "[first], in the context of his conception of human iconicity, secondly, in the context of his conception of human personhood, which links personhood directly to dignity, and thirdly, in his use of the term *dignitas*, as it appears in other anthropologically relevant contexts," see Guerrero van der Meijden, *Person and Dignity*, 288–95.

68   EES, 305; emphasis added. Stein does not treat the concept human dignity (*Menschenwürde*) or personal dignity (*persönliche würde*) in any of her writings, even while she evidently had an appreciation for the exceptional value of the personal subject and his being. For an expansive treatment of Stein on the question of the person and dignity, which also treats of Aquinas's understanding, see Guerrero van der Meijden, *Person and Dignity*; and for a study on human dignity informed by Stein's

using "bearer" simply as a translation of Aquinas's "*subsistere* [to subsist]" in correspondence with her manner of her interpretation of the classical definition and its associated terminology. Yet, given her developed understanding of the personal meaning of being a bearer, and the related ontological and actual bearing of the personal I, we surely find new accentuation to the meaningfulness of personal dignity. Since all personal bearing returns to the personal I as its actual, ontological root, and since the personal I is thereby established as the new focal point, a new aspect of the dignity of the person is unveiled and underscored in its axiological significance. Though, like Aquinas, Stein recognizes that personal dignity is grounded in the individual who subsists in a rational nature, in contrast to Aquinas, Stein reveals that such dignity is further rooted in the personal I bearing the rational nature in the subsistence of a primary substance. Yet, while this certainly introduces a new accentuation to personal dignity, an accentuation that adds further inflection to the dignity of being a personal substance, there is nothing in Stein's attention to the personal I as bearer that detracts from Aquinas's position regarding the dignity of subsisting in a rational nature. Rather, Stein's development merely extends our understanding of the meaning of personal dignity by including the personal *kind* and *mode* of bearing involved in being a personal subject, with dignity now centered on the personal I as the singular center of personal being.

Finally, I propose that we find a further sphere of coherence between Stein and Aquinas when we attend to the dynamism of personal life. As indicated above, in addition to bearing the rational nature, and as a natural consequence of this bearing, the personal I ordinarily comes to bear the dynamism of personal life in all personal acts, and in all else subject to rational freedom in the essential structure of his being. As a spiritual being, the person is capacitated to understand his own nature and to further understand the natures of the things of the natural world. This dual understanding foundationally conditions all further personal actions, as well as all personally expressive bodily activity. Thus, the person is naturally capacitated with the potential to personally embrace his nature, both through charting the course of his personal life, and through mediating the development of his personality—in metaphysical *and*

---

phenomenological perspective, see Mette Lebech, *On the Problem of Human Dignity: A Hermeneutical and Phenomenological Investigation* (Würzburg: Königshausen & Neumann, 2009), esp. 223–89; together with its associated anthology, *European Sources of Human Dignity: A Commented Anthology* (Oxford: Peter Lang, 2019); and the shorter exposition of Lebech in *Phenomenology to Metaphysics*, 49–64.

psychological senses—through his free activity. This means that the personal I has the capacity to attain personal possession of his being and nature, and has a corresponding capability to freely determine the course of his unfolding. Thus, Stein says, "We held the 'person' as bearer in a preeminent sense, because she not only possesses and encompasses her essence, but 'possesses' it in a very peculiar sense, i.e., is master of herself and can dispose of herself freely."[69] This Steinian presentation has perfect accord with Aquinas's conception of the significance of the person, which he argues is found in the ability of the person to freely determine his actions. Indeed, Aquinas argues that the term "person" signifies subsistent individuals that "have dominion over their own actions," and expressly says that the term has been coined in view of this rational dominion.[70] This means that Aquinas holds that the person is significant precisely because he is the kind of being that not only acts out of its nature, as do all individual substances, for action is always the action of an individual, but also acts out of himself as this very individual, as the subsistent source of his own actions.[71]

Thus, in manifold interrelated ways, all of which can be organized around the "personal I" as "bearer," we see that Stein introduces new conceptual depth to our understanding of the person, conceptual depth that invariably leads to an enhanced understanding of the human person. Through her Augustinian way of philosophizing, Stein expands the presentation of the person in the writings of Aquinas by refocusing the conceptual content on the Boëthian definition of the personal I as bearer. Whereas Aquinas accounts for the objective metaphysical structure of the person, Stein develops this objective structure by interweaving a phenomenologically developed understanding of the personal subject. Whereas the conception of Aquinas provides a robust metaphysical description of the structure of the person, Stein deepens our understanding of this structure by folding in the significance of personal subjectivity. In Stein's renewed conception, the personal I stands at the center of the structural whole as the interior pole of conscious experience and spiritual stirring, the new linchpin that conceptually expands all essential elements of

---

69   EES, 345–46; see also EES, 307–9; and AMP, 78ff.
70   ST, I, 29.1, co.
71   Again here, and perhaps particularly here, Stein and Wojtyła proceed in parallel ways. See esp. Wojtyła, "The Personal Structure of Self-Determination," in *Person and Act*, 457–66; and indeed the whole of *Person and Act* itself.

the definition—thus "renovating" the classical conception from within. In this way, Stein brings to light a previously unexamined depth of the person as classically conceived and focuses our attention on the subjective significance of this depth. The personal I is established as the interior pole of the "subsisting" personal "individual", the luminous apex of conscious life and spiritual stirring, and the actual, ontological bearer of the "rational nature."

Conclusion:
The Person and the Personal I

By adopting and gradually assimilating the essential core of the classical definition, Stein attains basic accord with Aquinas's understanding of the person while also moving beyond Aquinas's presentation by attending to the unique way the personal subject is bearer. Stein reconsiders the classical definition from the perspective of the personal I as bearer of conscious experience and spiritual activity, and thereby discloses the specific way personal being is found to be something subsistent, a supposit, and hypostasis. By placing the accent of understanding on the significance of personal subjectivity in this way, the classical conception comes to be viewed from a distinctly modern perspective. This results in Stein presenting the personal I as the ontological bearer of the rational nature, the actual and dynamic bearer of conscious experience and spiritual stirring, with the corresponding capacity to attain free rational possession of his personal being and nature. The personal I is thus given as the ontological bearer of the personal nature with the further potential to become the dynamic bearer of that same nature through the course of a life lived in a genuinely personal way. Accordingly, I suggest that Stein has wrought something of a "personalization" of the Thomistic understanding of human nature, a personalization brought about by her reconsideration of human nature from the perspective of the classical definition with the accent now placed on personal subjectivity. Consequently, I propose that the classical definition can now be reformulated with the following distinctively Steinian supplement: "The person is an individual substance of a rational nature *borne by a conscious I.*"[72] This expansion of the classical definition highlights the

---

72 I choose "conscious I" over "personal I" in the definitional formula since it is precisely in bearing the rational power/nature that the conscious I is personal.

complementarity of phenomenology and metaphysics in working together toward achieving a fully rounded conception of the person, one that clearly delineates the objective metaphysical structure of the person while at one and the same time identifying the vital significance of personal subjectivity, a subjectivity at which—according to Wojtyła—*we should pause*.[73]

---

[73] See Wojtyła, "Subjectivity and 'the Irreducible' in Man," in *Person and Act*, 536–45, esp. 541–43; and above, "Preface." As indicated, Stein's phenomenological development of the classical conception can usefully be compared to the developed presentation of personal subjectivity in the thought of Wojtyła, esp. Wojtyła, "Thomistic Personalism," in *Person and Community*, 165–76; and Wojtyła, "The Personal Structure of Self-Determination"; and the just-mentioned "Subjectivity and 'the Irreducible' in Man," in *Person and Act*, 457–66, 536–45; and the longer phenomenological study, Wojtyła, *Person and Act*, esp. 105–48. Betschart also notes that Stein's inclusion of the I in the metaphysically detailed structure of human nature shows the beneficial complementarity of phenomenology and metaphysics in conceiving of the human person. See Betschart, *"Person,"* in *Stein-Lexikon*, 278–81.

Chapter Two

Human Unity and Bodily Formation

> The personal I is properly at home in the innermost of the soul.
>
> —*Edith Stein*[1]

The problem of the unity of the human being stands at the center of Stein's investigation of the structure of human nature in her later works.[2] Through reflection on the nature of one's own being as it is given in experience, Stein argues that the human self is given as a personal substance structured as a unity of spirit, soul, and living-body. Yet, since reflection on this same personal substance also discloses its structure as a complex of spirit, soul, and living-body, what exactly is the character of the unity of the human being, and what is the principle of this unity? Stein turns to this question in the penultimate chapter of *The Structure of the Human Person*, a chapter titled, "The Soul as Form and Spirit," and takes Aquinas's defense of the substantial unity of the human being as her point of departure. In the opening paragraph Stein puts

---

1 EES, 370.
2 An earlier iteration of a substantial portion of this chapter is found published in Robert McNamara, "Edith Stein's Conception of Human Unity and Bodily Formation: A Thomistically Informed Understanding," in *American Catholic Philosophical Quarterly* 94, no. 4 (2020): 639–63; and short sections are also found in a still earlier article on a related topic in Robert McNamara, "Human Individuality in Stein's Mature Works," in *Edith Steins Herausforderung heutiger Anthropologie*, ed. Hanna-Barbara Gerl-Falkovitz and Mette Lebech (Heiligenkreuz: Be&Be, 2017), 124–39.

the question in the following way, "What about the unity and simplicity of the human soul, and the unity of the substantial form, both of which are affirmed by Thomas?"³

In the previous chapter, after a wide range of investigations into human nature, Stein has finally achieved a comprehensive understanding of the specifically human in contrast to the merely material, organic, and animal—that is, the spiritual and the personal, which she understands as the final component in her systematic analysis of the human person.⁴ Having thus completed her investigation of the *structure* of human nature, Stein finally turns her attention to the question of the *unity* of the human being before bringing her investigation to a close.⁵

Stein understands the unity taught by Aquinas to imply that there is no plurality of substantial forms in the human being, but that everything that formally comprises the human individual is reduced to one form, the rational or intellectual soul, which is the substantial form of the human individual as one whole, inclusive of the material body as a living body.⁶ According to his

---

3   AMP, 93. By unity, we are to understand "that which is undivided," and by simplicity "that which is uncomposed." These notions are evidently closely related, inasmuch as that which is uncomposed is necessarily undivided, even while that which is undivided is not necessarily uncomposed. See below, chap. 4, 126–170, and chap. 6, 204–245, for a fuller unfolding of the meanings of unity and simplicity.

4   Though Stein turns directly to this question only in chapter VII of AMP, the question has been percolating in the background in all previous chapters. See AMP, 39–41, 53–55, 69–71, and 83–84. Lebech describes this chapter of AMP as a critique of Thomas's doctrine of the unity of substantial form; I would rather describe its contents as a critical appropriation of Aquinas's teachings, one that retains the outline conceptual content of Aquinas's teachings even while the meaning of his teachings are judiciously adjusted. See Mette Lebech, *The Philosophy of Edith Stein: From Phenomenology to Metaphysics* (Oxford: Peter Lang, 2015), 96–97.

5   Already in her earliest work, PE, Stein is attentive to the distinctive unity of the human being, and there details the living-body as the "zero point of orientation" with reference to the surrounding world which is given to consciousness via the living-body. See PE, 56ff.; and also, Jadwiga Guerrero van der Meijden, *Person and Dignity in Edith Stein's Writings* (Berlin: De Gruyter, 2019), 144–48. I am grateful to Guerrero van der Meijden for bringing to my attention this aspect of Stein's understanding in PE.

6   See AMP, 93–106. For this and following, see John F. Wippel, *The Metaphysical Thought of Thomas Aquinas: From Finite Being to Uncreated Being* (Washington, DC: The Catholic University of America Press, 2000), 312–75, esp. 320n96; Joseph Bobik, *Aquinas on Matter and Form and the Elements* (Notre Dame, IN: University of Notre Dame Press, 1998, repr. 2006), esp. 159–67; George Klubertanz, *The Philosophy of*

hylomorphic understanding of the composition of material substances, Aquinas argues that the rational soul is that which makes the human being human. As one essential part in composition with prime matter, the naturally simple soul immediately and directly informs the purely potential prime matter as the act of its potency, thus constituting the human being as a living bodily being, a unified substance of the human kind. The human soul is thereby established as the formal foundation of the being and unity of the human substance, precisely since, as Aquinas maintains, "the soul communicates that being in which it subsists to the corporeal matter, from which [matter] and the intellectual soul there results a unity, so that the being of the whole composite is yet the being of his soul."[7] Aquinas is here closely following Aristotle's teaching of the unity of natural (living) material substances as a unity of form (soul) (μορφή (ψυχή)) and matter (ὕλη) joined in an act-potency relation, and he argues that this kind of joining of metaphysical principles results in unity of the highest degree since act-potency compositions are "most of all one."[8] Thus, for Aquinas, the rational soul is both that which determines the human being as human, as this very human individual, and that which determines the materiality of the

---

Human Nature (New York: Appleton-Century-Crofts, 1953), 12–38, 298–303, 309–10; and Étienne Gilson, *Spirit of Mediaeval Philosophy*, trans. A. H. C. Downes (New York: Charles Scribner's Sons, 1936; repr. Notre Dame, IN: University of Notre Dame Press, 1991, repr. 2008), 168–88; and *The Christian Philosophy of St. Thomas Aquinas* (Notre Dame, IN: University of Notre Dame Press, 1956, repr. 2010), 187–99. In what follows, I use the terms rational and intellectual interchangeably, even while both Stein and Aquinas recognize subtle differences in their meanings when used technically, with rational signifying discursive thinking, and intellectual signifying simple intuition and understanding—that is, the motile discovery of truth versus the restful apprehending and comprehending of truth.

7   ST, I, 76.1, ad 5; see also ST, I, 76.4; and SCG, 2.57, nos. 5–16.
8   Meta, 5.6, 1016^{b}2–3; see also DA, 2.1, 412^{a}12–15. Evidently, the body here mentioned must be understood as the *result* of the soul's formation of matter, where the concept "body" (or, more precisely, "living body") includes the formative action of the soul, inasmuch as the most basic meaning of body for Aquinas is "formed (or ensouled) matter," and likewise the concept "soul" must be understood to include its formative action relative to the body, inasmuch as the most basic meaning of soul for Aquinas is "form of a living body," since "to be united to the body is fitting for the soul by reason of itself." ST, I, 75.1, ad. 6; see also QDA, 15, arg. 14. Indeed, in his commentary on Peter Lombard's *Sentences*, Aquinas goes as far as to say, "the soul is the nature of the body itself," thus indicating that *what the body is* (its nature) is consequent to the soul's formative actuality. Sent, I 3.2.3, ad. 1.

body as a living human body. The rational soul is then not only the substantial form of the human being, the principle of its being and unity, but precisely as such is also the form of the material body, so that the unity of human nature as a spiritual-material composite is finally accomplished in the unmediated formation of the material body by the naturally simple rational soul.

Stein is aware of the significance of this teaching in Aquinas's anthropology, of its controversial character in the late medieval period, and of the vigorous defense Aquinas makes of this particular teaching throughout his works.[9] Moreover, Stein recognizes that this teaching is of vital significance toward establishing a realistic philosophical anthropology, and she accepts both that the human being is a substantial unity through the rational soul and that the rational soul is the final formative principle of the material body, as well as accepting their common foundation in a hylomorphic understanding of the relation of soul and body.[10] Finally, Stein recognizes that these paired teachings—the rational soul as principle of substantial unity and as form of the body—are closely related and the resolution of the difficulties of each are settled only through a unified solution, a solution finally accomplished by attending to the way the rational soul *informs* the material body as a living human body. However, notwithstanding this basic agreement, Stein also reconsiders the meaning

---

9 See AMP, 95; and also, ST, I, 76.1–4. Daniel A. Callus provides a presentation of the medieval debate surrounding the question of a plurality of substantial forms and its source in the contradictory proposals of Avicenna (Ibn Sīnā) and Avicebron (Ibn Gabirol), and he notes that while the controversy preceded Aquinas, with Aquinas "the debate entered a new phase" and it was Aquinas who "gave the problem its full significance." See Daniel A. Callus, "The Origins of the Problem of the Unity of Form," in *The Thomist: A Speculative Quarterly Review* 24, no. 2 (1961): 257–85: 260. In light of developments in the natural sciences, the question of the unity of substances is again a burning question for philosophers, especially those embracing or considering hylomorphism, and several proposed (at least partial) solutions are provided in William M. R. Simpson, Robert C. Koons, and Nicholas J. The, eds., *Neo-Aristotelian Perspectives on Contemporary Science* (New York: Routledge, 2017).

10 Stein is also aware of the dogmatic definition originally affirmed at the Council of Vienne (1311–12), establishing the rational soul as the form of the body as a teaching to be definitively held by Catholics. The definition, formulated in the negative, prohibits assertions that "the rational or intellectual soul is not the form of the body through itself and essentially [*anima rationalis seu intellectiva non sit forma corporis humani per se et essentialiter*]." See WIM, esp. 6–11; and Heinrich Denzinger et al., *Compendium of Creeds, Definitions, and Declarations on Matters of Faith and Morals*, ed. Peter Hünermann, 43rd ed. (San Francisco: Ignatius Press, 2012), §902, 290.

of human unity and bodily formation in light of a fresh phenomenological investigation. As a result, Stein comes to understand human nature as a formally complex structure that attains progressively layered formations as material, organic, animal, and spiritual, with all ultimately subordinated to the personally determined spiritual soul as the final formative principle of the complex human whole. And so, though Stein certainly follows Aquinas in affirming the unifying and formative primacy of the rational soul, in contrast to Aquinas she argues that the substantial configuration of the human being is best described as a "formal structure" of manifold formal determinations, which is finally secured as a unity through the personally determined spiritual soul.[11]

Investigating Human Unity and Bodily Formation

Stein's investigation of human unity and bodily formation begins with ordinary human experience, the experience of the human being as it is announced in inner and outer experience. From such experience rationally investigated according to the aforementioned Augustinian and Aristotelian ways of philosophizing, Stein argues that it is evident that the human being is a complex structure with life manifest in three primary ways, organic, animal, and spiritual. Yet, notwithstanding this complexity, Stein argues that it is also evident that the human being is a thoroughly unified whole, with a unity manifest in the inner experience of the ensouled body and its coordinated living operations, and in the outer experience of the material body and its enclosed and coordinated organization. These givens of lived experience are matched by the presentation of the composite and unified character of human nature in the writings of Aquinas, who conceives of the human being as a microcosm of the cosmos, uniting in one nature the many diverse regions of being, material, vegetative, sensitive, and rational.[12] In accord with his broader metaphysical framework,

---

11 AMP, 131–32; EES, 182–89. By my use of determination I am indicating the ontological boundary or limit of finite being, the meaningful *terminus* establishing each and every finite being as *what* it is. As indicated above (lxixn84), my use corresponds to Stein's use of "*Bestimmung*" and Aquinas's use of "*determinatio*."

12 See AMP, 26, 29–31, 40. The term Aquinas uses to designate human nature as a microcosm is *minor mundus* (literally, little world), and he gives two separate reasons, namely: (1) the structural similarity between the composition of human nature and the totality of kinds in the natural world; and (2) the analogy between the way the human being is master of his bodiliness with formative immediacy, and the way God is Lord of the material cosmos to which he is immediately present. See QDV, 24.5, sc;

Aquinas argues that throughout the hierarchical cosmos the more perfect forms contain in themselves the formative powers of the less perfect forms, and since human nature is a recapitulation in micro of the entire cosmos, the substantial form of human nature contains in itself the various perfections of less perfect forms, material, vegetative, and sensitive, in a unity of nature that is also rational. Consequently, Aquinas argues that the rational soul as substantial form "virtually contains" sensitive and vegetative forms of life, as well as inferior material forms, "and itself alone does whatever the imperfect forms do in other things."[13]

Stein attends to this multi-layered composition as manifest in lived experience and presented in the conceptualization of Aquinas, and investigates each of the strata in a progressively ascending sequence. By performing this investigation Stein seeks to understand the formation of each layer and thereby come to a more comprehensive understanding of the structure and unity of the human being. This is most evident in *The Structure of the Human Person* when she analyzes the human being in a sequentially layered fashion, "as material body, living essence, soulish essence, [and] spiritual essence."[14] The investigation of each layer involves an abstractive isolation of the layer from the phenomenal whole, according to which only the formation following upon the particular layer is at first conceptually detailed. In this way, Stein can focus on the primary formative undertakings of all layers while comparing and contrasting each layer with natures finally determined and classified according to that particular region of being. Stein thereby discloses the many formative determinations of human nature, clearly delimiting each one while simultaneously attending to the extent of their mutual interconnectedness. This provides Stein with an enhanced potential to detail the manifold formations that take place in human

---

27.3, arg. 13; 5.5, sc 7. For a more expansive treatment of Aquinas on this matter, and for Stein's employment of this same notion, as well as the (likely) initial transmission of the idea to her through Scheler, see Guerrero van der Meijden, *Person and Dignity*, 162–70.

13 ST, I, 76.3, ad 4; I, 76.4, co.; see also QDSC, 3, ad 13.

14 AMP, 23; see also AMP, 33, 40. For brief outlines of the progression of Stein's analysis from material thing to spiritual person, see Marian Maskulak, *Edith Stein and the Body-Soul-Spirit at the Center of Holistic Formation* (New York: Peter Lang, 2007), 61–72; Lebech, *Phenomenology to Metaphysics*, 93–94. What follows is set forth in an earlier iteration in McNamara, "Human Individuality in Stein's Mature Works," 126–29.

nature, and to highlight the corresponding ordered unity of this manifold, while clearly identifying the ontological priority of the specifically human within the structural whole.[15]

As a result of this abstractive investigation, Stein specifies four basic meanings of formation in human nature:

(1) At a first level, there is a rudimentary bodily formation of already formed material components (corresponding to the corporeal form (*forma corporalis*) of Aquinas), wherein a variety of material elements are structured as a unified whole, a material structure that is "in itself enclosed, indivisible, and incompatible with any other shape."[16]

(2) Following upon this most basic level of bodily formation is an organic formation of the material body (the vegetative soul (*anima vegetativa*) of Aquinas), wherein the structured material whole is organized and animated by a living inner form, now identified with the soul as *organic*—here understood as the formative principle of organic life and the many operations of such life.[17]

(3) At a still higher level, there is an animal formation of the organic body (the sensitive soul (*anima sensitiva*) of Aquinas), wherein the organized and animated whole is further enlivened with sensation and motility through the presence of the soul as *animal*—now understood as the formative principle of sensitive and motile life and the many operations of such life.[18]

(4) Finally, at the highest level of formation, there is a specifically spiritual formation of the sensitized organic body (the rational or intellectual soul (*anima rationalis* or *intellectiva*) of Aquinas), wherein sensation and motility are elevated into an integrated unity with what is specifically human, rationality and freedom, through the presence of the soul as *spiritual*—now understood as the formative principle of rational life and the many operations of such life.

---

15 In EES, 310–21 (together with the earlier discussion of form and matter, 194–238) Stein performs her investigation of the layered structure without the same explicit abstractive analysis of AMP.
16 AMP, 33.
17 See AMP, 33, 38, 42–43.
18 See AMP, 46–47, 52–53, 54–55. Stein's designation of this layer as animal (*animalisch*) rather than sensitive (*sensitiv*) is plausibly intended to highlight the specifically human over against the animal in general.

In just this way, following the path of her abstractive analysis in tandem with the conceptual apparatus of Aquinas, Stein details the manifold formative undertakings taking place in human nature, moving from the material through to the organic and up to the animal, before proceeding to the specifically human.

However, though Stein thereby highlights four basic meanings of formation, these distinct formations are not to be understood as isolated strata within the structure of human nature, taking place without any defined relation to one another. Rather, Stein's analysis shows that within the layered structure of human nature, each higher layer presupposes and is only possible on the foundation of the lower layer(s), since each higher layer relies upon and employs the formative outcomes of the lower layer(s) in its own formative undertakings. On the other hand, Stein's analysis shows that the lower layers, as so ordered to and employed by the higher, lose their independence in becoming subject to the formative undertakings of the higher.[19] Moreover, Stein's analysis shows that the formative powers of the higher layers permeate and pervade the lower layers in such a way that they undergo a characteristic elevation through their integration into the formative goals of the higher. Therefore, and importantly, the subordination of lower to higher does not destroy the formative undertakings of the lower or short-circuit their specific formative goals, even while they become thoroughly integrated in the formative undertakings and goals of the higher. Indeed, this integration is accomplished precisely through the hierarchical way the layers are arranged and regulated. Thus, Stein argues that "in the structure of the human being [...] all lower levels undergo a specific modification in the higher," so that the overall formation of the whole comes to be understood as an integrated layering of formations, with all ultimately subordinated to the spiritual and personal, the final formative layer of human nature and that which secures the coordinated unity of the whole.[20]

In broad correspondence to the latter three meanings of formation, Stein also identifies three basic meanings of soul (*Seele*) when considering the formation of the living-body:

(1) In general agreement with Aquinas, Stein reasons that the soul identifies the "living inner form" or, simply, the "inner form," where it is understood as the organizing and animating principle of the human individual

---

19   See AMP, 98–99.
20   AMP, 74.

as a substantial whole inclusive of the living-body.[21] In this sense, the soul is the principle of life and the many operations of life, whether they be organic, animal, or spiritual.

(2) Moving beyond the presentation of Aquinas, Stein reasons that the soul identifies the sensitive interior, here understood as the inner locus of sensitive receptivity to the sensible world and a corresponding basis of active motile engagement with the world (both substantial and postural).

(3) Progressing still further beyond the presentation of Aquinas, Stein reasons that the soul identifies the spiritual interior, now understood as the inner locus of spiritual receptivity to the meaningful world and a corresponding basis of active engagement with the world, an active spiritual engagement that is also worked out bodily.

Thus, when considering human nature, Stein provides manifold meaning for the term soul, which takes cognizance of the varied ways the human soul structures and animates the living-body, while duly prioritizing the way the spiritual dimension is given for and experienced by the personal subject. Yet, notwithstanding this manifold, upon the basis of her Augustinian point of departure in first-person experience, Stein reasons that the term soul primarily signifies the interiority of the self and conceives of this interiority as something both sensitively and spiritually "expansive," in addition to possessing its own distinct sensitive and spiritual characteristics.[22] The whole of this sensitive and spiritual expanse is then presented by her as the interior "space" within which the personal I "dwells" and out of which it enters into free, rational engagement with the experienced world, its persons, things, events, and states of affairs. Thus, Stein reasons that the personal I stands within the structure of the soul's interiority in a position of dynamic preeminence, embracing the life of the soul by drawing all of the soul's power into an organic unity of being and living. I return to this aspect of human interiority and the indwelling

---

21 See AMP, 39, 46, 87, 99; and EES, 125, 218, 226. Stein attributes the latter designation to Aquinas even though, to my knowledge, Aquinas never uses this particular phrase to designate the inner principle of living being, even while he certainly does conceive of the soul as an inner principle of formation and life.

22 See above, 18–19. Moreover, as intimated above, with the presence of the spiritual dimension in human nature, there is a natural elevation of the sensitive dimension through its integration with and permeation by the spiritual, so that the sensitive also comes to bear a trace of the distinctive marks of spiritual being and life.

priority of the personal I when further detailing the unity of the human being immediately below.[23]

And so, in correspondence to the results of her abstractive analysis, Stein concludes her investigation into human unity and bodily formation by arguing, on the one hand, that human nature is a "*formal structure [formale Aufbau]*" of manifold formal determinations, and on the other hand, that human nature is a formally unified whole through a final formal determination that makes of the complex an integrated "formal framework [*Formgefüge*]."[24] This final determination is that layer into which all lower layers are arranged so that the entire complex is coordinated as a thoroughly unified whole. Stein identifies this final determination as the "*ruling* form [herrschende *Form*]" of the complex structure, or the "dominating principle of form [*dominierende Formprinzip*]" within this formal whole, precisely since it encompasses all subordinate determinations and frames them as an integrated unity.[25] And

---

23 See below, "The Personal Formation of the Living-Body." Stein's understanding of the meaning of soul is subtle and complex, and the meanings here set forth are not intended to be exhaustive; and neither do I intend to detail (either here or below) Stein's understanding of the "spiritual matter" of the soul. For a summary of the complexity of Stein's understanding of the soul, see Betschart, "Seele," in *Edith Stein-Lexikon*, ed. Marcus Knaup and Harald Seubert (Freiburg i. Br.: Herder, 2017), 334–38; Angela Ales Bello, "Edmund Husserl and Edith Stein: The Question of the Human Subject," trans. Antonio Calcagno, *American Catholic Philosophical Quarterly* 82, no. 1 (2008): 143–59: 152–53; and Donald Wallenfang, *Human and Divine Being: A Study on the Theological Anthropology of Edith Stein* (Eugene OR: Cascade Books, 2017), 157. Like Stein, Aquinas and Aristotle also recognize a manifold of meaning for the terms soul and body but regard these meanings as various coordinate ways of *conceiving* of soul and body and not as various ways of identifying soul and body according to distinct formative layerings with structural significance. In particular, Aquinas recognizes the human being to be a composite of soul and body, not merely a composite of spiritual soul and prime matter, and thereby signifies the already formed body as something in composition with the soul, with soul now understood as the sensitive and rational (virtual) parts of the soul that wield command over the formed and animated body and its member organs. See DEE, 2.6–7; ST, I, 7.3; Meta, 7.10; and for an expansive account, see Joshua Hochschild, "Form, Essence, Soul: Distinguishing Principles of Thomistic Metaphysics," in *Distinctions of Being: Philosophical Approaches to Reality*, ed. Nikolaj Zunic (Washington, DC: American Maritain Association, 2013), 21–35.

24 AMP, 131–32. In EES, instead of "*Gefüge*" Stein uses the term "*Gerüst*" to describe the formal structuration of substances, which, like "*Gefüge*," can be translated as framework, structure, or scaffold. See EES, 182–89; and compare PA, 60.

25 EES, 182–89.

since the spiritual dimension takes precedence over all else in human nature, in *The Structure of the Human Person* Stein identifies this ruling form with the "spiritual soul [*geistige Seele*]."[26] So considered, the spiritual soul takes its place in the formal structure in a commanding and regulating position as that formal principle which provides the encompassing unity of the human structure as a material, organic, animal, and spiritual nature. Accordingly, Stein completes her investigation in *The Structure of the Human Person* by arguing, on the one hand, in contrast to Aquinas, that human nature is a complex formal structure of manifold formal determinations, and, on the other hand, in correspondence to Aquinas, that human nature is an integrated substantial unity through the dominance of the spiritual soul.[27]

Examining Stein's Conception of Human Unity

To properly understand what Stein means by formal structure and framework, it is necessary to set her understanding of human nature against the background of her conception of the formal structure of being in general. For Stein every finite being that is not a simple form (what she calls the "simple essentialities") is a complex formal structure that has unity provided by an encompassing formal principle embracing and framing the totality. The structure is itself comprised of various formal determinations of differing kinds, all those formal determinants that enter the makeup of each thing and meaningfully determine its *what*, with various sub- and super-ordinations within the interlocking manifold. The structural whole is arranged as a unity via a most foundational determination that provides the definitive enclosure of the compounded whole so that it stands in being as a framed unity. This ruling principle is that into which the various subordinate formal determinations are comprehensively integrated with the kind of lawful articulation that makes of the whole a framed unity. In *Finite and Eternal Being*, Stein describes this final principle as an empty-form (*Leerform*) since it must be filled by the subordinate formal (and material) contents that comprise the particular thing, each according to

---

26 EES, 182–89. As indicated above, when speaking of the expanse of the soul in these contexts, whether spiritual or sensitive, this and related terms should be understood metaphorically.

27 In the above, I have refined what I presented in McNamara, "Human Unity and Bodily Formation," 639–63, by shifting the emphasis in the way the spiritual soul frames the structure of the human soul.

its kind. She says, "Finally, we call the 'form' (= empty-form) the 'framework [*Gerüst*]' of the whole thing (and the parts of the framework) in relation to that which gives it content and determines it as *this* individual thing."[28] The empty-form encompasses the structural whole and makes of the complex a unity at the highest level of formal determination. And since human nature is given as a complex ultimately determined by its spiritual character, Stein reasons that the material, organic, and animal determinations that make up human nature are framed and unified by the spiritual soul as the empty-form of the complex whole.

As suggested by Sarah Borden Sharkey and Christof Betschart, Stein's understanding of the relation of formal determinations in the structural whole can be interpreted in light of the phenomenological understanding of parts and wholes as set forth by Husserl in his *Logical Investigations*.[29] Though Stein does not explicitly refer to Husserlian mereology when explaining the relationship of formal parts within the whole, it is helpful to view her account of the formal structure and framework against this background. So considered, the various parts of the structure can be taken as "formal moments" of the complex with reference to their final integration in the spiritual soul as that which frames the whole. All lower determinations are understood as dependent and inseparable parts of the whole, essentially interwoven by the spiritual soul as ruling principle of the being and unity of the substance.[30] Yet, though so

---

28 EES, 189; see also EES, 66, 188ff., 250–51, and 314n28.

29 See Sarah Borden Sharkey, *Thine Own Self: Individuality in Edith Stein's Later Writings* (Washington, DC: The Catholic University of America Press, 2010), 127–43; and Christof Betschart, "The Individuality of the Human Person in the Phenomenological Works of Edith Stein," in *Edith Stein: Women, Social-Political Philosophy, Theology, Metaphysics and Public History* (Cham: Springer, 2016), 73–86: 76; *Unwiederholbares Gottessiegel: Personale Individualität nach Edith Stein* (Basel: Reinhardt, 2013), 174; and also Edmund Husserl, *Logical Investigations*, 2 vols., trans. J. N. Findlay (New York: Routledge, 2001, repr. 2008), 2:1–45.

30 This requires some qualification. Though human nature requires all formal determinations—material, organic, animal, and spiritual—for the completion of the nature, Stein recognizes the separability of the human soul from the materiality of the body, as well as the natural transition of material components constituting the body through ingestion and excretion (and, we should also include, inhalation and exhalation). Therefore, since the material dimension is evidently less tightly integrated into the substantial whole, we can deduce that the mode of dependence is not entirely the same for all formal parts. More details regarding this are given below.

interwoven in a tightly structured way, this dependence and inseparability should not be understood as if there is an order of derivation of parts from the spiritual soul, since the dependence and inseparability is not like that of accidental (in the Thomistic sense) formal content. Rather, the formal parts are integrated in a lawfully regulated manner through the framing provided by the spiritual soul without the spiritual soul in any way grounding them as a basis from which they could be derived. Rather, the spiritual soul unifies and integrates the formal (and material) determinations that duly fill out the essential fullness of human nature, which fullness is needed by the spiritual soul precisely as an empty-form.[31] Thus, Stein understands all formal determinations to have distinct ontological significance within the structure, a significance that is evident in their formative shaping of the human individual in the layered manner indicated by her abstractive analysis, even while they are still conceived as unified formal moments of the complex structural whole. The ontological significance of such formal moments then provides a fitting explanatory basis for eidetically and conceptually grasping—as well as linguistically expressing—the complexity and interwoven character of human nature, since the structural layers and their arrangement ground the manifold ways human nature is known and understood, in its complexity and in its unity.

What conception of soul (Seele) *is operative here?* Evidently, by her use of the term "spiritual soul" in this context, Stein does not intend to designate the whole of the human soul but rather only one dimension, the specifically human, the spiritual and the personal. Whereas the human soul as one whole is the living inner form of the human being, the spiritual soul is merely the dominating principle of form, the ruling formality that encompasses the structure and definitively determines its being and unity. The spiritual soul is but one part, even if the dominant part, of a complex structure that includes in itself the lower dimensions determining organic and animal operations of life, as well as the incorporated matter comprising the living-body. Yet, since the human soul is definitively determined by the spiritual soul as its ruling form and since this form pervades all lower framed subdeterminations, Stein

---

31 Some caution should be exercised here. Since Stein appears to hold that there is a real distinction of formal parts within the formal structure, and a corresponding real integration of the parts as a unified whole through the unifying function of the final formal determinant, the formal subdeterminations of the structure should not be understood merely as moments differently determined in meaning within an actually simple formal whole.

maintains that the human soul as one whole is itself something spiritual and she identifies the human soul as a "spiritual kind of soul [*Geistseele*]."³² Therefore, we can say that for Stein the human soul is still but *one* soul, even if this one soul has an inner complexity and structural arrangement of partial determinations; and, moreover, it is this one soul *as a whole* that informs the human substance and organizes and animates the living-body. Yet, in neither of these senses—as "spiritual soul" or as "spiritual kind of soul"—does Stein simply equate the soul with the substantial form of the human being, if by substantial form we are to understand the completed formal determination of the human substance. Since neither the spiritual soul nor the spiritual kind of soul singularly determine the whole of human nature, even while both in their own way determine the being and unity of the human substance, neither can be identified with the substantial form of the human being without further ado. In the first case, the "spiritual soul" does not by itself determine the whole of the human being, even while it embraces and pervades the entire human structure with its material composition. In the second case, the "spiritual kind of soul," though now formally determining the human being as one whole, does not do so without the co-determinative impact of the already formed material elements which are incorporated into the composition of the living-body.³³

What conception of form (Form) *is operative here?* In her later works, Stein uses the term form *(Form)* according to two basic senses, each of which traces its roots to the different traditions of Stein's own formation. In accord with her phenomenological formation, Stein is considering form primarily from the perspective of consciousness, as the meaningful determination of an intentional object apprehended in an intentional act. In accord with her Thomistic formation, Stein is considering form primarily from the perspective of actual being, as the intrinsic principle determining each being as *what* it is and, secondarily, *how* it is. Yet, in both senses, the phenomenological and the Scholastic, form is understood to be something intelligible, which has a determining and unifying role relative to its particular matter; where matter is understood as something correlative to form, as the relatively indeterminate yet determinable substrate of form.³⁴ In her mature thought, bringing these

---

32   AMP, 84.
33   See AMP, 41, 111, 130–32; EES, 164–65. I take up this formal co-determination of the material elements of the body on a number of occasions below.
34   For phenomenology, with its focus on consciousness, "matter" includes all possible

somewhat contrasted perspectives into confrontation, Stein develops a multifaceted understanding of the meaning of form that is expressly attentive to both positions.[35] When considering the formal structure and framework, as well as the mutual interconnection of formal parts within the whole, Stein is approaching form primarily from a phenomenological perspective. Yet, this use of form has its counterpart in Scholasticism, in the "diverse modes of understanding [*diversos modos intelligendi*]" or "diverse notions [*diversas rationes*]" according to which each thing can be abstractly considered.[36] Such formal notions are understood to be intentionally paired with the partial determinations of the completed form of the known thing, precisely inasmuch as these determinations can be abstracted from the whole. Conversely, when considering the formal structure of any actual substance in general, or the living inner form of living beings in particular, Stein is considering form primarily from a Scholastic perspective. Yet, similarly, this use of form also has its counterpart in (realist) phenomenology, as the actual form that inwardly determines the actual thing as a formal whole, which is also the intelligible correlate of an intentional apprehension of the object as a whole.

And so, though both phenomenology and Thomism consider form with primary reference to the contrasted perspectives of consciousness and being—in the ways here all too briefly outlined—Stein evidently does not consider these perspectives to be mutually exclusive, and rather understands them as complementary stances that capacitate her for a more comprehensive presentation of the structure of being, inclusive of the human being.[37] Along these lines,

---

contents of intentional acts, all formal and qualitative content grasped intentionally as the "act-matter" (in contrast to the "act-quality," as that which determines the intentional act in kind), and this includes spatially extended sensual content (matter in the ordinary sense). For Scholasticism, with its focus on the real, "matter" ordinarily means spatially extended stuff, a principle of "pure" potency that is apt to be actualized by substantial form (and remains present in the substance as an intrinsic cause); then, in an extended sense, "matter" includes the substance as subject of accidental form, and in an analogical sense anything (relatively) indeterminate and (further) determinable. Compare EES, 413n47.

35 See esp. EES, 194–237; and PA, 21–25.
36 DV, 2.1, co.
37 For an outline of Stein's conception of form traced to its phenomenological, Scholastic, and Greek sources, see Betschart, "Form," in *Stein-Lexikon*, 119–22. The complementarity of perspectives in this area deserves further examination not possible within the confines of the present study.

according to Stein's phenomenological training, the entire formal structure of human nature can be understood to be something that is first thought by God—whose knowledge is the principle of the human being, and who knows human nature according to all formal aspects—then actually determines the human individual as a human substance—as that by which the human being *is* and *lives* as a complex whole—and subsequently becomes the possible object of thought according to a limited but extensive manifold—as that according to which the human being can be variously considered in thought.[38] Yet, notwithstanding this complexity, both ontological and epistemological, according to Stein's Thomistic understanding the actual form of human nature is understood to be a unified whole, a living inner form or soul, which as spiritual is immediately created by God and contains all formal subdeterminations. Thus, in the complexity of the soul as formal structure, and in the unity of the soul as inner form, both of Stein's uses are brought together to provide a fully comprehensive conception of human nature. I will return to this synthesis of phenomenological and Scholastic stances below and there detail more fully how Stein differs from Aquinas when it comes to the structure of the human soul as form.[39]

The Personal Unity of the Human Being

In *Finite and Eternal Being* Stein extends the investigation begun in *The Structure of the Human Person* by proposing that the spiritual unity of the human being should be understood as a properly personal unity. As was shown above in her Augustinian point of departure, Stein reasons that the human individual is first given in experience as a unity of spirit, soul, and living-body in the living unity of the personal I. The personal I was there seen to be that dimension of human nature wherein the life of the individual is concentrated, the indubitably given core of conscious life, which has at its immediate disposal

---

38 Gregory Doolan shows that the divine ideas of Aquinas not only represent the various formalities that comprise the formal structure of all actual and possible beings—as something proper to divine speculative knowledge—but also represent the multiplicity of ideas of all actual individual things according to their full essential and accidental structures—as something proper to divine practical knowledge in the divine creative knowing of creatures. Thus, for Aquinas, the divine ideas are to be understood, ultimately, as exemplar causes of actually created finite beings. See Gregory Doolan, *Aquinas on the Divine Ideas as Exemplar Causes* (Washington, DC: The Catholic University of America Press, 2008), esp. 143–47, 190–99.

39 See below, 91ff.

the properly spiritual powers of thinking, willing, and spiritual feeling. Yet, as was also shown above, Stein argues that the personal I is not given in experience as a bare pole of consciousness, something that possesses the stream of experience but which is itself without any inner ground or depth. Rather, she convincingly shows that the personal I rises to the wakefulness of conscious life from a transcendent "inner world," and fittingly describes this inner world as a complex of spirit, soul, and living-body.[40] Moreover, Stein reasons that this structural whole is not exhaustively described when account is given of the ontological role of the soul as form of the living-body, or indeed, through the further detailing of the ordered array of spiritual, animal, and organic powers of the soul—significant as both these accounts of human nature undoubtedly are. Rather, as detailed above, in accord with her Augustinian way of proceeding from first-person experience, Stein reveals that the human soul possesses an interior expansiveness of both a sensitive and spiritual kind, an interiority within which the personal I "dwells" and out of which it engages the outer world via the many spiritual and sensitive powers at its disposal.

It is worth here quoting at length the fascinating way Stein describes this indwelling presence of the personal I within the expanse of the soul, while also integrating the mystical presentation of St. Teresa of Avila into her philosophical conception of human interiority.

> The soul is the "space" in the middle of the bodily-soulish-spiritual whole [*leiblich-seelisch-geistigen Ganzen*]; as a sensitive soul it dwells in the living-body, in all its members and parts, receives from it and has a shaping and preserving affect upon it; as a spiritual soul [*Geistseele*] it rises above itself, looks out into a world beyond itself—a world of things, persons, events—and by understanding, enters into communication with the world and receives from it; as soul in the most proper sense, however, the soul dwells with itself, the personal I is at home in the soul. Here everything that enters in from the sensory and from the spiritual world is gathered, here an inner confrontation takes place with what enters into the soul, from here a position is taken upon what enters in, and here is gained what becomes its most personal property, an integral part of its very self—what (figuratively speaking) "becomes its flesh and blood." The soul as "interior castle,"

---

40 See esp. EES, 66, 188–94, 247–49, and 314n28; and AMP, 131–32.

as our Holy Mother Teresa describes it, is not point-like, as is the "pure I," but rather is a "space"—and, indeed, a "castle" with many dwellings—within which the I can move about freely, sometimes moving outwards, sometimes withdrawing more into the interior. And it is not an "empty space," even though a fullness can enter into it and be taken up by it; indeed, it must be so if the soul is to unfold its own peculiar life.[41]

Much can be said about this significant passage that appears late in *Finite and Eternal Being*—especially given its synthetic character, as an account at once Augustinian, Thomistic, and Carmelite—but I wish here to focus only on the way Stein reveals the dominant position of the personal I within the completed structure and dynamism of the soul. Since the personal I has the ability to move about freely within the interior expanse of the soul, and thus take up its position in the innermost depth of the soul, from where it can embrace the collected power of the soul, and since the personal I has the ability to encounter the experienced world via its spiritual and sensitive powers, and thus inwardly engage the outer world from which it receives both meaning and values, the personal I evidently holds sway over the entirety of the soul.[42]

---

41 EES, 317–18; and also Teresa of Avila, *The Interior Castle*, trans. Kieran Kavanaugh and Otilio Rodriguez (Washington, DC: Institute of Carmelite Studies, 1987). It is worth noting that Stein here resolves something of a problem embedded in the text of *The Interior Castle*. By making a distinction between the personal I of the soul and the soul as interior space, and showing how the personal I both inhabits and moves about within the expanse of the soul with its many dwelling places, she resolves the difficulty of accounting for how an inner journey to the depth of the soul is possible by identifying the one making the journey with the personal I. At the same time, she significantly adjusts Teresa's conception of the soul by showing that the structure of the soul unfolds through time via lived experience and the sensory and spiritual "incorporation" of meaning from the transcendent worlds, that the castle is, so to speak, progressively "built" over the course of life lived in an authentic manner. For a comparison with Wojtyła on the interior expanse of the soul and the indwelling I, see Wojtyła, *Love and Responsibility*, trans. Grzegorz Ignatik (Boston, MA: Pauline Books and Media, 2013), 3–7, 68, 96–100, 103–4, 185–92, 244.

42 Evidently then, the inner expanse of the soul is not like a vacant warehouse, but is rather something with definition and order, a reality that has an already given determinate architecture, even while it is also something that unfolds this architecture only through the course of time.

Indeed, as implied in all above anthropological analyses, this dynamic command of the personal I within the expanse of the soul bespeaks of an actual and ontological predominance of the I in this same structure, with the consequence that when Stein returns to the question of human unity in *Finite and Eternal Being*, she further refines her understanding and there shows that the unity of the human individual should be understood as a personal kind of unity, with substantial unity grounded in nothing other than the personal I. Though this conclusion is implied already in Stein's reflection on the primordially given self of first-person experience, inasmuch as such experience discloses the structural unity of the human being in and through the immediately given unity of the conscious I, only late in *Finite and Eternal Being* does Stein finally clarify that the priority of the I is something not merely dynamic but also structural, and there argues that the personal I should be taken as the definitive empty-form that encompasses the essential fullness of human nature.[43] With this further refinement, we can say that while the spiritual soul is formally dominant within the structure of human nature as a material, organic, and animal structure, the personal I is itself formally dominant within the structure of the spiritual soul, with the further consequence that the personal I has a position of dominance within the structure of human nature as a whole.

This I take to be Stein's finally worked-out and fully mature position. However, in what immediately follows, in correspondence to the presentation in *The Structure of the Human Person*, where human unity and bodily formation is detailed more expansively, I proceed by analyzing these two important teachings from the perspective of the spiritual soul without always adverting to the distinction of personal I within the soul.[44] Yet, out of consideration for the further precision introduced in *Finite and Eternal Being*, I often identify the spiritual soul as the "personally determined spiritual soul." In subsequent chapters, when directly exploring the question of the

---

43 See esp. EES, 320, 420.

44 Though Stein nowhere, to my knowledge, precisely details the ontological relation of personal I and spiritual soul, even while she frequently details the phenomena of the personal I indwelling the spiritual expanse of the soul, as well as showing the I as the inner pole wielding the powers of the spiritual soul, in EES she definitively states that the personal I is the final formal determination of any and all personal forms of life, inclusive of the human being. For a brief description of the complexity of the personal structure, and its relation to the structural whole of human nature, see Claudia Mariéle Wulf, "Ich," in *Stein-Lexikon*, 187–88.

being-individual and individuality of the human being, I again take up the question of the priority of the personal I and there show definitively in what way the personal I is the ultimate formal principle accounting for the unity of the human being.

The Personal Formation of the Living-Body

Having now summarized the results of Stein's investigation of human formation and concluded to the unity of the human being through the personally determined spiritual soul, we are in a position to provide further details about Stein's conception of the soul's formation of the body, a Thomistic teaching succinctly captured by the traditional Latin formula, "*anima forma corporis.*" By unpacking the meaning Stein attributes to this important proposition of the Catholic tradition, we see clearly how Stein's novel presentation of human unity has considerable import for our understanding of the *personal* significance of the human body.

As shown above, first and foundationally, in basic agreement with Aquinas, Stein argues that the human soul as a whole, according to its essence as soul, is the form of a materially composed body that it organizes and animates as a living-body *(Leib)*—actualizing the material body as *what* it is, a living human body. Yet, as also shown above, in some contrast to Aquinas, Stein reasons that the human soul forms the body in a layered manner in correspondence to layered structure of the soul itself, first organizing the body according to the requirements of the powers of each layer and then animating the body with the powers of these same hierarchically ordered layers. In further contrast to Aquinas, she also argues that the already formed material elements that are incorporated into the living-body retain their structural distinction in addition to their formative power, even while they lose their independence as distinct substances in their subordination to the higher formative outcomes of the human organism. This contrasts with Aquinas inasmuch as he argues for the immediate formation of prime matter by the one and simple human soul, even while he recognizes that incorporated material elements remain virtually present in the body and are retrievable upon death and the material dissolution of the *post-mortem* body.[45]

---

45   Of the full significance of this particular disagreement, I treat in greater detail below. See "Assessing the Potential Benefits of Stein's Novel Proposal."

Beyond this first meaning of bodily formation for Stein, where the soul is understood to be *one* with the living-body, even if informing and animating already formed material elements, Stein attributes to the proposition "*anima forma corporis*" a further manifold of meaning. Since the living-body is the locus of sensitive interaction with the world in all cognitive and appetitive responsivity, as well as the sensitive instrument of active engagement with the world, Stein argues that the already formed living-body undergoes a higher level of sensitive formation beyond the foundational organization and animation of the living-body and its organs. This further formation is brought about first by the gradual habituation of the sensitive and motile powers and their respective bodily organs, according to which these powers together with their organs become ever more acute and agile in their operations. This sensitive formation of the body is brought to completion when the peculiar character of the sensitive interior of the soul leaves an enduring impress on the body, through the progressive expression of this character via sensitive interaction with the world.[46]

At a still higher level, and a level of most import in human life, the living-body undergoes a further level of formation of a properly spiritual and personal kind. Since the living-body is the locus of all spiritual interaction with the world in all cognitive, appetitive, and affective responsivity of a spiritual kind, as well as the material instrument of active spiritual engagement with the world, the already formed living-body undergoes a higher level of spiritual formation beyond the foundational organic and animal formation of the body. This specifically spiritual formation presupposes and elevates the prior organic and animal formations, determining these undergirding formations in new and higher ways through the dynamism of spiritual life, in consequence of which the body gradually comes to bear the impress of the spiritual and personal. This additional formation is brought about first through the further habituation of the sensitive and motile powers and their organs according to the needs of spiritual cognition and movement, and through the enduring impress the peculiar character of the spiritual interior leaves upon the living-body as it is expressed more and more through time in all spiritual interaction with the meaningful world. This spiritual formation finds its highest determination in the potential for the living-body to be formed in a properly personal manner, when the body comes to be impressed with

---

[46] See AMP, 46–47, 52–53, 54–55. One can perhaps consider Stein's understanding of the particular character of the sensitive interior to be something analogous to the traditionally given psychological temperaments, or indeed, contemporary psychological classifications of the same psychological realities.

the freely determined character of the personal I, together with the qualitative individuality of the personal spirit, both of which are brought about in and through all specifically personal action and expression.[47]

Thus, Stein attributes manifold related meanings to the adopted proposition "*anima forma corporis*," meanings sequentially layered in correspondence to the formal structure of the human soul. In summary, Stein reasons that the soul is the form of the body in the following ways: (1) as organizing and animating the material body as a living human body; (2) as sensitively habituating the living-body and leaving an enduring sensitive impress upon the living-body; and (3) as spiritually habituating the living-body and leaving an enduring spiritual and personal impress upon this same living-body. Yet, and importantly, as already indicated, Stein does not conceive of these formative undertakings as discrete layerings with radical separation from one another. Rather, in correspondence to her understanding of the formal unity of human nature, she maintains, "The whole human being receives its impression through the *actual life of the I* and is 'matter' for formation through the *activity of the I*."[48] And again, "[The conscious and free I] has a formative influence on its body and soul, [such that] the whole of his own 'human nature' belongs to the domain of his mastery."[49] In this way, the human body gradually comes to bear the impress of the personal soul, according to both its sensitive and its spiritual nature, and according to the freely determined character of the personal I together with its particular qualitative individuality (as detailed below).[50]

The layers of bodily formation are then obviously both *ontologically* and *dynamically* significant for Stein, ontologically, inasmuch as they comprise the substantial structure of the human being, and dynamically, inasmuch as this already given substantial structure receives its completion only through the dynamism of personal life. One would then expect the human body to come to bear the peculiar "*Gestalt*" of the personal individual more and more through the

---

47 In part II below, I take up the question of human individuality, both with respect to the individual being of the human person, according to which human individuals are rendered distinct from one another in being, and with respect to the qualitative individuality of the human person, according to which distinct human individuals are rendered qualitatively different from one another.
48 AMP, 83.
49 EES, 320.
50 See chap. 4 below.

course of life. This would then progressively reveal the individual human body to be something properly unique, not only because of each individual's bodily constitution—determined as it is by genetic inheritance and life's developmental course—but also through the impress it receives of the sensitive, spiritual, and personal character of the individual. If brought to completion, the living-body would become a profound and rich manifestation of the person—of *who* he is in himself—and thus comes to represent not merely some*body*, but rather the *body* of some*one*. The human individual would then attain the fitting spiritual and personal elevation of the organic and animal formations of the living-body. And indeed, for Stein, this is a key aspect of the end or τέλος (*telos*) of human formation: the thoroughgoing personal formation of the living-body.[51] The individual personal I is then best understood as the final "bearer" of the living-body, as the *one* tasked with the responsibility of forming *his* living-body in a personal way, a formation that first illustrates the profound ontological unity of human nature, and realizes the proper completion of this unity as a personal and ethical task in and through the dynamism of personal life.[52]

Reframing all this in ordinary terms might here be helpful: Since the appearance of the body is shaped by the human individual in a dynamic way through the course of life, and particularly in and through all personal expression and action, one would expect that the body would come to bear—more and more over time—the inner constitution of the human individual, making this inwardness visible (i.e., sensible) in and through the figure of the body, its posture, gait, and resting expression. In this way, the body would come to manifest something of the truth of the individual, of his inner life and dispositions, of his response to meaning and value, together with his personal bearing toward the vagaries of life, with all its weal and woe. Eminent in this bodily manifestation is the face, since the human face is that bodily part that most clearly makes present the being of the person as such, both through the

---

51 See AMP, 74–75, 80–81, 83–84.
52 For an account of the order of human formation with a focus on personal responsibility, see Anna Maria Pezzella, "Bildung und Selbstbildung der menschlichen Person," in *Edith Steins Herausforderung heutiger Anthropologie*, ed. Hanna-Barbara Gerl-Falkovitz and Mette Lebech (Heiligenkreuz: Be&Be, 2017), 256–68: 257–63; and, with a focus on the continuity of spiritual and personal formation with psychic and bodily formation, see René Raschke, "Self Realization of the Human Being," in *Edith Steins Herausforderung heutiger Anthropologie*, ed. Hanna-Barbara Gerl-Falkovitz and Mette Lebech (Heiligenkreuz: Be&Be, 2017), 269–90: 273–83.

high density of facial muscles facilitating facial expression, and through the expressivity of the eyes, the so-called windows of the soul. Indeed, of the human eyes, Stein says,

> I look into the eyes of a human being and his look answers me. He permits me to penetrate into his interior or defends himself against me. He is master of his soul and can open or close its gates [...] If two human beings look at one another, then one I and another I stand opposite one another. It can be an encounter at the gates or an encounter in the interior [...] The look of a human being speaks. An *autonomous, aware I* looks at me from within. Therefore, we also say: a *free spiritual person*.

And have we not all encountered individuals like this: those, usually the elderly, whose eyes and faces—and sometimes indeed their whole bodies—have come to bear their individual personal being and dynamic course of life, manifesting their person in an incredibly clear way? We could here think of St. Teresa of Calcutta, an individual all but universally known, whose eyes, face, and whole body most clearly bore the unique character of her personal identity, as well as her life given to Christ and the materially and spiritually dispossessed—such that to see her photograph is, so to speak, to see her person.[53]

Assessing Stein's Conception of Human Unity and Bodily Formation

Given Stein's independently developed presentation of the substantial unity of the human being, taken together with the related manifold of meanings she attributes to the proposition "*anima forma corporis*," we can now directly address how Stein's understanding compares with its adopted foundation in Aquinas's thought. This comparison will show clearly in what way Stein's proposal corresponds to

---

53 Wojtyła's Thomistically inspired conception of the profound personal significance of the human body clearly parallels Stein's understanding (even though his is worked out in a theological context as a theology of the body), and this is plausibly because both accounts depend upon and are shaped by the principle *anima forma corporis*, even though Wojtyła's conception does not include the hierarchical and layered detail of Stein's. In particular, see John Paul II, *Man and Woman He Created Them: A Theology of the Body*, trans. Michael Waldstein (Boston: Pauline Books and Media, 2006).

that of Aquinas and the Thomistic tradition while also setting her distinctive proposal into relief, without in any way overlooking the remaining tensions—even contradictions—to be found between their positions. Such a comparison is best performed, I suggest, by exploring Aquinas's reasons for arguing for the rational soul as principle of human unity and bodily formation and examining Stein's proposal with reference to these same reasons, in view of its ability to satisfy Aquinas's criteria, and perhaps account for them with greater facility. This analysis is completed by examining certain benefits that arise from conceiving of human unity and bodily formation after the manner of Stein.

In the most mature work with which Stein was familiar, his *Summa theologiae*, Aquinas's arguments for the substantial unity of the human being and the soul as form of the body are fashioned on the basis of the kind of being possessed by the human being and the way we think and speak about this being—that is, according to the orders of being and predication.[54] In *Summa theologiae* (I, 76), in the context of examining the union of the soul and body over the course of eight articles, Aquinas forcefully argues for the *simplicity* of the soul and for the substantial *unity* of human nature through the rational soul's immediate formation of the material body.[55] By simple (*simplex*) Aquinas means that which is without composition, so that the simplicity of the human soul should be taken to mean that the human soul is not composed of a series of (substantial) forms concurrently informing the material body and/or parts of the material body; and by unity (*unum*) Aquinas means that which is without division, so that the unity of the human being should be taken to mean that there is no actual division of the rational soul from the materiality of the body.[56] For our purposes, Aquinas's arguments can serviceably be resolved into the following series of questions, which we can pose of Stein's alternate solution to the same anthropological problem. Concerning the order of being: Does Stein's proposal provide an ultimate principle of being and unity in human

---

54 See ST, I, 76.1–8.

55 More precisely, Aquinas argues that the intellectual principle is united to the body as its form; that each human individual possesses a separate intellectual principle; that there is in the human being just one substantial form and one soul, and this soul is the intellectual soul; that the intellectual soul is directly and immediately united to the body as its form, and that the formation of the body is proper to the intellectual soul; and, finally, that the whole intellectual soul pervades the whole body, even while its faculties or powers are localized in various organs of the organized and animated body.

56 See ST, I, 3; I, 76; SCG, 1.31, 2.90.

nature corresponding to the rational soul?[57] Can this principle account for the simple generation of the human individual?[58] And can it also provide an explanation for the unified ground of human activity?[59] Concerning the order of predication: Does Stein's proposal account for the essential predication of all generic determinations of the human being?[60] And does it account for the attribution of a particular act of understanding to a particular bodily individual?[61]

First, concerning the order of being: With her proposal of the personally determined spiritual soul as the dominant formal principle encompassing the entire structure of human nature, Stein provides a principle of being and unity for the human being, which includes the formation of the material body as a living body. Insofar as the spiritual soul is the ruling form into which all subordinate determinations are integrated, the spiritual soul provides the final principle of the *being* and *unity* of the human substance. This means that the human substance has an ultimate principle of being that provides substantial unity to the whole, a unity that is secured by the personally determined spiritual soul through its regulated framing of all formal and material subdeterminations, whether animal, organic, or material. In so holding to the substantial unity of the human being through the spiritual soul, notwithstanding the manifold of subordinate determinations, Stein avoids arguing for a plurality of substantial forms or souls, each providing formation for the different regions of bodily life, and having to find a further principle to unify them—a concern explicitly raised by Aquinas.[62] Rather, as shown above, Stein argues that the human soul is still but *one* soul, even if formally complex in its inner structure, and it is this one soul that immediately informs the material body, even while the material components of the body remain co-determinative. In the very same way, then, Stein can account for the simple generation of the human individual since the generation of the whole occurs through the appropriate formal and material filling of the personally determined spiritual soul as the encompassing formal framework. Thus, in like manner to the way the rational soul is by its nature correlated with prime matter for the completion of human nature in

---

57 See ST, I, 76.3, co.; SCG, 2.68; QDA, 2; and QDSC, 2–3.
58 See ST, I, 76.4, co. See also QDA, 11; and QDSC, 3.
59 See ST, I, 76.3, co.
60 ST, I, 76.3, co.; and also, QDA, 11.
61 See ST, I, 76.1, co.; QDA, 2; and QDSC, 2.
62 See ST, I, 76.3, co.

Aquinas, so too the personally determined spiritual soul is naturally correlated with the formal and material fullness of human nature in Stein. Accordingly, for both thinkers, the human individual comes into being as one substantial whole according to all required formal and material parts, even while each thinker proposes a different way of understanding the composition of formal and material principles, and notwithstanding the further degree of complexity introduced by Stein's proposal of the formal structure.[63]

Stein also argues for a unified basis for human activity by appealing to the notion of "life-power [*Lebenskraft*]," a concept she already developed in her early phenomenological works to account for the diverse kinds of causality in which human life is immersed.[64] Through an investigation of the impact of generically different kinds of causes on the dynamism of life, Stein argues that there is a finite reserve of life-power available to the human individual for his living operations. This life-power is consumed through its conversion into living experiences and actions, and augmented through its reception from

---

63 At this point it is worth adverting to the aspects of Stein's position that appear to coincide with teachings of Scotus, specifically: (1) his stance on the possibility of a plurality of substantial forms comprising one substance through an ordered layering under some highest formal unity; and (2) his recognition of a formal distinction in addition to real and logical distinctions. Although there is some alignment between Stein and Scotus on these points, in AMP or EES Stein does not reference him in her investigation of human unity and bodily formation and their positions do not track one another perfectly. In relation to the former, (1) Stein does not argue for a plurality of *substantial* forms comprising one substance, even while she does propose an interconnected layering of distinct formal determinations under one ruling form that frames the whole (though this difference could arguably be taken as something more terminological than conceptual). In relation to the latter, (2) there is certainly alignment, since both recognize the objective distinction of actually inseparable formalities within one formal whole, even while Stein pays particular attention not only to the distinct structural reality and interwoven formative undertakings of each formal layer, with a significance both ontological and dynamic, while also attending to their tightly framed actual unity. A separate extensive analysis not possible here would be required to detail the precise range of similarity and difference between Stein's and Scotus's clearly comparable positions. For more on Scotus on these points, see Thomas Ward, *John Duns Scotus on Parts, Wholes, and Hylomorphism* (Boston: Brill, 2014), 76–109; and Allan B. Wolter, "The Formal Distinction," in *Studies in Philosophy and the History of Philosophy, vol. 3: John Duns Scotus, 1265–1965*, ed. John K. Ryan and Bernardine M. Bonansea (Washington, DC: The Catholic University of America Press, 2018), 45–60.
64 See PK, 21–34, esp. 64–80.

various material and spiritual sources.[65] In her later thought, Stein integrates this phenomenologically developed understanding with Aquinas's presentation of the faculties of the soul, and she argues that a unified ground of action is revealed in the way life-power is consumed across the diverse faculties of the soul as they transition into action with varying degrees of intensity.[66] Though life-power is divided across the different layers of the soul, the available power for action is given in experience as a limited unitary reserve through the reciprocal impact or the consumption of power by any one faculty has on the ability of other faculties to transition into experience and/or action with appropriate intensity.[67] Thus, for Stein, the human being is given in experience as a dynamic unity of life-power, possessing a unified ground of activity and living operations, inasmuch as all layers of the human complex are given as one via their common "tapping" of unitary reserve. However, though Stein in this way establishes a unified ground of human activity, one with clear alignment with the parallel reasoning of Aquinas regarding the reciprocal impact of the exercise of the faculties, this argument leaves untouched the validity (or not) of her proposition of a formal structure and framework, even while it manifests the inherent coherency of her proposal.

Concerning the order of predication: Since the personally determined spiritual soul as ruling form presupposes certain definite formal determinations, and is that which frames these partial formal determinations as an integrated unity, Stein's conception permits all generic attributions—living, animal, etc.—to be predicated essentially of the human being. This is possible because of the way

---

65   See AMP, 108, 111–13, 118–19, 121–22. Wallenfang identifies power with the "substance of the soul" and further identifies the substance of the soul with the "soul of the soul." However, this double identification obscures important distinctions in Stein's thought. See Wallenfang, *Human and Divine Being*, 107–10.

66   See AMP, 52–53, 76–77, 123–25; and also, EES, 358–59, 366–67. Following the Latin terminology of Aquinas and the Scholastics, Stein denominates these inherent faculties (powers, capabilities) as "*vires, virtutes, facultates,*" and variously translates them into German as "*Anlagen, Kräfte, Vermögen, Fähigkeiten* [translatable in English as: tendencies, powers, faculties, capabilities]" (AMP, 124). For a brief treatment of the Aristotelian-Thomistic inspiration of Stein's understanding of the faculties of the soul, see Sarah Borden Sharkey, "Capacity or Castle? Thoughts on Stein's Creative (Carmelite) Contribution to Discussions on the Soul," in *Edith Steins Herausforderung heutiger Anthropologie,* ed. Hanna-Barbara Gerl-Falkovitz and Mette Lebech (Heiligenkreuz: Be&Be, 2017), 203–14.

67   See AMP, 108, 110–11, 118–19, 120–21, 124–25.

Stein conceives of the dependence and inseparability of formal parts within the formally framed whole of human nature. As noted above, this dependence and inseparability is not like that of certain kinds of accidental content (as surface is presupposed by color, as implied in the meaning of color), and should not be understood as if there is an order of derivation of the formal parts within the formal whole, so that there could only be a derivative manner of predication of generic attributions of the human being. Since formal frameworks have a lawfully defined order of integration, the ruling form can be filled only by certain formal determinations, and only in a certain tightly regulated order of arrangement. This regulated order is essential to the framework and is that whereby the various subdeterminations become defined essential parts of a defined essential whole, fitted together in a defined order of arrangement. When this general picture is applied to human nature, we see that the personally determined spiritual soul presupposes certain definite formal determinations, those material, organic, and animal, as subdeterminations necessarily required by the spiritual soul for the completion of its particular being, according to which all subdeterminations become essential parts of the integrated whole of human nature. The essential fullness provided by the formal and material parts should be understood as that which *fills* the completed structure of the human essence inasmuch as they are required by the spiritual soul for the completion of the essence. Consequently, all generic determinations of the human structure can be predicated essentially of the human being as properly pertaining to the human essence according to the first manner of essential (*per se*) predication of the Scholastic tradition—a concern explicitly raised by Aquinas when addressing the question of substantial unity.[68]

---

68 Following Aristotle, Aquinas recognizes two manners of essential predication: according to the first, only those features belonging to the essence as such—and the definition corresponding to and expressing the essence—are predicated essentially, "when that which is attributed to another pertains to its form"; according to the second, also those elements that include in their meaning—and thus their corresponding definition—a reference to the essence are predicated essentially, "when [...] that to which something is attributed is its proper matter and proper subject." Aquinas, InPA, 1.10 (referring to Aristotle, PAn, 1.4, 73^{a}34–^{b}26). An example of the first would be the way line is predicated of triangle: since line is included in the meaning and definition of triangle, line is predicated according to the first manner, "as pertaining to its form." An example of the second would be the way curve is predicated of line: since curve presupposes and implies line but is not included in the meaning and definition of line as such, curve is predicated according to the second manner, "as to its proper subject."

Finally, according to the very same reasoning, the act of understanding, an act proper to the personally determined spiritual soul, can licitly be attributed to the particular bodily individual, since this very bodily individual is one and the same being, in an essentially regulated unity, as the one who understands.[69] Otherwise stated: since the personally determined spiritual soul is both the functional basis of understanding and the formal principle of the being and unity of the living-body, a particular act of understanding is properly predicated of the particular bodily individual. Socrates's act of understanding is an act predicable of the bodily individual identifiable—with the pointing finger—as Socrates.[70]

For Stein's understanding of the relation of genera and species to the individual, see the relatively lengthy reflection in EES, 127–37, esp. 135–37.

69   See ST, I, 76.1, co.

70   Out of concern for the reintroduction of a Platonic understanding of the soul as motor, John Goyette defends Aquinas's position against contemporary Thomists who are inclined to argue for a plurality of forms in light of developments in contemporary science. Goyette suggests that the introduction of such a plurality erroneously presents form and matter as things rather than as principles of being, with the consequence that form is misunderstood as the efficient cause of movement rather than as the formal cause of being. Consequently, Goyette proposes that "we can either accept the hylomorphism of Aristotle and Thomas and affirm the unity of substantial form or we can adopt the Platonic view of the soul as the sailor in the ship and posit a plurality of movers." See John Goyette, "Thomas on the Unity of Substantial Form," in *Nova et Vetera* 7, no. 4 (2009): 781–90: 786. Terence L. Nichols (the most recent Thomistic thinker Goyette references) is attempting to establish the meaning of the unity of the substantial form in terms of a rapprochement with modern science. He proposes a reconsideration of the presence of a plurality of forms in the substantial whole, which forms he argues should be understood as hierarchically arranged in a part-whole relationship he calls "subsidiarity." See Terence L. Nichols, "Aquinas's Concept of Substantial Form and Modern Science," *International Philosophical Quarterly* 36, no. 3.143 (1996): 303–18: 316–17. In light of the above presentation, I suggest that Stein's conception of the hierarchical arrangement of formal subdeterminations through the formal framing of the spiritual soul surpasses Nichols's presentation of subsidiarity while explaining the very same findings of contemporary science for which Nichols wishes to account. At the same time, Stein's conception of the lawful arrangement of formal determinations bypasses the mutually exclusive dichotomy set up by Goyette and does not fail his legitimate concern for the preeminent place of a formal unifying principle in substantial wholes. Though the fittingness of Stein's proposal to account for contemporary scientific findings is beyond the scope of this study, I believe that Stein's adjustment of Aquinas's teachings in the ways here presented, while still holding to substances and their unity, could well be a fruitful place of dialogue with

In light of this ability of Stein's proposal to account for the concerns raised by Aquinas when considering the substantial unity of the human being, I suggest that Stein's conception of a formal structure and framework satisfies the foundational criteria established by Aquinas's arguments for the substantial unity of the human being through the rational soul, even while her solution diverges from Aquinas in the way she accounts for this unity. According to the order of being, Stein's proposal provides a singular principle of being and unity within the composite structure of the human substance, a principle that accounts for the simple generation of the human being and the unified ground of human activity. According to the order of predication, Stein's proposal provides for the essential predication of all generic attributions of the human being, as also for the attribution of the particular act of understanding to the embodied individual. Moreover, in addition to meeting these criteria, Stein's conception does not fail to address Aquinas's concern that the distinction of "formal notions or logical intentions [*diversas rationes vel intentiones logicas*]" would be confused with the distinction of natural things, each with its own substantial form, and has not muddled the distinction of the orders of knowing and being.[71] Indeed, her solution provides a neat explanation of the relation of these orders by simultaneously accounting for the close correspondence of the ontological and intentional orders. Since the various determinations of the formal structure are *not* to be understood as distinct substantial forms (or souls), but rather should be conceived as partial subdeterminations of a framed whole, Stein can account for the given ontological complexity of human nature while concomitantly disclosing the structural principles by which the human being can be known—both with regard to its complexity and with regard to its unity. In this way, the various formal notions corresponding to the order of knowing, the intentional order, are understood to mirror the formal complexity and unity of the order of being, the ontological order, so that Stein's proposal satisfies both orders, that of being and knowing, while simultaneously accounting for their close correspondence through the intentional relation of knower and known.

---

the natural sciences. For other presentations of the unity of hylomorphic substances that engage contemporary science, see Christopher J. Austin and Anna Marmodoro, "Structural Powers and the Homeodynamic Unity of Organisms," and Christopher J. Austin, "A Biologically Informed Hylomorphism," in *Neo-Aristotelian Perspectives on Contemporary Science*, 169–84, and 185–210, respectively.

71 See ST, I, 74.3, ad 4.

Given this understanding of the substantial unity of human nature, what of the simplicity of the soul so vigorously defended by Aquinas? Inasmuch as Stein provides a final principle of being and unity in the personally determined spiritual soul, Stein grants a relative simplicity to the human soul, even if this simplicity is now qualified. Since the simplicity of the soul is now grounded in the simplicity of the personal I finally determining the spiritual soul, the simplicity of the personal I is communicated to the remainder of the formal structure through the lawful integration of all formal (and material) subdeterminations. But this must be qualified. Since the soul also possesses a formally complex interior structure, Stein's conception certainly lacks the radical simplicity found in the presentation of Aquinas, a simplicity that resolutely establishes the unity of the human being as a hylomorphic composite. Though Aquinas recognizes that the human soul possesses vegetative, sensitive, and rational manifestations of life, since he argues that the rational soul virtually contains these lower forms, he presents the human soul as radically simple in being, and thus secures the profound unity of human nature through the essential determination of the whole of the human substance by the soul as a simple whole.[72] Therefore, even if one should grant that Stein's novel proposal

---

72 To say that the rational soul immediately informs prime matter is to imply both that the first composition of a material substance is substantial form and prime matter, and that the ultimate subject of substantial form is prime matter; notwithstanding that, for Aquinas, the principle of individuation for material substances is designated matter (*materia signata*). This manner of distinguishing prime and designated matter is possible for Aquinas because he does not position designated matter in opposition to prime matter, but rather understands designated matter to be prime matter subject to (indeterminate) dimensions—that is, matter marked off and apportioned as "this matter." And though designated matter, through (indeterminate) dimensive quantity, provides the founding condition of the existence of a material individual, the ultimate potency in which substantial form inheres as the act of its potency is prime matter. Consequently, in ST, I, q. 76, a. 4, ad 3, in response to an objection that the human soul would be imperfect if it "inhered immediately to prime matter," Aquinas replies that the substantial form, as giving all degrees of perfection, inheres "to matter immediately"; and again, in ST, I, q. 75, a. 5, ad 1, he states, "Prime matter receives individual forms"; and finally, in ST, I, q. 77, a.1, ad 2, now from the perspective of matter, he says, "The act to which prime matter is in potentiality is the substantial form." See also G. E. M. Anscombe, part II of "Symposium: The Principle of Individuation," in *Proceedings of the Aristotelian Society, Supplementary Volumes*, 27 (1953): 69–120: 88: "Matter only has identity in so far as it is designate, earmarked; in itself it is indefinite (ἀόριστος)." In some correspondence to this division of matter, Aquinas then makes a distinction

satisfies Aquinas's concerns for human unity and bodily formation, Stein's formally complex solution diverges significantly from Aquinas's coordinate solution to the same metaphysical problems with respect to the question of simplicity. Yet, as noted, since Stein does provide a qualified simplicity to the human soul—through the grounding of the human soul in something that is itself radically simple in being, the personal I that finally determines and encompasses the soul—Stein can be understood to guarantee a qualified simplicity to the human soul (and being) through the radical simplicity of the personal I.

Assessing the Potential Benefits of Stein's Novel Proposal

In the end, Stein proposes the formal structure of the human being as a *fitting* explanation of the complexity of human nature, while simultaneously securing the unity of the human being through the framing provided by the spiritual soul. By considering human nature to be a structure of lawfully arranged formal determinations, Stein accounts for the evident complexity of human nature, as it is given in ordinary experience and attested to by Aquinas. By further arguing for the integration of these determinations in a lawfully framed arrangement of sub- and super-ordination, Stein accounts for the evident unity of human nature, as is also given in ordinary experience and attested to by Aquinas. Moreover, by meeting the challenge of Aquinas's rationale for arguing for the unity of human nature through the rational soul as substantial form, Stein's solution pays respect to the importance of human unity as such, in addition to clearly highlighting its central importance in the Thomistic tradition. However, the benefit of her independent solution is found only when we consider the specifically personal, both with respect to the impact of the personal throughout human nature, and with respect to the complementary impact of the material, organic, and animal on the person. That is to say that the dominance of the personally determined spiritual soul explains the comprehensive penetration of the whole of human nature by the spiritual and personal—a "top-down" influence—without ignoring the ongoing inverse impact

---

within form, between the form of the part (*forma partis*), identifiable with the rational soul in human nature, and the form of the whole (*forma totius*), identifiable with "humanity" in the human and which includes in its meaning matter abstractly considered.

of all lower layers, material, organic, and animal, upon the spiritual and personal in human life—a corresponding "bottom-up" influence. Stein neatly captures this complementary top-down and bottom-up influence when she says, "The soul thoroughly penetrates the living-body, and through this penetration of organized matter, not only does the matter become a thoroughly spiritualized living-body, but the spirit also becomes a materialized and organized spirit."[73] Here we see clearly how Stein recognizes the complexity of human nature without losing sight of the profound unity of the human being, and also gives account of the priority of the specifically personal in human nature while simultaneously paying due regard to the various material, organic, and animal determinations of the whole.[74]

The mutual influence of spiritual soul and material body is also something for which Aquinas is eager to account, and as indicated above he explains this given of experience with what has come to be called "virtual presence."[75] Though Aquinas only briefly adverts to the significance of virtual presence when detailing the structure and unity of human nature in *Summa theologiae*, he evidently sees the necessity to account for lower kinds of formation in higher kinds of substances, as seen in his thematized explanation of virtual presence in *De mixtione elementorum* when investigating the problem of the structure of material substances.[76] In *Summa theologiae*, in accord with

---

73 AMP, 107.
74 Evidently then, Stein argues in accord with the above-noted dogmatic definition regarding the soul's formation of the body (see above, 46n10), by affirming that the rational soul *is* the form of the body "through itself and essentially." Indeed, in the theological work paired with AMP, WIM, Stein forthrightly summarizes her understanding of the dogmatic definition, there saying, "That the rational soul which is a substantial form of the body [*Körper*], is essentially and not accidentally joined to the body, means, on the one hand, that the human living-body [*Menschenleib*] owes what it is as a living organism and a human living-body to this indwelling soul, that for the human being it is not only the principle of his thinking and spiritual activity in general, but rather of his entire being and life, and, on the other hand, that it is not external to and accidental for the soul to be joined to the body, but rather that it belongs to its own essence, that it would no longer be a soul if it did not have this unity with the body." WIM, 10–11. Not only does this quote reveal dogmatic orthodoxy, but also the closeness of her interest, insight, and conclusions to those of Aquinas and the subsequent Thomistic tradition, including Wojtyła.
75 See Wippel, *Metaphysical Thought*, 350–51; and Klubertanz, *Human Nature*, 26–28.
76 See DME. In this work in detail, as in ST in brief, Aquinas strives to account for the significance of the manifold of prior formations undergone by matter before its

the general understanding of material composition detailed in *De mixtione elementorum*, Aquinas argues that the substantial form of the human being "virtually contains" the various perfections of the less perfect forms, whether material, vegetative, or sensitive, and "itself alone does whatever the imperfect forms do in other things."[77] This means that the rational soul includes the formal determinations of all lower forms in a simple formal unity, in a manner analogous to the way more complex geometrical figures sequentially contain less complex figures, and itself provides for the entire formal determination of the unitary whole—"so neither is Socrates man by one soul and animal by another, but by one and the same he is both."[78] Thus Aquinas accounts for the various degrees of commonality of the human substance with other material substances, whether inanimate bodily substances, or animated vegetative and sensitive living-bodies, while also attending to the way material elements are incorporated into and recoverable from the human body, without thereby doing away with the unity of human being and the simplicity of the soul—both of which, as we have seen, are energetically defended by him.[79] This is obviously quite different from Stein's proposition of the above-detailed pairing of formal structure and framework. Yet, in terms of accomplishing something of a rapprochement between Stein and Aquinas in this area, it is interesting to note that he uses the phrase "*virtute continet*" when detailing the kind of presence of lower forms in the structure of higher forms, thereby implying that the rational soul contains or holds together (*continet*) the manifold of

---

fitting integration into the substantial unity of higher-order substances including the human being.

77 ST, I, 76.4, co.
78 See ST, I, 76.3, co.
79 As is evident, Aquinas not only recognizes but profoundly respects the significance of all prior formations of matter before its incorporation into the greater substantial whole of the human being, a significance that is in some way foundationally important for the structure of the human body. Moreover, in tandem with Stein, Aquinas recognizes that the significance of material forms for the whole (via virtual presence) differs from the significance of vegetative and sensitive forms within the whole, since the primary material elements are "retrievable" from the composed substantial whole through *post-mortem* bodily corruption (or, indeed, through excretion), while vegetative and sensitive forms are not so separable and retrievable. See SCG, 3.22, nos. 7–8; and also, Bobik, *Aquinas on Matter and Form*, esp. 125, 131–37, 140, 144–52; and Christopher Decaen, "Elemental Virtual Presence in St. Thomas," in *The Thomist: A Speculative Quarterly Review* 64, no. 2 (2000): 271–300.

formative virtues or powers (*virtutes*) of lower forms in the integrated unity of one simple substantial form. Evidently then Aquinas maintains that lower formal determinations are present in their power, *virtute*, in the substantial whole of human nature, even while he also argues that they are not substantially present—that is, that their structural significance is entirely supplanted by the polyvalent substantial formality of the rational soul. This explanation is certainly descriptively close to the coordinate explanation of Stein, since it clearly accounts for the ongoing formative significance of elemental material forms, as well as that of the vegetative and sensitive functional parts within the substantial whole of the human. Yet, though Stein was aware of this teaching of Aquinas, rather than endorsing it, or indeed disagreeing with it, she prefers to account for the complexity of human formation in terms of the here detailed formal structure and framework.[80] This is plausibly due to the facility Stein sees in these paired concepts to comprehensively account for the complexity of human nature while simultaneously securing its unity.

This facility is seen first in the above-detailed explanatory force of Stein's solution to account for human unity and bodily formation, inasmuch as she provides a proposal that elegantly accounts for the ontological and intentional orders, while also providing a fine-grained explanation of the way the human body is formed as material, organic, and animal. However, it is most clear in Stein's identification of the structural and functional priority of the spiritual and personal within the complex arrangement of human nature. Whereas Aquinas presents human nature as spiritual and personal primarily from the perspective of the rational power of the soul, Stein distinguishes the personal I from the rational power, while also distinguishing both from the spiritual expanse of the soul itself, and she argues that the personal character of human nature should be approached also from the perspective of the personal I indwelling the expanse of the soul. In further identifying the personal I as the bearer of the rational powers, and in highlighting the ability of the personal I to move about freely within the expanse of the soul, Stein confirms the personal I as the central dimension of human life, the spiritual soul and the human being in totality. Thus, the personal I comes to be understood as that dimension which holds a position of actual and ontological priority relative to the personal nature that is borne, with the corresponding potential to realize a dynamic bearing of his personal being through the free rational possession of the entirety of

---

80 See EES, 181, 221–23.

his nature, a self-possession that is completed in the above-detailed personal formation of the living-body. By so prioritizing the specifically personal in the structure of human nature, we find in Stein's presentation of human unity and bodily formation a defined benefit, one that simultaneously appeals to the objectivity of personal subjectivity, and to the corresponding axiological significance of the bearing of the personal subject.[81]

A number of further benefits are seen in Stein's considerations of claims for and against the substantial unity of the human being late in *The Structure of the Human Person*, claims that serve to illustrate both the structural complexity of human formation and the profound unity of the human being.[82] In conceiving of the human soul as a complex formal structure unified by the spiritual soul, as that which frames but does not negate the presence of integrated subordinate forms, Stein's conception can account for the following phenomena: (1) the fact that the soul as spiritual begins its existence in a material body which has already received an initial formation through the inherited matter of conception, an inheritance that foundationally conditions all further human development and formation; (2) the fact that throughout the bodily life-cycle of the human organism, the living-body transitions material components through its nutritive, assimilative, and growth functions, so that the body should be understood as perpetually built up by diverse kinds of already formed material components; (3) the fact that the human body experiences many material changes not determined or further determinable by the soul, alterations that are not entirely within the soul's power to regulate or overcome, such as those caused by defect, injury, or disease; and, finally, (4) the factual disharmony that can occur in certain individuals between the character of the spiritual and sensitive soul and that of the living-body, such that, for example, Stein maintains that one can find vigorous souls in frail bodies and, *vice versa*, frail

---

81   See EES, 304–7, 309–10, 320–21, 345–46; and PA, 17, 84–86. The importance of the personal unity and formation of human nature is most clear when it is considered from the perspective of the human *individual*, precisely since the person is an individual by definition, and indeed is eminently individual in being. Though I treat the individual in greater detail below, we can identify this importance already here in brief by focusing our attention on the fact that not only is human nature essentially personal—with the consequence that all individuals in possession of this nature are persons—but that each and every human individual personally possesses his human nature in a personal manner via the wholistic bearing of the personal I—first ontologically, and then, given the right conditions, dynamically.

82   See AMP, 96–98, 130–31, 143.

souls in vigorous bodies.[83] On the other hand, in conceiving of the personally determined spiritual soul as the unifying form, framing the complex structure as one integrated whole, Stein's conception can account for the following phenomena: (1) the experience of the material, organic, and animal living-body as an essential part of the human being in profound unity with the spiritual and personal dimension of human life; (2) the experience of the personal I indwelling the human whole, inclusive of the living-body—so that, in addition to saying, "*I* think, will, and feel," one can also say, "*I* eat and digest, grow and develop, sense and move," etc.; and finally, (3) the fact that upon bodily death the body loses its structural integrity and decomposes into previously incorporated material components (elements and compounds) that disperse into the cosmos for incorporation into other substances.

In accounting for these seven givens of experience, Stein's solution to the question of bodily formation has evident explanatory force. This force is seen in the way Stein's proposal accounts for the structural complexity of human nature without thereby jeopardizing the unity of the human being, but rather manifesting the kind of unity fitting for the human being as a personal substance. However, I would like to suggest that the first two of the first listing are of particular significance, since they exhibit the ongoing formative influence of already formed matter on the completed structure of the living whole. This is seen initially in the profound impact that bodily inheritance has on the further development of the individual, where inheritance foundationally determines all further formation, even formation of a properly spiritual and personal kind. This is evinced in the conditioning influence of bodily inheritance on both temperament and personality, and on certain aspects of character development and virtue formation. The second is seen in the ongoing impact of material and environmental factors on bodily growth and development, such that only certain material components can be incorporated into the living-body, and upon their incorporation they decisively condition subsequent growth and development, often leading to a basically healthy or unhealthy body.[84] Of the second listing, the first two are also of some significance, since everyday human experience not only discloses the distinction of the spiritual and personal

---

83 Obviously, Stein here means soul as sensitive and spiritual rather than as living inner form (even while she also holds that this living inner form is one and the same as the sensitive and spiritual soul).

84 See AMP, 41, 111, 130–31; and EES, 164–65. See also Schulz, "Theory of Identity," 161–76: 171.

within the structure of human nature, but also discloses the profound unity of the spiritual and personal with the material, organic, and animal living-body, so that the human individual ordinarily experiences his material body with its living functions as "*my*" body—even if at times certain personal and social factors overlay this elementary experience and one feels alienated from one's own body. And so, for Stein, notwithstanding the fact that all lower formations lose their independence in their subordination to the personal spirit, she provides a robust explanation of how such lower formations remain co-determinative of the living personal whole.[85]

Conclusion:
The Personal Unity and Formation of the Human Being

Through performing a fresh phenomenological investigation of human nature, Stein attains a comprehensive understanding of the meaning of human unity and bodily formation, while simultaneously incorporating two key teachings of Aquinas's anthropology—namely, the rational soul as principle of substantial unity and the rational soul as form of the material body, together with their shared hylomorphic foundation. By adopting these closely related teachings in their broad conceptual outline, Stein's anthropology is situated against the backdrop of Aquinas's anthropology and lies in decisive continuity with its chief propositional formulations.[86] However, through thoroughly investigating

---

85 As noted above, this ongoing formative impact of the material components means that Stein understands the formal determination of the material part within the human structural whole differently than she understands the formal determination of the organic and animal formal parts, since the material parts comprising the materiality of the human whole are more loosely integrated into the whole. This is seen especially in the way the material components of the living-body can be retrieved from the living-body upon bodily death (as well as through the process of excretion and exhalation).

86 Scarpelli Cory argues that the substantial unity of the human being is something of a *sine qua non* of Aquinas's anthropology and its authentic reception, and together with Gyula Klima highlights the significance of the spirit-matter composition of this unity, describing it as a unity that straddles the primary division of being and thereby provides a unique horizon in the created cosmos. See Therese Scarpelli Cory, "The Distinctive Unity of the Human Being in Aquinas," and Gyula Klima, "Aquinas' Reception in Contemporary Metaphysics," in *The Oxford Handbook of the Reception of Aquinas*, ed. Matthew Levering and Marcus Plested (Oxford: Oxford University Press, 2021), 581–95, and 565–80, respectively.

human formation, Stein reconsiders the meaning of these teachings and attains a conceptually expanded understanding of their significance. By first abstractly attending to the way the human being is formed as material, organic, animal, and spiritual, Stein argues that human nature is a formal structure of material, organic, animal, and spiritual parts; by further attending to the dominant position of the spiritual and personal within this structure, Stein argues that human nature possesses a substantial unity through the formal framing provided by the personally determined spiritual soul. The significance of Stein's original conception of human unity comes forcefully to the fore in her reinterpretation of the meaning of bodily formation, when she attributes an interconnected manifold of meaning to the proposition that the rational soul is the form of the material body, and again secures all in the personally determined spiritual soul. In this way, Stein not only shows that the ontological unity of human nature is a personal unity, but also reveals that each individual bears responsibility for the proper completion of the unity of his person.

Though this understanding of human unity and bodily formation clearly differs from that of Aquinas, I have suggested that Stein's expanded conception need not be understood as squarely opposed to Aquinas, inasmuch she continues to hold to the teachings according to their basic propositional formulation, while simultaneously satisfying the criteria established by Aquinas for securing human unity and bodily formation in the rational soul. Though Stein exchanges the naturally simple unity of the rational soul and the radical immediacy of material formation for a complex formal structure with a corresponding complexity of bodily formation, I suggest that Stein's solution presents, precisely as a factor of its complexity, a more adequate account of human nature, especially in the face of the findings of contemporary natural science. On the other hand, I also propose that by holding her phenomenological investigation in tension with the positions and arguments of Aquinas, Stein's solution remains suitably anchored in the philosophical tradition of the *philosophia perennis* and can rightly be understood as an offshoot and development of this same tradition.[87] As repeatedly noted

---

87 This is especially important when considering certain corollary issues bound up with the question of human unity and the simplicity of the human soul, issues that are not only practical or ethical in character but also theological, as evinced in the vigorous debate surrounding this question in the late medieval period and in the ecclesial condemnation of positions thought to be problematic to the Christian faith. For an historical overview of these condemnations as they bear reference to the thought of Aquinas, see Jean-Pierre Torrell, *Saint Thomas Aquinas*, vol. 1: *The Person and His*

above, the development Stein introduces here is most evident in the preeminent position she grants to the spiritual and personal within the complex structure of human nature. Through identifying the dominant position of the spiritual and personal, Stein clarifies the responsibility that falls to each individual to receive and accept the gift of his already determined humanity, including the inherited material body as a living-body, and work toward the proper personal possession of that same nature through its thoroughgoing personal formation, finally completed in the intensive personal formation of the living-body.

Accordingly, again here, I submit that Stein has wrought a fundamental "personalization" of our conception of human nature via her personalization of the substantial unity of the human being and of the meaning of bodily formation, which personalization can to some degree be separated from the differences she introduces into the conceptual schema of Aquinas regarding the unity of the human being and simplicity of the soul. And indeed it is precisely here that we see most clearly the beneficial import of Stein's understanding of human unity and bodily formation, since she secures the unity of the human being as a personal unity via the personal formation of the entirety of the human structure, while simultaneously accounting for the way this structure is inextricably interwoven with the structures of other natural material substances in the natural cosmos—something absolutely necessary for accounting for human unity in the face of varied findings of contemporary natural science.[88]

Work, trans. Robert Royal (Washington, DC: The Catholic University of America Press, 1996, repr. 2005), 298–308.

88 In terms of signaling some important areas for further research, I suggest that Stein's understanding of human unity and bodily formation has defined significance for our understanding of human nature in the contemporary world, especially in the face of natural scientific developments that tend to reduce the human being to the elementary structures and forces of matter, as well as the (oft-related) cultural and social dynamics that tend to depersonalize and variously destroy the personal identity of the body, with both movements of thought conceiving of the human body as little more than a complex mechanism without inherent meaning and available for manipulation at will. I believe Stein's presentation of the ongoing formative impact of lower forms in human nature, whether material, organic, or animal, while simultaneously highlighting the position of the spiritual and personal within the structural whole, could readily meet these contemporary challenges to the profound spiritual and personal meaningfulness and identity of the human body, notwithstanding its materially composed character and the fact that its arrangement and operativity can be understood and modeled mechanically.

Conclusion to Part I:
Human Nature as a Personal Nature

The point of departure for Stein's objective investigation is the most original knowledge of the being of the conscious I, the always present "I am" that is given in first-person inner experience. Phenomenological reflection on this elementary datum of experience opens upon a transcendent depth underlying consciousness, indicating that the being of the self is given as a personal substance structured as a complex unity of spiritual soul and living-body. In order to adequately detail the reality of the personal substance thus unearthed in experience, Stein adopts certain teachings of Aquinas and the Thomistic tradition and progressively incorporates them into her mature anthropology. In this way, Stein situates her mature phenomenological anthropology against the backdrop of the metaphysical anthropology of Thomism and presents a conception of the human person that lies in decisive continuity with that of Aquinas according to its primary propositional formulas. However, as shown above, Stein does not leave the conceptual content of Aquinas's teachings undisturbed but reconsiders each of them in light of a fresh phenomenological investigation of human nature according to the complementary ways of philosophizing she identifies as Augustinian and Aristotelian, with an initial, though not unqualified, priority given to the Augustinian way.

The first consequence of this reconsideration is a novel approach to the conceptual content of the so-called classical definition of the person, brought about directly by Stein's attention to the personal I as the inner locus of personal life. Stein's phenomenological mode of approach enables her to identify the significance of the personal I as the ontological bearer of the rational nature and the dynamic bearer of rational life, so that all aspects of the classical conception come to be understood from the new coordinating perspective of the personal I. The second consequence is a thorough reinterpretation of the meaning of human unity and bodily formation. By reconsidering the substantial composition of the human being as a formal structure with substantial unity secured through its formal framing, Stein accounts for the progressively layered formation that takes place in human nature while simultaneously holding to the unity of the human being through the personally determined spiritual soul. This leads to a deepened understanding of the formative role of the personal throughout the whole of human nature, inclusive of the living-body, with the consequence that the human individual comes to be understood as the formative bearer of the whole of his nature and tasked with its thoroughgoing personal formation. This developed conception also leads to a subtle and refined understanding of the way the human soul is the form of the material body, an understanding that has significance not only for our understanding of the formation of the human body, but also for our recognition of the body as an essential dimension of the human person, and indeed a thoroughly *personal* reality.

For the mature Stein reinterpreting the received teachings of Aquinas, human nature comes to be understood from the coordinating perspective of the personal subject, in terms of its essentially personal character and personal course of unfolding, and the corresponding formative dominance of the personal throughout the substantial whole. Consequently, I have proposed that Stein brings about a fundamental "personalization" of the conceptual content of the received anthropology, in such a way that this personalization can be understood to represent an original expansion of certain decisive anthropological teachings of Aquinas, Thomism, and the *philosophia perennis*, one key aspect of which is the intensive focus on subjectivity—a focus that I argue is entirely coherent with the corresponding objective focus of Aquinas and Thomism. Indeed, I suggest that Stein's grafting of personal subjectivity onto the anthropology of the *philosophia perennis* is foundationally beneficial for this tradition of philosophizing, precisely inasmuch as it represents the fitting phenomenological complement of the metaphysical anthropology of Aquinas and Thomism.

Part II

The Human Individual

> In a more special and perfect way, the particular and
> the individual are found in rational substances,
> which have dominion over their own actions.
>
> —*Thomas Aquinas*[1]

Stein's understanding of the human individual takes shape in the broader context of her understanding of human nature in general, and in like manner as her understanding of human nature is developed with aid received from Aquinas, so too her understanding of the human individual is informed by the reception of certain metaphysical principles and teachings from Aquinas and the Thomistic tradition. However, in contrast to her basically harmonious incorporation in the sphere of human nature, Stein's investigation of the human individual leads to conclusions that expressly contradict Aquinas, even while her own understanding remains to some degree harmonious with basic principles of the Thomistic tradition and that of the *philosophia perennis*. In part II I explore this critical engagement with Aquinas by first examining the foundational principles and teachings she incorporates, before examining her independently developed conception of the material individual in general and the human individual in particular. The analysis is divided into two chapters. In the first, I analyze Stein's assessment of the standard Thomistic presentation before immediately moving to a presentation of Stein's contrasted conception of the material individual. In the second, I present Stein's original

---

1 ST, I, 29.1, co.

conception of the human individual, before concluding with an examination of the contrast between Stein's original proposal and that of Aquinas and the Thomistic tradition.

Through this staged analysis, I show that while Stein incorporates certain basic teachings and principles from the broader metaphysics of Aquinas and the Thomistic tradition, largely through the mediation of the Thomistic commentary of Josef Gredt, she also draws from Thomistic principles to critique the Thomistic account of material individuation via designated matter, and she finally proposes that the "being-individual" and "qualitative individuality" of both the material individual and the human individual have formal rather than material bases. As becomes clear in what follows, by being-individual (*Einzelsein*) I mean the principle according to which the individual *is* an individual—that is, that by which the individual stands in being as something distinct—and by qualitative individuality (*Individualität, Singularität, Einzelheit*) I mean the principle according to which several specifically alike individuals are dissimilar from one another—that is, that by which individuals of the same kind are different from one another. Thus, by being-individual I understand *distinction*, and by qualitative individuality *difference*.[2] After so

---

2   Although "*Einzelsein*" translates literally as "being-singular," Stein takes the terms "*Einzeln* [singular]" and "*Individuum* [individual]" as equivalent in referent when considering substances in general; and though Stein includes "being-individual" in the meaning of "individuality," I deliberately distinguish "individuality" from "being-individual" in order to highlight the distinctively qualitative aspect of individuation. Christof Betschart uses the terminology of "formal individuality [*formale Individualität*]" (further identified as "numerical individuality [*numerische Individualität*]") and "material individuality [*materiale Individualität*]" (further identified as "content individuality [*Inhaltliche Individualität*]") to designate the realities here designated as "being-individual" and "qualitative individuality." See Christof Betschart, *Unwiederholbares Gottessiegel: Personale Individualität nach Edith Stein* (Basel: Reinhardt, 2013), esp. 14–15, 233, 283. In his work tracing the influence of Scotus on the thought of Stein, Francesco Alfieri renders the same distinction with the terminology of "individual being" and "qualitative fullness" though with an appreciably different presentation than here given. See Francesco Alfieri, "The Presence of Duns Scotus in the Thought of Edith Stein: The Question of Individuality," trans. George Metcalf, in *Analecta Husserliana*, 120 (Cham: Springer, 2015), eBook, esp. 103–16. Borden Sharkey does not extensively detail "being-individual" and largely attends to questions of individuation and individuality from the perspective of "individual form," a term I largely avoid since its traditionally loaded meaning threatens to obscure the precise character and novelty of Stein's conception. See Sarah Borden Sharkey, *Thine*

detailing Stein's contrasted position to Aquinas and Thomism with regard to material individuation in general, I proceed to show that it is ultimately through her attention to the personal in human nature that she is led to propose an original conception of the human individual that diverges from the standard Thomistic position, when she argues that the human being is individual via the spiritual and personal structure, and that this spiritual and personal structure has its own characteristic uniqueness.

Own Self: Individuality in Edith Stein's Later Writings (Washington, DC: The Catholic University of America Press, 2010), esp. 20–22, 115–25. In the Stein *Lexikon* there is no entry for "being-individual [*Einzelsein*]," and in the short entry for "individual/individuality [*Individuum/Individualität*]," where attention is almost entirely given over to detailing the human being as an individual, no express mention is made of "being-individual," though descriptions of both dimensions—being-individual and individuality—are included and subsumed under the term "*Individualität*." See Urbano Ferrer, "Individuum/Individualität," in *Edith Stein-Lexikon*, ed. Marcus Knaup and Harald Seubert (Freiburg i. Br.: Herder, 2017), 195–98. And though the related entry of "*Tode ti* [this what]" does mention "being-individual" (when directly quoting Stein), since the entry is focused upon differentiating Stein's and Aristotle's conceptions of τόδε τί, "being-individual" remains without sufficient treatment. See Martin Hähnel, "*Tode ti*," in *Stein-Lexikon*, 366–67. See also Robert McNamara, "Human Individuality in Stein's Mature Works," in *Edith Steins Herausforderung heutiger Anthropologie*, ed. Hanna-Barbara Gerl-Falkovitz and Mette Lebech (Heiligenkreuz: Be&Be, 2017), 124–39, where I use the related but not yet fully clarified terminology of "individual mode of being" to identify what I here designate simply in Steinian terms as "being-individual." In what follows, I translate Stein's use of "*geschieden*" as "divided," "*abgeschieden*" as "separated," "*verschieden*" as "different," and "*unterschieden*" as "distinct"; each term is significant toward appreciating Stein's understanding of the material individual.

Chapter Three

The Material Individual in General

> An individual is what is in itself indistinct yet distinct from others. [...] according as it implies incommunicability.
>
> —*Thomas Aquinas*[1]

In the final chapter of *Finite and Eternal Being*, toward completing her conception of the meaning of being, Stein performs an extended investigation of the meaning of being an individual, titled "The Meaning and Foundation of Being-Individual." The goal of this chapter, having already completed an understanding of the meaning of being in general, is to accomplish a fully rounded understanding of the human being. Stein says, "If we are to understand the essence of the human being, his place in the order of the created world, and his relation to divine being," then we must understand the "being-individual (the individuality) of the human being."[2] To accomplish this goal, Stein grounds her understanding of the human individual in the broader context of an investigation of the material individual in general and expressly situates her investigation against the backdrop of the conception of material individuation in the writings of Aquinas and the Thomistic tradition, taken alongside its hylomorphic basis in the thought of Aristotle.[3]

---

1   ST, I, 29.4, co.; and ST, I, 29.3, ad 4.
2   EES, 395. Compare AMP, 20–24.
3   Though I focus my analysis on the investigation in EES, since it represents Stein's matured position in which her engagement with Aquinas and Thomism is most fully

Stein begins her inquiry by clarifying the meaning of the term "individual" by marshalling several notions of the individual taken from the *philosophia perennis*, and thereby appropriately demarcates the sphere of her investigation.[4] Following Aristotle, she identifies the individual as "τόδε τί (this there [*Diesda*])"—an identification that requires use of the pointing finger, and which cannot be further named because all further naming typically possesses universal significance.[5] In accord with the decisive feature of the individual noted by Aquinas, Stein explains that the individual must include in itself not only the general essence of the species of which it is a member, but must also include something proper to itself as this very thing, as a particular member of the species, and thus must possesses something incommunicable (*unmitteilbar*)[6]—that is, something without the possibility of being imparted

---

worked through, Stein's attention to the human individual is paralleled in a number of Stein's later works, including the other works here under investigation; for example, see PA, 168–76; and AMP, 130–33.

[4] In the introduction to his magisterial work, Jorge Gracia presents multiple varied ways the individual has been understood throughout the history of the Western tradition, and he separately investigates its meaning with respect to indivisibility, distinction, division of species, identity, and impredicability, before finally settling on non-instantiability as the decisive feature of the individual as such. This feature is largely equivalent to Stein's and Aquinas's use of incommunicability (*Unmitteilbarkeit* and *incommunicabilitas*, respectively). See Jorge Gracia, "Introduction: The Problem of Individuation," in *Individuation in Scholasticism: The Later Middle Ages and the Counter-Reformation, 1150–1650*, ed. Jorge J. E. Gracia (Albany, NY: State University of New York Press, 1994), 1–20.

[5] EES, 395. Though Stein translates τόδε τί as "this there/here [*Diesda*]," a literal translation of the Greek would render as "this what." Stein clarifies that the "pointing/indicating" function of the term "this" is the meaning implied by Aquinas (and Avicenna) in their use of *signare/designare* (literally, to point out, to indicate), which is then imported into the meaning of designated matter as the principle of individuation.

[6] EES, 395, citing ST, I, 29.3, ad 4; see also EES, 79; and compare ST, I, 11.3: "It is manifest that whatever makes any singular thing this particular thing is in no way communicable to many"; and QDP, 9.9, ad 1. Aquinas receives his notion of incommunicability—and, more precisely, the incommunicability of the person—from Richard of St. Victor, saying, "Richard of St. Victor reforms [*corrigere*] this definition [of Boëthius] by saying that Person, when speaking of God, is an incommunicable existence of the divine nature [*divinae naturae incommunicabilis existentia*]" (ST, I, 29.3, ad 4). See Jadwiga Guerrero van der Meijden, *Person and Dignity in Edith Stein's Writings* (Berlin: De Gruyter, 2019), 3n10, 180n107. The German term *unmitteilbar* translates literally as "in-divisible-with" or, more simply, "un-sharable," and thus helps

The Material Individual in General 93

to or made common with another.⁷ Finally, following the basic definition of the individual given by Aquinas and the Scholastic tradition more generally, Stein defines the individual as "that which is in itself undivided yet divided from all else," and immediately interprets "in itself undivided" as "unity or being-one."⁸ Having in this way established an outline meaning of being an individual—an understanding that guides all subsequent analysis and governs her fully developed conception of the individual—Stein proceeds to examine the presentation of the material individual in Aquinas and the Thomistic tradition, primarily through engaging the Thomistic commentary of Josef Gredt in his magisterial work *Die aristotelische-thomistische Philosophie*.⁹

---

us to understand the native meaning of incommunicable as something incapable of being rendered common.

7 The notion of incommunicability is somewhat controverted, as is its use in resolving the question of the individual and individuation, though I here sidestep much of this controversy by focusing on the thought of Stein and Aquinas and their particular understandings of the concept. The notion is taken up repeatedly below; and, as we will see, this notion is central to Stein's understanding of the individual—as it is for Aquinas.

8 EES, 395–96. The German translation of Aquinas is taken from Gredt. See Josef Gredt, *Die aristotelische-thomistische Philosophie*, 2 vols. (Freiburg i. Br.: Herder, 1935), 1:80, citing ST, I, 29.4, co.: "Individuum autem est quod est in se indistinctum, ab aliis vero distinctum." As will be shown below, this interpretation of "in itself undivided" as "unity or being-one" establishes one of the key parameters for Stein in her investigation and is of central significance in understanding her divergence from Aquinas in this area.

9 See Gredt, *Philosophie*, 1:241–51. Stein also garnered her understanding of the Thomistic position from other works—including "the thorough study" (EES, 395n1) of Marie-Dominique Roland-Gosselin, *Le "De ente et essentia" de saint Thomas d'Aquin* (Paris: Paris Librairie philosophique J. Vrin, 1948)—though most of her investigation in EES relies heavily on the presentation of Gredt in *Philosophie*. Alfieri argues that Stein's understanding of the human individual echoes the teaching of Scotus in arguing for an intrinsic, positive, and unique principle of individuation, even while he also clarifies that Stein's familiarity with the thought of Scotus is largely mediated by a pseudo-Scotus source (which turns out to be that of Vitalis de Furno). Alfieri's thesis is partially confirmed by Stein in EES (408n42) when she indicates the closeness of her own understanding of the individual to that of Scotus and his conception of individuation resting upon "something positive [...] that separates the individual essential-form from the general." See Alfieri, "The Question of Individuality"; see also Betschart, *Unwiederholbares Gottessiegel*, 289–92; and Borden Sharkey, *Thine Own Self*, esp. 146–51. However, as will become clear in what follows, Stein's conception of the individual is developed with primary reference to Aquinas and the Thomistic tradition, as is evident in her express and repeated reference to Aquinas and Thomistic

Standard Thomistic Position on Material Individuation

According to Gredt, the individual essence (*Einzelwesen*) of a material substance is itself structured as a composite of matter and form. In such composed essences, form takes the active role of determining the individual as an actual thing of this or that kind, and matter takes the passive role of restricting and limiting the form to this or that thing.[10] Whereas form is a principle of commonality, inwardly determining a plurality of substances as members of the same species, matter is a principle of distinction, diversifying these specifically identical substances from one other. Since matter is a principle of distinction that lies beyond or outside the form, but which is nonetheless essential to the composition of the substance, matter provides the possibility of multiplying formally identical material individuals. Thus, a plurality of individuals of like kind are rendered distinct from one another through their material principle while remaining like one another through their formal principle. The foundationally incommunicable nature of matter, via quantitative extension, then renders the substance incommunicable to another, preventing the actual form of this or that concretized individual from being communicated to or shared by any other individual. In precisely this way, according to the Thomistic commentary of Gredt, matter provides for the differentiation of things not only *in* species, through formal distinction, but also *within* species, through material distinction.[11]

---

sources throughout her investigations. Consequently, and given the delimited range of the present study, as well as the already extant scholarship on Stein's apparent alignment with Scotus, I will not here treat Stein's convergence with and divergence from the thought of Scotus and Scotism more generally. For a concise exposition of Scotus's conception of individuation, see Allan B. Wolter, "John Duns Scotus," in Garcia, *Individuation in Scholasticism*, 271–98; and Étienne Gilson, *John Duns Scotus: Introduction to His Fundamental Positions*, trans. James G. Colbert (London: T&T Clark: 2019), 345–70.

10   EES, 399, citing Gredt, *Philosophie*, 1:244. In what follows, I assume the Thomistic interpretation of Gredt that essence in Aquinas and Thomism should be considered as something both general and individual—that is, that essence designates not only the common determination of a plurality of specifically identical individuals, but also the singular determination of each actual material individual (as something individuated in the individual by designated matter). See DEE, 2:5, and esp. DEE, 2:85–7, where Aquinas says, "The difference between the essence of Socrates and the essence of man lies solely in what is designated and not designated."

11   See EES, 403, citing Gredt, *Philosophie*, 1:245; and also PA, 29.

Significantly, for Gredt, as for Aquinas and Thomism more generally, the matter here considered is not identified with prime matter (*materia prima*) but rather with matter designated by extension (*materia signata quantitate*), which Gredt describes as a "prior preparation of matter" for its formation as a material substance.[12] Whereas prime matter is the completely indeterminate substrate of material being, undergirding all actual material substances as their ultimate substratum, designated matter is prime matter "distinguished or separated through extension."[13] This distinction of matter is a "partitioning" that renders it "distinct and divided from all remaining matter" insofar as it is "distinguished and divided from every other extension through position."[14] As a consequence of this partitioning, designated matter is capable of individuating form by contracting and limiting it to *this* particular extension with its *exclusive* position in place. The form is then "this and that [form] solely because it is in this and that matter."[15] The precise relation of form and matter in the individual essence is then further explained by Gredt via a Thomistic teaching that has come to be called the "transcendental relation." Gredt says, "*Each [form] is this form through a transcendental relation, intrinsic to [the form], to the matter designated by extension.*"[16] By using "transcendental" here, Gredt is indicating that material forms (i.e., forms of material substances) have an inherent relation to designated matter, which is proper to the form as such, and to the matter in its correlation to form. This means that the earlier mentioned

---

12 EES, 398, citing Gredt, *Philosophie*, 1:242–43. See also, AMP, 94. To my knowledge the exact phrase *materia signata quantitate* does not actually appear in Aquinas's writings, though this phrase certainly represents the standard reading of Aquinas by Thomistic thinkers and represents a fair reading of his texts.
13 EES, 398.
14 EES, 398. As with other Thomistic interpreters, Gredt acknowledges that this extension should not be understood to imply determined "size and shape," precisely inasmuch as such features follow upon the material individual as quantitative accidents of the actual individual.
15 EES, 403, citing Gredt, *Philosophie*, 1:245.
16 EES, 403. The term "transcendental relation," though not of Aquinas's own formulation, is used by later Thomistic commentators to designate the kind of correlation of form and matter in the structure of material substances implied in Aquinas's works. Since the correlation cannot be described as accidental or predicamental—as something inhering in or predicated of form—it is identified as transcendental—as something beyond form—to which form has an inherent and necessary relation. See John F. Wippel, *The Metaphysical Thought of Thomas Aquinas: From Finite Being to Uncreated Being* (Washington, DC: The Catholic University of America Press, 2000), 320n96.

"prior preparation of matter" through which it is partitioned is transcendentally required by the form for the instantiation of the individual, since extension "is a condition for the individuation of substance, which, as an extension transcendentally required (*ut connotata*), designates the parts of the matter and, as a partitioned extension, divides them from one another."[17]

Thus, according to the Thomistic conceptual schema related by Gredt, designated matter is the intrinsic and radical principle of individuation for material substances, inasmuch as it provides the passive potential required for the multiplication of form in a plurality of specifically identical individuals. Moreover, since designated matter renders the substance (and form) incommunicable through its extension and corresponding exclusive position, such matter further functions as the intrinsic principle of being an individual. The individual essence so comprised is then established in being as an *actual* individual for Gredt by two further principles of the substance—namely, self-dependence (*Selbstand*) and existence (*Dasein*).[18] Gredt first reasons that self-dependence belongs to the individual essence as a positive perfection of that essence, which definitively encloses the essence as something fully determined in itself with relative independence from all others, whether alike or different. Self-dependence then capacitates the individual essence for the reception of the actuality of being, through which the individual essence attains the further perfection of existence, becoming something that stands in being as an individual. With these two further perfections of the material substance, we have a finished understanding of the constitution of the material individual, since the actual substance so completed is established in being as a τόδε τί, something in itself undivided yet divided from all else, and inherently incommunicable.

In what follows, I take the position of Gredt to be representative of the Thomistic tradition and designate it the "standard" Thomist position on material individuation.[19]

---

17 EES, 403, citing Gredt, *Philosophie*, 1:246. Thus, Gredt affirms both that matter is designated by extension in view of the transcendental relation and that form is individuated by the so transcendently designated matter. Stein (not Gredt) italicizes this last sentence, and this particular Thomistic principle becomes the focus of her critique of the conclusions of Thomism with regard to material individuation.

18 See EES, 399–401, citing Gredt, *Philosophie*, 1:244, and *Philosophie*, 2:114, 116–17. Compare the similar treatment of Maritain regarding personal subsistence in Jacques Maritain, *Degrees of Knowledge*, trans. Gerald B. Phelan (Notre Dame, IN: University of Notre Dame Press, 1998, repr. 2014), 246.

19 By denominating it standard I do not intend to exclude other interpretations

Critically Questioning the Standard Thomistic Position

Stein poses the following series of questions of the position of Gredt:

(1) Can matter by itself really perform the work that is here attributed to it?
(2) Does the form only effect the determination of the species and nothing further?
(3) Is being-individual "presupposed" to self-dependence and existence, as Gredt seeks to prove?[20]

Through questioning in this manner, while also performing an objective investigation of material formation, Stein assesses the cogency of the Thomistic position and eventually concludes to a position that stands in direct opposition to the Thomist conclusion, a conclusion Stein succinctly summarizes as "*individuum de ratione materiae*, the individual by reason of matter."[21] However, Stein develops her opposition not by proposing a solution based on new grounds, but rather by continuing to employ conceptual apparatuses of Aquinas and Thomism—namely, the hylomorphic composition

---

of Aquinas, but rather wish to highlight the representative character of Gredt's presentation of the Thomist position. For contemporary confirmation of this presentation as representative, see Wippel, *Metaphysical Thought*, 351–75; "Metaphysics," in *The Cambridge Companion to Aquinas*, ed. Norman Kretzmann and Eleonore Stump (Cambridge: Cambridge University Press, 1993), 85–127; Jeffrey E. Bower, "Matter, Form, and Individuation," in *The Oxford Handbook of Aquinas*, ed. Brian Davies and Eleonore Stump (Oxford: Oxford University Press, 2012), 85–103; and Lawrence Dewan, "The Individual as a Mode of Being according to Thomas Aquinas," in *The Thomist: A Speculative Quarterly Review* 63, no. 3 (1999): 403–24. Betschart corroborates the standard character of Gredt's presentation and ventures that Stein's work in EES is "a critical confrontation with the standard Thomistic understanding." See Betschart, "Überlegungen zur Menschenwürde und zu ethischen Konsequenzen von Edith Steins Verständnis der menschlichen Individualität," in *Edith Stein Jahrbuch*, 21, ed. Ulrich Dobhan (Würzburg: Echter, 2015), 114–31, and 116n247, where he cites lexiconic articles on Gredt from M. Hoegen in *Lexikon für Theologie und Kirche 4* (Freiburg: Herder, 2001) and David Berger in *Biographisches-Bibliographisches Kirchenlexikon 21* (Nordhausen: Traugott Bautz, 2003), with both identifying Gredt's general presentation of Thomism as standard.

20 EES, 404.
21 AMP, 65, 94, 131; compare EES, 426. To my knowledge Aquinas does not use the exact phrase as cited by Stein.

of material substances, the definition of the individual as something in itself undivided, and the notion of the individual as incommunicable—even while she adjusts the meaning and import of certain adopted concepts together with their conceptual interconnections. Moreover, Stein develops her opposition through a critique of the Thomist position on Thomistic grounds and according to Thomistic metaphysical principles—namely, the kind of undividedness possessed of the individual, and the ontological priority of the form in the structure of material substances.[22] In brief, Stein argues that the determining priority of form in the structure of the individual, taken together with its actualizing and unifying function relative to matter, means that the being-individual and qualitative individuality of the material individual cannot "rest" upon designated matter, but rather must be rooted in the form. In what directly follows, I detail and examine her critique of the Thomist position, before turning to an examination of her original proposal regarding the being-individual and qualitative individuality of the material individual in general. In the next chapter I move to a consideration of the human individual.

In agreement with Gredt, Stein immediately rules out prime matter as a candidate for material individuation, since prime matter, as the wholly *indeterminate* substrate of material being, cannot function as the *determining* ground of the individual.[23] Stein reasons that only matter equipped with extension has the expansiveness and corresponding divisibility needed to render matter capable of grounding the material substance. However, in contrast to Gredt, Stein maintains that the idea of expansive and divisible matter already includes the notion of a "first formation [*erste Formung*]," and she calls this first formation of matter its "generic nature [*Gattungsnatur*]."[24] Thus, in similarity to Gredt, Stein reasons that matter must receive initial preparation "through its ordination to extension" so that it can receive the formation needed to establish the substance as a quantitatively extended whole. Yet, in contrast

---

22 Ales Bello suggests that Stein critiques Aquinas's conclusions in a way that does not essentially contradict him, but rather "that Thomas is brought into greater agreement with himself" through Stein's critical interpretation and adoption. Angela Ales Bello, "Thomas von Aquino in Edith Steins Interpretation," in *The Hat and the Veil: The Phenomenology of Edith Stein*, Ad Fontes: Studien zur frühen Phänomenologie, 3, ed. Jerzy Machnacz et al. (Nordhausen: Traugott Bautz, 2016), 15–25: 24.
23 See EES, 404–6.
24 EES, 404–6; see also, EES, 408–9; and PA, esp. 195–98, where Stein already uses the phrase *erste Formung* but does not identify it with spatially extended matter.

to Gredt, Stein argues that this initial preparation should be identified as the generic determination of extended matter, both since it involves the inward ordination of matter toward formal determination, and since material substances so grounded comprise "a *genus* of beings determined in content: that of the extended, place-filling, and divisible [*Ausgedehnten, Raumfüllenden und Teilbaren*]."[25] However, Stein clarifies that this generic determination is "*not yet a form*," since such extended, place-filling, and divisible matter "still lacks the determination that is necessary for actual being."[26] Though "the generic nature of matter is a condition of the possibility of its fragmentation into individual things," for Stein, "the generic nature [of matter] is not a sufficient reason for the actual fragmentation [of matter into individual substances]."[27] And so, while Stein grants to such generically prepared matter a *kind* of initial formation through its ordination to extension, this should not be understood as if such matter were actualized in being with a kind of determinate reality. The generic nature merely provides a preparatory stage toward the actualization of the material individual, giving matter its intrinsic potential to be further determined by the kind of formation that renders it an actual individual. And so we see that for Stein, even at the most foundational level of matter designated by extension, now reinterpreted as extended matter under a generic nature, the notion of *formation* is already included in the material grounding of the individual.[28]

Stein continues her investigation by examining the close correlation of form and matter in the diverse kinds of material beings constituting the hierarchical cosmos and argues for a progressively layered formation of matter in the formal structure of material substances. This layered formation begins with the formation of matter into primary elements and compounds, continues with its formation into larger shaped entities, those of the natural environment, and concludes with its organized and animated formation in living substances,

---

25 EES, 405; compare AMP, 94; emphasis added.
26 EES, 406.
27 EES, 405–6. Wippel similarly describes the designation of matter in terms of formation, saying, "Matter is rendered divisible and designated insofar as it is *informed* by indeterminate dimensions" (emphasis added), while also mirroring Stein's caution that this "informing" should not be understood as its temporally prior actuality and determination. See Wippel, *Metaphysical Thought*, 364.
28 Stein's conception of matter, here only briefly detailed, deserves much greater investigation and is arguably one of the areas of her most profound development of Aristotelian-Thomistic hylomorphism.

what Stein regards as the highest stage of material formation.²⁹ Based on this analysis, and considering the earlier identified determining features of the individual, Stein argues that the material individual is first found only at that level of formation wherein something "is set out by itself with its own being and action."³⁰ Neither the generic nature of matter nor the formation of matter into material elements and compounds qualifies as the kind of formation necessary to constitute a material individual, since neither kind of preparatory formation provides the possibility of the separate and active mode of being necessary to constitute a "genuine 'substance' or πρώτη οὐσία (*prote ousia*)."³¹ Though such formations are necessary for the material grounding of all higher levels of formation, Stein does not consider them sufficient to account for the determinate and self-enclosed wholeness of the material individual.³²

---

29   See EES, 164–65, 218, 417–19; PA, 164–65, 208–10; and AMP, 38–39. Though Stein only mentions certain kinds of material elements in EES, "gold, iron, etc.," in PA she notes and assumes (while not endorsing) the findings of contemporary physics and chemistry, where each species of matter is understood to be constituted by a plurality of atoms (and, more broadly, molecules) of the same kind. See EES, 405–10; PA, 195–201; and AMP, 33–35.

30   EES, 406; compare PA, 25–26. This conception of the inherent dynamism of the individual as a subject of being and action partially mirrors contemporary conceptions of the individual in the biological sciences and in corresponding philosophical considerations of the data of the biological sciences, where the individual is picked out and identified in terms of its dynamic unity over time. See Christopher J. Austin and Anna Marmodoro, "Structural Powers and the Homeodynamic Unity of Organisms," Christopher J. Austin, "A Biologically Informed Hylomorphism," and Janice Chik Breidenbach, "Action, Animacy, and Substance Causation," in *Neo-Aristotelian Perspectives on Contemporary Science*, ed. William M. R. Simpson, Robert C. Koons, and Nicholas J. The (New York: Routledge, 2017), 169–84, 185–210, and 235–60, respectively.

31   EES, 406. This does not necessarily preclude the possibility of singular atoms (or molecules) being actual individuals if they were to be separated out from the larger entities they compose, though this would depend to some degree on the relative stability that such isolated atoms (or molecules) would or could have in and of themselves over time. This is significant precisely because atoms (or molecules) are usually identified as individual only when temporarily separated out from larger wholes via various experimental procedures.

32   Though the finer detail of Stein's understanding of the layered formation of matter represents a divergence from the thought of Aquinas, Aquinas also recognizes the prior formation that matter receives before its incorporation into higher-order substances, prior formation that then foundationally conditions its incorporation and, moreover,

Consequently, she argues that material being is realized as a genuine individual only with the presence of what she calls the essential-form (*Wesensform*)—and intends the same reality identified by the substantial form (*forma substantialis*) of Aquinas and the *morphe* (μορφή) of Aristotle.[33] The paradigmatic kind of material individual is then found among living things, since, in contrast to all merely material things, which are often decisively shaped by their environment, the living individual receives its determinate and self-enclosed shaping from within—thus becoming an exemplary τόδε τί, in itself undivided, and incommunicable.[34] Finally, to complete her understanding, following the Thomistic lead of Gredt, Stein reasons that the so compounded individual form-matter essence must be embraced by the further perfections of self-dependence and existence if it is to stand in being as an *actual* material individual, where the enclosure of the essence provides the perfection of self-dependence, and the reception of being provides that of existence.[35]

Evidently, for Stein, the essential-form is proper to the individual, inasmuch as it informs the material substrate and meaningfully determines the individual essence. Yet, the essential-form is also that through which the material individual is numbered as a member of its species. Accordingly, Stein argues that the essential-form partakes (*teilhaben*) in the formal determination of the species by including in its determination the meaningful determination of the species, and she identifies this meaningful determination as the pure

---

whether or not the substantial form is well received, such that an "indisposition of matter" can result in a deformity of the higher-order substance. See SCG, 3.10, no. 8; 3.73, no. 2; QDV, 23.2, co; and DP, 3.10, co.

33 See esp. EES, 140–42, 162–64, 199, 232–38, 408. Stein does not use *Wesensform* extensively in PA (or at all in AMP), and when detailing the formation of living being prefers to use the Greek term ἐντελέχεια (*entelecheia*)—literally, having completion or being at completion—a term specially coined by Aristotle to denominate the same reality identified by Stein with *Wesensform*.

34 As already indicated, the essential-form of the living thing is understood by Stein to be a living inner form and soul.

35 Moreover, like Gredt, Stein conceives of these further principles of the material substance as positive perfections that follow upon the definitive enclosure of the essence (resulting in the perfection of self-dependence) and its reception of the actuality of being (resulting in the perfection of existence), even while this requires some qualification when it comes to detailing Stein's understanding of the ultimate formal basis of being-individual; this qualification is treated in greater detail below, see "Stein's Original Conception of the Material Individual" and "Assessing Stein's Original Conception of the Material Individual."

form (*reine Form*) of the species—and intends the same reality identified by the *eidos* (εἶδος) of Aristotle.³⁶ The formal determination of the material individual can then be considered from two distinct, through inherently related perspectives, that of the essential-form of the individual, and that of the pure form of the species, which Stein identifies with the Aristotelian *morphe* and *eidos*, respectively. Whereas the essential-form powerfully shapes the individual, structuring and ordering the matter as a self-enclosed and independent whole, the pure form represents the meaningful determination of a plurality of specifically identical individuals. Whereas the pure form of the species makes possible a plurality of specifically identical individuals through its meaningful communication to a number of essential-forms, these individual essential-forms actually determine their corresponding material individuals, actualizing them in being and determining them as *what* they are without being in any way communicable to another. The essential-form is then both that through which the material individual *is* and is *what* it is—has *being* and is *determined* in kind—and that through which the material individual is numbered as a member of a particular species.³⁷

Consequently, Stein argues that the essential-form is not only something individual—as that which actually determines the material individual—but is also that through which the individual is an individual—as that which determines the separated being and unity (as well as determination) of the

---

36 See EES, 408; and also, EES, 140–42; compare AMP, 48–49, 62–63. Borden Sharkey identifies three distinct senses of "species form" in the thought of Stein: (1) as a biological classification; (2) as an inner principle of determination of formally alike individuals; and (3) as an atemporal ideal structure. Stein's use of the concept encompasses all three with priority in the ideal structure, the pure form of the species, as that which grounds all the other senses. See Borden Sharkey, *Thine Own Self*, 33–36.

37 In contrast, Borden Sharkey identifies the essential-form (denominated substantial form) as the principle of individuation rather than the principle of being-individual. She also highlights a distinction in Stein between *Einzelwesen* and *individuelles Wesen* and designates the latter "individual form" in a way that emphasizes the possible kinship of Stein's position with the philosophical tradition of individual forms. See Borden Sharkey, *Thine Own Self*, xxixn4, 117; and EES, 140–50, 199. However, I maintain that this designation obscures the distinction between the individual essential-form and individual essence (comprised of the individual essential-form and informed matter) and risks highlighting only apparent similarities between Stein and the philosophical tradition of individual forms. Moreover, Stein heavily prefers *Einzelwesen* and uses *individuelles Wesen* only in areas where she is detailing the relation of the actual individual to the pure form of the individual.

individual. Thus, she concludes, "we ascribe being-individual [*Einzelsein*] to the form of the thing."[38]

In correspondence to her analysis of being-individual, Stein also argues that differences in qualitative content among specifically identical individuals cannot be found on the side of matter, as indeterminate substrate, but rather must be sought on the side of form, as determining principle.[39] Such differences in qualitative content, she reasons, are due to a number of closely related factors, namely: (1) the elemental composition of material substances; (2) the material features of their environmental setting; and (3) the creative activity of personal beings. Yet, in all these areas, form has an evident priority, since: (1) elementally formed matter is in potency to higher levels of formation in a manner foundationally determined by the preparatory formation it has already received; (2) alterations brought about by the material environment are due to the formative powers of already formed material and living entities; and (3) all efficient causal activity of (personal) subjects are due to the (embodied) formative powers of these same (personal) subjects. Accordingly, Stein argues that all differences in qualitative content among specifically identical individuals must lie on the side of form, in the already undergone formations of incorporated matter and in the formative impact of the environment, both natural and personal. Upon this basis, Stein proceeds to argue that living individuals have certain qualitative differences that are to be accounted for by the natural variability of the form of the species among individual members of the species. Stein's reasoning relates to the way she understands the form of the individual partaking in the form of the species, and she argues that the forms of living species are differently realized in individual members of each species, and not only because of the way the essential-form inheres in already formed matter but also because of the inbuilt "room for play [*Spielraum*]" of the form of the species as it is differently realized in each individual.[40]

---

38 EES, 408. Stein proposes a second argument for the formal grounding of the individual based on her understanding of the individual being of pure geometrical figures, which further substantiates her argument for the formal basis of the individual as such, precisely inasmuch as all fully determined pure geometrical figures represent the ideal limits of the extended figures of the actual world. Since this additional argument is not necessary toward understanding Stein's conception of the material individual, I do not treat of it here. See EES, 410–12.

39 EES, 416–17.

40 The pure form of the species then functions somewhat like an archetypical blueprint, an outline formal determination that allows for certain predefined variations among the

Therefore, in like manner to the being-individual of the material individual, Stein ascribes the qualitative individuality of the material individual to form and formal difference, rather than matter and material difference.

And so, in summary: In agreement with the standard Thomist position of Gredt, Stein argues that the form of the material individual is itself an individual, precisely as individuated in the individual; yet, in contradiction of the Thomist position, she argues that the form of the individual is also that through which the individual is an individual. Since the form is that which establishes the individual in being and makes of the individual a self-enclosed unity, distinct and separate from all else, a τόδε τί with its own being and action, Stein argues that the being-individual of the material individual must have a formal basis. While she agrees with Thomism that matter is a necessary condition for the becoming and being of the material individual, she disagrees that matter is a sufficient condition for this becoming and being. This means that though she grants the necessity of a material basis for the concretion of the material individual, she does not grant that designated matter individuates the common form of the species in the material essence, but rather argues that the individual essential-form must individuate the individual essence and establish the individual in being as a distinct and unified whole, an individual of this or that kind, perfected by self-dependence and the actuality of being.

Then, with regard to the characteristic differences among specifically identical individuals, Stein again agrees with Aquinas and Thomism that matter plays a conditioning role in determining differences among specifically identical individuals; yet, she also argues that all qualitative differences should be traced back to form and formal differences. Since prior formation not only determines the differentiability of incorporated matter, but also determines

---

individuals ranged under its common formality, without thereby disturbing the species unity of the individuals so ranged via their individual essential-forms. This account of the relationship of the essential-form to the form of the species is precisely what makes it necessary to distinguish between biological species and the pure form of the species, and also provides a partial explanation of the possibility of the evolution of biological species, inasmuch as evolution can be accounted for by progressive minor adjustments of essential-forms in ancestrally related individuals according to the free play of the pure form of the species in individually instantiated essential-forms. See EES, 406–9; AMP, 57–73; PA, 186–207; and also, Borden Sharkey, *Thine Own Self*, 30–43. The question of how exactly an evolutionary transition of species would eventuate from such a process would require closer examination of Stein's thought in both AMP and EES, which is not here possible.

the actual (living) individual inasmuch as the essential-form (soul) differently instantiates the form of the species, and since other variations among material individuals can be resolved to the formal actuality of the material environment, Stein argues that the qualitative individuality of the material individual must have an encompassing formal basis.[41]

Examining Stein's Critique of the Standard Thomistic Position

A number of questions should be posed of Stein's novel proposition regarding the material individual. Is Stein's investigation successful in showing the formal basis of the being-individual of the material individual? And the further formal bases of its qualitative individuality? What is the precise location of the divergence between Stein and Aquinas and Thomism that leads to such a contradiction in conclusions? What place if any does Stein grant to the principle "*individuum de ratione materia*, the individual by reason of the matter"?

I propose to answer these questions by approaching Stein's critique of the standard Thomist position from a consideration of the Thomistic commitment to the ontological priority of form in the structure of the material substance, first as this relates to extended matter, then as it relates to the undividedness of the material individual, and finally as it relates to incommunicability. For this analysis, I make my own Stein's understanding of the meaning of being an individual, an understanding she holds together with the *philosophia perennis*. This includes the way an individual is identified, as τόδε τί, how the individual is defined, as in itself undivided yet divided from all else, and the decisive feature of the individual, as something possessing incommunicability.

As shown above, according to the standard Thomistic presentation of Gredt, matter is designated by extension by virtue of the transcendental relation, and designated matter performs the function of individuating form by virtue of the same transcendental relation.[42] This means that, on the one hand, the

---

41 In her conclusions Stein has some evident alignment with the thought of Scotus on individuation, through her recognition of a positive, formal basis of the being-individual of the material individual, thus aligning with Scotus's treatment of the individual in terms of "*haecceitas* [thisness]," though of course such alignment should not hastily be understood as simple agreement without further ado. See Gilson, *Duns Scotus*, 357–58.

42 See Gredt, *Philosophie*, 1:244–6, cited in EES, 403–4.

transcendental requirements of form dictate that matter be designated for the sake of the inherence of form, and on the other hand, the so-designated matter performs the inverse function of contracting the common form of the species to this particular individual. So understood, the transcendental relation indicates that form and matter should be understood as complementary causal principles in the structure of the individual—both in terms of its first becoming, and in terms of its continuation in being—where matter is first designated according to the transcendental requirements of the form, and form is then individuated by these same requirements working in reverse.[43] In this way, the common form of the species is contracted to this or that material individual by the limiting potency of matter—so that the form becomes this or that individuated form, and the essence this or that individuated essence—and an indefinite plurality of formally identical individuals is established through their extension and exclusive position in place.[44] With this standard Thomistic presentation of the relation of form and matter Stein partially agrees, yet she queries the ability of matter to perform the work of division and distinction. In opposition to the conclusion that matter individuates by force of the transcendental relation, Stein argues that the notion of the transcendental relation implies not that "the form is this and that [form] solely because it is in this and that matter," but rather the inverse, that "the matter is this or that matter because it *belongs* to this or that form."[45]

The crucial basis of Stein's reasoning lies in her conception of the priority of form in the structure of material substances, a priority that is affirmed by Aquinas and Thomism in its presentation of form as the intrinsic principle of both being and unity, in addition to its role in determining the essence of material substances. While granting the truth of the transcendental relation, and

---

[43] Wippel provides a coordinate explanation to Gredt when he describes "the distinct lines of causality [...] at work in this explanation, i.e., material or receiving, and formal or actualizing." Wippel, *Metaphysical Thought*, 364.

[44] It seems to me that a fully comprehensive conception of designation and individuation (in the Thomistic presentation of both Gredt and Wippel) is had only when both designation and individuation are presented together with a consideration of the causal activity of the generating agent. This is to say that we can make sense of the reciprocal lines of causality involved in the concretion of the material individual only by introducing the further causality of the agent that generates the individual through introducing a determinate form to a designated portion of matter, which matter then receives and contracts the form to this very individual through its material extension and exclusive position in place.

[45] EES, 404; emphasis added.

reconsidering it in tandem with the ontological priority of form, Stein reverses the individuating polarity of the relation and argues that the being-individual of the material substance must have its basis in the form rather than in the matter. Since form is that which makes the material individual an actual being of a determinate kind, a unified and discrete whole that is distinct and separate from all else, Stein reasons that we must affirm that being-individual is due to the essential-form rather than to the designated matter. Indeed, she supports her reasoning by quoting a principle she adopts from Aquinas, namely, "Since matter is *only* for the sake of form, material *distinction* is *only* for the sake of formal *distinction*," which she takes to imply, among other things, that the distinction of individuals must lie on the side of form.[46] Thus, Stein argues that the distinction of the material individual rests not on any distinction of matter but rather on the distinction of form—or, more precisely, not on any distinction of designated or generic matter but rather on a distinction of the essential-form. Hence, as shown above, Stein reasons that the essential-form is not only something individual through being individuated in the material individual but is actually the root cause of the being-individual of the individual.

This reversal of the individuating polarity of the transcendental relation is a critical point for Stein in establishing the cogency of her critique of the standard Thomistic presentation, and her conclusions here foundationally support all subsequent argumentation for the formal basis of the being-individual of the individual, as well as the related issue of its qualitative individuality. If transcendental polarity can reasonably be reversed in this way—or indeed if it *should* be reversed—then Stein's conclusion of the formal basis of the material individual follows unavoidably.

Is such a reversal reasonable? As indicated above, Thomism allows that the form of the material individual is itself something individual, as individuated in the individual by virtue of the contracting and limiting potency of designated matter.[47] Yet it is the then individuated form that provides the individual substance with its *actuality* and *unity*, "for through form, which is the act of the matter, matter becomes an *actual being* and this *particular thing*," and "according as things have being, they have *unity* [...] for according as

---

46 EES, 416, citing ST, I, 47.2, co.; emphasis added. To this, and in relation to what follows, we could also add Aquinas's understanding that "matter is the principle of substanding [for accidents], and form is the principle of subsisting [for the subject]" (ST, I, 29.2, ad 5.).

47 See DEE, 5, 131–40; and also, EES, 404, citing Gredt, *Philosophie*, 1:246.

anything is a being it is *likewise one*."[48] And so, even though Aquinas holds that the form of the individual is individuated by the receiving potency of (designated) matter—according to which the individual is set apart with an exclusive position in place—he also holds that the so individuated form provides the material individual with its being and unity—through which the material individual is an undivided whole with its own distinctive being and action. Indeed, since Thomism also holds that (designated) matter is a potency that is of itself radically divisible—this seems to be the very reason why it is understood to provide for the possibility of material individuation—(designated) matter certainly cannot be that which accounts for the determinate actuality in being and undivided wholeness of the individual. Accordingly, in his Aristotelian-Thomistic commentary Gredt pointedly formulates his conclusion regarding material individuation in the following way: "[Matter] *multiplies* the form and the substance as a whole *purely in number*."[49]

Obviously, the question Gredt is answering, as was Aquinas before him, is the question of the instantiation of the same form in a plurality of specifically alike individuals in view of accounting for the manifest plurality of material individuals bearing one and the same species determination. Theirs is a question of the principle of individuation (*principium individuationis*), understood as the metaphysical basis whereby one and the same form can be instantiated and multiplied in a plurality of alike individuals within a hierarchical cosmos of formally differentiated kinds.[50] And since form is patently the principle

---

48 DEE, 2, 31–32; CT, 1.71; emphasis added; see also DEE, 4, 45–46: "Matter and form are so related that form gives being to matter."
49 EES, 403, citing Gredt, *Philosophie*, 1:246; emphasis added. This formulation by Gredt is echoed in the explanation of Wippel who formulates the question of the material individual in the following way: "what intrinsic principle (or principles) accounts for the fact that one individual material substance is *numerically* distinct from other members of the same species?" Wippel, *Metaphysical Thought*, 352; emphasis added.
50 See SCG, 4.10, no. 7; ST, I, 75.4, co.; QDP, 9.6, ad 1; DEE, 2, 67–84. John Finley, referencing Gracia, makes a similar point by attending to the grammatical use of individuation (*individuatio*) and argues that its meaning in Aquinas is grammatically like that of creation and generation, as suggestive of "the process or determination whereby something becomes individual." See John Finley, "The Problem of Individual Being," in *Selected Papers on the Legacy of Edith Stein's Finite and Eternal Being*, ed. Sarah Borden Sharkey (= *Quaestiones Disputatae*, 4.1 (2013)), 107–20: 109–3, referencing Garcia, *Individuation in Scholasticism*, 1–20: 4–5. However, given Aquinas's Aristotelian understanding of causation (where causes are temporally coincident with

of commonality—identifying a plurality of individuals as members of one and the same species—the principle of distinction must be found outside the form and in the receiving potency of its material correlate.⁵¹ In precisely this way Thomism regards designated matter as a necessary condition for the instantiation and multiplication of form, and consequently argues that the individuation (*Vereinzelung*) of material substances is accomplished by designated matter.⁵² Yet, even here, it is still the individuated form that makes of the substance an actual undivided whole.

Accordingly as noted above, Stein recognizes the foundational role of matter in the becoming and being of the material individual, and she grants that a

---

their effects), it would seem better to interpret Aquinas's conception of individuation as implying not only the causal becoming of the individual but also its causal continuation in being, since the substantially intrinsic causes of matter and form remain causally concurrent with the actual being of the individual substance.

51   Since designated matter then also provides the material substance with its exclusive position in place, designated matter renders the material whole something inherently incommunicable.

52   For a sampling of texts, see ST, III, 3.7, ad 1; SCG, 2.80, nos. 7–17; QDA, 7, co.; and CT, 1.52. For further confirmation of this reading of Aquinas, see the following: Kevin White, "Individuation in Aquinas's *Super Boetium De Trinitate*, Q.4," in *American Catholic Philosophical Quarterly* 69, no. 4 (1995): 543–56: 547: "Aquinas here seems to regard the term 'individuation' as interchangeable, if not precisely synonymous, with the expressions 'numerical diversity,' 'numerical plurality' and 'unity of individual substance'"; Armand Maurer, "Introduction," in *Faith, Reason and Theology, Questions I–IV of his Commentary on the De trinitate of Boëthius*, trans. Armand Maurer (Toronto: Pontifical Institute of Medieval Studies, 1987), xxxv: "Matter plays a passive role in individuation, making possible the multiplication of form in many individuals"; Christopher Brown, "Aquinas on the Individuation of Non-Living Substances," in *Proceedings of the American Catholic Philosophical Association* 75 (2002): 237–54: 238, who argues that apart from the question of incommunicability, the question of individuation for Aquinas is about "numerical identity," and formulates the question in the following way, "What accounts for x being numerically distinct from y, when x and y share the same species?"; and also, when treating of human individuation, Michael Waldstein, "Personal Individuality According to Thomas" (unpublished article [2005]): 1–5: 3–4: "Form—and in a different perspective, '*esse*'—is the primary principle of individuality in a being. Form is what accounts for a being's inner unity and thus also for its division as one being from others […] The rational soul gives to a human being the most perfect way (*modus*) of individuality, which is signified in the word 'person' […] Prime matter is a principle of individuation not on the side of being and unity, but on the side of diversity, distinction, division and, therefore, multiplicity."

material substratum is necessary for the instantiation and multiplication of material substances. Yet, as also indicated above, she questions the sufficiency of matter to causally ground and anchor the individuation of the individual. Unlike Aquinas and Thomism, Stein is not primarily interested in the instantiation and multiplication of the form of the species in a specifically identical plurality, and rather is more focused on the intrinsic principle through which the material individual has being as an undivided and distinct whole, set apart with its own being and action. And so, in contrast to the Thomistic interest in identifying the principle of individuation relative to the form of the species, Stein is interested in identifying the principle of the individual relative to its being and undivided wholeness. Hers is a question of the being-individual (*Einzelsein*) of the material individual as a distinct and unified whole, rather than the individuation of the common form of the species in a plurality, and she reasons that designated matter is insufficient to the task since it is a radically divisible, receptive potency. Indeed, it is only form that can provide the material substance with its actuality and unity, and it is only form that can set the material substance apart as a distinct whole. This difference of foci when investigating the problem of the individual—between the instantiation and multiplication of the form of the species, and the intrinsic ground of the being and unity of the individual—evidently changes the aspect taken upon the question of the material individual, with the foreseeable consequence that when Stein comes to the question of the material individual, she reasons to an expressly opposed solution to Aquinas and Thomism.[53]

This difference at the level of essential principles has even deeper roots in a more fundamental difference over the manner of conceiving of the meaning of undividedness or unity. Whereas Aquinas maintains that "to be one is to be indivisible," a fundamentally negative notion, and equates the unity of the material individual with numerical unity, Stein maintains that "unity or being-one" is something notionally and ontologically positive and argues that the unity of the individual as such is distinct from and also grounds numerical unity. Though Aquinas does not present a separate treatise on

---

53 The material individual could "rest" on spatially extended matter only if this were the secondary matter of artificial objects, matter which already has its being as this or that kind of natural material substance, and which is then further shaped and structured as an artifact in a wholly exterior manner. Yet, even here, it is the form that sets the artifact apart as an actual individual, as this thing here, an undivided whole divided from all else.

unity, it is clear that he follows Aristotle (and Averroes, contra Avicenna) by noting both transcendental and numerical kinds of unity, where transcendental unity is understood to come together with being and traverse all regions of being, and numerical unity to be the principle of number and plurality, found eminently realized in the category of quantity from where it is extended to the other categories.[54] Thus, Aquinas identifies the "in itself undivided" of the individual with numerical unity and, in correspondence, conceives of the question of material individuation to be one of instantiation and multiplication. Yet, for Stein, the undividedness of the individual cannot be identified with numerical unity without further ado, since numerical unity extends beyond the individual and encompasses anything that can be objectified and numbered, and therefore also applies to objects that are not individuals, either by not being "in themselves undivided," or by not being "divided from all else."[55] Moreover, Stein reasons that the undividedness of the material individual cannot simply be identified with transcendental unity, since transcendental unity is also possessed by the universal standing opposite the individual, as something communicable to many individuals even while itself remaining undivided in meaning. Consequently, she proposes a distinct kind of "unity or being-one," a primitive unity that furnishes the intrinsic positive ground

---

54 See esp. InMeta 10.1, nos. 13, 17; and 10.4, no. 1 (Meta, 10.1, 1052^{b}16, 1052^{a}32; and Meta, 10.3, 1052^{b}16); and EES, 395–96. This fundamental division is not intended to exclude intentional kinds of unity, such as specific, generic, and analogical unities; and neither is it intended to preclude recognizing further distinctions within unity, such as those between simple and composite unities, essential and accidental unities, and intrinsic and extrinsic unities. Rather, in tandem with Stein's own analysis, and in terms of her comparison with Aquinas, I focus on transcendental and numerical kinds of unity as the primary division of unity with respect to actual being. See InMeta 10.1–4 (Meta, 10.1–3). See also David Svoboda, "The *Ratio* of Unity: Positive or Negative? The Case of Thomas Aquinas," in *American Catholic Philosophical Quarterly* 86, no. 1 (2012): 47–70: 47–49, 65–66; and Bernhard Blankenhorn, "Aquinas on the Transcendental One: An Overlooked Development in Doctrine," in *Angelicum* 81, no. 3 (2004): 615–37; Wippel, *Metaphysical Thought*, 74, 264, 356; George Klubertanz, *Introduction to the Philosophy of Being*, 2nd ed. (New York: Appleton-Century-Crofts, 1963), 220–22; and Joseph Owens, *An Elementary Christian Metaphysics* (Milwaukee, WI: Bruce, 1963; repr. Houston: Center for Thomistic Studies, 1986, repr. 2013), 117–18.

55 Anything that can be objectified can be taken as a numerical unity and counted as one element of a numerical plurality—"so one can group 'number,' 'color,' and 'weight' together as 'three objects' (in the widest sense of 'object')" (EES, 396).

of both numerical and transcendental unities, and ascribes such unity to the individual.[56]

This understanding of unity foundationally coordinates Stein's understanding of what qualifies as the essential principle of the individual, so that when she approaches the question of material individuation, now understood as a question of the being-individual of the material individual, Stein argues for its formal basis in the essential-form rather than in the divisible substrate of designated matter. Since the essential-form is the intrinsic principle of the being and unity of the substance, Stein argues that the individual essential-form is the only component of the substance that can actually account for the *being-one* of the individual, and therefore also for its being as this very individual. In the conceptual schema of Aquinas and Thomism, where the unity of the individual is first understood negatively—at least notionally, even if not ontologically—and further identified with numerical unity, the question of the material individual inevitably becomes one of the instantiation and multiplication of the common form of the species in separated numerable wholes.[57] Such a question is aptly answered by the potency of designated matter, precisely inasmuch as it has the potency to divide and multiply the common form of the species by contracting and limiting it to this or that piece of matter. Yet, given Stein's contrasted positive understanding of unity, and her corresponding understanding of the primitive unity of the individual, the question of the material individual becomes one of locating the intrinsic ground of the unified being of the individual, its being-one. Stein's question is decidedly one of the *being-individual* of the material individual in contrast to its *individuation*, and such a question can only be answered by the essential-form unifying the material individual as a distinct and separated whole. Thus, and following through on the Thomistic principle of the ontological priority of

---

56   From here forward, I will identify the unity of the individual detailed by Stein as "primitive," since it is something primary and original in the structure of the individual and, moreover, is something irreducible to any other principle or feature.

57   Again here, Stein's analysis appears to closely track that of Scotus, and both with that of Avicenna. See Victor M. Salas, "Edith Stein and Medieval Metaphysics," in *American Catholic Philosophical Quarterly* 85, no. 2 (2011): 323–40: 330–31; though Salas finally argues that Stein's position is actually closer to that of Henry of Ghent (similar to her position on essential being). The question of the unity of the individual is taken up again below in greater detail; see esp. "Assessing Stein's Original Conception of the Material Individual."

form, Stein argues against Aquinas and Thomism and proposes a formal basis for the being-individual of the material individual.

What about the incommunicability of the material individual? Since matter with its extension and exclusive position in place is inherently incommunicable, and the form of the species is evidently communicable to many, must Stein not grant with Aquinas and Thomism that the material individual is rendered incommunicable through its material principle? Though Stein follows Aquinas in conceiving of incommunicability as the decisive feature of the individual—precisely inasmuch as the individual *must* possesses something not common to many—given her above-detailed reconsideration of the priority of form she need not rely on matter to provide the incommunicability of the individual.[58] Since the essential-form is both that through which the individual is an actual thing, and that through which it is included as a member of its species, the form of the individual can cause not only the specific determination of the substance but also its individuated formal actuality. Though Stein recognizes that the pure form of the species is universally communicable to an indefinite plurality of individuals of that species, she argues that the essential-form is inherently incommunicable to any and all other individuals by virtue of its formal actuality, since precisely as something actual it cannot be made common and shared among a plurality.[59] Accordingly, Stein maintains that the essential-form is not only actually incommunicable to another but is also the intrinsic principle of incommunicability.

This certainly represents an express domain of disagreement with Aquinas and Thomism, yet it also has some accord with the Thomistic distinction of abstract and real considerations of form, a distinction highlighted by John Finley in a paper examining the disagreement between Stein and Aquinas over individuation.[60] Finley marshals the distinction between the formal unity of the species, an abstract consideration, and the formal unity of the supposit, a concrete consideration, to show the greater range of agreement between Stein and Aquinas. According to an abstract consideration, form is understood from

---

58 "Now it is manifest," Aquinas says, "that the reason why any singular thing is this particular thing is because it is not directly communicable to many" (ST, I, 11.3, co.). See also, I, 29.4, ad 3; and I, 30.4, ad 3. Again, as noted above, to be incommunicable is—for both Stein and Aquinas—to possess something that is not and cannot be simultaneously common to a plurality of individuals.
59 See EES, 408–9, 416.
60 See Finley, "The Problem of Individual Being," 107–20, esp. 115–18.

the perspective of its universal formality through which it is communicable to many individuals, thus possibly constituting a plurality of specifically identical material individuals. According to a real consideration, form is understood from the perspective of its formal actuality through which it is itself something individual, possessed by this individual alone and incommunicable to any other. Finley argues that this distinction is left unclarified in Aquinas and is further veiled in the Thomistic commentary of Gredt, with the consequence that the more nuanced position of Aquinas and Thomism regarding the role of form in the individual is not sufficiently illumined for Stein when she prepares to appropriate the Thomistic conceptual schema. Yet even should this confusion be granted, the standard Thomistic presentation still holds that the form of the material individual is individuated by virtue of its (transcendental) relation to the designated matter, according to which the so-composed essence is rendered inherently incommunicable through the incommunicability of the matter—and thus an individual. Hence, the fundamental disagreement between Stein and Aquinas over formal versus material bases stands.

What place, if any, does Stein grant to the Thomistic principle, "individuum de ratione materiae, *the individual by reason of matter"?* With Aquinas and Thomism, Stein acknowledges that all kinds of material individuals require matter as a necessary basis for their initial becoming as well as their continuation in being. And since this matter cannot be identified with prime matter—as the wholly indeterminate substrate of material being—Stein reasons that the matter incorporated by material individuals must have received prior preparation. As shown above, this prior preparation begins with the generic nature of spatially extended matter, includes its elementary formation into primary elements and compounds, continues with its formation into the larger shaped entities of the natural world, before its inclusion in all higher levels of formation wherein the individual is found, as paradigmatically realized in plant, animal, and human substances. As a consequence of this prior preparation through which the matter is already formed in a determinate way—a prior formation Borden Sharkey helpfully identifies as the formative history of matter—Stein reasons that such prior determinations continue to play a foundational role in the structure of the material individual by co-determining its fully completed structure.[61] Thus, for Stein, matter continues to be significant for the material

---

61 Borden Sharkey describes designated matter as having a "history" of formations that foundationally conditions its subsequent formation in the structure of the individual material substance. See Borden Sharkey, *Thine Own Self,* 36–38, 121.

individual, both in terms of its being-individual—where matter remains a condition of the possibility of the becoming and being of the individual—and in terms of its qualitative individuality—where the formative history of matter foundationally conditions the qualitative distinctiveness of the substantial whole so comprised. Accordingly, we see that Stein extensively employs the Thomistic principle "*individuum de ratione materiae*" even while she significantly adjusts its application by showing that even here all differences ultimately reduce to formal differences.[62]

Having now treated many difficulties related to the question of the material individual, we are in a position to provide Stein's answers to the series of questions earlier posed of the standard Thomistic presentation.[63]

(1) "Can matter by itself really perform the work that is here attributed to it?" Given the ontological priority of form in the structure of the material individual, as that principle by which the being and unity of the individual is secured, taken together with the passive potency and radical divisibility of matter, Stein reasons that designated matter cannot perform the task of grounding the material individual in being. Consequently, she argues that the being-individual of the material individual cannot "rest" on the material principle but must be sought in the formal principle.

(2) "Does the form only effect the determination of the species and nothing further?" Given the relation of the individual substance to the species of which it is a member, Stein reasons that the form of the individual not only determines its species classification through participation in the pure form of the species, but also determines the actual being and unity of the material individual, even should all individuals of the same species be formally identical. Therefore, she argues that the being-individual of the individual is determined by the individual essential-form, which form can be considered more or less equivalent to the individuated substantial form of Aquinas and Thomism.

(3) "Is being-individual 'presupposed' to self-dependence and existence, as Gredt seeks to prove?" Given the ontological priority of form in the structure of the individual, Stein reasons that being-individual is ontologically prior to the perfection of self-dependence, as something presupposed to self-dependence, with both ontologically prior to the perfection of existence, as perfections

---

62   Compare Betschart, *Unwiederholbares Gottessiegel*, 193–94.
63   See above, 97, citing EES, 404.

presupposed to the reception of the actuality of being, the ultimate perfection. Therefore, she argues, being-individual is something fundamental in the ontological structure of finite being, as already signaled by the primitive kind of unity of the material individual.[64]

And so, through an objective investigation of the structure and formation of material being, Stein argues definitively that the being-individual and qualitative individuality of the material individual has formal bases. Though she continues to follow Aquinas and Thomism in conceiving of the individual essence as a hylomorphic composition, she departs from Aquinas and Thomism in her understanding of the way the material individual is concreted via the transcendental relation of form and matter, by recognizing the unqualified priority of form in the layered structure of the hierarchical cosmos, by tracking the priority of form in composite being, and ultimately, by reversing the individuating polarity of the transcendental relation.

Stein's Original Conception of the Material Individual

Having in this way received and critically incorporated the hylomorphic schema of Aquinas and Thomism, and concluded to formal bases for being-individual and individuality, Stein proceeds to develop an independent position with regard to the ultimate principle of being-individual. Given her already developed understanding of the formal structure of being, where the essential-form is understood to be a formally complex structure of manifold formal determinations, Stein argues that the root principle of being-individual is to be found in the empty-form "thing" that frames the structural complex of the essential-form together with its correlated material fullness.[65] As the final formal

---

64 For each answer, see EES, 405, 408; 408–9; and 412–13 (and note that its 2nd edition of 2013, 404nn32–34, incorrectly lists the related page numbers as 440, 445, and 446ff.). In the realm of ideal formal being, the conclusion to the last question is somewhat different, since Stein reasons that both being-individual and self-dependence are rooted in the formal structure of the individual as an ideal formal structure, with neither ontologically prior to the other, and both ontologically prior to existence. Evidently then, Stein also grants existence to ideal forms, precisely inasmuch as they have an essential mode of being. See EES, 412–13.

65 See EES, 182–84, 188–89, 221–23, 240–48. For the following, also compare the coordinate presentations of Betschart, *Unwiederholbares Gottessiegel*, 227–35, 238–41; and Alfieri, "The Question of Individuality," 86–87. In *Thine Own Self*, Borden Sharkey

determination of the structure, Stein reasons that the empty-form encompasses the essential fullness with a formal unity and consequent formal indivisibility. The empty-form thereby closes off the formal structure as a discrete whole and renders it something formally separate from all else. And since the empty-form "thing" has this ontological priority within the structure of the essential-form, Stein reasons that this empty-form is itself something incommunicable to another, and indeed is that through which the individual essential-form is rendered formally incommunicable. That is, since the empty-form encompasses the essential-form and makes of it a self-dependent whole, the empty-form is that which makes of the unified structure an incommunicable whole, so that the incommunicability of the complex structure is reducible to the incommunicability of its empty-form. Hence, Stein argues that the empty-form "thing" sets the (material) individual apart by encompassing the formal and material fullness of the individual, grounding the individual essence as "this individual thing [*dieses Einzelding*]," an "individual object [*Einzelgegenstandes*]," or simply, an "individual [*Individuum*]."[66]

To further elucidate the role of the empty-form in the structure of the individual, and to develop a fully rounded understanding of what it means to be an individual, Stein introduces the concept "bearer" to clarify the formal basis of the individual, and she argues that "being-bearer [*Trägersein*]" provides just this conceptual clarification.[67] By being-bearer, Stein first intends that which is "set out on its own," an individual thing or object, so as to exclude that which is borne by the bearer, namely, all other formal and material determinations of any kind whatsoever. Being-bearer then initially corresponds to the first meaning of bearer detailed above, where bearer identifies the individual thing

---

largely disregards the question of the empty-form with the unfortunate side effect that her work is foreshortened in its explanatory force. See Borden Sharkey, *Thine Own Self*, esp. xxxn5, 116–18.

66   See EES, 189, 192. As noted above (25n47), the empty-form "thing" can be identified as "object" (in the narrower sense applicable only to things, and not to anything that can be objectified as a unity), and "individual thing" or simply "individual." Again here, I note the closeness of Stein's conclusions with those of Scotus, in his proposal of an *ultimate* basis of actuality, determination, and, consequently, individuation in the (material) individual, in the "*differentia ultima*" as the final actuality of the form. See Timothy B. Noone, "Individuation in Scotus," in *American Catholic Philosophical Quarterly* 69, no. 4 (2010): 527–42; and Gilson, *Duns Scotus*, 357–61. See below, 132n74, for some more detail.

67   See EES, 399, 413; see also Betschart, *Unwiederholbares Gottessiegel*, 246–47.

taken in completion with all of its structural parts, precisely since the individual thing bears itself and bears its own being and essence in itself. Yet, since the empty-form bears the essential-form together with its material correlate as one whole, the individual thing as a substantial whole is ultimately borne by this empty-form. So considered, the individual essential-form is itself something individual precisely because of the bearing of the empty-form "thing," which encloses the formal structure and sets it apart as an incommunicable whole. Thus, Stein reasons, "We [...] have found the *root-principle* [Wurzelpunkt] of being-individual in the formal structure of objects as such: in that the bearer enclosing its essence as an empty-form is incommunicable."[68]

And so, again here, as in the investigation concerning human nature, through usefully employing these closely correlated concepts—those of empty-form and bearer—Stein fulfills the previously established criteria for identifying the individual provided by the tradition of the *philosophia perennis*, that the individual be a τόδε τί, something in itself undivided yet divided from all else, and inherently incommunicable. This resolution of being-individual to the empty-form as bearer can be understood as Stein's conclusive answer to the problem of what constitutes an individual, an answer to the question she earlier poses should the formal basis of the individual be granted—namely, "Is [being-individual] something supervening [to the form] or does it belong inwardly to [the form] and constitute it?"[69] Evidently, given what we've just seen, being-individual belongs inwardly to the form and constitutes it, precisely inasmuch as being-individual is traceable to the empty-form enclosing the essential-form and its material correlate. Moreover, Stein employs this conceptual apparatus in such a way that she can utilize it as a universal explanation of being-individual applicable across all regions of being, whether identifying spiritual or material individuals, or describing individuals possessing essential or non-material actual being, precisely inasmuch as the empty-form has this universal malleability. The being-individual of the individual is then something properly distinctive in the ontological structure of being—or, more pointedly, the being-individual of the individual is just that, its *being-individual*.

---

68   See EES, 416. See also EES, 189–92; PA, 22–25; and AMP, 61–62.
69   EES, 408–9.

Assessing Stein's Original Conception
of the Material Individual

Given the obvious differences between Stein's original conception and that of Aquinas, is Stein's position squarely opposed to that of Thomism, or are there avenues toward the partial reconciliation of their alternate positions? I propose to approach this question through an examination of the rationale behind Stein's proposition that the individual essential-form is an individual via the empty-form as bearer, since this brings to light the very heart of the disagreement between Stein and Aquinas over individuation, as well as indicating the several places where no disagreement is found.

The reason Stein proposes a formal structure unified by the empty-form "thing" is based on the simple given that all actual individuals appear in abstract intentional acts as formally complex wholes that share the abstract form "thing."[70] Though each material individual is distinct in being and separated from all else, all material individuals no matter their essential determination share in the empty formality of being this or that thing. This formality can be said to be formally common to all individuals of any and all kinds even if it is actually proper to each and every individual. As a result, the common formality "thing" can be abstracted from all actual individuals, conceptually formulated as the universal concept "thing," and then attributed to these very same individuals in acts of intellectual judgment and predication. So far, what is said contains no contradiction of the teachings of Aquinas and Thomism, as this accords with the Thomistic understanding of the way things can be abstractly considered in intentional acts, whether they be acts of understanding, conceptualization, or judgment. Yet, for Stein, the common formality "thing" is not merely abstractable from each actual individual, a notion the intellect finds in its most general consideration of the distinction of beings. Rather, she presents it as an actual formal determination of the structure of the individual, a distinct formal dimension that determines each thing, with the essential fullness of each furnished by all further formal determinations received by this empty formality. Indeed, she holds that it is only because this formality is part of the formal structure that the knowing intellect can abstract it from the

---

70   For the moment I prescind from detailing the empty-form "personal I" (in contrast to "thing") and treat this further dimension of Stein's thought when detailing the human individual as a material substance below (127ff.).

individual, formulate it conceptually, and then predicate it of the individual, since, Stein concludes, "the forms of entities [*Gebilde*] of thought (= logical forms) must correspond to forms of being (= ontological forms)"—that is, if we are to really *know* reality.⁷¹ Therefore, Stein argues that the formality "thing" is not merely a form of thought, concept, and predication, but a form that determines each individual as an individual, so that "the being-individual of one thing does not differ from that of another through any content," and rather "belongs to its 'empty-form.'"⁷²

Given this rationale for the empty-form, is any reconciliation at all possible between Stein and Aquinas? As shown above, Stein's mature understanding of form is developed through the confrontation of phenomenological and Scholastic conceptions of form, where form is considered primarily from the contrasted perspectives of consciousness and being. However, as also indicated above, this contrasted primacy does not exclude their complementary opposites. When considering the distinct formal determination of the structure of the individual, Stein is using form in a typically phenomenological sense, and when considering the individual form as the essential-form of an actual being, Stein is using form in a typically Thomistic sense. However, as shown above, the phenomenological sense has its counterpart in Scholasticism in the diverse "formal notions or aspects" of actual individuals, precisely inasmuch as all things can be variously considered in differing abstractions. Such abstract considerations provide the basis for the Thomistic understanding of universals, where universals are fashioned after some or other formal aspect abstracted from a delimited open range of actual individuals, before being conceptually expressed and intellectually attributed to these same individuals. Though universals have an intentional mode of being for Aquinas—in the *one* notion-concept-word *turned toward many* objects of understanding, after the Latin *uni-versus*—they have their ontological basis in the things from which they are abstracted, their foundation in things (*fundamentum in re*).⁷³ Thus, a clear avenue opens toward

---

71   EES, 183; compare PA, 26.
72   EES, 409.
73   See esp. DEE, 3, 120–46; and InDA, 2.12, esp. nos. 5–8 (DA, 2.5, 417ᵇ19–27). As indicated above, such formal notions can be understood to have their primordial mode of intentional being in the intellect of the Creator, who first thinks the forms of all actual things according to their universal similarities and individual differences, prior to creating each actual individual as a formally determined whole that shares various overlapping formal determinations with other actual individuals of alike and different kinds.

a partial reconciliation of Stein and Aquinas, inasmuch as the *fundamentum in re* of universal notions-concepts-words can be considered analogous to Stein's conception of formal structures with their manifold formal determinations, all ultimately united under the empty-form "thing" encompassing the formal whole and found present in all individuals. Since the abstraction of the formal notion "thing" from the material individual signifies the presence of a formality common to all individuals, so that a universal notion applicable to all individuals is arrived at through this abstraction with its *fundamentum in re*, we have the ground of a properly formal notion of the individual. On the other hand, Stein's conception of the complex structure of forms need not be understood as unequivocally antithetical to the Thomistic conception of the unity and simplicity of substantial forms. In the formal structure of the individual essential-form, the empty-form "thing" has a final and radical formal priority, uniting the structure as a discrete whole through the regulated order of arrangement of all subdeterminations. This means that each complex structure is determined as a unified whole with a relative simplicity as an *actually* indivisible whole via the empty-form encompassing the structural complex with its primitive unity, something that renders the essential form a unified whole with its own qualified simplicity. Nevertheless, even if this partial accord between Stein and Aquinas should be granted, Stein's proposition of the distinct structural reality of each partial formal determination within the framework of the structure clearly departs from Aquinas's proposition of the unqualified simplicity of substantial forms.[74]

---

74 Even though universals can be understood as partial formal subdeterminations of the formal unity that actually informs the things so universally considered, Aquinas and Thomism does not grant to them a distinct structural reality within the formal unity of the thing. As noted above (69n63), Stein's position here is comparable with Scotus's explanation of form and structure, with the consequence that her similar critique of Aquinas on individuation has several further parallels with Scotistic analyses of the problem of the individual and Scotist-inspired critiques of the Thomistic position. Among others, see Noone, "Individuation in Scotus," 527–42; Salas, "Edith Stein and Medieval Metaphysics," 323–40; O. J. Brown, "Individuation and Actual Existence in Scotist Metaphysics: A Thomistic Assessment," in *The New Scholasticism*, 53, no. 3 (1979), 347–361; and James Reichmann, "Edith Stein, Thomas Aquinas, and the Principle of Individuation," in *American Catholic Philosophical Quarterly* 87, no. 1 (2013): 55–86. Yet, in Stein locating the root principle of being-individual in the empty-form "thing," and in her related understanding that this formal determination can be intellectually abstracted from all (actual) individuals, she clearly departs from

When we further consider the formal basis of the individual from the perspective of the empty-form as bearer, we get a further avenue toward partial reconciliation. Following Gredt, Stein maintains that self-dependence follows immediately upon being-individual, and also that the individual essence and the self-dependence of that essence, though not actually separable, are "*objectively distinct* [sachlich verschieden]."[75] This means that the individual essence that possesses self-dependence is objectively distinct from the possessed perfection of self-dependence and, consequently, that self-dependence is notionally and conceptually distinguishable from the individual. Though the essence is individual through the formal structure itself, only when the individual essence is fully determined by the union of the essential-form and matter does the individual essence of material being have the positive perfection of self-dependence, and only then does the individual essence receive the actuality of being and stand in existence as an actual individual.[76] However, whereas Gredt identifies the distinction between the individual essence and its self-dependence as "objectively *modal* [modal *sachlich*], as opposed to absolutely objective [*schlechthin sachlichen*],"[77] Stein argues that this distinction is best conceived according to her distinction of "being-bearer" and "being-borne"—that is, between the bearer of the formal and material fullness, and the corresponding formal and material fullness borne. Since the empty-form of the individual bears the essential fullness as the final formal determination of its distinct and unified structure, the empty-form is not actually separable from the formal and material fullness it bears, even while it remains objectively distinct and notionally distinguishable from this formal and material fullness. Hence, while recognizing Gredt's Thomistic presentation of the distinct perfection of self-dependence, Stein argues that Gredt's identification of the distinction as modal parallels her distinction of bearer and borne, where self-dependence follows immediately upon the formal encompassing of the essential form by

---

Scotus's conception of individuation and our knowing of individuals. As noted above, given the focus of this study, excepting these brief outlines in footnotes, I refrain from further comparison of Stein and Scotus.

75   EES, 401; see also EES, 247–48. For this and following, compare the similar analysis of Betschart, *Unwiederholbares Gottessiegel*, esp. 287–89.

76   As noted above, this requires some qualification when dealing with pure forms, and indeed with the human soul, which as spiritual endures separation from the body in bodily death and the subsequent dissolution of the material remains of the body.

77   EES, 401–2. See the largely similar presentation of Finley, "The Problem of Individual Being," 107–20: 117–19.

the empty-form, which empty-form also already grounds the being-individual of the essence.[78]

Finally, what is the relation of the empty-form to the unity of the individual? The empty-form is that which provides the formal structure with the kind of unity I have described as primitive, a "unity or being one" that establishes the individual thing as something formally undivided in itself and distinct from all others. In this sense, the empty-form encompasses the structure as one whole with the kind of unity that makes of the complex a unity at the highest level of determination. This is important for Stein, because while Aquinas recognizes *ens* (being, as noun) and *res* (thing) among the transcendentals as positive conceptions, *unum* (one) is conceived by him only negatively as undividedness—since, as above mentioned, "to be one is to be indivisible"—at least in notion, even if not in being.[79] In contrast, Stein reasons that transcendental unity should be conceived as something notionally and ontologically positive.[80] Stein's rationale follows the ontological necessity that an undivided whole indicates the presence of some positive

---

78   See EES, 401; and also, EES, 247–48.
79   See above, 110–12. By her use of the empty-form "thing," Stein does not intend to identify *res* (thing) as it is understood in the Thomistic conception of the transcendentals, as notionally designating the *what* of actual being in contrast to *ens* (being) which notionally designates being precisely *as* being. Rather, thing is here understood as a denominator of the individual in a region of being that does not exhaust all being, since Stein also includes the essential kind of being of universals and essentialities in her comprehensive portrait of being. See EES, 245–47, esp. 245n16. With this interpretation, Stein also stands opposed to Gredt's interpretation of the "noun-participle" distinction contained in the phrase *ens ut ens* (being as being) mapping the distinction "what-is." See EES, 246–47.
80   Though this appears to be expressly opposed to Aquinas's position, there may actually be ground for accord here. Focusing on transcendental unity, Svoboda presents the weight of evidence that Aquinas conceived of unity as a negation or privation of division, but also argues that given his other metaphysical commitments—the relation of unity to the actuality of being, the degrees that are possible for unity, and the fact that substantial beings guard their unity—Aquinas must have understood unity as having positive ontological significance, i.e., as a positive perfection of being. This is supported by the manner in which Aquinas often explains the metaphysical reality of unity in terms of the deficiencies in the human mode of apprehending, since he argues that human beings comprehend simple things only via comprehension of compounded things, which compounded things are the proper objects of human cognition. See Svoboda, "The *Ratio* of Unity," 47–70: 69–70; and, for a sampling of Aquinas's later texts on unity, see ST, I, 10.1, ad 1; I, 11.1–4, esp. I, 11.2; and ST, I, 29.1, ad 3.

principle through which it is undivided, and the further logical necessity that negation follows upon, and indeed *must* follow upon affirmation.[81] Consequently, if the negative of *un*dividedness is to be fittingly grounded, Stein argues that the unity of the individual must be positive in being, and must also be conceived positively as being-one (*Eines-sein*). This kind of unity is had by the material individual, and it is this unity that grounds both the transcendental unity of the individual as a discrete and separate whole, and the numerical unity of the individual as a potential or actual member of a numerable plurality. Consequently, in disagreement with Aquinas, Stein concludes, "We should consider unity as a *form* that must find a determinate filling in every individual being, and indeed not only as a form of being [*Seiend*] but rather of *being* [Sein] to which unity belongs originally."[82] The unity of the individual is then evidently an original kind of unity, an ultimate ontological and logical principle of each substance, and is thus a unity that is *sui generis* and irreducible to another. Accordingly, again here, but now in higher resolution, we see why Stein's conception of unity coordinates her conception of the individual and decisively distinguishes her position from that of the standard Thomist presentation.[83]

Conclusion: The Formal Basis of the Material Individual

Through performing an objective investigation of the material individual within the hierarchically layered formation of the material cosmos, Stein mounts a systematic critique of the Thomistic conception of material individuation via designated matter upon the basis of Thomistic metaphysical principles. In light of this critique, she presents an independently developed understanding of the formal basis of the being-individual of the material individual in the individual

---

81 And so, for Stein, transcendental unity is possessed of *ens, res,* and *aliquid,* since "*ens* designates the being as a whole: 'that which *is* [*das, was* ist]' highlights being, '*res*' emphasizes the what [*das Was*], and *aliquid* the that [*das Das*]; '*unum*' is a formal property [*formale Eigenschaft*] belonging equally to the that [*zum Das*] (= object [*Gegenstand*]) as to the what [*zum Was*] and to being [*zum Sein*]." EES, 251.
82 EES, 250; see also EES, 245–46, 250–51.
83 One could perhaps also call this kind of unity "simple" inasmuch as the empty-form is itself noncomplex and provides the formal framing of a structure that it then renders relatively simple. However, given that the empty-form enters into composition with a complex formal structure that it frames and unifies, I choose primitive as preferable to simple.

essential-form, before finally proposing an original conception of the ultimate formal basis of being-individual in the empty-form "thing." In this way, Stein provides an ultimate explanation of the formal basis of the material individual that fulfills the criteria established by the *philosophia perennis* in general, and Thomism in particular—namely, that the individual be identifiable as τόδε τι, definable as something "in itself undivided yet divided from all else," and established in being as something incommunicable. This original conception evidently contradicts the received metaphysical tradition of Aquinas and Thomism, which accounts for material individuation via designated matter with its extension, exclusive position in place, and incommunicability.

Yet, I have suggested a number of avenues toward a partial rapprochement of Stein's position with that of Aquinas and the Thomistic tradition—namely: (1) by considering Stein's conception of the formal structure of being as akin to Aquinas's conception of the various formal notions or aspects of being, according to which all actual material individuals are conceived as formally complex with respect to intellectual acts of abstraction and conceptualization, and all corresponding predications; and (2) by considering the Thomistic conception of self-dependence as an objectively distinct positive perfection as akin to Stein's conception of self-dependence via the bearer, where all actual material individuals are understood to be definitively enclosed with the perfection of self-dependence by the empty-form "thing" before the reception of the actuality of being and perfection of existence. Yet, even should these avenues be granted, Stein's reversal of the individuating polarity of the transcendental relation, and her further grounding of being-individual in the empty-form "thing," represents a significant departure from the Thomistic conceptual schema and consequent contradiction of the standard Thomistic presentation of material individuation, a departure that bears intimate reference, I have argued, to Stein's opposed conception of the primitive "unity or being-one" of the individual.

Chapter Four

The Human Individual in Particular

> The being-individual of the human being—
> as every spiritual person—
> differs from the being-individual of all non-personal things.
>
> —*Edith Stein*[1]

> And when the Revelation of John says,
> "To him who conquers I will give [...] a white stone,
> upon which is written a new name which
> no one knows except him who receives it."
> Shouldn't that name be a proper name in the full sense
> of the word, a name that speaks forth the innermost
> essence of the recipient and unlocks for him the
> mystery of his being hidden in God.
>
> —*Edith Stein*[2]

Having in this way critiqued the standard Thomistic position on individuation and developed an independent understanding of the being-individual and qualitative individuality of the material individual in general, Stein proceeds to

---

1 EES, 420.
2 EES, 422–23, quoting Revelation 2:17.

investigate the human being in particular. In doing so, Stein continues to situate her investigation against the backdrop of the conceptual apparatus of Aquinas and the Thomistic tradition, and she uses this apparatus in the adjusted form detailed above while also introducing further significant conceptual features specific to personal being. These new features are resolutely grounded in Stein's phenomenological understanding of the human being as a personal subject, and her consequent recognition of the preeminent position of the personal I within the structure of human nature. In light of these phenomenological insights, cultivated via her Augustinian way of philosophizing, Stein develops an understanding of the human individual that locates his being-individual and qualitative individuality in the personally determined spiritual soul. In what follows, I detail these new conceptual features by first briefly considering the human individual as a material individual, thus showing the continuity of the human being with other material beings, before considering the human being as a spiritual person, where I show how Stein provides an insightful exposition of the inescapable givenness of the personal individual as such. I conclude this analysis by proceeding to examine her independently developed position with reference to the alternate position of Aquinas and Thomism within the broader context of the *philosophia perennis*.

The Human Being as a Material Individual

Stein says, "Thomism considers the human being a species of the genus 'living being' and makes no distinction between plants, animals, and human beings in the grounding of being-individual."[3] This equation of the being-individual of the human being with that of non-personal beings is a conclusion that Stein cannot accept, since she understands the essentially personal nature of the human being to be the decisive feature and finally determinative of the human individual as such. Yet, Stein also recognizes that the human being shares a certain kinship of nature with non-personal beings, whether they be material, organic, or animal, so that the being-individual and individuality of the human being ought not to be understood in isolation from that of such

---

3   EES, 419. See also, EES, 402–3, 417–21, esp. 420–21; and AMP, 40, 48–49, 93–95. For this and following, also see an earlier iteration in Robert McNamara, "Human Individuality in Stein's Mature Works," in *Edith Steins Herausforderung heutiger Anthropologie*, ed. Hanna-Barbara Gerl-Falkovitz and Mette Lebech (Heiligenkreuz: Be&Be, 2017), 124–39: 126–33.

non-personal beings. Indeed, when detailing the completed constitution of the human individual she continues to use the conceptual apparatus earlier developed, and in this way highlights the radical continuity of the human being with material beings in general. Ultimately this means that while Stein recognizes that the human individual shares a kind of being-individual with all material beings, as also a characteristic individuality that is determined by material factors, she simultaneously distances herself from the final resolution of human individuation to such material factors in isolation, to the Thomistic principle, *individuum de ratione materiae*.

First, with regard to the being-individual of the human being: Stein argues that the human individual has a specifically material, organic, and animal determination of being-individual. As material, the human individual is a spatially extended material shape that is "in itself enclosed, indivisible and incompatible with another shape."[4] As animated, the material structure is comprised of a living essential-form and incorporated matter, where the essential-form organizes the incorporated matter as a unified living-body of the human kind. As shown above, this essential-form has its own intrinsic structural complexity according to which the living-body is formed in a layered manner as organic, animal, and human: as organic, the living-body is organized as an articulated whole so that the completed structure permits of no natural conjoining or dismembering; as animal, the living-body has a higher degree of unity brought about by the sensitive organization of the organic body, both for the sake of the exterior-interior interchange of sensation, and for the sake of the local movement of the bodily whole in place, and the corresponding postural movement of bodily members; finally, as human, the living-body is further unified by the formal framing of the personally determined spiritual soul, a framing that elevates all lower levels of formation and arranges them as a tightly integrated personal unity, while also granting to the living-body a qualified simplicity of being via the simplicity of the personal I.[5]

From this brief overview it is clear that for Stein an intensification of being-individual occurs as the hierarchy of being is ascended, an intensification that is evident in the progression of unity wrought by each subsequent layer of formation: beginning with the material unity of continuous extension and shape, progressing to the animated unity of wholistic organization, progressing

---

4   AMP, 33. For the following, see AMP, 38, 44–73.
5   This distinctively personal kind of being an individual is treated in detail immediately below.

still further to a sensitive and motile kind of unity in place, before finally being completed by a spiritual and personal kind of unity. In tandem with this intensification of unity, there is also a corresponding intensification of incommunicability as the hierarchy is ascended: beginning with the incommunicability of matter, progressing to the incommunicability of organic and animal living-forms—that is, souls—before being finally completed in the incommunicability of the spiritual person as such.[6]

Then, with regard to the qualitative individuality of the human being: In correspondence to the above-detailed layered structure of bodily formation, Stein argues that the human individual has an individual distinctiveness shared with beings finally determined as material, organic, and animal.[7] As material, the human individual is co-determined by the elementary material constituents of the body, first through the genesis of the human individual in an already formed product of fertilization, then through the ongoing process of nutrition by which organic matter is incorporated into (and excreted from) the developing, growing, and healing structures of the living-body.[8] As animated, the living-body is conditioned by various features of the material environment within which life is situated and with which the individual responds interactively in all living operations, its geography, climate, nutritive resources, etc. The human body is then also a member of an ancestral series of common descent, receiving bodily distinctness from this ancestry through the branching of humanity into "races, peoples, tribes, lineages, [and] families."[9] This branched diversity into varying kinds Stein understands in a manner similar to that of other living kinds which are diversified into varieties among themselves, inasmuch as the common determination of the human species is variably expressed in each bodily individual through the inherent room for play of the form of the species. And since this free play also bears reference to the features of the material environment within which the transmission of bodily inheritance occurs, such formally determined material-environmental factors are significant for the

---

6 By my use of "intensification" here I mean to signify that these features of being—unity and incommunicability, and therefore being-individual—are rendered more profound in kind and degree as the hierarchy of being is ascended, becoming stricter and tighter at each subsequent level of the hierarchy up to and including the personal, where they attain their fully defined kind and degree.
7 See EES, 419–20, 428–29; and AMP, 19, 96–97, 111, 141–42.
8 One could also here include hydration and oxygenation.
9 EES, 420.

variable expression of the form in the individual. Finally, the living-body of the individual can come to bear the impression of the personally determined spiritual soul, a distinctively individual impression that would ideally elevate all lower levels of formation by their integration with all that is properly spiritual and personal.[10] It is clear, then, that an intensification of individual distinctness also occurs as the hierarchy of being is ascended, an intensification that is evident in the compounded manner that human distinctness is wrought by each subsequent layer of formation, before being united under the specifically spiritual and personal.

In just this way, Stein conceives of the human individual as sharing a kind of being-individual and qualitative individuality with all other kinds of material beings, whether material, organic, or animal, while also recognizing that the human being surpasses these other kinds, first through the intensification of unity and incommunicability as this hierarchy is ascended, then through the way the so unified and incommunicable human individual possesses qualitative distinctiveness in a layered manner. Yet it is also evident that Stein recognizes that the being-individual and individuality of the human being cannot be reduced to such common features in isolation, precisely since the human being transcends what is material and bodily in his structure. Thus, Stein reasons that the being-individual and individuality of the human individual outstrips the shared bases of being-individual and individuality in the natural world through what is properly spiritual and personal. To this important specificity we now turn.

The Personal "Being-Individual" of the Human Being

To develop a fully comprehensive understanding of the human individual as a spiritual person, Stein performs an involved phenomenological analysis of the human being from the perspective of personal subjectivity.[11] She begins with

---

10   This distinctively personal kind of qualitative individuality is treated in detail below ("The Personal 'Individuality' of the Human Being").
11   See EES, 413–22; compare PA, 85–86. Stein performs this investigation first as an abstract consideration of personal being in general before applying this analysis to the human being in particular. For this and following, compare the similar presentations of Christof Betschart, *Unwiederholbares Gottessiegel: Personale Individualität nach Edith Stein* (Basel: Reinhardt, 2013), 190–92; "The Individuality of the Human Person in the Phenomenological Works of Edith Stein," in *Edith Stein: Women,*

the cognitive *distinguishability* of the human being as it is given in conscious life, and from there discloses the actual *distinction* of the human being as a spiritual person. Beginning with the primordial givenness of the personal I, Stein reasons that the personal I is distinguishable for himself as an individual in all conscious experiences and spiritual stirrings. Through the natural reflexive transparency of intentional acts, the personal I discovers himself as the enduring subject of experience, something distinguishable from experience itself, from the intentional acts and contents of experience, and from every transcendent object of experience. Indeed, the personal I discovers himself to be the necessary condition of all conscious experience whatsoever, and, more importantly, to be the actual inner foundation of his own spiritual acts. The personal subject thereby discovers himself to be something absolutely *distinguishable* from everything that takes shape in experience, its acts and objects—simply the subject discovers himself to be an *I* and thereby comes to distinguish himself from *everything* else, from all else actual, and all else possible. The grammatical function of the "I" indicates the special character of this inward awareness, precisely inasmuch as the "I" is a reflexive pronoun that can be explained only from the perspective of first-person self-awareness: first, when the person inwardly experiences himself as a subject, that is, as the subject of his own conscious, intentional life; then, when the person consciously intends himself in a reflexive intention by which he takes himself as an object—both of which yield the self precisely as an *I*.[12]

As noted above, this inward awareness of the I is a cognitively rich experience, an experience that not only unveils the *distinguishability* of the

---

Social-Political Philosophy, Theology, Metaphysics and Public History (Cham: Springer, 2016), 73–86: 74–76; "Quid and Quale: Reflections on Possible Complementarity between Metaphysical and Phenomenological Approaches to Personal Individuality in *Potenz und Akt*," in *Intersubjectivity, Humanity, Being: Edith Stein's Phenomenology and Christian Philosophy*, ed. Mette Lebech and Haydn Gurmin (Bern: Peter Lang, 2015), 211–28: 214–16. Some of the following was presented at conferences where I received valuable questioning and feedback that informs the presentation below, and much of the following text can be found in an earlier version in the published proceedings of one of those conferences, the Hildebrand Project conference on Christian Personalism (2018). See Robert McNamara, "The Cognition of the Human Individual in the Mature Thought of Edith Stein," ed. Elisa Grimi in *Philosophical News: Dietrich von Hildebrand and Christian Personalism* 16 (2018): 131–43, esp. 137–42; and see also, "Human Individuality," 124–39: 133–39.

12 See above, 6n5.

I, but also reveals its actual *distinction*. Since the personal I lives his spiritual life in and through conscious experience, and since all spiritual stirring has an inherently self-referential, transparent character, the distinct kind of being of the I is manifest to the I himself in and through these same conscious experiences. Together with the cognitive distinguishability of the personal I via the reflexive transparency of spiritual life, the actual basis of the distinction of the personal I is concomitantly given in the corresponding transparency of spiritual life, so that the personal I is given for himself as actually distinct from everything else in these same experiences. This means that the personal I discovers himself to be something *essentially distinct in kind* and *actually distinct in mode*, precisely when he discovers himself to be *this-very-being-and-no-other*, and thereby comes to recognize his radical distinction from everything else. Thus, through the inherently self-referential nature of spiritual life together with its inherently transparent character, the personal I is disclosed for himself as some*one*, a being who stands in existence as an individual with consciousness entirely his own, radically distinct and distinguishable from all else personal and non personal alike, and inherently in possession of himself. Accordingly, Stein says, "Only a being that in his own being is inwardly aware of his being, and at the same time of his being-distinct from every other being, can call himself 'I.'"[13]

This "being-distinct" has three primary dimensions. First, in conscious experience, the I recognizes himself as a "τόδε τί," as this very conscious subject set apart in the world with his own being and action. As the pole of conscious

---

13 EES, 294. As noted above, although the I can be considered in abstraction from the personal structure as the pure I of Husserlian phenomenology, precisely as such an abstraction it has no independence in being and, consequently, no being-individual. Therefore, in the human being, it is not the abstractly considered pure I that is the ground of the being-individual of the individual but the personal I that bears the essential fullness of human nature. See Betschart, *Unwiederholbares Gottessiegel*, 233–34, 246–51, and esp. 287–89, 340; and *"Quid* and *Quale,"* 211–28: 214–17. For the relation of this conception of being-individual to the personal identity of the human subject in Stein, considered from both phenomenological and metaphysical perspectives, see Peter J. Schulz, "Toward the Subjectivity of the Human Person: Edith Stein's Contribution to the Theory of Identity," trans. Christina M. Gschwandtner, in *American Catholic Philosophical Quarterly* 8, no. 1 (2008): 161–76: esp. 169–76; and Angela Ales Bello, "Edmund Husserl and Edith Stein: The Question of the Human Subject," trans. Antonio Calcagno, *American Catholic Philosophical Quarterly* 82, no. 1 (2008): 143–59: 151–59.

experience, the I is given as possessing a "punctual" kind of being, the kind of being that is eminently undivided in itself—and, indeed, actually indivisible—while also being eminently distinct from all else, personal and non-personal alike. Finally, by wielding spiritual stirrings, the I discovers his spiritual being to be his own proper possession, a possession that is absolutely incommunicable to another, again, personal and non-personal alike.[14] Accordingly, through these three elementary givens of first-person experience, all mutually implicated, the actual *being-individual* of the personal I is disclosed for the conscious subject—in both kind, as personal, and in mode, as bearer. Moreover, this experience of the kind and mode of being an individual is indubitable, precisely since *being-this-individual* is given together with the indubitability of conscious experience. This means that the personal I is foundationally capable of distinguishing himself from any and all other things in an evidently infallible way, with the same infallibility as the indubitably given self. Indeed, no other individual of any kind is more present to the personal I than the personal I is to himself, since his recognition of himself as an individual is inseparable from the consciousness of all other individuals. One can then say that the experience of one's own being as individual—the experience, "I am me," or more simply, "I am," or more profoundly, "I am who I am"—is the most evident human experience, an experience that the human individual cannot sidestep, overcome, or deny.

Two somewhat lengthy quotations, one from *Potency and Act* and the other from *Finite and Eternal Being*, serve to forcefully illustrate what Stein means. In *Potency and Act*, she says,

> The I as such *is* individual, apart from the bond with a material body, and without consideration for the species that qualitatively distinguishes him from others. The being-separate from all others lies in his own being and is graspable for himself in being-conscious of himself,

---

14 Indeed, earlier Stein forthrightly affirms, "Every I is unique [*ein Einmaliges*]; he has something that he shares with no other being, something *"incommunicable* [*Unmitteilbar*]" (EES, 294), and she clarifies in parentheses that this incommunicable aspect of the individual is "the Thomistic interpretation of individuality." Similar to the above interpretation, Wallenfang says, "Subjectivity itself is non-transferable [...] human subjectivity reveals the impenetrable and unrepeatable *sui generis* character of each and every human soul." Donald Wallenfang, *Human and Divine Being: A Study on the Theological Anthropology of Edith Stein* (Eugene OR: Cascade Books, 2017), 163.

which is something unmistakably different from all consciousness of anything else: Only an I can call himself "I," and thus "have" himself so that he can say "I."[15]

Then, in *Finite and Eternal Being*, she writes,

That every person can distinguish [*Unterscheidung*] himself from every other person, whether they live at the self-same time or at another time, whether they are specifically alike or different, is grounded in the peculiarity of being-self-conscious [*Eigentümlichkeit des Selbst-Bewußtseins*], which belongs to the personal being-I [*persönlichen Ichsein*].[16]

Thus, Stein reasons that the personal I is given for himself as eminently individual, as one who can enunciate the personal pronoun "I" in an unequivocally singular way—notwithstanding the universality of its use by all personal individuals. Again here, the grammatical function of the "I" vividly illustrates the significance of this experience, since it is precisely in the unity of knower and known—all contained in the enunciation "I"—that the unmistakable identity of the human individual is given. Indeed, the compelling force of Stein's argument is found in the immediacy of first-person experience, where the personal I is given for himself as this very self, radically undivided in himself and distinct from all else, and absolutely incommunicable to another. Hence, through introspective reflection on primordial experience, Stein can resolutely conclude "that the being-individual of the human being—as every spiritual person—differs from the being-individual of all non-personal things."[17]

To complete her understanding, Stein proceeds to correlate this personal kind of being-individual with the already developed formal basis of being-individual in general. Assuming the empty-form "thing" as a universal formal basis of being-individual, Stein extends its conceptual content to include the personal structure by proposing that the role of the empty-form "thing" in material being in general is replaced by the empty-form "personal I" among

---

15 PA, 86.
16 EES, 415; emphasis added. See also Claudia Mariéle Wulf, "Ich," in *Edith Stein-Lexikon*, ed. Marcus Knaup and Harald Seubert (Freiburg i. Br.: Herder, 2017), 185–88, for the distinguishability and consequent self-identification of the I as an I.
17 EES, 420.

personal beings in particular.[18] The personal I is then taken to be the final formal determination of the structural whole of the personal nature, that which encompasses and frames the formal (and material) fullness of this nature as its ultimate formal determination. And since the personal I bears this entire formal (and material) structure as something radically undivided and absolutely incommunicable, the empty-formal unity and incommunicability of all personal individuals is traced back to the formal unity and incommunicability of the personal I. This replacement of the empty-form "thing" with "personal I" was earlier deduced from Stein's phenomenological disclosure of the radical priority of the personal within the structural whole of human nature and is here definitively justified by the unmistakable recognition of the evidential givenness of the being-individual of the personal I.

By so rooting the being-individual of spiritual persons in the personal I as empty-form, Stein not only retains the basic continuity of being-individual across all regions of being, but also highlights the eminent kind of being-individual of all personal kinds of being, precisely since, as indicated above, the unity and incommunicability of the personal individual is intensified in the unity and incommunicability of the I: First, since the unity of the personal I is "punctual," the primitive unity of the empty-form is intensified by the point-like character of the I—which intensified unity is communicated to the whole personal nature encompassed by the I. Then, since the incommunicability of the personal I is a spiritual kind of incommunicability, the incommunicability of the empty-form is also intensified by the rational and free character of the personal subject—an intensified incommunicability that is also communicated to the whole of the personal nature borne by the I.[19] In this way, Stein can conceive of the personal individual in a way analogous to that of all other kinds of material beings, and an analogous community of being-individual

---

18 See esp. EES, 320, 420. Compare Betschart, *Unwiederholbares Gottessiegel*, 246–51, 257–61; McNamara, "Human Individuality," 124–39: 136–37; and Urbano Ferrer, "Individuum/Individualität," in *Stein-Lexikon*, 195–98; and Wulf, "Ich," in *Stein-Lexikon*, 188. The analysis here concludes adjudication of the earlier problem introduced over the relative priority of the personal I in relation to the spiritual soul in the formal structure of human nature (see above, 58–62).

19 This intensification of being-individual can be understood to extend throughout the whole of spiritual soul and living-body, first actually and ontologically, according to the being and essential structure of the human being, then potentially and dynamically, through to the course of personal living, ideally leading to a fully integrated human individual whole.

is recognized for all kinds of individuals, while simultaneously stressing the personal way being-individual is possessed by spiritual persons.[20]

An interesting corollary of Stein's proposal as it is developed from the perspective of consciousness is that the personal individual can be understood from two distinct but closely related perspectives, that of the personal *kind* of being-individual, an essential or ontological way of being-individual, and that of the personal *mode* of being-individual, an actual or real way of being-individual.[21] *With regard to the personal kind of being-individual*: Considering the nature of personal being, the personal I as empty-form grounds the being-individual of the person by encompassing the entire formal and material fullness of the personal nature, setting the individual apart as a formally unified and incommunicable whole through a personal kind of being-individual. This *ontological* way of being-individual has its basis in the distinction and corresponding distinguishability of the formality of the personal I as empty-form. *With regard to the personal mode of being-individual*: Considering the being of personal being, the personal I with the actuality of being stands in existence as someone from whom consciousness and spiritual life radiate, setting this individual apart as a distinct and incommunicable whole according to a personal mode of being-individual.[22] This *actual* way of being-individual has its basis in the distinction and corresponding distinguishability of the actuality of the personal I as an existent spiritual reality. Evidently then, the personal mode of being-individual is ontologically determined by the personal kind of being-individual, and conversely, the personal kind of being-individual is actually

---

20 Beyond the differences here indicated in the contrasted intensities of unity and incommunicability, the kinds of empty-form are primarily diversified though the different kinds of formal and material filling possible for each, which at a foundational level would be differentiated into rational versus nonrational contents.

21 This kind and mode of being-individual directly relates to the above-mentioned personal kind and mode of bearing of the personal I, where the personal I is understood both to bear the personal essence with an essential kind of bearing, and to bear the personal actuality of being with an actual mode of bearing, a mode of bearing that directly refers to the actuality of being (*Sein, esse*). See above, 36–39.

22 See esp. EES, 294. Ferrer notes, "Without the self-dependence of a singular essence [*singulären Wesens*] there would be no self-consciousness." Ferrer, "Individuum/Individualität," in *Stein-Lexikon*, 195. In contrast to Ferrer, I here focus not so much on self-dependence but on the actuality of being, since according to my reading of Stein (and Aquinas) a self-dependent human essence does not yet constitute an actual personal I.

disclosed in and through the personal mode of being an individual. These are two distinct but inseparable perspectives on the being-individual of the personal subject—one focused on essence, the other on being—where the ontological kind of being-individual conditions the actual mode of being-individual, and the actual mode of being-individual existentially announces the ontological kind of being-individual.[23]

From this we can see that Stein's proposal regarding the human individual can be understood as a phenomenological resolution of a metaphysical problem she detects in the thought of Aquinas and Thomism, that of accounting for human individuation via the material principle. Moreover, this phenomenological resolution is brought about by turning to consciousness itself, and the consequent cognitive distinguishability of the personal I as it is disclosed in first-person inner awareness according to an Augustinian way of proceeding. This datum of personal experience is given together with the self-evidence of one's own being in the unmistakable "I am" of first-person inner awareness, such that the personal individual is given for himself as some*one* in an evidently infallible way. Indeed, the compelling force of Stein's proposal is found in the experience of *the actual self*, in being someone who is always already given for himself as this very individual, *as* himself and *in* himself (even if not *from* himself).[24]

---

23 Borden Sharkey worries that Stein's focus on essential being results in downplaying the importance of actual being. Though this worry is to some degree warranted by the absence of a thematized analysis of being (*"esse"* in Aquinas) or the act of being (*"actus essendi"* in Aquinas) in Stein's investigation of being-individual, or indeed in her metaphysical investigations more broadly, I would argue that Stein's delineation of essential being actually assists and enhances her understanding of the significance of actual being and its placement in her fully developed conceptual framework, as it is presented in EES, precisely inasmuch as she comes to recognize that only certain self-dependent essences have received an act of being and thereby possess the actuality of existence. Indeed, as becomes clear in part III below, Stein follows Aquinas in recognizing that the primary composition of finite being rests on the real distinction of essence (*Wesen, essentia*) and being (*Sein, esse*) in every actual finite being (*Seiend, ens*). See Sarah Borden Sharkey, *Thine Own Self: Individuality in Edith Stein's Later Writings* (Washington, DC: The Catholic University of America Press, 2010), 223. Bénédicte Bouillot similarly claims that Stein does not sufficiently engage with Aquinas's understanding of the *actus essendi* in terms of assessing his understanding of individuation. See Bénédicte Bouillot, *"Materia signata quantitate,"* in *Stein-Lexikon*, 239–40.

24 Evidently then, being incommunicable in this context means ontologically

The Personal "Individuality" of the Human Being

Notwithstanding this manner of distinguishing personal individuals, Stein recognizes that such first-person experience cannot disclose the distinguishability required to differentiate *other* spiritual persons.[25] Since the distinction and distinguishability here manifest is grounded in the experience of the personal self, this mode of cognizing the individual is exclusive to the personal I as a private experience. And while Stein grants such cognitive distinguishability to all personal Is, so that the actual distinction of every personal I is factually secured, she acknowledges that this cannot be a basis for distinguishing other personal Is from one another. And though she further grants that the *human* personal I is distinct and distinguishable via the living-body, since the personal I is also a bodily I, she reasons that this manner of distinguishing human individuals cannot be the ultimate ground of their differentiation.[26] Rather, in accord with her understanding of the intensification of qualitative distinctiveness as the hierarchy of being is ascended, Stein argues that the ultimate basis of distinguishability among spiritual persons must be found in the personally determined spiritual structure, and not in the above-detailed compounded distinctness of the material, organic, and animal layerings manifest in the living-body. And since this basis cannot be found on the side of the empty-formality of the personal I, inasmuch as the personal I is a universal form of personal life common to all persons, Stein reasons that it must be sought on the side of some qualitative determination of the spiritual structure. Such difference in qualitative content would then render the factual plurality of human personal Is—already interiorly distinguishable from a first-person experience, and exteriorly distinguishable

---

incommunicable rather than morally incommunicable, given that the moral communication of personal being is possible through voluntary personal self-gift (in marriage and consecrated life). And indeed, such moral communicability rests on the foundation of ontological incommunicability as its necessary foundation—i.e., personal self-gift is simply not possible with personal self-possession. For Stein on personal self-giving, see esp. EES, 382–91; and for Karol Wojtyła's comparable (even more insightful) presentation of the same, see Wojtyła, *Love and Responsibility*, trans. Grzegorz Ignatik (Boston, MA: Pauline Books and Media, 2013), 78–83, 278–85.

25 See EES, 415; compare PA, 86; and see also Betschart, *Unwiederholbares Gottessiegel*, 281–83.
26 It should be remembered that Stein first performs an analysis of the personal spirit in abstraction, and so also includes the personal being of pure spirits, before developing its applicability to the human being as a personal spirit.

via the materially extended living-body—also *spiritually* distinguishable from a second-person perspective.

To disclose the basis of this qualitative individuality, Stein again appeals to what is immediately given in conscious experience from a first-person perspective. However, this recourse to subjective experience is employed only to initially identify the spiritual basis of the qualitative distinction of persons, and as soon as this basis is clearly identified she immediately expands her reasoning to include the second person distinguishability of the spiritual person as such.[27] Stein says, "The innermost of the soul, what is most spiritual and most properly its own, is not colorless and shapeless, but rather has a peculiar characteristic: [the soul] feels this characteristic when it is 'with itself,' [when it is] 'recollected within itself.'"[28] Beginning with an inward awareness of one's own being and life, Stein reasons that the personal individual experiences himself to be in possession of a peculiar characteristic that determines the depth of his spiritual soul.[29] Stein identifies the act by which one accesses this characteristic as a "feeling [*spüren*]" and maintains that "this feeling bears its own warrant within itself as a special mode of original experience."[30] This feeling-act is a singular mode of conscious experience, something originary in the experiential life of the person, not founded on or reducible to any other kind of experience. To more clearly delineate the nature of this feeling, Stein describes it as a "spiritual perceiving [*geistiges Wahrnehmen*]," thus noting its intentional character, and further indicates this intentionality by affirming

---

27 For this and following, compare the detailed presentation of Betschart, *Unwiederholbares Gottessiegel*, 194–95, 230, 251–57, 280–83; "Individuality of the Human Person," 73–86: 74–76; "*Quid* and *Quale*," 211–28: 218–19, 224–25. See also Alfieri, "The Question of Individuality," 113–16; and Ferrer, "Individuum/Individualität," in *Stein-Lexikon*, 195–98.

28 EES, 420; compare PA, 118–19. Though Stein uses feminine pronouns when speaking of the soul, this is presumably because *seele* is grammatically feminine in German. I follow my typical use of neuter pronouns when speaking of the soul as *part* of human nature.

29 By her use of peculiar (*eigentümlich*), Stein does not intend to indicate that the characteristic is something strange or unusual in contrast to the normal and usual, but rather that it is exceptional and rare in contrast to the general and common. Maskulak similarly notes that peculiar identifies "something particular or singular." Marian Maskulak, *Edith Stein and the Body-Soul-Spirit at the Center of Holistic Formation* (New York: Peter Lang, 2007), 74.

30 EES, 421.

that it provides content for cognition, content that has "its own value for knowledge."³¹ Yet, she also maintains that this content "does not have the clarity and distinctness of a conceptually graspable insight of understanding," with the consequence that it cannot be identified with a name—at least insofar as human naming typically possesses universality of reference.³²

Evidently then, by her use of feeling, Stein does not intend to identify an affective state of the subject, and neither does she intend to relegate this experience to the realm of the exclusively subjective. Rather, she uses the term feeling only because the experience is what she describes as a "perceiving with the heart [*Wahrnehmen mit dem Herzen*]," which does not render a fully clarified object for cognition and allow for conceptual formulation and language-based communication.³³ To identify the peculiar characteristic so disclosed Stein uses both the Latin "*quale*" and the Greek "ποῖον," and she describes this characteristic as "the '*how* [Wie]' of the essence itself."³⁴ These identifiers mean that the characteristic should not be understood as an integral part of the structural determination of the essence, but rather as identifying something that *qualifies* the structure of the essence. To further illustrate its character and clarify its status as qualitative, Stein employs the metaphor of color by explaining that the *quale* or ποῖον "colors" the innermost structure of the personal spirit, and thus renders the individual qualitatively distinctive from the very depth of his being. This peculiar characteristic is then a simple determination of the person as such, something that colors the inner depth and ideally illumines the entirety of the personality with its peculiar hue.³⁵

---

31 EES, 421. For a summary exposition of Stein's understanding of the various kinds of affective experience, and the intentional content of certain kinds of affections, see Íngrid Vendrell Ferran, "Intentionality, Value Disclosure, and Constitution: Stein's Model," in *Empathy, Sociality, and Personhood: Essays on Edith Stein's Phenomenological Investigations*, ed. Elisa Magrì and Dermot Moran (Cham: Springer, 2017), 65–85: 71–6.
32 EES, 421. See also, EES, 420, 423.
33 EES, 421.
34 EES, 420, emphasis added; see also, PA, 256; and AMP, 87, 96. Again here we see why the conscious I cannot simply be identified with the qualityless pure I of Husserlian phenomenology, but rather must be identified with a spiritual being that is qualitatively determined in the very depth of the spirit. See McNamara, "Human Individuality," 124–39: 137–8.
35 Stein's use of the metaphor of color in this context is illustrative of the metaphysical nature of the personal quality, both in terms of its qualitative character, and in terms

In tandem with the personal quality, Stein also recognizes two further bases for the spiritual distinction of the person by considering the "openness" and "power" of the soul.[36] Under openness, Stein includes all that determines the earlier outlined "expanse" of the soul, its width, breadth, and depth, together with its structure as an interior castle "with many dwellings."[37] She identifies this aspect as *openness* only and precisely because its structure requires "nourishment" from the world if it is to unfold its already given determinate character, by receiving from the world that which becomes "its most personal property, an integral part of its very self [...] 'its flesh and blood.'"[38] Closely correlated with openness is the soul's power, a finite reserve that empowers the soul's receptive engagement with the world, which Stein reasons has a peculiar measure that determines the way the individual engages the world. Indeed, its measure foundationally conditions the spiritual life of the individual even

---

of its ability to manifest something for cognition. With regard to the first, colors are frequently understood as the paradigmatic kind of quality, ontologically and experientially irreducible to any other genera of being, something that can be indicated only by the pointing finger and perceived only by the power of sight. No amount of explanation or argumentation will "give" the experience of color if such an experience is not had with direct immediacy, only the simple seeing of this or that actual hue as it lies before the naked eye provides the experience of color, and a particular hue. With regard to the second, it should be noted that colors obviously manifest colored things, making them visible and thus revealing their existence and more acutely than the other senses their nature, without at all being constitutive of the structure of these things—thus, colors *show without structuring*. As will become clear in what follows, these two features of color make it a fitting metaphor for the personal quality, something irreducible and ineffable as an individual quality, and something with an exceptional potential to manifest the personal individual as such.

36 See esp. PA, 255–63; and compare AMP, 32, 80, 83–92. Though this aspect of individuality includes the sensitive dimension of the soul, for the sake of simplicity and clarity, I restrict my analysis to the spiritual dimension.

37 See above, 58–62, citing EES, 317–18.

38 EES, 317–18. One can understand this inward development of the spiritual soul according to the analogy of the living-body, where the meaningful contents of the world are received into the interior expanse of the soul and thereby become that through which the soul matures into its own already given structure, what Stein calls "its own peculiar life [*eigentümliche Leben*]." This aspect of human individuality, as something at least partially wrought through the openness of the soul in its capacity to receive shaping via experience, obviously includes the distinctness of the stream of experience and its individuating role in personal life, even while it certainly does not reduce human individuality to this purely experiential mode of distinction.

while it also admits of degrees of variation, being consumed and replenished throughout living engagement, and empowering the unfolding of the soul into its already given expansive structure. Thus, we see that each person is not only evidently individual in being through the ontological distinction of the personal I, but is also manifestly different from all other persons through the peculiar distinctness of his personal spirit, via the peculiarity of the personal quality, the openness of the soul, and the soul's power. However, though Stein grants to the spiritual soul these three dimensions of individuality, she definitively grounds the latter two—openness and power—in the personal quality. Even while "the full extent" of the individuality of the person includes the "*quale*, openness, and power" as distinct but inseparable determinations of the spiritual soul, "each *quale* will have its own specific openness and power."[39] Though Stein does not reduce individuality to the personal quality in isolation, she does argue that the *quale* is that which finally secures the qualitative distinctness of the individual as a personal spirit. Accordingly, Stein concludes that the personal individual is not only *spiritually* distinguishable from a first-person perspective, as is the case with the being-individual of the personal I, but is also spiritually distinguishable from a second-person perspective via the peculiar *quale* or ποῖον—taken together with the openness and power of the soul, in addition to the manifold material differentiations of the living-body.

And yet, since the *quale* only qualifies, but does alter the structural determination of the human essence, and since the openness and power of the soul are common features of all human individuals, even if quantitively variable, the common humanity of the multiplicity of differently qualified human individuals remains intact, and all individuals bearing their own peculiar qualities remain equal members of the one human species.

Thus, Stein argues for a complex array of distinguishing features determining the individuality of the human person. And while human individuality is fully determined by these features taken together, it is the personal quality that provides the ultimate ontological basis for the qualitative distinction and distinguishability of human beings. This is possible, for Stein, not only because the personal quality peculiarly determines the spiritual dimension of the soul, but also because the whole of the human individual

---

39 PA, 262. Notwithstanding the significance of these two further grounds of individual distinctiveness, I focus my analysis here on the decisive core of human distinctiveness in the *quale*. For further details on these dimensions, see Betschart, *Unwiederholbares Gottessiegel*, 176–83, 193–98; and "*Quid* and *Quale*," 211–28: 223–24.

is in potency to being colored by its peculiar hue. In all the ways that the spiritual depth of the person becomes manifest in personal expression and activity, the personal quality radiates outward throughout the layered structure of human nature, impacting the living behavior and character development of the individual. Unfolding outward in this way the personal quality begins to leave an enduring impress on the whole of the human structure, beginning with the interior expanse of the soul, and gradually moving outward through all dimensions of this structure, including the living-body. Thus, Stein reasons, the personal quality is apt "to impress its seal on every character trait of the human being and on all behavior, and is the *key* to building the structure of his character"—even to the point of becoming available for second-person perception via the living-body.[40] However, though mediated by the materiality of the living-body in this way, Stein argues that second-person perception of the *quale* is still a spiritual mode of perception, a perceiving of the personal spirit that takes place in the above mentioned "perceiving with the heart"—but now of the human other. Consequently, Stein maintains that every genuine "living encounter" involves "a more or less profound inner confrontation," which potentially includes the apprehension of one another's "*proper individual character* [individueller Eigenart]."[41]

Finally, beyond this manifold of distinguishing features, both bodily and spiritual, which serve to differentiate human individuals, both singularly and through their compounded intersection in the structural whole, Stein argues that the personal individual has the potential to directly influence his own developing individuality.[42] This self-shaping is already seen in the way the structure of the soul unfolds by receiving meaningful nourishment from the world, expanding or contracting in width, breadth, depth, enlarging or depleting its peculiar reserve of life-power, and providing developmental materials for its many dwellings. Such personal determination is seen analogously in the way

---

40 EES, 420; emphasis added; see also, EES, 420–25; and AMP, 21, 31, 96, 99. The personal quality can then also be expressed in an objective form detached from the individual subject in creative works, and it can thus endure with an objective form of existence independent of the actual individual; moreover, it can be approximated in varying degrees by the skilled biographer who captures an individual subject's peculiar gestalt. In both ways, the individuality of the human being becomes available, to a limited degree, to a third-person perspective.
41 AMP, 31.
42 See EES, 422ff.; and AMP, 32, 80, 83–92.

the structure of the living-body develops by engaging with the material world, according to which the already determined living-body is conditioned in its developmental unfolding and eventually comes to assume its characteristic figure. And while both of these determinations, spiritual and bodily, are foundationally conditioned by the environment within which the individual is alive and active, it is the individual's own free activity and freely determined receptivity that decisively controls how he unfolds within this environment, both spiritually and bodily. This personal shaping includes the already mentioned radiation outward of the personal quality, yet here to an even greater degree than with the other dimensions of individuality, the free cooperation of the individual is required to effect its unfolding. Indeed, Stein argues that the human individual *must* learn to live from the inner depth of his personal spirit with personal authenticity if the personal quality is to illumine the structure of the individual, and if the being and life of the individual is to take shape in a way that accords with this most personal possession.[43]

In just this way, Stein envisages the personal individual to have a profound influence on the way his already ontologically determined individuality takes shape in the completed structure of his being as he gradually matures through the course of time, a rational and free influence that decisively conditions his qualitative individuality on all levels, both spiritual and bodily. Yet, for Stein this free determination also bears close reference to the manifold of already given ontological determinations of human nature, so that even this free-willed conditioning of individuality is discovered to be grounded in an already given spiritual and bodily structure, as well as an already given material, social, and cultural environment. While decisively depending on the rational freedom of the individual, together with his choices and decisions, it receives a high degree of determination from the particular environment within which he lives, with its peculiar material, social, and cultural characteristics. From this we can see that the proper development of individuality rests on the interaction of freedom and environment, where both play intermeshing roles in the expression of individuality. Such free determination should then be understood as a *cooperative* kind of activity, according to which the unfolding of the ontological givens of one's own nature requires the free collaborative engagement of the self. And since the personal quality serves to distinguish the human individual in a primary way, while all other bases are structurally subordinate to the personal

---

43 See esp. EES, 422–23.

quality, such collaboration must respect this dimension of human individuality with priority, first according to its structured unity with the openness and power of the soul, then according to its hylomorphic unity with the genetic and material composition of the living-body, all of which can be appropriately mediated only by living from the depth of the spiritual soul. That is to say that in a life lived in a properly personal way, the compounded features of human individuality all come to bear the peculiar "hue" of the personal spirit in a fulsome historically conditioned realization of human individuality.[44]

Given this high understanding of individuality, does Stein thereby maintain that the human individual is unique? The above-detailed collage of individualizing features—at the level of the spirit: quality, openness, and power; at the level of the body: genetic inheritance, material composition, and material impact—certainly renders each human individual qualitatively distinctive, especially when these features are taken in their compounded intersection. Yet, while most of these bases of distinction—openness and power; genetic and material constitution and shaping—could in principle be replicated in a number of human individuals, Stein reasons that each human individual is absolutely unique via the uniqueness of the personal quality. Reflecting on the notional possibility of a *Doppelgänger*, and the natural aversion to such a thought being realized, Stein argues that "everyone feels himself in his innermost essence as something 'singular [*Eigenes*].'"[45] Considering what might be the source of such singularity, Stein rules out features related to the particular spiritual and material structure of the individual, as well as features related to his peculiar history and developmental unfolding, and she argues that the ultimate difference securing human uniqueness is found in the personal quality itself. Though she does not see any essential necessity for such uniqueness in an absolute sense, one that is available for rational elucidation and/or demonstration, and though she grants that the personal quality could in principle be communicated to many individuals, she nonetheless maintains that the personal quality is *factually* unique and the proper possession of the individual as such—a singular feature that gives the human individual his own proper "uniqueness [*Einzigartigkeit*]."[46] Hence, the personal quality can be understood as a second basis of the incommunicability of the individual, and it is awareness of *this* basis that grounds the natural aversion to a human

---

44   See esp. PA, 262–63.
45   EES, 421; compare PA, 262; and AMP, 48.
46   EES, 422–23; see also AMP, 22, 31.

Doppelgänger, precisely inasmuch as any duplication of the personal quality would mean the repetition of that which is the most personal possession of the individual. Moreover, she reasons that this uniqueness is apt to be perceived *in* other human beings and *by* other human beings in all genuinely personal encounters, so that not only does every human person feel himself to be unique in inner experience, but so too do "all those who have *actually* 'apprehended' him."[47]

But what is the basis of such factual uniqueness? Stein proposes that the personal quality (together with the openness and power of the soul) is bestowed directly by God and is something unique by divine intent.[48] She reasons that such uniqueness is a "special personal gift of God" which "represents the highest nobility of the human being" and establishes each individual in a unique relation to God as a singular reflection of the divine essence.[49] As a consequence of this divine grounding, Borden Sharkey maintains that the uniqueness of the human being is only extrinsically secured by divine choice rather than intrinsically by ontological necessity, so that the individual is not unique in the strong sense of ontologically unrepeatable but only in the weak sense of factually unrepeated.[50] At first sight, Borden Sharkey's assessment appears to be reconcilable with the text of Stein, both because Stein regards human uniqueness to be rationally indemonstrable, and because she grounds human uniqueness in the choice of God rather than in any ontologically unrepeatable characteristic. Yet, I suggest that Stein holds to a strong sense of human uniqueness, even if not by ontological necessity, both because of the *way* the personal quality is experienced by the person, and because of the *fittingness* that such a quality would remain unrepeated. With regard to the first, Stein claims that perception of the personal quality includes the datum of its uniqueness, since perception not only renders the quality *qua* quality, but also renders its qualitative content to be something

---

47 EES, 421; emphasis added. Indeed, for Stein, it is awareness of this incommunicable uniqueness of the human other that opens the privileged space for personal interactions of particular fullness, grounding such personal relations in the particular distinctiveness of individual *relata* who know (and love) one another's uniqueness.

48 See PA, 261–62; AMP, 31, 157; and EES, 422–23. In PA, Stein locates human uniqueness in the "*quale*, openness, and power" taken together as one compounded whole, while indicating that the uniqueness of the whole can reduce to one unique part; in EES, Stein largely abandons openness and power when considering human uniqueness and finally grounds uniqueness in the *quale* or ποῖον itself.

49 PA, 262.

50 See Borden Sharkey, *Thine Own Self*, 124–25.

singular. Indeed, Stein maintains that perception of this content as "one-off [*Einmalig*]" is included in the "warrant [*Rechtsgrund*]" of its perception.[51] But does this not contradict the ontological possibility that the personal quality would be repeated, something granted by Stein as a notional possibility when she says that "'communication' of such a proper character to a plurality of personal bearers is not completely inconceivable"?[52]

If Stein is not here contradicting herself, must we not conclude that perception of the personal quality includes awareness that it *ought* not be repeated? Otherwise stated, does not experience of the uniqueness of the human individual—of oneself and the known other—reveal that repetition of this particular quality would be unfitting or unseemly for the person, that it would in some strong sense be "out of place" in the world of persons? I suggest that this is precisely what is implied in the aversion to a *Doppelgänger*—either with respect to oneself or with respect to a truly known and loved other—since the presence of such a personal double would in some way "offend" the meaning of being a personal individual with personal individuality.

And so, I submit that the rational indemonstrability of human uniqueness is due to the kind of thing that personal uniqueness is rather than any "weakness" in its qualitative content, and that this represents a strength of personal uniqueness—a strength that is verified in every properly personal encounter. This reasoning is supported by how Stein understands the singularity of one's personal relation to the personal God, a singularity that is ontologically grounded by the uniqueness of the personal quality. Since she views the uniqueness of each individual to be a "special personal gift" that embodies "the highest nobility" of the human individual, the qualitative singularity of the human person flows directly from the will of God for the personal order of personal creatures, rather than following upon some pre-given ontological or logical necessity, or indeed upon the mere factuality of divine choice. That is to say that no ontological, logical, or notional necessity binds the hand of God in bestowing personal uniqueness. Rather, the unrepeatability of the personal individual comes forth from divine gratuity and abundance, the kind of gratuity that foundationally shapes the order of personal beings, including the relations among finite persons themselves, and between finite persons and their Creator. So considered, the divine choice that establishes the personal

---

51 EES, 421.
52 EES, 424.

quality has deep roots in the will of God for the order of personal creatures, in their relation to God, and in the corresponding status of each individual within the created order—where every individual is understood to represent *one* peculiar hue of the refracted fullness of divine white light.[53] In *The Structure of the Human Person*, Stein beautifully summarizes this divine source of the human individual—both with respect to his being an individual, and with respect to his individuality—when she says,

> The proper character [*Eigenart*] of the singular [human being], individuality in the strongest sense of the word, is that which is proper to the singular soul, and which, like the soul itself, originated from nowhere other than immediately from the Creator of all being [...] What the human being is, his deepest and most proper [*Eigenste*], he owes to God alone [...] There is in every human being a sphere that is free from earthly binding, which does not originate from other human beings and is not determined by other human beings. Here he stands alone before God. This is the innermost depth of the soul, the absolutely individual and free I, the personal.[54]

Thus, in freedom before God—in being oneself before the face of God—the meaning of human uniqueness is given.

---

[53] I note here that Stein's understanding of the human individual has parallels in the thought of Wojtyła and von Hildebrand, both of whom emphasize the significance of the human individual and human individuality for personal relationships and ethical interactions, though Wojtyła typically focuses on the unrepeatable human individual in the uniqueness of their being, while von Hildebrand typically focuses on the qualitative distinctiveness of the human individual as a unique whole. See esp. Wojtyła, *Love and Responsibility*, 67–71; and Dietrich von Hildebrand, *The Nature of Love*, trans. John F. Crosby (South Bend, IN: St. Augustine Press, 2009), 22–23, 72–76. As can be seen here, Stein then goes beyond both Wojtyła and von Hildebrand in different ways by providing an ultimate ontological basis for both the being-individual and the qualitative individuality of the individual in the personal I and personal quality, respectively. In a beautiful *Urbi et orbi* address shortly after his elevation to the papacy, Pope St. John Paul II puts the truth of the human individual in a way that highlights his philosophical insights and resonates deeply with Stein's presentation, "For God and before God, the human being is always unique and unrepeatable, somebody thought of and chosen from eternity, some called and identified by his own name." See Pope St. John Paul II, *Urbi et orbi*, Christmas 1978.

[54] AMP, 157.

This understanding of the unrepeatable character of human uniqueness casts further light on the nature of the "feeling" that renders the personal quality for cognition. As mentioned above, cognition of the personal quality does not provide a fully clarified object that permits conceptual formulation and enunciation with a humanely meaningful name. Since it has the property of being unique—that is, of being "one-off"—no concept with a universality of reference can be ascribed to the individual quality, precisely inasmuch as it cannot be meaningfully defined or described, and nor can it be meaningfully communicated in human language. Rather, the meaning of the personal quality can only be pointed to and unveiled in a *direct* and *immediate* personal encounter with the personal self or with the personal other. This makes the personal quality something properly ineffable for the human being, something that cannot be enunciated but rather only "felt" or "perceived" in some or other personal encounter.[55] Interestingly, because of this characteristic, and the above-detailed source of this quality in the choice of God to "refract" his image in a plurality of different personal creatures, Betschart suggests that such ineffability could lead to an apophatic anthropology with analogical likeness to the apophatic theology of the Christian tradition.[56] It is then not at all surprising that Stein reasons that the personal quality is brought to cognition only in and through something like an intuitive perception of an affective kind—a "feeling" or "perceiving with the heart." Only such an experience would, or indeed could provide evidence for the existence and nature of such a characteristic of human individuality. That is, in a manner not unlike one's perception of an individual hue of light, where the color is given only in immediate intuitive presence, perception of the personal quality is a mode of knowing that is always grounded in and needful of a face-to-face encounter, an encounter that one returns to—or at least wishes to return to—again and again. In brief, it is a *sui generis* cognitive act that is irreducible to any other mode of knowing; it is through and through a personal act.

---

55 However, though not humanly nameable (inasmuch as human naming has generality of reference), basing her reasoning in Christian Revelation (citing Psalm 32:15, and Revelation 2:17), Stein maintains that personal individuality is nameable for God. Thus, she argues that the human individual has a proper name (*Eigenname*), a name that surpasses human language and is known only to God, a name "that enunciates the innermost essence of the recipient and unlocks for him the mystery of his being hidden in God." EES, 423.

56 See Betschart, "Individuality of the Human Person," 73–86: 84.

Assessing Stein's Original Conception of the Personal Individual

It is immediately evident that Stein's conception of the human individual stands in marked contrast to and even in contradiction of the standard Thomistic presentation of the human being as an individual, and at first sight it would appear that there is no possible reconciliation between their divergent conclusions regarding the individual. However, I suggest that there are subtleties in Aquinas's presentation of human individuation that open avenues toward a degree of partial alignment with Stein, an alignment that leaves their initially divergent positions less squarely opposed. We find these subtleties when attending first to Aquinas's understanding of the special kind of individuation of the human form, and when also considering his broader metaphysics of the person, personhood, and personal life. Examining Aquinas's writings in these closely related areas reveals that his position on human individuation involves qualifications beyond those of material being in general, qualifications that indicate that his position regarding human individuals cannot simply be equated with that of sub-personal beings.[57]

This is seen initially in his understanding of the ontological priority of the rational soul in the structure of human nature, where his conception of the material composite receiving being via the substantial form, true of all kinds of material individuals, has deeper significance when considering the human soul as substantial form. As already noted, Aquinas maintains that "the soul communicates that being in which it subsists to the corporeal matter, from which [matter] and the intellectual soul there results a unity, so that the being of the whole composite is yet the being of his soul"; and he concludes this insight by arguing, "Because of this *the human soul retains its own being* after the destruction of the body," which is in no way true of merely material forms.[58] Thus, he argues that the human soul has its own act of being through which it subsists as an immaterial form. This act of being is proper to the intellectual

---

57   Facilitating the possibility of such alignment of positions, I prescind from introducing the conceptual apparatus of empty-form, formal structure, and formal framework in what follows. This is made possible because Stein's proposition of a personal kind and mode of being-individual through the personal I need not be explained by employing these related conceptual apparatuses since they do not necessarily depend upon them, even while Stein finds them to be the most fitting conceptual toolkit.

58   See above, 45n7, citing ST, I, 76.1, ad 5; emphasis added.

soul, even while it is communicated to the body through its formation of the body, which means that the human soul, precisely as spiritual, has a certain degree of independence from the body.[59] Consequently, in contradistinction to other kinds of material beings, the existence of the human individual does not ultimately depend upon the materiality of the body, but rather resides in the self-subsistence of the spiritual soul as an immaterial form—with the result that Aquinas concludes that the human individual is capable of existence in separation from the matter of the body. This conception of the enduring being of the individual soul is closely related to his understanding of the divine origin of the human soul. Unlike the souls of other living beings, which he says "are produced by some power of the body," Aquinas argues that the human soul requires an immediate creative act and is therefore directly "produced by God."[60] God is the immediate causal source of the spiritual for Aquinas, and the spiritual being created directly by God lives on as a self-subsisting form in separation from the body upon bodily death and the dissolution of its material constituents.[61]

---

59 For Aquinas, the human soul's enduring being as an individual is consequent upon the rational nature of the soul. Since being is proper to and naturally inseparable from any spiritual or immaterial form, once such a form has received the actuality of being it is naturally apt to persist unendingly. See ST, I, 75.6, co.; and also Joseph Owens, "Aquinas on the Inseparability of Soul from Existence," in *The New Scholasticism* 61, no. 3 (1987): 249–70: 262; Christopher Conn, "Aquinas on Human Nature and the Possibility of Bodiless Existence," *New Blackfriars* 93, no. 1045 (2012): 324–38; and Bernard J. Cantens, "A Solution to the Problem of Personal Identity in the Metaphysics of Thomas Aquinas," in *Proceedings of the American Catholic Philosophical Association* 75 (2002): 121–34, esp. 130–31.

60 ST, I, 75.6, ad 1.

61 There is much debate in recent Thomistic scholarship over the precise ontological status of the separated soul (*anima separata*) and whether Aquinas maintains that it can be identified as a "human individual" and a "person" in the interim state between bodily death and bodily resurrection. Since the separated soul is an incomplete human individual lacking the essential material constituent of prime/designated matter, "corruptionists" argue that the separated soul can no longer be identified as a *human* individual (i.e., an entity possessing the essential completion of human nature) or a *person* (i.e., an entity possessing the perfection of being signified by this term). Yet, since the separated soul still possesses the complete formal determination of human nature and stands in existence as a subsistent rational individual, "survivalists" argue that the separated soul is both a human individual (i.e., an entity possessing the full formal determination of human nature, even if lacking its material correlate) and a person (i.e., an entity fitting the definition of person as "an individual substance of

Confirming the special character of the human soul in *De ente et essentia*, but now with express attention to the individuation and consequent individual being of the spiritual soul, Aquinas says,

> Granted that [the intellectual soul's] individuation depends on the body as for the occasion of its beginning [*ex corpore occasionaliter dependeat ad sui inchoationem*], because it does not acquire its individuated being [*esse individuatum*] except in the body of which it is the act: still, it is not necessary that individuation perish when the body is withdrawn, because [the soul] has separate being [*esse absolutum*] once it has acquired its *individuated being* by having been made the form of a particular body, that being *always remains individuated* [semper remanet individuatum].[62]

In *Summa contra gentiles*, Aquinas puts this understanding still more forcefully when he says, "Human souls are individuated according to bodies [...] yet not as though individuation were caused by bodies [*non quasi individuatione a corporibus causata*]."[63] And again, in a later section, "The human soul is a form according

---

a rational nature" or "subsistent rational individual," even if imperfectly). In a recent paper proposing something of a reconciliation of these contrasted positions, while holding to a decidedly survivalist conclusion, Brandon Dahm and Daniel De Haan argue that the separated soul should be understood as an "incomplete human person," since the separated soul subsists through itself, is a rational supposit performing rational operations, which possesses operational, formal, existential, and suppositional completeness, even while it lacks the specific completeness of human nature. In what follows, I accept the position of Dahm and De Haan and present the separated soul as having a human and personal mode of being as a subsistent rational individual, even while this mode of being is imperfect due to the absence of its natural material part. This is to say that I hold that the separated soul can meaningfully be identified as a *human* individual and *person*, even if living in separation from the material body and thus in an unnatural state. For a representative presentation of the corruptionist position, see Turner C. Nevitt, "Aquinas on the Death of Christ: A New Argument for Corruptionism," in *American Catholic Philosophical Quarterly* 90, no. 1 (2016): 77–99; for a representative presentation of the survivalist position, see Mark K. Spencer, "The Personhood of the Separated Soul," in *Nova et Vetera* 12, no. 3 (2014): 863–912; and for the proposed survivalist reconciliation of these contrasted positions, see Daniel De Haan and Brandon Dahm, "Thomas Aquinas on Separated Souls as Incomplete Human Persons," in *The Thomist: A Speculative Quarterly Review* 83, no. 4 (2019): 589–637.

62 DEE, 5, 59–67; emphasis added.
63 SCG, 2.75, no. 6.

to its being independent of matter. Thus, it follows that souls are multiplied according to the multiplication of bodies, yet not that the multiplication of bodies is the cause of the multiplication of souls [*non tamen multiplicatio corporum erit causa multiplicationis animarum*]."[64] These quotations, across multiple works, clearly indicate that for Aquinas the human being is individuated not by matter alone, but also and foundationally by the act of being received by the rational soul, which is thereby made to stand in being as a self-subsistent form, something capable of continued existence in separation from the materiality of the body. Thus, even though matter provides the founding possibility of the coming into existence of the individual soul, for Aquinas, inasmuch as a material individual cannot come into being without a material principle, it is the then individuated soul subsisting via the received act of being that accounts for its enduring "individuated being" by which it "always remains individuated."[65]

---

64 SCG, 2.80, no. 8.
65 This exposition of Aquinas on individuation can be cross-referenced with many contemporary presentations of the Thomistic position, such as those of Joseph Owens and Etienne Gilson, and more recently, Montague Brown, Kevin White, and Linda Farmer. See esp. Joseph Owens, "Thomas Aquinas," in *Individuation in Scholasticism: The Later Middle Ages and the Counter-Reformation, 1150–1650*, ed. Jorge J. E. Gracia (Albany, NY: State University of New York Press, 1994), 173–194; Étienne Gilson, *The Elements of Christian Philosophy* (New York: Mentor-Omega Books, 1963), 222–40, and *The Christian Philosophy of St. Thomas Aquinas* (Notre Dame, IN: University of Notre Dame Press, 1956, repr. 2010), 187–99; Montague Brown, "St. Thomas Aquinas and the Individuation of Persons," in *American Catholic Philosophical Quarterly* 65, no. 1 (1991): 29–44; White, "Individuation in Aquinas," 543–56; Linda L. Farmer, "Human Individuation According to Aquinas: Resolving the Debate," in *The Modern Schoolman* 80 (2002), 55–61; and Michael Waldstein, "Personal Individuality According to Thomas" (unpublished article [2005]): 1–5. What becomes clear in each of these authors is the superior role of the form and the act of being in accounting for the individuation of the human being. Joseph Owens, perhaps the strongest representative of these interpretations, says the following, "Existence gives the thing its thoroughgoing individuation by synthesizing everything in the thing into a single unit, both on the essential and accidental levels [...] In material things the form remains prior to the matter it actuates, as well as to the dimensive quantity that marks the matter off into separate portions in the three dimensions required by the thing's nature [...] As principle of individuation, matter under dimensions is concerned in immediate fashion with the bodily aspects of the thing, in that generic abstraction. But form as the cause of individuation bears on the full accompaniment of qualities and endowments that fill out the richness of individuality, on the vital, sentient and rational levels as well as on the corporeal" ("Thomas Aquinas," 188). Montague Brown sums up this way of

Therefore, again here, but now more pointedly, we see that matter is the principle of individuation for Aquinas only inasmuch as it facilitates the instantiation of material individuals alike in kind—a numerical manner of conceiving of human individuation and plurality. Yet, once such individuation is accomplished, Aquinas holds that the human individual retains his own individual mode of existence through the self-subsistent being of the then individuated soul. Thus, while Aquinas certainly maintains that the human soul requires a material principle to come into being "from below"—being a necessary condition of the possibility of the genesis of every human individual—the subsistent being of the human composite is ultimately accounted for by the act of being received "from above"—an act belonging

> interpreting Aquinas while saying the following, "As the matrix between the material and the immaterial, we are individuated in the ways appropriate to both. Like material things, we are individuated by matter. Like immaterial things, we are individuated by our intellectuality. And like all created things, we are individuated by our existence (*esse*)" ("St. Thomas Aquinas and the Individuation of Persons," 41). Attempting to clarify and resolve the debate, Linda Farmer argues that whereas *esse* or being [existence for Owens] is the principle of being one *in* number (*unum numero*) for Aquinas, matter is the principle of being one *of a* number (*unum de numero*), with one in number and therefore *esse* having primacy, precisely since being one in number is prior to being one of a number (see "Human Individuation," esp. 55–56). As can be seen from these selections, these Thomists (among other contemporary Thomists) are not arguing that matter is without significance in accounting for human individuation (or material individuation more broadly), but rather that just as matter is not primary in accounting for the *being* and *unity* of the human substance, neither is it primary with respect to the individuation of the human being. In contrast to these alternate positions on human individuation, and directly debating the views of Owens and White, Lawrence Dewan argues that *esse* does not function in Aquinas's metaphysics in the way attributed to it by Owens and White, but rather that material individuation must be considered from the perspective of the mode of being of primary substances as subsisting beings, those beings which are incommunicable due to the material principle. See Lawrence Dewan, "The Individual as a Mode of Being according to Thomas Aquinas," in *The Thomist: A Speculative Quarterly Review* 63, no. 3 (1999): 403–24; compare Gilles Emery, "The Dignity of Being a Substance: Person, Subsistence, and Nature," in *Nova et Vetera* 9, no. 4 (2011): 991–1001. I take Dewan's presentation to be an accurate reading of Aquinas's express position, a presentation that correlates well with my reading of Aquinas with regard to the human soul as a self-subsistent form with an enduring relation to designated matter, even while I also recognize the significance of these alternate interpretations of what could be a Thomistic position—that is, a position that argues for a different principle of individuation from within the Thomistic metaphysical schema.

to the soul as substantial form and shared by the matter comprising the living body.[66] Yet, notwithstanding such subtleties when Aquinas adverts to the way the individual soul persists in being, it is clear that he also continues to argue for an intrinsic reference of the soul to matter. He says, "The being of the soul does not perish with the perishing of the body; and so the individuation of the soul does not perish with the body, even though it continues to have some *relation* to the body."[67] Later Thomistic commentators have interpreted this continued "relation" to the material body according to the aforementioned "transcendental relation," and they argue that the separated soul continues as an individual by virtue of its intrinsic relation to the designated matter of the body. Accordingly, we see that though Aquinas holds a nuanced position on the individual when it comes to the human being, even to the point of recognizing the individuated being of the spiritual soul, this does not amount to a recognition of the formal basis of being-individual for the human being, since the self-subsistent spiritual soul remains individuated by virtue of the individuating role of designated matter.

When this understanding of the subsistent being of the rational soul is considered with reference to the human being as a person, we find a further avenue toward the partial reconciliation of Stein and Aquinas. Aquinas conceives of the term "person" as a signifier of perfection inasmuch as a distinctive perfection of being is possessed by every individual subsisting in a rational nature. "Person," he says, "signifies what is most perfect in all nature, namely, the subsistent individual of a rational nature."[68] Indeed, Aquinas notes that the term "person" has been devised to signify subsistent rational individuals, because "in a more special and perfect way, the particular and the individual are found in rational substances, which have dominion over their own actions."[69] This recognition of the special manner the individual

---

66 See DEE, 5, 130–40. Stein also uses the terminology of dual limitation, from below (*von unten*) and from above (*von oben*), in both PA (216–17, 224–25) and EES (310), though it appears she received this terminology from Hedwig Conrad-Martius rather than Aquinas. See Hedwig Conrad-Martius, *Metaphysische Gespräche* (Halle: Max Niemeyer, 1921).

67 QDA, 1, ad 2; emphasis added.

68 ST, I, 29.3, co.

69 ST, I, 29.3, co.; and ST, I, 29.1, co. For a helpful personalist exposition of Aquinas's teaching regarding the significance of human action for personal determination, see Karol Wojtyła, *Person and Act: And Related Essays*, trans. Grzegorz Ignatik (Washington, DC: The Catholic University of America Press, 2021), and a shorter

is found among rational substances indicates that Aquinas also recognizes a significant difference between the individual kind and mode of being of personal individuals in contrast to all non-personal individuals. Indeed, in *Summa contra gentiles* Aquinas even says that "the individuation fitting for human nature is personality [*personalitas*]," and he is evidently here using the term in a metaphysical rather than a psychological sense, as signifying that which pertains to the personhood of the individual.[70] When he then indicates that this ontological perfection is manifest in the way rational individuals have dominion over their actions, it is clear that he regards the eminent individuation of human persons to bear close reference to that which is specifically personal, that is, free rational acts.[71] Thus, in a manner clearly analogous to Stein's demonstration of the personal mode of being-individual via the spiritual life of the personal I, Aquinas recognizes that the human being has a personal mode of being as an individual, and that this mode of being is manifest in the way the human being performs personal actions.[72]

We see from this that with regard to the personal nature of the human being, as also when considering the subsistent being of the spiritual soul, Aquinas introduces certain subtleties that expose avenues toward a degree of alignment with the contrasted position of Stein. Yet, since Aquinas touches upon these nuances only briefly, and since his express conclusions indicate that he maintains that human individuation is the result of designated matter in like manner to other material substances, these avenues toward alignment remain narrow, and the express disagreement between Stein and Aquinas over formal versus material bases of the human individual remain outstanding.

---

    article presentation of the same in "The Personal Structure of Self-Determination," in *Person and Act*, 457–66.

70 SCG, 4.41, no. 6. Aquinas is here arguing against the Nestorian heresy, which heretical doctrine stands in opposition to the orthodox position regarding the union of human and divine in the Person of Jesus Christ.

71 This personal mode of action obviously disposes the personal individual for the development of a dynamically realized individuality, a self-determined individuality, which could well represent an area of further accord between Stein and Aquinas.

72 Indeed, as Scarpelli Cory shows, with a specific focus on the act of knowing, Aquinas holds that knowledge of the individual self is given in first-person inner awareness in all intellectual acts, either implicitly in the act of cognition of extra-mental objects, or explicitly when the act of cognition is expressly attended to by the individual, thus revealing "an existing individual, concretely present to myself in my acts," such that "I understand myself as a whole (this individual existence, I)." See Therese Scarpelli Cory, *Aquinas on Human Self-Knowledge* (Cambridge: Cambridge University Press, 2015), 73, 217.

Assessing Stein's Original Conception of Personal Individuality

Like being-individual, Stein's presentation of human individuality is also clearly innovative in comparison to that of Aquinas and Thomism, especially when we come to the personal quality determining the depth of the personal spirit.[73] In what follows I focus my analysis on this central feature of human individuality, the *quale* or ποῖον, notwithstanding the manifold further bases of human distinction given in Stein's texts, especially that of the openness and power of the soul, since, as seen above, Stein herself regards this feature as the ultimate basis of human individuality, and it is also where she most differs from the presentation of Aquinas, Thomism, and the *philosophia perennis*.

As seen above, Aquinas argues that all human individuals belong to the same species according to an identical formal determination, where the form of the species and the form of the individual are taken to be formally identical, with the consequence that all differences between individuals are located beyond the form in the material dimension. Moreover, according to his broader metaphysical schema, basing his reasoning on Aristotle's understanding of form and species, if there were formal differences among individuals, Aquinas holds that such formal differentiation would cause an automatic adjustment in the degree of actuality and perfection of these individuals, together with a corresponding alteration of the species within the gradated hierarchy of natural kinds. Referencing Aristotle's *Metaphysics*, he says, "The species of natural things are like the species of numbers, according to which the addition or subtraction of a unit varies the species."[74] Elsewhere, again following Aristotle, he correlates the differences of natural species with the differences of geometrical figures, and he argues that each subsequent natural species in the hierarchy of being virtually contains lower forms in like manner to the way each subsequent geometrical figure in the geometric order virtually contains all prior geometrical figures.[75] Thus, according to this correlation of natural species with species of

---

73   Again here, in what follows I prescind from including the conceptual apparatus of formal structure, framework, and empty-form, since Stein's proposal of the personal quality need not be understood as dependent on this associated apparatus.
74   QDA, q. 7, co.; commenting on Meta, 8.3, 1043^{b}33–1044^{a}2.
75   This understanding is founded on the Aristotelian notion of specific difference through contraries in the intelligible structure of being, so that "whatever contraries are in the notion, that is, on the side of the form, cause difference according to species." InMeta,

quantity, both numerical and geometrical, Aquinas argues that the ordered cosmic whole of differentiated kinds is a progressively ascending sequence of actuality and perfection, wherein all grades "differ from one another in their degree of perfection according to their recession from potentiality and accession toward pure act."[76] This being so, every hypothetical formal difference between "human" individuals would necessarily involve an adjustment in actuality and perfection, and an automatic alteration of species. The natural consequence of this would be that formally different "human" individuals would no longer share a common formal determination and subsist together as members of one and the same human species.

Again here, the interests of Aquinas appear to be related to accounting for the possibility of a plurality of specifically identical individuals in an ordered hierarchical cosmos. However, while granting the hierarchical gradation of the cosmos, which Stein does, we can reasonably ask whether every formal difference does or must result in an adjustment of actuality and perfection, a corresponding ascension or descension in the hierarchy of being, and an automatic alteration of the determination of the species. Moreover, we can ask whether the numerical and geometrical examples used by Aquinas (following Aristotle) should be transposed into the domain of natural species without further ado—that is, whether all formal difference in natural things should be considered according to the discrete quantitative analogy of number or the continuous quantitative analogy of figure.[77] Clearly, Stein disagrees; and she comes to propose an alternate understanding of form and formal difference that envisages a different kind of relation between the form of the individual and the form of the species, which also provides a different way of conceiving of the relation of formal difference to actuality and perfection. Though Stein follows Aquinas in conceiving of the created cosmos as a gradated hierarchy of formally different kinds, wherein the various species of natural kinds are

---

10.11, no. 5 (Meta, 10.9, 1058^{b}1). Stein takes up this Aristotelian understanding in EES, 127–38.

76 DEE, 5, 105–15.

77 Of course, there is good reason to transpose this principle insofar as the genera of the natural realm obviously formally include all lower order genera in their completed formal determinations, i.e., plant including material, animal including plant, etc. Yet, we can still ask if this transposition keeps its import when it comes to formal differences as such, or whether it is possible that there could be alternated formal differences of the same degree of perfection and without being higher in the sequence.

hierarchically arranged according to their formal differentiation, she disregards the Thomistic (and Aristotelian) assertion that *every* formal difference causes an automatic adjustment in actuality and perfection and alteration of the species, and argues that a plurality of specifically identical individuals can be formally different from one another with differences that neither alter actuality and perfection nor destroy the common unity of the species. Since Stein understands the individual form to be a complex formal structure that includes but is not limited to the formal determination of the species, and since she further permits a free play of the form of the species in the plurality of formally alike individuals ranged under its specificity, Stein concludes that a plurality of material individuals can be formally different from one another while remaining equally members of the same species. Moreover, together with this reasoning, she maintains that not every formal difference need result in an adjustment of the grade of actuality and perfection, and rather recognizes kinds of formal differentiation that nonetheless exemplify the very same degree of actuality and perfection.

Consequently, Stein can conclude that human individuals are formally different from one another through the further specification of the form of the species in the form of the individual via the above-detailed personal quality, without disturbing the specific unity of human individuals.[78] This means that for Stein the further formal determination of the species in the human individual need not destroy the unity of the species, nor introduce anything that disrupts the equality of actuality and perfection needed to secure the basic unity of human individuals as a species. Though Stein recognizes that the presence of personal distinctness implies that the human individual comes to be, in a certain sense, of his "own-kind," out of concern for the unity of the species, in *Finite and Eternal Being* she refrains from identifying the human individual as a distinct species of the human genus sharing merely a generic commonality with other individuals.[79] A number of thinkers have noted

---

78 As indicated above, this differentiation of individuals is not limited to the personal quality, for Stein, even while the personal quality is the root feature of the distinctive differentiation of personal individuals, but also includes the characteristic openness and power of the soul.

79 See EES, 424–27. Though this is certainly true of EES, in PA Stein says, "Each individual human being is his own species [*eine eigene Spezies*], i.e., a spiritual person of specific proper character [*spezifischer Eigenart*]" (PA, 266). Notwithstanding this claim in PA, Betschart rightly notes that "Stein will refuse to speak of the human person

several concerns with Stein's introduction of formal differentiation between individuals, concerns of a personalistic, ethical, socio-political, and theological kind, all of which ultimately relate to the potential for formal differentiation to rupture the unity of the species and lead to axiological distinctions between individuals, as well as potentially obscuring the ability of human persons to properly understand and relate to one another.[80] Yet, given the interpretation

---

as a species of its own," while also showing clearly that she considers humanity to be a genus that is further specified by the difference introduced by the personal *quale*. Betschart, "*Quid* and *Quale*," 211–28: 121nn18–19. The accumulated sense of Stein's thought seems to be that humanity can be considered both generically and specifically so that the unity of the human species is adequately secured even while it is further specified in individuals through the formal difference of the personal quality.

80 For the most comprehensive enumeration and detailing of concerns, see Borden Sharkey, *Thine Own Self*, 153–84. In summary, if Stein's proposition were to rupture the unity of the species and lead to hierarchical distinctions among human individuals, then her proposal would certainly run into the following interconnected array of problems: (1) personalistic: since personal relationships are conditioned by mutual understanding, which is itself founded in commonality (as indeed are all kinds of relations), to the degree that persons differ from one another, especially if those differences be hierarchical, to that same degree mutual understanding and all further relating is impeded; (2) ethical: without substantive commonality among a plurality of individuals, ethical considerations of a normative kind—from either virtue or law—would be strained to the point of becoming ineffectual, since all norms would lose their universal applicability; (3) socio-political: given the essentially ethical character of human sociality and society, including the political order, should ethical matters be negatively impacted by (hierarchical) differentiation, then society and politics would be impacted in the very same ways by associated necessity; and (4) theological: given that the Christian faith holds that the salvation of humanity is wrought through the Incarnation and Redemption of Jesus Christ, should the human community be fractured by (hierarchical) differentiation, so too would the universal import of Christ's Redemption be threatened, as would the consequent communion of the Mystical Body of Christ. In response to these concerns, as shown above, Stein's proposal avoids running into these complications precisely because she continues to argue for the unity of the human species through the common possession of the species determination "being-human," while simultaneously recognizing that a differentiation of individuals can be grounded in a *qualitative* determination of species without any alteration of the structure of the essence in the individual—resulting in a differentiation that does not alter the nature commonly possessed or introduce any hierarchical disparity. This means that Stein's proposal can robustly differentiate persons at the level of the spirit in a way that does not frustrate mutual understanding and all relationships conditioned by mutual understanding; indeed, as she argues, her proposed personal quality actually

here set forth, it is evident that Stein's conceptual apparatus avoids introducing such problems. Indeed, it is precisely through her conception of the relation of the form of the individual to the form of the species that Stein secures the personalistic, ethical, socio-political, and theological unity of the species while also subtly accounting for characteristic differences between individual members of the species—differences that then become key features involved in the way human individuals understand themselves and relate to one another, personally, ethically, and theologically, and even socio-politically. Therefore, notwithstanding the formal differentiation of individuals introduced by the unique personal quality, I submit that Stein does not stand squarely opposed to Aquinas on such fundamental questions as the unity of the species and the concomitant equality of actuality and perfection among human individuals.[81]

By approaching Stein's conception of human individuality from the perspective of its *qualitative* character, it is possible to show from another perspective that Stein's position is not antithetical to the broader conceptual schema of Aquinas (or that of Aristotle), or that it inadvertently introduces the above-mentioned list of concerns. Since Stein conceives of the personal quality as something that colors the spiritual person with its peculiar hue, the personal quality is not to be understood as an integral part of the structure of the essence, but rather as something that qualitatively determines the spiritual dimension

---

redounds to the good of personal relationships since it provides another base upon which these relationships can be founded, a base that arguably proves decisive in the loving relationships of friendship and spousal union. Moreover, for the very same reasons, her proposal does not complicate ethical, social, or political matters, since it does not differentiate human individuals in a way that would be ethically, socially, or politically significant, precisely since it maintains the unity of human individuals through their common possession of human nature with all its entailments and implications. Finally, and again for the very same reasons, Christ's Incarnation and Redemption continue to have their universal import, both with regard to the universal applicability of salvation and with regard to the potential of all individuals to enter the Mystical Body, both of which Stein reflects upon at length in the final chapter of EES, a chapter dedicated to the meaning of being an individual—a meaning, it should be noted, she ultimately locates in the mystery of Christ and his Mystical Body.

81 Noting Borden Sharkey's concerns, Betschart similarly argues that Stein avoids such difficulties and argues that Stein's position need not be understood as excluding the Thomistic conception but rather can be understood as complementary to the standard Thomistic position. See Betschart, "Individuality of the Human Person," 73–86: 79–80; and "*Quid* and *Quale*," 211–28: 219–21.

of the personal essence, thus becoming something that qualifies but does not constitute the essence.[82] So considered, Stein's understanding overlaps with the Thomistic (and Aristotelian) understanding of "quality" as an accidental category of being and predication. According to the Thomistic schema, the accident of quality (*quale*) inheres in substance without being a constituent feature of the essence of the substance, even while certain accidents always come together with their substances as something proper to the species or genus of the substance. Therefore, in locating individuality in the personal quality, it is clear that Stein does not differentiate human individuals in a way that destroys the unity of the species or cause a corresponding hierarchical disparity of between human individuals.[83] Since the personal quality is a differentiated "hue" on the same level of actuality and perfection across human individuals, the specific and axiological commonality uniting human individuals remains intact.

Yet, even should this crossover be granted, the personal quality of Stein cannot simply be inserted into the metaphysical division of accidents proposed by Aquinas, where accidents caused by intrinsic principles are divided into those following upon form, and common to the genus or species as something proper to and inseparable from genus or species, and those following upon matter, though in its relation to form, and particular to the individual, whether as something separable or inseparable.[84] Even though the personal quality possesses

---

82 Borden Sharkey proposes that we could describe this quality as "adverbial individuality," presenting human individuality as something that qualifies the *way of being* and/or *living* of the human individual. However, in line with the above presentation, while also following the lead of Borden Sharkey, I suggest that the personal quality is best described as "adjectival individuality," precisely since it is something that qualifies the individual essence ontologically and actually before subsequently becoming adverbial by potentially qualifying the individual's way of being and living. See Borden Sharkey, *Thine Own Self*, 190–91.

83 I here correlate Stein's understanding of the personal quality with the third species of quality recognized by Aquinas, namely, as an accidental mode of determination of the subject via the potentiality of the subject, and which is then often later identified by Thomists as "affection/passion" or "affective quality/passible quality"—that is, an accidental determination apt to *affect* the cognitive faculty. See ST, I, II, 49.2, co.; and also Joseph Owens, *An Elementary Christian Metaphysics* (Milwaukee, WI: Bruce, 1963; repr. Houston: Center for Thomistic Studies, 1986, repr. 2013), 170–71, 177.

84 See esp. DEE, 6, 50–97. This division applies to accidents caused by intrinsic essential causal principles in contrast to accidents introduced from without by extrinsic causal

features recognizable in this Thomistic division, it also resists simple insertion into one or other branches of the division, both because the personal quality is something purely formal, even if apt to be impressed upon the materiality of the body, and because the personal quality is proper to and inseparable from the individual, rather than something proper to genus or species. Therefore, though Stein's conception of the personal quality can be aligned with the Thomistic (and Aristotelian) understanding of quality as an accidental mode of being and predication—and her adopted terminology of "*quale*" (and "ποῖον") certainly implies that it should—since the personal quality fails to fit readily into the Thomistic division of accidents, this alignment can only ever be partial—unless, that is, the Thomistic (and Aristotelian) schema be expanded to include another division: that of accidents following upon the form and proper to the individual.

Finally, does Stein's understanding of human individuality represent any benefit over against that of Aquinas? Stein's proposal certainly represents a heightened conception of human individuality when compared with that of Aquinas and Thomism. By placing the ultimate basis of individuality at the level of formal difference, even if qualitative, Stein maintains that human individuality relates more to determinacy, actuality, and perfection rather than indeterminacy, potentiality, and imperfection. Thus, Stein presents human individuality in a way that corresponds to the eminent position of the human being in the cosmic hierarchy of being—an ontological and axiological position granted by Aquinas and Thomism—and forcefully exhibits the intensification of individuality that occurs as this hierarchy is ascended, up to and including the superior position of the human being as a spiritual person. Furthermore, by placing individuality at the level of the personal structure, both with respect to the personal quality, and with respect to the related openness and power of the soul, Stein maintains that individuality is a specifically personal feature, one that is proper to the human being as a spiritual person rather than as a material living-body, whether organic or animal. Should we further reflect on the ontological and axiological significance of such an account of human individuality, we immediately see the great value in Stein's insights and corresponding exposition of human uniqueness. In providing an account

---

principles. See John F. Wippel, *The Metaphysical Thought of Thomas Aquinas: From Finite Being to Uncreated Being* (Washington, DC: The Catholic University of America Press, 2000), 266–75.

of personal uniqueness that places the decisive feature in the spiritual and personal, while also arguing for the pre-given *a priori* character of the personal *quale* or ποῖον—that the character is prior to any experience or choice—Stein provides an explanation of human uniqueness that enables us to account for the prevailing sense of uniqueness that comes to the foreground in all kinds of personal relationships, especially those of friendship and spousal love, where the beloved stands before the lover as someone absolutely unrepeatable—and therefore irreplaceable.[85]

In such loving relationships, the uniqueness of the human individual becomes a focal point of human experience and the ultimate coordinating feature of the personal relationship, inasmuch as the lover comes to love the beloved to the exclusion of all others—and, therefore, precisely as an individual distinct and separate from all others. It is love that most fully *gives* the person, first cognitively and affectively, in one's fulsome recognition to their being and value, then volitionally, in one's free affirmation of this being and value—indeed, it is only love that provides the definitive affirmation of the being and value of the person. While discussing the nature of love, and its proper completion in self-giving, Stein explains,

> Giving [*Hingabe*] tends toward becoming one, it comes to completion first through acceptance on the side of the beloved person. Thus, for its completion, love requires the reciprocal gift [*Wechselhingabe*] of persons. Only in this way can love be total affirmation [*Jasagen*], since one person opens and reveals himself to another only by giving. Only in becoming one is genuine knowledge of persons possible. Love, then, in its highest fulfilment, includes knowledge.[86]

Stein here shows that it is precisely the union of love, effected through reciprocal self-gift, that testifies most properly to the significance of the individual—a union differently realized in friendship and spousal love—by first providing privileged access to knowledge of the beloved, before being completed in a

---

85 On this point, see the brief but beautiful explanation of Borden Sharkey in *Thine Own Self*, esp. 185, 234.

86 EES, 382. This clearly resonates with the similar insights of Wojtyła, when he reasons that love in its completed form is found in reciprocal self-gift, and that "affirmation of the value of the person as such is contained in the essence of love." Wojtyła, *Love and Responsibility*, 26.

properly fulsome affirmation of the beloved. Through the interpenetration of cognition, affection, and volition, working distinctly and in tandem, the beloved is *given* for the lover as someone irreplaceable—in and through the lover's self-*giving*. Though a loving friend may certainly have other beloved friends, and though a loving spouse may marry another upon the death of their first love, this does not overcome the irreplaceability of the beloved. Individual irreplaceability, then, seems to be interwoven essentially with personal love. And it is this very irreplaceability that is ultimately secured by Stein's proposal of personal uniqueness, since the unrepeatable uniqueness of the personal quality renders the beloved ontologically irreplaceable—with an irreplaceability anchored in the personal dimension of the spiritual soul and potentially pervading all dimensions of the individual. Thus, Stein reasons that it is precisely this uniqueness that motivates the lover to seek the beloved, and it is this character too that inwardly grounds their personal union.

One might argue that such irreplaceability is already found in the beloved's uniqueness as *this* very individual—that is, according to his *being-individual*—and that it is love of the individual in his *being* that matters. However, while not denigrating the significance of this truth of love, which I certainly grant, Stein's reasoning for the qualitative differentiation coordinating love and loving unions reveals a further depth of significance of human relationships, one that differentiates the loving relationship of unique *relata*. Though we could place the basis of qualitative distinction grounding love in bodily constitution, in the historical context of the individual's genesis, in the circumstances of his life, and/or, with even greater right, in the particular complex of free choices made by the individual throughout life, these differentiating features stand at varying degrees of remove from the spiritual and personal dimension of human nature, the first because it is bodily rather than spiritual, the second and third because these factors lie outside the structure of human nature even while they shape the unique development of the individual, and the last because human actions follow upon and are secondary to the structure of the personal individual, even while such actions are properly personal and of paramount significance for the development of the individual. Therefore, in contrast to these many interlocking bases of individuality, and while recognizing their qualitative import, Stein provides a robust ontological grounding of human uniqueness that accounts for the above-mentioned features of loving relationships—that is, that the beloved stands before the lover as some*one*, a being "absolutely" irreplaceable. By further detailing the "divine" character of human uniqueness and unrepeatability, by both grounding individuality in divine choice and clarifying its status as a unique and unrepeatable imaging of God, brought about through the abundant gratuity of God as befitting the personal order, Stein not only shows the closeness each individual has to God but simultaneously reveals a key aspect of the "divine" character of human love, where love of the other participates in one's love of God insofar as it is illumined by the particular hue of the beloved as *imago Dei*.[87]

Conclusion:
The Human Individual and Human Individuality

After presenting an originally developed universal conception of being-individual through the empty-form "thing" as bearer of the formal and material whole of the individual, Stein expands her conceptual apparatus to include the being-individual of the human being as a personal spirit. In light of the formal dominance of the personal I within the structure of human nature, as it is given in conscious experience phenomenologically investigated, Stein reasons that the being-individual of the human being is grounded in the empty-form "personal I" as that which encompasses and bears the essential fullness of human nature. Yet, notwithstanding this formal ground, it is only when the personal I is completed as a self-dependent whole of spiritual soul and living-body that the human person can stand in existence as an actual individual—at least *pre-mortem*—having his own distinctive being and action. Together with the living-body the personal being-individual of the human being is then exteriorly manifest for second-person perception through the living-body and living personal expression and activity. In this way, Stein conceives of the being-individual of the human being in full continuity with the being-individual of finite being in general, via the empty-formal bearer, while also revealing the way the human being surpasses all non-personal beings, via the unifying and incommunicable formality and actuality of the personal I.[88] Beyond this personal

---

[87] For more detail on the axiological and ethical consequences of Stein's understanding of human individuality, see Betschart, "Überlegungen zur Menschenwürde und zu ethischen Konsequenzen von Edith Steins Verständnis der menschlichen Individualität," in *Edith Stein Jahrbuch*, 21, ed. Ulrich Dobhan (Würzburg: Echter, 2015), 87–109. As previously noted, Stein does not thematize human dignity in her works and more research is needed to draw out the full significance of Stein's conception of the human individual for this important topic.

[88] Betschart proposes a useful tabulation of the layers of Stein's complex conceptualization

presentation of the being-individual of the human being, Stein introduces a further dimension of human distinctness by developing an original conception of the qualitative individuality of the individual, and finally proposes that such distinctness is ultimately determined by a unique personal quality that "colors" the personal spirit and renders the human individual qualitatively irreplaceable and unrepeatable. As with being-individual, this personal quality is naturally apt to be impressed on human nature as one whole through its progressive unfolding in personal expression and action, whereby it comes to exterior expression and availability for perception via the living-body.[89] However, though manifest via the body in this way, this personal kind of distinctness is nonetheless a spiritual qualification that is recognized by perceiving with the heart. According to both dimensions, then, that of being-individual and qualitative individuality, Stein argues that the human individual is not merely some*thing* but rather is decidedly some*one*.

With her independently developed conception of being-individual and individuality, Stein's mature conception of the human individual meets all the requirements of the individual enumerated by the Thomistic tradition and the *philosophia perennis*, namely, that the individual be identifiable as a τόδε τί, something in itself undivided yet divided from all else, and inherently incommunicable. However, her original conception is certainly also considerably different from and even opposed to the standard presentation of the material individual in the thought of Aquinas and Thomism, where all kinds of material being, including the human individual, are understood to be individuated by the designated matter comprising the material body. Yet, it is likewise clear that for Aquinas the human soul as spiritual is characteristically different than all other substantial forms, with the consequence that the human individual

---

of the features comprising the human being as an individual (as found in PA and AMP). See Betschart, *Unwiederholbares Gottessiegel*, 196, fig. 12; 233, fig. 13.

89 In PA and AMP, Stein draws together the two poles of the incommunicability of the individual through her use of the concept "core of the person [*Kern der Person*]," though she entirely drops the terminology of core in EES when speaking of persons. See PA, 122–47; and AMP, 96, 103; and also the earlier works, PE, 127; IC, 227, 246, 271; and EPh, 134–36. For more detail, see Christof Betschart, "Kern der Person: (Meta-) Phänomenologische Begründung der menschlichen Person nach Edith Steins Frühwerk," in *Europa und seine Anderen*, ed. Hanna-Barbara Gerl-Falkovitz, René Kaufmann, and Hans R. Sepp (Dresden: Thelem, 2010), 61–72; *Unwiederholbares Gottessiegel*, 190–92; Borden Sharkey, *Thine Own Self*, 10–12; Schulz, "Theory of Identity," 161–76: 172–4; and McNamara, "Human Individuality," 124–39: 132–33.

attains his individuated being directly from God and is capable of subsisting as an individual in separation from the designated matter of the body. Moreover, it is clear that for Aquinas the personal individual is revealed as eminently individual through rational activity, and he concomitantly maintains that the individuation fitting for human nature is personality. And so, even while Aquinas maintains that the spiritual soul is individuated by virtue of its relation to the matter of the body, a narrow degree of partial alignment is found between Stein and Aquinas and Thomism in these two related areas: that of the spiritual and the personal. On the other hand, when consideration is made for the alternate way Stein conceives of the relation of the form of the individual to the form of the species, as well as the qualitative (= accidental) character of human individuality, the unique distinction of individuals Stein argues for need not be understood as disrupting the formal unity of the human species and its corresponding equality, something definitively secured by Aquinas and Thomism. Yet, notwithstanding these narrow avenues toward partial rapprochement, the disagreements between Stein and Aquinas over the metaphysical bases of being-individual and qualitative individuality remain considerable—that is, all the difference of form and matter.

Conclusion to Part II:
Personal Being-Individual and Individuality

In continuity with her chosen method of investigation, the being of the personal I is the ever-present foundation to which Stein's analysis of the human individual bears reference. In direct consequence of this undergirding point of departure, Stein's understanding of the human individual is decisively shaped by the cognitive givenness of the personal I. This stands in marked contrast to the mode of approach in the thought of Aquinas and Thomism, where consideration of the human being as an individual is largely determined by broader metaphysical and cosmological considerations. However, notwithstanding this divergence, Stein's conception of the human individual is framed by the broader conceptual schema of Aquinas, with the foreseeable consequence that a large domain of foundational agreement is found between Stein and Thomism—much greater than is ordinarily granted in this area. This agreement spans the hylomorphic composition of the material essence together with the above-noted substantial perfections of self-dependence and existence, and it encompasses the Thomistic definition of the individual as "in itself undivided yet divided from all else," as well as the decisive feature of the individual as something incommunicable.

Yet, according to the results of her phenomenological investigation, Stein reconsiders the relationship of form and matter in the structure of the individual essence and reverses the individuating polarity of the transcendental relation, so that the formal component comes to assume unqualified priority in the structure of the material substance. As a result, Stein concludes to a formal basis for the "being-individual" of the material individual via the individual essential-form—more or less synonymous with the substantial form (*forma substantialis*) of Aquinas and the *morphe* (μορφή) of Aristotle. When this conclusion is taken together with her reconsideration of the relation of the form of the individual to the form of the species, as well as her understanding of the material and environmental factors that condition the fully developed shape of the material individual, both genetically and dynamically, Stein also concludes to a formal basis for the qualitative individuality of the material individual. This collection of conclusions represents the central, broad range of disagreement between Stein and Aquinas and that of the Thomistic tradition. Yet, while these conclusions stand opposed to the standard Thomist position, Stein presents her own position as basically coherent with the broader metaphysical commitments of Aquinas and the Thomistic tradition. This is especially true when considering the ontological priority of form in the structure of material substances, where the form is understood to be the principle of both being and unity, in addition to its (species) determining role, and is further understood to be the universal principle of intelligibility, thus grounding our ability to understand the individual.

Beyond this domain of central and broad disagreement, the fine-point of disagreement is found in Stein's proposition that the being-individual of the essential-form is itself rooted in the empty-form "thing" for material being in general, and empty-form "personal I" for personal being in particular. By reflecting on the cognitive givenness of the spiritual life of the conscious subject, Stein comes to understand the being-individual of the human individual to be decisively determined by the personal I, as that which formally encompasses and bears the whole of the human individual as a complex formal and material structure. The personal I is that in which the being-individual of the essential-form is finally rooted, with the consequence that this specifically personal kind of being-individual pervades the entire formal structure of human nature—via the hylomorphic relation—and renders the human whole something eminently individual in a properly personal way. A further fine-point of disagreement is found in Stein's claim that the human individual is determined as qualitatively unique via a peculiar characteristic of the spiritual and personal structure of the soul, a personal quality that distinctly determines the individual and renders him unique and unrepeatable from the innermost depth of his being. By reflecting on the cognitive givenness of spiritual life, Stein reasons that this peculiar spiritual characteristic is perceptible via a perceiving with the heart, both through inner awareness of one's own depth, a private *sui generis* personal experience, and through outer awareness of the personal other via the living-body, a public but still *sui generis* personal experience.

These two final conclusions regarding the personal individual are evidently different than anything found in the presentation of Aquinas and Thomism, and at first sight they appear directly opposed to the received teachings. Yet, when considering the being-individual of the human individual, the examination here performed indicates certain subtleties in Aquinas's thought—considering the self-subsistence of the spiritual soul and the special mode of being personal—which unveil a number of narrow avenues toward their partial reconciliation. Moreover, with regard to human individuality, Stein's understanding of the personal quality as something that does not destroy the unity and equality of the human species, nor introduce disparities making mutual understanding between individuals difficult or impossible, means that Stein's alternate solution secures fundamental truths robustly protected by Aquinas and the Thomistic conceptual apparatus. However, even should these narrow avenues be granted, there remains considerable disagreement between Stein and Aquinas over the principles by which the human being is determined in being as an individual, whether they be the spiritual principles of personal I and personal quality, or the material principles of designated matter and material content.

Part III

The Human Being's Relation to God

> Once he has grasped it, the idea of Pure Act or Eternal Being becomes for the I the measure of his own being.
>
> —*Edith Stein*[1]

Stein does not investigate human nature in separation from its insertion into the natural world as one nature among a plurality of natural kinds, and neither does she investigate the human individual in radical isolation from human community and the exceptional range of relations possible for the human being as a person. Yet, in her mature thought, the most important natural human relation, and that which is foundational for all other actual and possible relations, is the natural creaturely relation to God the Creator. To explain the basic structure of this relation Stein has recourse to key metaphysical teachings of Aquinas and the Thomistic tradition, namely, the Thomistic demonstration of the existence and attributes of God and the Thomistic conception of the analogy of being understood as an analogy of proportionality. In her characteristic way, Stein reconsiders the meaning of these teachings by independently investigating this creaturely relation, in consequence of which she significantly expands their conceptual content in specifically personal terms. In this part III, according to a mode now familiar, I analyze Stein's reception of these teachings by first exploring her assimilation of the conceptual content

---

1   EES, 59.

of each teaching before turning toward assessing her reconsideration of their meaning and reinterpretation of both in personal terms. The analysis is divided into two chapters. In chapter 5, I examine Stein's understanding of how we attain philosophical knowledge of God the Creator and show how Stein's understanding is supported by Thomistic argumentation for the existence and attributes of God. I then analyze Stein's initial phenomenological mode of approach to the analogy of being before detailing her critical questioning of the Thomistic conception of the analogy of proportionality. On the basis of these analyses, I proceed in chapter 6 to explore Stein's recasting of the analogy of proportionality in distinctly personal terms, by examining how she expands the conceptual content of this most important apparatus to include the personal nature of human and Divine Being. Finally, I conclude by arguing that Stein's reinterpretation of analogy greatly enhances the (anthropological) significance of this central teaching of the Thomistic tradition, by revealing in what way the human person is always already established in a profound personal relation to the personal God.

Chapter Five

Philosophical Knowledge of God

> The *analogia entis*, understood as the relation of temporal and Eternal Being, is already visible in this starting point [—that of the personal I].
>
> —Edith Stein[1]

In both the later completed *Finite and Eternal Being* and the earlier preparatory inquiry *Potency and Act*, "the *question of being* stands at the center" of Stein's investigations.[2] In these works being is understood to encompass both finite and Eternal Being and is conceived in decidedly Thomistic terms according to the overarching perspective of the "analogy of being [*analogia entis*]," which Stein describes as "the basic law [...] governing all being."[3] The predominating concepts employed by Aquinas in his approach to being are the paired concepts of act (*actus*) and potency (*potentia*), yet even these most basic concepts, and *a fortiori* all further concepts, are intersected by a division demarcating their attribution to creature and Creator, so that "*nothing can be said in the same sense of God and creatures.*"[4] However, this division distinguishing the conceptual content of every term simultaneously authorizes the attribution of these very same terms of creature and Creator according to an analogical form of predication. Thus, together with establishing the fundamental conceptual *distinction* of the creature *from* the Creator, this analogical form of predication

---

1 EES, 42.
2 See EES, 4, 9; see, PA, 7.
3 EES, 4, 9.
4 EES, 9–10, citing QDP, 1.1; compare PA, 7.

inaugurates the primary way of describing the fundamental conceptual *relation* of the creature *to* the Creator. And since the conceptual apparatus by which being is conceived ideally mirrors the ontological structure of being, this analogical form of predication provides a most primary way of conceiving of the actual distinction of creature from Creator while concomitantly identifying the profound relation of creature to Creator. Accordingly, the analogy of being provides Stein with the appropriately universal perspective "to seize on the entire manifoldness of all that which is" so that her inquiry into the meaning of being has the requisite generality—encompassing all being, both finite and Eternal.

Yet, since the analogy of being rests on prior confirmation of the actual existence and attributes of God, before Stein can proceed with her investigation of analogy, she must first attain a conceptual grasp of God from a properly philosophical perspective. Such a grasp provides the suitably grounded conceptual framework for speaking of Creator and creation, as well as the fitting foundation needed for investigating the corresponding relation of creature to Creator. And so, after initially approaching the question of God from a purely phenomenological perspective, Stein briefly but decisively turns to the metaphysical reasoning of Aquinas to support her knowledge of God as Creator with the argumentative rigor of Aquinas's demonstrations of the existence and attributes of God.

The Existence and Attributes of God

As shown above, Stein develops her understanding of finite being via an Augustinian mode of investigation by beginning with reflection on the conscious life of the personal subject.[5] Such reflection immediately reveals two transcendent (in the phenomenological sense) worlds on which the personal I depends for his own characteristic being—namely, the transcendent "inner world" of the personal self and the transcendent "outer world" of sensibly

---

5   See above, chapter 1: "Point of Departure in the 'Life of the I.'" As stated, such rational reflection discloses the presence of three transcendent (in the phenomenological sense) worlds beyond what is immediately given in conscious experience, the inner world of the self undergirding the life of consciousness, the outer world filling consciousness with its intentional contents, and the world above announced together with the finitude of consciousness.

given things. However, in addition to these transcendent worlds experienced horizontally, so to speak, Stein argues that reflection on first-person experience also reveals a transcendent "world above" disclosed together with the "inner and outer worlds."[6]

How so? The personal I is given in experience as an actual individual standing in existence—the "I am" of first-person experience—as is clearly manifest in any and all conscious experience whatsoever, and the personal I is given as having a characteristic fullness of being and life—as is likewise manifest in the experiential fullness of spiritual life to which all being is intentionally given. Yet, the personal I is also unveiled for himself as the kind of being that does not adequately account for his own being, but rather discovers himself as a being suspended between being and nonbeing, possessing a radical dependency on the three transcendent worlds which are given together with conscious experience. First and foundationally, the personal I becomes aware that he has an *actual* dependence on the "inner world" for his very being and life as a conscious I, and a further *dynamic* dependence on the "outer world" for the meaningful contents of his intentional life. Then, complementing and completing these horizontal experiences, the personal I discovers that he also has a *possible* dependence on the world above, a transcendent realm of being that is vertically announced together with all conscious experience. That is to say that in the very finitude of his own being and life, in its experienced admixture of potentiality and actuality, and its corresponding essentially temporal character, the personal I becomes aware that while he has being *in* himself as a subsistent rational individual, his being is not and cannot be absolutely independent, precisely inasmuch as he does not have being *from* himself. Consequently, the personal I realizes that he is radically dependent in being and becomes aware that he has a possible dependence on a transcendent realm of enduring being in the world above.[7]

---

6   PA, 18; see also, EES, 57. Stein's understanding here parallels that of Husserl. See Edmund Husserl, *Ideas Pertaining to a Pure Phenomenology and to a Phenomenological Philosophy*, 2 vols., trans. W. E. Pohl, T. E. Klein, and F. Kersten (The Hague: Martinus Nijhoff, 1983, 1989), 1:133–34.

7   Ian Leask proposes a similar reading and presents Stein's analysis of the Thomistic doctrine of act and potency as "nothing less than a phenomenological re-working of the Augustinian movement from a primal 'self'-awareness, to a wider being-certainty which any self must presuppose, to the divinity which this being-certainty seems to suggest (but can never prove)." Ian Leask, *Being Reconfigured* (Newcastle upon Tyne:

Closely connected with this experience, the personal I "comes to the *idea of fullness*, through striking-out from his own being what he himself is conscious of as a privation."[8] By negating the various actual and temporal limitations of his own being by way a kind of *via negativa*, the I alights on the idea of being without limit, what Stein variously describes as "the *idea of Eternal Being*" and "the *idea of True Being*," and, in typically Thomistic terms, as "the *idea of Pure Being*" and "the *idea of Pure Act*."[9] The personal I comes to these ideas in his own conscious experience, yet not as the immediate content of any experience. Rather, through reflecting on the fleeting character of experience, and through further reflecting on the nature of his own finite being, Stein reasons that the personal I comes upon the idea of a completed fullness of being and life by negating all that is finite about his own being and fleeting about his own life. More precisely, through the direct experience of his own finite being and fleeting life, and through forming corresponding ideas with finite meaning, the personal I indirectly confronts the idea of an infinite and enduring fullness of being, a being that does not have any finitude of being nor any corresponding frailty of life. Once this idea of the "changeless-eternal" has been grasped by the personal I, Stein reasons that it becomes the implicit "*measure* [Maß]" of his own being and experiential life, a kind of absolute standard by which the I begins to assess and evaluate all that he is, all that he has, and all that he experiences.[10]

Cambridge Scholars, 2011), 81; see also 113–17, 128. As will be clear in what follows, though I align with Leask in understanding this access to divinity as something *suggested in* and *by* experience phenomenologically investigated, I disagree with Leask that this suggestion cannot be followed through with inferential reasoning that proves the existence (and attributes) of God; rather, I argue that a metaphysical mode of reasoning completes this suggestive phenomenological approach with demonstrative clarity. And though I further agree with Leask that Stein to some degree presupposes a "faith-full intentionality" throughout EES (117, 128) and other works, I also maintain that she grants that intentional access to Divine Being can be something natural, even if it is—at least initially—mediated by metaphysical reasoning.

8   EES, 58.
9   See esp. EES, 42, 50, 57–61; PA, 10–12; AMP, 102. For a sampling of Aquinas's use of these terms, see ST, I, 3; I, 9; I, 12; QDP, 1.2, co.; 7; 10; QDV, 21.5, co.; DEE, 4, 127–47; and SCG, 1.16, no. 5, where he variously refers to God as *actus purus* (Pure Act) and *esse purum* (Pure Being) or *esse tantum* (Being Only/Alone). Reviewing Aquinas's *corpus*, one sees that these are the most frequently used philosophical identifiers for God in his writings.
10 See EES, 59. Given what Stein says elsewhere, "measure" should obviously be taken in a

In precisely this way, Stein argues that Divine Being first announces itself in experience, an announcement that takes place in and through what is immediately given in conscious experience, even while what is so announced does not form an immanent part of the content of experience. In a beautiful passage of *Finite and Eternal Being*, Stein puts this complex of insights in the following way,

> My being, as I find it in myself and find myself in it, is a null being, I am not from myself and of myself I am nothing, every moment I stand before the nothing and from moment to moment must be given being anew. And yet this null being is still being, and with it at every moment I touch the fullness of being. Becoming and perishing, as we find it in ourselves, as earlier mentioned, reveal to us the idea of true being, the changeless-eternal.[11]

In these and similar passages, Stein phenomenologically clarifies the precise character of this experiential openness to the possibility of Divine Being. In analyses of the finitude and temporality of conscious experience, which clearly resonate with insights found in Martin Heidegger's *Being and Time*, Stein reveals just how *full* and at the very same time how incredibly *frail* the life of the I actually is. The fullness is given in the conscious and spiritual form of the life of the I, which reveals that the I has a dual kind of preeminence, an ontological preeminence relative to what is borne by its intentional life, and a temporal preeminence in the present "now" relative to the past that is no longer and the future that is not yet. Yet, together with this experience of preeminence, Stein shows that we simultaneously experience "the powerlessness and frailty of this 'preeminent' being."[12] Note the profound paradox. As a being suspended between being and nonbeing in the temporal flow of conscious life, surrounded by the *already-passed-away* and the *as-yet-to-be*—even while the personal I is that to which all else is given via intentionality—the personal I is nonetheless brought "face-to-face with the nothing [*das Nichts*]" through

---

metaphorical sense, because the Divine Being is incommensurable and therefore could not perform the function of measuring anything, and moreover, because the finite personal I has no direct cognition of the essence of God and thus cannot directly refer his being to Divine Being.

11 EES, 57.
12 EES, 56.

the frailty of his personal life. Stein says that we experience "how little reason there is in the self for security and how much [our being] is in fact exposed to the nothing."[13] However, in contrast to Heidegger, Stein reasons that it is precisely this "powerlessness and frailty" that opens the space in experience for the dawning of the "the *idea of Eternal Being*." That is to say, inasmuch as the being of the self represents a "most extreme contrast to the self-possession [*Selbstherrlichkeit*] and self-transparency [*Selbstverständlichkeit*] of a *being from itself*," the idea of Divine Being is precipitated in conscious life.[14]

Nonetheless, even while Stein argues that "a philosophy based on natural knowledge has here a legitimate point of departure," the mere *idea* of God does not yet provide the evidential basis required to establish the *reality* of such a Divine Being.[15] Indeed, the world above is not given in experience with luminous certainty; instead what we have is an incipient and inchoate, even if suggestive, announcement of a dependence on the possible existence of such a world. This possibility is first one that stands opposite the impossible, as something that "can-be" but which also "can-not-be," a basic logical opposition. But it is also one that stands together with the actual, as potential for the actual, as something that opens toward and intimates its possible fulfillment in the actual. Accordingly, Stein reasons that the personal I must thoughtfully take hold of his own being in an attempt to unveil what is indirectly given in experience. This means that the finite personal I must find a rational basis in experience that enables him to bridge the gap between his immanent idea of Divine Being and the very actuality of God, a bridge that would also reveal in what way the finite personal I depends on the transcendent world above for his own characteristic being. This bridge is philosophically established by pursuing "the way of inferential thinking that follows *evidence for God* [Gottesbeweise]," what Stein calls "the way of philosophical knowledge," and it is theologically established by following "the way of faith" in personal surrender to the self-revelation of God, as is found historically in the religious traditions of Christianity and Judaism.[16] Both ways—the philosophical and

---

13   EES, 59, citing Heidegger, *Sein und Zeit*, 184ff., in the first quotation.
14   EES, 56–57.
15   EES, 42.
16   EES, 60. Compare PA, 17–18, where Stein speaks of the former as the way of logical procedure (*logischen Verfahrens*) and natural knowledge (*natürlichen Erkenntnis*). Even while Stein understands the ideas disclosed in consciousness as a starting-point for a natural knowledge of God, she does not proceed to use them as a basis for an ontological argument, and indeed follows Aquinas in questioning the validity of such

the theological—provide a rational bridge to the completed fullness of being already disclosed in the experiential life of the self, precisely inasmuch as both ways confirm and clarify the relation of the personal I (and all finite being) to God via the act of creation and the concomitant distinction and relation of creature and Creator. In her life and thought, Stein follows both ways and readily recognizes the complementary coherence of what is known distinctly via both ways, though the validity of her philosophical investigations rest on the way of philosophical knowledge, even while these same investigations are guided by the light and grace of divine Revelation.

To follow the path of philosophical knowledge, which is here of interest, Stein has brief but decisive recourse to Aquinas's metaphysical demonstrations of the existence and attributes of God. Stein's use of Aquinas in this area is especially brief and the demonstrations she references are presented in greatly abridged form. In *Potency and Act* she only cursorily refers to Aquinas's demonstrations, and in *Finite and Eternal Being* only cites Aquinas in footnotes associated with her own partial reformulation of his arguments. Nonetheless, Stein's recourse to Aquinas has crucial significance for her further philosophical investigation of God, as also her corresponding conception of the relational dependence of the creature upon the Creator.[17] The three demonstrations Stein

---

ontological arguments, precisely inasmuch as she reasons that we are not "naturally capable to know purely spiritual essences (God or angels) without mediation, that is, without recourse to the experience of temporal-actualities," and further argues that we are naturally unable to attain any "fulfilling intuition" of the essence of God, and consequently of the coincidence of essence and being in God. EES, 99, 103–4; see also, PA, 17n2. For an alternative discussion of the place of ontological arguments in Stein's thought, as well as her apparently negative evaluation of cosmological arguments, see Walter Redmond, "A Nothing That Is: Edith Stein on Being without Essence," in *American Catholic Philosophical Quarterly* 821, no. 1 (2008): 71–86; "Edith Stein's Ontological Argument," in *Intersubjectivity, Humanity, Being: Edith Stein's Phenomenology and Christian Philosophy*, ed. Mette Lebech and Haydn Gurmin (Bern: Peter Lang, 2015), 247–68.

17 Although Stein also believes in the existence of God as a matter of faith, since she separately investigates many articles of faith in a philosophical way, it is plausible that she would have done so here also, especially given the philosophical value of assenting to such knowledge naturally. Moreover, notwithstanding Stein's stronger conception of Christian philosophy (see above, xxxiiin15), where she argues that the believing philosopher can licitly seek assistance from the supernatural contents of Revelation, it is unlikely that Stein thinks that this includes the very existence of God, especially given the fact that she clearly designates demonstrations of God as "the way of philosophical knowledge," and was also surely aware of the dogmatic definition affirming the

expressly references are the following: (1) Aquinas's proof of the unreceived and self-necessary being of God, demonstrated in *Summa theologiae*, I, 2, while proving the existence of God; (2) Aquinas's proof of the essential actuality of God as Being Itself, a conclusion reached while arguing for the simplicity of God in *Summa theologiae*, I, 3; and (3) Aquinas's proof of the oneness of God, and the corresponding impossibility of multiple Gods, demonstrated in *Summa theologiae*, I, 11, as something that follows upon the earlier proved simplicity of God.[18]

Before overviewing Stein's recourse to Aquinas, I here provide a concise outline of the arguments as they are found in the texts of Aquinas.[19] In the third way of Aquinas's famous *quinque viae*, the existence of an unreceived and self-necessary being is argued for on the basis of the possible (*possibili*) and the necessary (*necessario*) and has its point of departure in the actual existence of the finite things of the natural world, "certain things that are possible to be and not to be."[20] Natural things certainly are, which evinces their essential possibility, but natural things also could not be, which evinces their contingency; yet if all

---

possibility of demonstrating the existence of God (see below, 183n31), not to mention the scriptural affirmations of the same.

18   See EES, 60nn51–53, citing ST, I, 1.2; I, 3.4; I, 11.3. Compare PA, 18, where Stein approvingly references "the way of the Thomistic demonstrations of God."

19   Of course, in summary form, it is not be possible to fully detail let alone substantiate and support the reasoning of each of the arguments, or indeed engage the various intra- and extra-Thomistic controversies surrounding their interpretation. Moreover, since Aquinas provides several demonstrations of the simplicity and unity of God, only the one that forms the ground of Stein's abbreviated reasonings is here summarized. Extensive commentary of all of Aquinas's arguments can be found in many Thomistic commentaries, in books and articles, where one or more of these arguments are presented, interpreted, and defended; one such resource is John F. Wippel, *The Metaphysical Thought of Thomas Aquinas: From Finite Being to Uncreated Being* (Washington, DC: The Catholic University of America Press, 2000), esp. 442–500, 501–75, which contains details on each conclusion here referenced and provides a good overview of the arguments themselves, their interpretation, and related controversies, while also providing valuable references for other Thomistic resources.

20   In this context, since both *possibili* and *necessario* are adjectives qualifying things, by "possible" we are to understand some *thing* that is not repugnant to being, but rather has a nature or essence that can stand in existence, and by "necessary" we are to understand some *thing* that cannot not be, but rather is unchanging with respect to being. See John F. X. Knasas, "'Necessity' in the Tertia Via," in *The New Scholasticism* 52, no. 3 (1978): 373–94; and Lawrence Dewan, "St. Thomas and the Possibles," in *The New Scholasticism* 53, no. 1 (1979): 76–85.

things were of this sort, beings that of their nature are indifferent to being and nonbeing, there would be no way to account for the actuality of the beings of the natural world. Therefore, there must be one necessary being in addition to the numerous merely possible, yet also actual beings of the natural world; and, moreover, there must be one *self*-necessary being, a being that has not received its necessity from another, precisely since one cannot proceed to infinity in caused necessary beings.[21] This unreceived and self-necessary being Aquinas calls God. After so demonstrating the existence and attributes of God in this and many other ways, in the very next question of *Summa theologiae*, together with demonstrating the simplicity of God, Aquinas argues that in God it is impossible "that being [*esse*] be one thing and essence [*essentia*] another." He reasons that if being differs from essence in any given thing, the being of that thing must be caused, because no thing suffices to be the cause of its own being through its own essence—for it would then have to be prior to its being. And since God has already been shown to be the first efficient cause (*prima causa efficiens*), this means that *to be God* must simply be *to be*—that is, the divine *essentia* must be coincident with the divine *esse*.[22] Finally, in question eleven, Aquinas proceeds to demonstrate the unity or oneness (*unitas*) of God "from the infinity of his perfection." Since God possesses the total perfection of being, as shown in *Summa theologiae*, I, 4, and as manifest in the "name" of God as Being Itself (*ipsum esse*), it is impossible for there to be more than one such being, because any plurality of such wholly perfect beings would have to be distinct from one another through some perfection possessed exclusively, or indeed through some privation of perfection in one in comparison to the other—or else such a hypothetical plurality would necessarily collapse into

---

21 As with several of his arguments for the existence of God, Aquinas reasons that one cannot proceed to infinity in *per se* causal series (sometimes identified as essentially or hierarchically ordered series), in contrast to *per accidens* causal series (usually identified as accidentally ordered series), where the distinguishing feature is that all consequent members of *per se* causal series have their causal power derivatively rather than essentially, and so causally rely on the prior member(s) of the series in an absolute causal sense. See Gaven Kerr, "Essentially Ordered Series Reconsidered," in *American Catholic Philosophical Quarterly* 86, no. 4 (2012): 541–55.

22 Thus, God is identifiable as Being Itself (*ipsum esse*), the total perfection of being as such and all that is entailed in such perfection. Though Aquinas does not use the phrase in this particular question, in the immediately following question, relying on argumentation of this question, he refers to God as *ipsum esse*. The Latin *esse* is literally the infinitive "to be," though it is often used as a noun by Aquinas, and hence its translation as "being" and its use as a noun.

one indistinguishable unity of being. Therefore, God not only *is* and is Being Itself, the unreceived and self-necessary totality of perfection, but precisely as such is also One—indicating both that there is only one God, and this One God is supremely one and absolutely simple.[23]

Stein's significantly abridged but parallel reasoning closely tracking the thought of Aquinas proceeds in the following way. She first reasons that the transcendent "ground and author [*Grund and Urheber*]" of finite being must not *have* being as something received from another, but rather must simply be *from itself* without any dependence on another.[24] In contrast to the dependent mode of being of finite being, which does not have being from itself but rather necessitates the reception of being, the ultimate ground of being cannot be dependent on the reception of being for its own existence, but rather must be through its own being and therefore must be by necessity—and indeed by its very own necessity. Stein summarizes, "It must be from its own self; a being that cannot—like everything that has a beginning—not be, but rather, is necessary."[25] Furthermore, unlike finite being, which radically depends on the constant provision of being from its ground and author, "there can be no separation in this being [*Seiend*] between *what* it is (and what it could or could not be) and its being [*Sein*]."[26] Since the author of being does not need to receive being, but rather has being as something proper to itself, Stein reasons that the author of being must simply just *be*, and so must be by essence, and therefore must be Being Itself (*Sein selbst*).[27] Finally, there must be only one such being, "for if there were a plurality, there would have to be a distinction between what differentiates one from the others and makes it this one, and what it has in common with the others."[28] To have a plurality of such beings would require some principle of distinction, and since no principle of distinction can be found outside the realm of being, there must be only one ground and author of finite being—and this being must be *one* in a preeminent sense, having in itself no division and separation. Therefore, for Stein, tracking and parallel

---

23 That is, though God possesses transcendental unity in an absolute way, and thus is supremely one, God is beyond the order of numerical unity, since there can be only one God. See esp. ST, I, 11.4, ad 2.
24 EES, 60n51, citing ST, I, 1.2.
25 EES, 60n51, citing ST, I, 1.2.
26 EES, 60n52, citing ST, I, 3.4.
27 EES, 60n52, citing ST, I, 3.4.
28 EES, 60n53, citing ST, I, 11.3.

reasoning of Aquinas, God the Creator must be Being Itself, the unreceived and self-necessary being, both supremely one and absolutely simple.[29]

In so marshaling the assistance of Aquinas, Stein does not systematically set forth the demonstrations of Aquinas, and neither does she expansively detail them in her own preferred formulations. Rather, in *Potency and Act* she simply references the arguments as the Thomistic way to God (in comparison to the Augustinian way), and in *Finite and Eternal Being* she merely recasts Aquinas's arguments in her own summary formulations while citing the corresponding texts. Is this brevity reason to think that Aquinas's demonstrations were philosophically insignificant for Stein? I do not think so. Notwithstanding the severely abridged character of Stein's reasoning, there is reason to believe that her recourse to Aquinas here has crucial significance for her subsequent philosophical investigation of God and creation, as also for her further examination of the relational dependence of the creature upon the Creator according to the analogy of being. This is most obvious in the way she introduces her abridged formulations of the demonstrations as "the way of philosophical knowledge [*der Weg der philosophischen Erkenntnis*]," a way that is traversed by "inferential thinking [*schluẞfolgernden Denkens*]" that follows evidence for the existence of God.[30] We should also note the obvious point that Stein plainly follows Aquinas in holding that the existence of God is philosophically demonstrable, and also that a basic subset of divine attributes is deducible from the conclusions of the demonstrations and their associated reasonings.[31] Indeed, Stein patently follows Aquinas's conclusion that the most

---

29 Though Stein does not expressly reference the simplicity of God in this context, she references the question of ST where Aquinas proves divine simplicity while also concluding to God as Being Itself, and she employs the simplicity of God in her later investigations of Creator and creation. It should also be noted that conceiving of God as entirely or absolutely simple (*simplex omnino*) is dogmatically defined by the Catholic Church—first by the Fourth Lateran Council (1215) and again by the First Vatican Council (1869–70)—and is evidently something for which Stein would have had a philosophical concern to properly understand and clarify, given her understanding of Christian Philosophy as above detailed (9n15). See esp. EES, 290–96; and Denzinger, §§ 800, 3001, 266, 601.

30 Emphasis added.

31 That the existence and attributes of God are philosophically demonstrable is something scripturally asserted (see Romans 1:19–20, and Wisdom 13:4–5) and ratified by the Catholic Church in the First Vatican Council's *Dei filius*, § 2, and therefore is a teaching of the Catholic faith to which Stein would certainly have assented.

foundational philosophical truth inferred about God is the affirmation that he is *ipsum esse* (Being Itself)—*esse subsistens* (Subsisting Being) or *ipsum esse subsistens* (Being Itself Subsisting) in Aquinas's own terminology.[32] This identification of God as Being Itself is a vital centerpiece of Stein's recapitulation of Aquinas's teaching, and it undergirds much of her later thinking about God, as also her conception of the natural creaturely relation of the human being to God via analogy.[33]

We should also observe that the pattern of reasoning by which Stein infers truths about God follows the same pattern as the comparable reasoning of Aquinas. Though Stein does not draw attention the provenance of her reasoning, but rather simply cites the corresponding source texts, her own formulations take the same shape as the prior reasoning of Aquinas and achieve conclusions in perfect accord with the conclusions attained by Aquinas. Stein evidently does not feel the need to comprehensively detail the demonstrations given by Aquinas; she neither alters nor amends, opposes nor contradicts, expands nor improves upon the demonstrations. Rather, she seems to accept Aquinas's prior reasoning in completion while simply restating the pattern of reasoning in abridged form. Finally, and most importantly, Stein nowhere separately demonstrates that the possible transcendent world above inchoately disclosed in the conscious life of the personal I is an *actual* transcendent world, and nowhere does she separately demonstrate that the finite personal I, or finite being in general, *receives being* from God the Creator. Yet, Stein evidently proceeds in both *Finite and Eternal Being* and *Potency and Act* as if: (1) the transcendent fullness of being ideationally disclosed is shown to *actually exist*; (2) this being has the basic subset of attributes provided by the demonstrations of Aquinas and recast in her own summary form; and, finally, (3) this being is not on the horizontal plain of finite being but rather represents the totally transcendent other, the infinite ground and author of

---

[32] For a sampling of texts of Aquinas on this point, see ST, I, 4.2, co.; SCG, 3.19, no. 3; QDV, 21.5, co.

[33] After paralleling the demonstrations of Aquinas, Stein succinctly describes the ideal, essential, and actual necessity of a transcendent ground and author of finite being in a pithy restatement of the position of Hedwig Conrad-Martius, saying, "Everything temporal is, *as such*, fleeting, and requires eternal support." EES, 60, citing Conrad-Martius, *Die Zeit*, 371ff. One can think of this pithy formulation as the temporal analogue of the more general proposition, "Since becoming necessitates being, if becoming, then being."

being as such. Indeed, in her subsequent investigations, Stein freely uses the conclusions attained here as the fundamental conceptual apparatuses to frame her understanding of the relation of creation to Creator, together with the corresponding absolute dependence of the creature upon the Creator. This conceptual apparatus includes the unreceived and self-necessary being of God, the identity of God as Being Itself, in whom there is no composition of essence (*Wesen, essentia*) and being (*Sein, esse*), and the corresponding supreme unity and absolute simplicity of the Divine Being (*Seiend, ens*). Indeed, this latter truth regarding the simplicity of God is indispensable to Stein in her later reconsideration of the Thomistic conception of the analogy of being as an analogy of proportionality.[34]

And so, we may reasonably conclude that Stein does grant that the transcendent "ground and author" of finite being announced in first-person experience is effectively accounted for by the Thomistic mode of arguing for the existence and attributes of God. Moreover, we may also reasonably conclude that Aquinas's inferential reasonings provide Stein with the conceptual clarity needed to proceed with her philosophical inquiry into the nature of God as Creator, in addition to providing her with the conceptual basis required for treating of the relational dependence of the finite person upon the Creator.[35] Indeed, the possible relation of the finite person to the completed fullness of being disclosed in first-person experience cannot be *rationally* completed without recourse to such metaphysical inferences, and it is in and through

---

34 As is evident by now, I translate the *esse* (literally, "to be") with "being" taken as a verbal noun, as Aquinas uses the term to signify the actuality of being, while I also translate *ens* with "being" but now taken as a plain noun, and signifying the thing possessing the actuality of being. Though *esse* is often translated as "existence" (presumably since it can also mean "the fact of being" in addition to "the act of being"), I believe this translation obscures the meaning intended by Aquinas for whom *esse* is arguably the key principle of his metaphysics, and who also uses the Latin cognate of "to exist," that is, *existere* (literally, to step out/come forth).

35 The assistance rendered to Stein by Aquinas stands as true notwithstanding the apparently negative evaluation she gives to the effectiveness of these demonstrations in leading people to a natural knowledge of God or to a living faith in God. Indeed, though Stein negatively evaluates the practical import of arguments for God, there is no reason to believe she doubts their theoretical validity—and, as indicated, surely assents to the Catholic declaration of their liceity (see above, 183n31). This may well be one reason why Stein anchors knowledge of God the Creator in the first-person experiences of the human subject and provides these demonstrations with a corresponding personal slant rather than restating them in a cosmological way. See PA, 17–18; EES, 104.

metaphysical reasoning that the first-person perspective attains its proper *rational* satisfaction—something obviously important for the human being as a person, that is, as a *rational* being. Consequently, when Stein supplements her phenomenological insights with the conceptual apparatus of Aquinas, she attains rational confirmation of the actual existence of the completed fullness of being, and conceptual clarity over the character of the relation of the finite personal I to this transcendent ground of being. On the other hand, by situating her phenomenological inquiry against the backdrop of the demonstrations of Aquinas, Stein gives these Thomistic demonstrations a significant personal twist. In contrast to Aquinas's mode of reasoning, which begins with the activities and natures of the finite beings of the natural world, Stein concentrates her attention on the finitude of the personal I, beginning with the admixture of potentiality and actuality in the inherently temporal conscious life of the finite subject. In so doing, Stein refocuses Aquinas's inferential reasonings on the conscious experiences of the I—with its potentiality, finitude, and temporality—and thereby expands their range of meaning to explicitly include the experiential life of the personal self.[36] The conscious experience of oneself then becomes a new demonstrative basis for the rational deduction of the Creator, a new "first premise" for a mode of reasoning that leads to the existence and attributes of God. Thus, Stein's reconsideration of Aquinas's reasonings can rightly be understood as providing a phenomenological reinterpretation of the metaphysical demonstrations of Aquinas, a reinterpretation that involves expanding their conceptual content to explicitly include the personal life of the human subject.

Again here, then, it is possible to say that Stein achieves something of a "personalization" of the received teachings of Aquinas. Though Stein provides only summary parallels, her express personalization of Aquinas's mode of reasoning is undoubtedly significant for the human individual, precisely since

---

36 As Stein unpacks her phenomenological investigation in the opening sections of EES, it is clear that while she attends to the potentiality and finitude of the personal self, she is primarily interested in doing so from the perspective of temporality. In focusing on the temporality of finite being in this way, like Heidegger, as well as on the essential finitude and potentiality of temporality itself, Stein is making it clear that temporality provides a defined pointer to the meaning of finite being in its contrast to Eternal Being—indeed, this contrast is found already in the title of the work. Moreover, she is indicating that the personal meaning of temporality is touched upon in an ultimate sense by the unfolding discovery that the origin and end of the finite self—the two definite and ultimate boundaries of the finite personal I—are to be found in God.

it provides a new point of departure for attaining philosophical knowledge of God in that which is closest to each and every human individual: the interior life of the personal self. In beginning with the being and life of the self, with the finitude of this being and the frail and fleeting character of one's experiential life, Stein provides a path to God from the most intimate sphere of human life, that which is the most proper possession of every individual. Stein's development in this sphere can then be understood as bringing together the contrasted Thomistic and Augustinian ways of concluding to the existence of God, insofar as the Thomistic way involves inferential reasoning that begins with the contingent beings and activities of the outer world, while the Augustinian way involves concentrated attention to the experiential givens of the inner world (notwithstanding that both Aquinas and Augustine recognize and value, each in their own way, the possibility of the alternate). This complementing with the Augustinian perspective and simultaneous personalization furnishes Aquinas's metaphysical demonstrations with a clearly defined existential significance, one that has the potential to *grip* the personal subject in fresh and compelling ways—emboldening the individual to say, together with Stein, "The being-secure that I feel in my fleeting being points to an immediate anchoring in the ultimate hold and ground of my being";[37] and again, "Despite this fleetingness, I *am* and I am *preserved in being* from moment to moment, and in my fleeting being I embrace enduring [being]."[38]

A Phenomenological Approach to the Analogy of Being

Notwithstanding her recourse to the demonstrations of Aquinas, in both *Finite and Eternal Being* and *Potency and Act* Stein is clearly more interested in investigating the Thomistic conception of the analogy of being than she is in presenting a demonstrative basis for the existence of God. As above mentioned, the analogy of being is the predominating concept overarching her investigation of being in these works and is employed by her to clarify the

---

37 EES, 61. Stein references Heidegger's conception of *Dasein* being "thrown" toward the "nothingness," but reinterprets Heidegger's insight by arguing that it would be more "rational" to conceive of the self (and all finite beings) as "held" in being. See below, 237–39; and also, Leask, *Being Reconfigured*, 87ff.; Lidia Ripamonti, "Being Thrown or Being Held in Existence? The Opposite Approaches to Finitude of Edith Stein and Martin Heidegger," in *Yearbook of Irish Philosophical Society* (2008): 71–83.
38 EES, 59; see also, PA, 17–18.

creaturely relation of the human person to God. However, Stein's use of analogy is properly founded only in tandem with her reliance on the metaphysical demonstrations of Aquinas, since Aquinas's reasonings provide the basis for recognizing the conceptual duality included in the analogy of being, that of the concomitant *distinction* and *relation* of creature and Creator conceptually embraced by analogy.[39] The Thomistic conception of creation as the provision of the actuality of being (*esse*), with the implied *distinction* of the creature *from* the Creator, and the simultaneously implied *relation* of the creature *to* the Creator, provides the intrinsic demonstrative basis required to undergird the analogy of being. Yet, on the other hand, the conception of creature and Creator established in the demonstrations is conceptually clarified for Stein, as it was for Aquinas, only by employing the conceptual apparatus of the analogy of being.[40] This means that the demonstrations of the existence and attributes of God and the analogy of being are paired intellectual apparatuses, where the demonstrations first argumentatively reveal the basis of the analogy of being embracing creature and Creator, and the analogy of being then conceptually clarifies the distinction and relation rationally established by the demonstrations.

In what immediately follows, I investigate Stein's preliminary mode of approach of the analogy of being in two stages. In the first I outline Stein's phenomenological approach to the analogy of being, and in the second I examine Stein's interpretation of the Thomistic conception of the analogy of being as an analogy of proportionality, together with her critical questioning of a central dimension of the apparatus. In the next chapter, I proceed to detail and examine Stein's innovative conceptual expansion of the Thomistic understanding by approaching it from a specifically personal perspective.[41]

---

39   See ST, I, 4.3 co.
40   Compare Wippel, *Metaphysical Thought*, 544, 568–69; and Jacques Maritain, *Degrees of Knowledge*, trans. Gerald B. Phelan (Notre Dame, IN: University of Notre Dame Press, 1998, repr. 2014), 249–50.
41   I note here that though Stein's reading of Przywara's *Analogia Entis* undoubtedly impacts her understanding of analogy (as indicated by her reference to his work in her works), given the focus of my investigation, as well as the involved and complex character of Przywara's work, I do not treat in detail of his impact on Stein beyond brief reference to their commonality and difference in footnotes, which commonality and difference is highlighted by Przywara in his "Edith Stein and Simone Weil: Two Fundamental Philosophical Themes," included in "Part II" of the English translation of *Analogia Entis*. See Erich Przywara, *Analogia Entis: Metaphysics—Original Structure and Universal Rhythm*, trans. John R. Betz and David Bentley Hart (Grand Rapids,

Stein begins by venturing a phenomenological analysis of the fundamental character of analogy by considering it from the perspective of the finitude of the personal I, since "the *analogia entis*, understood as the relation [*Verhältnis*] of temporal and Eternal Being, is already visible in this starting point."[42] This phenomenological point of access is already given in the above-detailed manifold ideas that are unveiled in the frail life of the I, ideas of the "finite, temporal, and mutable" in contrast to ideas of the "infinite, eternal, and immutable." Since these ideas are paired ideas, they form the ideational basis for attaining outline knowledge of a *possible* completed fullness of being not directly experienced, and inasmuch as they are paired in mutual opposition to one another through their meaningful relation, the ideas furnish preliminary access to the kind

---

MI: Eerdmans, 2014), 596–612. For some historical context of Stein and Przywara's shared thought world, see Philip Gonzales, "*Analogia Entis* and Creatureliness: Stein and Przywara's Refutation of Heidegger," in *The Hat and the Veil: The Phenomenology of Edith Stein*, Ad Fontes: Studien zur frühen Phänomenologie 3, ed. Jerzy Machnacz et al. (Nordhausen: Traugott Bautz, 2016), 119–30. First here, and then more decidedly in his recent monograph, *Reimagining the* Analogia Entis: *The Future of Erich Przywara's Christian Vision* (Grand Rapids, MI: Eerdmans, 2019), Gonzales treats primarily of the significance of the *distinction* established by the analogy of being, whereas my analysis here places the accent on the *similarity* and corresponding *relation* concomitantly established, even while I, following Stein, respect the "still greater" dissimilarity at the heart of the *analogia entis*—something Gonzales denies of Stein by starkly contrasting her typically modern approach (from the perspective of the conscious I) with what he calls the theocentric approach of Przywara. For more regarding Przywara and Stein, as well as Przywara and Gonzales's interpretation of Stein, see below, 208–9nn10–11.

42 EES, 42; compare PA, 10. Several scholars have referenced Stein's development of analogy in the context of conscious experience and in terms of the consequent implicit orientation of the finite I toward Divine Being; among others, see Christof Betschart, *Unwiederholbares Gottessiegel: Personale Individualität nach Edith Stein* (Basel: Reinhardt, 2013), esp. 345–51; Marian Maskulak, *Edith Stein and the Body-Soul-Spirit at the Center of Holistc Formation* (New York: Peter Lang, 2007), 49–50; Mary Catherine Baseheart, *Person in the World: Introduction to the Philosophy of Edith Stein* (Boston: Kluwer Academic, 1997), 110–23; See Karl Schmidt, "Edith Stein, Apophatic Theology, and Freedom," in *Selected Papers on the Legacy of Edith Stein's Finite and Eternal Being*, ed. Sarah Borden Sharkey (= *Quaestiones Disputatae* 4, no. 1 (2013)), 21–30: 24–28; Michael F. Andrews, "Stein: Beyond Reason, Faith, and Ethics," in *Edith Steins Herausforderung heutiger Anthropologie*, ed. Hanna-Barbara Gerl-Falkovitz and Mette Lebech (Heiligenkreuz: Be&Be, 2017), 383–99: 386–93; and Glenn Chicoine, "Present Potential in Edith Stein's Finite and Eternal Being, Chapter Two," in Sharkey, Selected Papers on the Legacy of Edith Stein's Finite and Eternal Being, 31–44: 39, 43–44.

of analogy that could *possibly* exist between finite and Eternal Being. This is best understood first from the perspective of the correlation of the finite and the infinite. The idea of the infinite is referred to the idea of the finite, since the infinite is *similar* to the finite, as founded in the idea of the finite, even while it is *dissimilar* to the finite, as formed by the negation of the finite. Thus, the infinite and the finite are meaningfully implicated by one another even while they are negatively counterpoised to one another—and, indeed, even as they are counterpoised on opposite ends of the spectrum, so to speak, as radically dissimilar. This same reasoning can be applied to the eternal and immutable in their contrast to the temporal and mutable, or indeed to any other complementary pair of ideas forged in the conscious life of the I, inasmuch the limited member of the pair would provide the meaningful ground of its complementary opposite via the negation of its particular kind of limitation. Each pair then contains one idea that is essentially limited and one idea that is essentially unlimited, possessing similarity to one another through their correlated meaningfulness, while possessing a still greater dissimilarity to one another through the contrast of limited versus unlimited.

Yet, since these paired ideas qualify *being*, with one of each pair qualifying the actual being of the finite personal self, and the other qualifying the possible being of the radically transcendent "other," these paired ideas provide an *ideal kind* of analogy of being, and an *ideational confirmation of the possibility* of an actual analogy of being. That is to say that since one idea of each pair is discovered relative to the actual being of the self, the being of the self as variously qualified in limited ways—as finite, temporal, mutable, etc.—provides the basis for attaining a corresponding idea of a being that is without limited qualification—as infinite, eternal, immutable, etc.—or, more precisely, the idea of a being that is unqualified. But since one of each pair qualifies the actual being of the self, while its paired opposite only qualifies the possible being of the radically transcendent "other," this form of analogy initially resides on the level of the *ideal* and *possible* rather than on the level of the *real* and *actual*.[43] However, when this ideational insight is taken together with the above-detailed metaphysical deduction of a completed fullness of being with actual existence as Being Itself, this ideal kind of analogy becomes the ideational basis for the

---

43 Since this analogy is both ideal and possible, and since essential being grounds all ideation and possibility, Stein's ideal analogy of being is also an essential analogy of being; of this dimension of analogy, I treat no further here. I thank Mette Lebech for bringing this insight to my attention.

actual analogy of being. And so, after exploring her initial phenomenological access to analogy, Stein turns to the metaphysical conceptual apparatus of Aquinas to clarify her already developed ideal conception, and thereby fittingly explicates the character of the actual relation of the finite personal I—as all finite beings—to God the Creator.[44]

The Thomistic Conception of the Analogy of the Being

In a dedicated subsection of chapter VI of *Finite and Eternal Being*, Stein introduces her thematized reflection on the analogy of being with the Aristotelian basis of analogy, before immediately proceeding to the understanding of Aquinas since Aristotle does not have a philosophical conception of creation and Creator and does not present analogy as embracing the distinction and relation of creature and Creator.[45] Aquinas's understanding is presented by

---

44 Evidently, then, even in her opening phenomenological analysis of the analogy of being—in the ideational contrast of finite and infinite, temporal and eternal, and mutable and immutable—Stein clearly aligns with the dogmatically defined "still greater dissimilarity" at the heart of the analogy of proportionality (Fourth Lateran Council, 1215). See below, 209n11, for more detail.

45 See EES, 288–89. For a brief but comprehensive history of the development of the use of analogy (ἀναλογία) in ancient Greece, from its mathematical roots with the Pythagoreans, through to its collation and precise formulation by Euclid, up to and including its conceptual expansion in the Academy and Lyceum, especially in the scientific investigations of Aristotle, see Roger M. White, *Talking About God: The Concept of Analogy and the Problem of Religious Language* (Surrey: Ashgate, 2010), 11–72. White shows how analogy began as a mathematical representation of the similitude of quantitative ratios, representable with four terms in the following way: "as A is to B, so C is to D"; and symbolically: "A / B = C / D" or "A : B :: C : D." Yet, this similitude of ratios possesses a rich and variegated useability by virtue of its potential to facilitate not only the handling of commensurable quantities but also naturally incommensurable quantities and naturally incommensurable things and kinds. This flexibility enables Aristotle to employ analogy as a conceptual apparatus of general scientific use for the comparison of relations across categories and classes of being, becoming especially useful in the biological sphere for drawing comparisons across species and genera boundaries, what White calls trans-categorial alternation. In such cases, the symbolic mathematical formula is then better expressed in a more general form that explicitly identifies the relation itself, "R (A, B) = R (C, D)." Since the relation among paired terms now bears significance toward correctly grasping the conceptual import of analogy, such a representation enables one to signify both the things analogically related and the analogical proportion itself. However, though

Stein through the inclusion of lengthy quotations from *Quaestiones disputatae de veritate*, 2.11, and *Summa theologiae*, I, 3.3–4, I, 50.2, which quotations she analyzes—with brief but decisive help from Josef Gredt—in an effort to properly understand the Thomistic conception. In this way, Stein attempts to get to the heart "of the peculiar *relation* [*des eigentümlichen* Verhältnisses] of finite and Eternal Being which makes it possible on the basis of a common stock of meaning to speak here and there of 'being [*Sein*].'"[46]

Immediately, Stein identifies the kind of analogy appropriate to the relation of creature and Creator as an analogy of proportionality, which she denominates with the German *Verhältnisgleichheit*, literally "likeness of proportion," and identifies this conception with the Latin *analogia proportionalitatis*.[47] Stein calls this kind of analogy the "Thomistic conception" since it embraces the close relation of the creature to the Creator while concomitantly respecting

---

analogical naming enables the gathering of heterogenous things under one concept in this way, White cautions that such a unified concept does not possess the definition and clarity ordinarily possessed of concepts, but rather contains an inbuilt vagueness. Finally, White notes that analogy is not first a linguistic phenomenon for Aristotle, but a conceptual and linguistic signification of actual things and kinds, and the relations between actual things and kinds, where analogical conceptualization and language neatly transposes the relations of the actual world. See White, *Talking About God*, esp. 13–16, 18–20, 29–37, 53–54, 58–60, 67–68. For an historical overview of analogy with a consciously Christian (even Catholic) *telos*, see Przywara, *Analogia Entis*, 238–306; in summary in Betz's "Translator's Introduction" to the same, esp. 30–43, and for more on the development and understanding of analogy in Ancient Greece, see Eva Brann, *The Logos of Heraclitus* (Philadelphia: Paul Dry Books, 2011), 31–36.

46 EES, 288; emphasis added. Though Stein here introduces analogy as a way of speaking ("naming"), given her understanding of the close correspondence of speech, knowing, and being, I take her to understand the analogy of being as something proper to language, thought, and being in their intimate correspondence. Moreover, I maintain that she here follows Aquinas, even though this reading of Aquinas is not without controversy. See ST, I, 4.3 co.: "And it is in this way," i.e., "according to some kind of analogy [*secundum aliqualem analogiam*]," "that those things which are from God, the first and universal principle of all being [*esse*], are made similar [*assimilantur*] to Him insofar as they are beings [*entia*]," where he applies his understanding of the various ways an effect resembles its cause, in order to account for analogical likeness of creatures to their Creator cause.

47 EES, 289. *Verhältnisgleichheit* can also be translated as "equality of relation," but the context clearly indicates "likeness of proportion." Przywara parallels Stein in identifying the kind of analogy of being relating the creature to the Creator as an analogy of proportionality.

the radical distinction of the creature from the Creator, a tension of profound relation and radical distinction that Aquinas readily and vigorously defends throughout his philosophical (and theological) works. Though Aquinas never actually uses the precisely formulated phrase, *analogia proportionalitatis*, or indeed, *analogia entis*, these technical terms introduced by later Scholastics—such as Thomas de Vio Cajetan, Francisco Suárez, and John of St. Thomas—helpfully clarify the conceptual content of Aquinas's writings about Creator and creation.[48] The principal figure associated with the analogy of proportionality is Cajetan, who distinguishes analogy into "analogy of inequality, analogy of attribution, and analogy of proportionality," and further distinguishes the latter into analogy "according to metaphor" and analogy by way of "proper proportion," understanding only the latter as analogy strictly speaking, and equivalent to later thinkers' use of the "analogy of proportionality."[49]

---

48 I note that the phrase *analogia entis* has an earlier provenance. For an overview of its development from different sides, see John R. Betz, "The *Analogia Entis* as a Standard of Catholic Engagement: Erich Przywara's Critique of Phenomenology and Dialectical Theology," in *Modern Theology* 35, no. 1 (2019): 81–102; Garrett R. Smith, "The Analogy of Being in the Scotist Tradition," in *American Catholic Philosophical Quarterly* 93, no. 4 (2019): 633–73; E. J. Ashworth, "Suárez on the Analogy of Being: Some Historical Background," in *Vivarium* 33, no. 1 (1995): 50–75.

49 See Thomas de Vio Cajetan, *De Nominum Analogia*, trans. Joshua P. Hochschild, "Appendix," to *The Semantics of Analogy according to Thomas De Vio Cajetan's De Nominum Analogia* (unpublished diss., University of Notre Dame, 2001), esp. 1.3, 211; 3.25–27, 220–21; 7.17–27, 242–43; 9.95–97, 251–52. For general accounts of the Thomistic conception of analogy, see George P. Klubertanz, *St. Thomas Aquinas on Analogy: A Textual Analysis and Systematic Synthesis* (Eugene, OR: Wipf and Stock, 2009); Wippel, *Metaphysical Thought*, 74, 543–72; and Joseph Owens, *An Elementary Christian Metaphysics* (Milwaukee, WI: Bruce, 1963; repr. Houston: Center for Thomistic Studies, 1986, repr. 2013), 86–94. Klubertanz and Wippel maintain that Aquinas likely changed his position and discreetly discarded the analogy of proportionality for the analogy of proportion in his later writings, those after QDV. See Klubertanz, *Aquinas on Analogy*, 93–96; and Wippel, *Metaphysical Thought*, 553–55. I do not here enter the debate regarding the question of the kind of analogy maintained by Aquinas, or of the possible development that takes place in his writings, or indeed that of the exact nature of Cajetan's presentation of analogy, whether Thomistic or not; rather, in consort with examining Stein's engagement with Aquinas and the Thomistic tradition, I restrict my analysis to the texts Stein cites and critically engages. However, I note that Hochschild convincingly argues that Aquinas maintained his position on the analogy of proportionality according to the presentation in QDV, 2.11 (a text heavily employed by Stein) throughout the entirety of his writings, even while he tailors his

With the help of quotations from Aquinas and Gredt, Stein begins her investigation by explaining that the analogy of proportionality indicates an agreement (*Übereinstimmung*) between distinct things because of some *similarity of proportions* between these things, in consequence of which the same term can be predicated truly of each. Yet, when the same term is so predicated, no determinate relation is signified between the things denominated, thus securing the (possibly still greater) disagreement (*Nichtübereinstimmung*) between the things identified as proportionally similar to one another. A text of Aquinas quoted by Stein uses the example of number to illustrate the nature of this form of indirect proportional agreement in its distinction from the mutual agreement implied by direct proportion.

> Agreement according to proportion is possible in two ways, and according to these two ways analogical community follows. For there is a certain agreement between things having a mutual proportion, to the extent that they have a determinate distance or some other habitude to one another, just as two and one, insofar as it is its double; likewise, agreement sometimes follows not because of some proportion between two things themselves, but rather between two mutual proportions, as six agrees with four because six is double three, as four is two. Therefore, the first agreement is proportion, but the second proportionality.[50]

While the agreement of "two" to "one" is given as the determinate relation "double," according to the direct proportion between the terms of the relation—since "two" is double "one"—"double" can also be predicated of "six" and "four," but now by virtue of the similarity of proportions between these two terms and two other terms—since "six" is double "three," and "four" is double "two." Accordingly, the predication now signifies only an *indeterminate agreement*

---

presentation to the needs of each context. Joshua P. Hochschild, "Proportionality and Divine Naming: Did St. Thomas Change His Mind about Analogy?," in *The Thomist: A Speculative Quarterly Review* 77, no. 4 (2013): 531–58; *The Semantics of Analogy Rereading Cajetan's De Nominum Analogia* (Notre Dame, IN: University of Notre Dame Press, 2010), esp. 122–64. I would like to thank Brandon Dahm for drawing my attention to the work of Hochschild on analogy in Cajetan and Aquinas.

50 See QDV, 2.11. Aquinas's numerical example is especially fitting given the mathematical origins of analogy.

between the two significant terms—"six" and "four"—precisely inasmuch as these two terms have an *indeterminate relation* to one another through their direct proportion to two other terms. Thus, we have a four-term analogy that can be represented in the following way: as "six" is to "three," so "four" is to "two"—or, more formally, as "A" is to "B," so "C" is to "D."

Since the two significant terms have a kind of indeterminate relation to one another, this form of analogy is appropriately denominated as an analogy of proportion*ality*, in contrast to the determinate relation signified by the direct proportion of the analogy of proportion. When the same term is predicated of two things indeterminately related in this way, the meaning of the term signifies both the basic similarity of relational agreement and the potentially still greater dissimilarity of distinguishing disagreement. Because of this concomitance of agreement and potentially greater disagreement, this kind of analogy is especially fitting for capturing the unique kind of relation of creature to Creator, inasmuch as the same terms can be truly predicated of both creature and Creator without ignoring the radical distinction of the creature from the Creator. Since the Creator is the completed fullness of being, Being Itself Subsisting, *Ipsum Esse Subsistens*, the Creator is in no way limited by any *terminus* that would introduce a de*terminate* relation of the creature to the Creator, a relation that would in some way de*termine* the Creator. As a result, the analogy of proportionality respects the radical distinction of the creature from the Creator even while it simultaneously captures the deep agreement of creature and Creator. This means that while analogous terms signify the intrinsic relational likeness of the finite creature to the Creator—through a basic similarity of proportions—they concurrently signify the infinite distance separating the creature from the Creator—through a radical dissimilarity of being—a form of predication that embraces both the basic similitude (*similitudo*) and the still greater dissimilitude (*dissimilitudo*) of creature and Creator. Consequently, Aquinas reasons that analogous terms "signify the divine substance, yet imperfectly, even as creatures represent it imperfectly."[51]

---

51 ST, I, 13.2, co. In the Thomistic tradition the dissimilarity conceptually signified by the analogy of proportionality is partially explained by making a distinction between the thing signified (*res significata*) and the mode of signification (*modus significandi*). However, since this distinction is not expressly treated by Stein and does not have special significance for her critical engagement with the analogy of proportionality, in what follows I do not attend to this central Thomistic insight. Yet, I note that Stein certainly

To complete her understanding, Stein quotes an important principle provided in the Thomistic commentary of Gredt, a principle that succinctly captures the Thomistic conception of this kind of analogy, namely "as the creature relates to its being [*Sein*], so God relates to his being [*Sein*]."[52] This formulation is of special significance because of the way Gredt grounds the proportional similarity of creature and Creator in the way both creature and Creator relate to their respective acts of being (*Sein, esse*), the created act of being of the creature and the uncreated act of being of the Creator. To further clarify the nature of this agreement, Stein marshals Gredt's explanation that this basic similarity is further grounded in the proportion of their respective essences to their respective acts of being, saying, "Created being [*geschaffene Sein*] is the act of the created essence and that through which it exists, and divine being [*göttliche Sein*] is the act of the divine essence and that through which it exists."[53] The act of being is that whereby both the creature and the Creator stand in existence, since both creature and Creator have existence because an act of being actualizes their respective essences, the creature possessing a created act of being, and the Creator possessing an uncreated act of being. And since both have this direct relation to their respective acts of being, both creature and Creator can be understood together according to an analogical form of conceptualization. This means that the creature can be understood to have an indeterminate relation to the Creator by virtue of the determinate relation of its finite essence to its finite act of being in its proportional agreement to the infinite essence of God actualized by an infinite act of being. Because of this similarity of proportions, an analogical likeness is established between the creature and the Creator, and like terms can be properly and truly predicated of creature and Creator via an analogy of proportionality.[54]

---

    does interpret and develop the analogy of proportionality in accord with this distinction, and she holds that God can neither be known directly nor conceptually comprehended, with the consequence that all terms indicating true perfections of God, though primarily predicable of God in terms of what they signify, the *res significata*, fall short of God in the imperfect manner of their signification, the *modus significandi*, precisely inasmuch as they are conceptually developed from the perspective of the perfections of creatures as various imperfect similitudes of God, and therefore cannot signify God in his perfection if they continue to possess their creaturely mode of signification.

52 EES, 290, citing Josef Gredt, *Die aristotelische-thomistische Philosophie*, 2 vols. (Freiburg i. Br.: Herder, 1935), 2:7; see also, Gredt, *Philosophie*, 2:5–6.

53 EES, 290.

54 The analogy of proportionality does not necessarily imply the causal relation

Accordingly, the first term usually predicated of creature and Creator is the term "being," and all transcendentals of being—namely, "one," "true," "good," etc., since both creature and Creator have the actuality of being, and both are one, true, good, etc., inasmuch as they possesses this actuality.[55] In this way, the creature is given as sharing a basic community of being (*Seiend*, *ens*, henceforth plain noun, "n") with the Creator through the correspondence of their relations to their respective acts of being (*Sein*, *esse*, henceforth verbal noun, "v"), which community grounds all further forms of agreement of creature and Creator, inasmuch as all further similarity presupposes and follows upon the actuality of being (v) and the consequent proportion of essence to this grounding actuality.[56] However, in union with Aquinas and Gredt, Stein notes that the creature has or possesses being (v) in a manner radically different from the way the Creator has or possesses being (v), with the result that both are beings (n) in ways radically dissimilar to one another.[57] Since the Creator is Being Itself (*ipsum esse*), wherein there is a perfect unity of essence and being (v), God does not so much "have" or "possess" being (v) but rather just "*is*" without further ado. Indeed, this "*is*" of the Creator has an infinitely packed

of creation, or indeed any causal relation; yet, given creative causation and the corresponding causal analogy inaugurated via creative causation, the relation of creature and Creator is best explained by the analogy of being understood as an analogy of proportionality. See ST, I, 4.3, co.

55 See ST, I, 13.5, ad 1; I, 13.2, co. As indicated by this analogous form of predication, God is not conceived by Aquinas *merely* as another being (n) among beings (n)— that is, as an individual instantiation of a universal kind, generically and specifically determined as a member of this kind—but rather, as Being Itself through the very purity of his being God is understood to be utterly different than and distinct from all other beings (n). I note here that though being (n) can be predicated of God also according to an analogy of attribution, so that the predication of being of God and creature is a case of mixed analogical predication, since Stein treats only of the analogy of proportionality, in what follows I too expressly deal only with this form of analogy.

56 From here forward I identify the distinction of being (*Sein*, *esse*) and being (*Seiend*, *ens*) with the shorthand of (v) and (n), respectively (except where it is beyond question what is signified).

57 See EES, 290; and Josef Gredt, *Elementa philosophiae Aristotelico-Thomisticae*, 13th ed. (Rome: Desclée, Lefebvre et Soc., 1899; Freiburg i. Br.: Herder, 1961), 2, 7; see also Owens, *Christian Metaphysics*, 93. Earlier in EES Stein notes the radical difference between *becoming* and *being*, as well as the necessary grounding of all becoming in "*true being*, being in the full sense of the word"; she further indicates the distinction of *becoming-being* from *pure-being*, as well as noting that the relation of becoming-being to pure-being must be understood according to the analogy of being. EES, 49.

signification, since it does not simply signify the mere factuality of existence—as the binary affirmation or negation, "God is" versus "God is not"—but rather signifies the unreceived and self-necessary actuality of Being Itself, the absolute and unlimited fullness of the existential actuality of being (v). Whereas the Creator's essence simply is "to be", such that the Creator is an essentially infinite being (n) possessing an unlimited act of being (v), the creature's essence has or possesses a received "to be" in a contracted and limited fashion, such that the creature is an essentially finite being (n) possessing a limited act of being (v).[58] This means that in contrast to the infinite fullness of Being Itself that is God, the creature is always determined by an essentially finite creaturely *kind of being* together with an actually finite creaturely *mode of being*, a finite essence contracting and limiting a finite act of being (v).[59]

And it is precisely in consequence of the radical differentiation of the proportion of essence to being (v) in the creature when compared to that of the Creator that we have the basis of the still greater dissimilarity encompassed by the analogy. Since the Creator is absolutely simple, the being (n) in whom there is a perfect coincidence of essence and being (v), anything predicated of the Creator while meaningfully signifying the divine essence concomitantly signifies the divine act of being (v), and so also the Divine Being (n) Itself. Consequently, anything that is truly predicated of God signifies something that is immediately coincident with God, identifying the being (n) of God, the essence of God, and the being (v) of God, all in the absolute simplicity of the One who is

---

58   This evidently means that not only do essence and being (v) perfectly coincide in the Divine Being (n), but so too do both coincide with the Divine Being (n) itself, all of which can be stated in the following symbolic relation:

> Divine Essence (*essentia*) = Divine Being (*esse*) = Divine Being (*ens*)
> In contrast, since essence and being (v) are distinct in finite being (n), both are also distinct from the finite being (n) itself, which can be stated symbolically in the following form:
> creaturely essence (*essentia*) ≠ creaturely being (*esse*) ≠ creaturely being (*ens*)

59   As is obvious from my interpretation of Aquinas, I understand the "real distinction" of Thomism to be a distinction of essence (*essentia*) and being (*esse*), *not* essence (*essentia*) and existence (*existentia*), even while this later distinction necessarily follows upon the former, since if any thing's essence differs from its being, so too does that thing's essence differ from its existence, i.e., its "standing forth" in being as something real. Thus, as previously noted, the *factuality* of being—a feature of the existent—should be contrasted with the *actuality* of being—a metaphysical principle of the existent, which grounds and establishes the existent's factuality.

Being Itself. Accordingly, the Creator actualizes all perfections of being (v) in their unlimited fullness, or rather *is* all perfections of being (v) without limit. And so, God does not so much have "unity," "truth," "goodness," etc., the various transcendental perfections of being, or "life," "wisdom," "justice," etc., and many other perfections of being, by *possessing* these perfections as distinct attributes, but rather *is* "Truth" and "Goodness," "Life" and "Wisdom," etc., through *being* these very perfections.[60] In contrast to this absolute simplicity, creaturely being (n) necessarily implies a composition of essence and being (v), so that anything truly predicated of the creature is not coincident with the creaturely act of being (v), or with the creaturely being (n) itself. Since the creature is a finite essence actualized by a received and contracted act of being (v), the creature distinctly *possesses* this or that perfection, and does so in an essentially limited fashion—and so, the creature is "true" and "good," "alive" and "wise," etc., by merely participating in "truth" and "goodness," "life" and "wisdom," etc.

This mode of conceiving of the dissimilarity of the creature from the Creator in proportion to their contrasted possession of being (v) is captured in the succinct formula of Aquinas when he says, "It is impossible that the creature attain something [and we could say, *anything*] in the same way as God, just as it is impossible the creature attain the same being [*esse*]."[61] Indeed, it is this very impossibility that grounds the ontological distinction embraced by the analogy of proportionality even while it inaugurates the creaturely relation to the Creator via the received act of being (v). Thus, the analogy of proportionality completely respects the indeterminacy of the relation of creature to Creator, since it embraces the similarity of the creature to the Creator through the possession of being (v), while simultaneously embracing the indeterminacy of this similitude through the indirect character of the proportional relation, so that it in no way signifies that the Creator is determined by this similarity. The analogy of proportionality thereby respects the radical distinction of the creature from the Creator even while it simultaneously sets the creature in radical relation to the Creator through the reception of the actuality of being

---

60   Stein notes that making such statements about God follows a human mode of proposition since the judgments undergirding propositions are strictly speaking not possible, "for every judgment involves a dismembering, but the perfectly simple does not allow for dismembering" (EES, 293); accordingly, Stein argues that "God is—God" (EES, 293) is the best possible statement, the most true, and indeed, the most full.

61   QDV, 2.11, co.

(v) and the corresponding likeness of creature and Creator. Thus, all perfections that follow upon the aboriginal perfection of being (v) are predicated of the creature and the Creator in the very same way that being (n) is predicated—that is, analogically via proportion*ality*, while the terms so predicated according to some "common stock of meaning" in no way signify a limiting *terminus* of God.⁶²

Critically Questioning the Thomistic Conception

In this way, in tandem with the Thomistic conception conveyed by Gredt, Stein interprets the analogy of being as an analogy of proportionality and understands this apparatus to be the conceptual toolset best crafted to represent the relation of creature and Creator, while simultaneously respecting the infinite distance separating the creature from the Creator. However, she also critically questions the Thomistic conception and enumerates several concerns with the Thomistic formulation of the distinction and relation of creature and Creator. Stein is initially concerned with the complex of relations inherent in the finite creature between the individual thing, its individual essence, and the self-dependence of that essence, since this complex of relations bears close reference to the proportion of essence to being (v) in creaturely beings (n), with the consequence that the Thomistic presentation of analogy is insolubly bound-up with this complex.⁶³ For Thomism, as related by Gredt, the self-dependence of the individual relates differently to the essence when it is material or immaterial, being tied to the principles of matter and form respectively, where each is separately identified as the principle that bears the essence in the self-dependent individual, whether material or immaterial. Yet, Stein questions the rationale behind this localizing of self-dependence differently in material and immaterial beings, a questioning that is obviously related to her reconsideration of the role of form in the structure of the individual, and in her corresponding reconsideration of the meaning of self-dependence via the concept of bearer.⁶⁴ And since the dissimilitude of creature and Creator

---

62 See EES, 288: "But '*ens*'—like all transcendental names—is valid for Him only in an analogous sense."
63 See, for example, ST, I, 3.3–4.
64 As detailed above, Stein presents a renovated understanding of self-dependence—both in terms of the self-dependent essence borne by the actual individual, and in terms of the self-dependent essence enclosed by the empty-form "thing" or "personal I," in

embraced by the analogy of proportionality is anchored in the contrast of the absolute simplicity of the Creator as Being Itself versus the actual and ontological complexity of creatures—as essence-being composites and, if material, as further form-matter composites—conceptual clarity regarding the analogy of being is closely tied to how this complex of ontological relations is worked out.

However, Stein is at first content simply to indicate the domain of the problematic and leaves all related questions temporarily unexamined and unresolved. Though attaining clarity over the precise character of these relations is important to her toward properly understanding the analogy of being, especially that of the bearer of the self-dependent essence, the decisive problem that troubles Stein about analogy bears reference to the apparent coincidence of essence and being (v) in God, a coincidence Stein grants throughout *Finite and Eternal Being*. She puts her critical questioning in the following way: "Does it make any sense to speak of the 'act' of the divine essence or of a 'proportion' of essence and being (*essentia* and *esse*) if essence and being fully coincide [*zusammenfallen*]? Is not the basis for a proportion missing here, and thereby also [the basis] for the likeness of proportion?"[65] Throughout her subsequent investigation Stein repeats this "riddling question [*Rätselfrage*]" in a number of different formulations, obviously convinced that an answer to this question will help her to get to the bottom of the analogy of being.[66] Though she certainly follows Aquinas and Thomism in recognizing the evident difference of *meaning* of essence and being (v) in creature and Creator, in addition to their actual distinction in the creature, as also the difference of their relation (v) in the creature and the Creator, nevertheless she deliberately poses the question in this way in order to expose a lacuna she perceives in the Thomistic conceptual apparatus, a lacuna she intends to fill by reconsidering the analogy of proportionality "from a completely

---

consequence of which she conceives differently than Aquinas and Thomism of the relations between the individual thing, its individual essence, and the self-dependence of the essence.

65 EES, 290.
66 For example, Stein says, "But does this already imply that God's being and essence *mean* the same thing?" (EES, 293); and again she asks, "Whether God's being *is* his essence, or—expressed differently—whether in God essence and being not only belong together necessarily but rather *mean* the same thing?" (EES, 296); emphasis added.

different point."[67] The different point she chooses is the adjusted perspective of the personal. Through approaching the question of analogy from a personal vantage point, Stein eventually comes to conceive of the analogical agreement of the creature to the Creator in a distinctly personal way. Moreover, through approaching the analogy of proportionality from this personal perspective, Stein partially resolves the "riddling question" of the coincidence of essence and being (v) in God, and thereby also brings to resolution the questions she earlier posed (listed above) and left temporarily unresolved. In the next chapter, we turn to this independent investigation of the analogy of being from a personal perspective, and there discover the area in which Stein most significantly develops the Thomistic conceptual schema to the defined benefit of the *philosophia perennis*.

Conclusion:
Stein's Recourse to the Philosophical Theology of Aquinas

In her attempt to understand the relation of the finite personal I to the vertically given transcendent world above, Stein has recourse to the metaphysical demonstrations of Aquinas to provide the pattern of reasoning by which she concludes to the actual existence and attributes of God the Creator. Though Stein only briefly references the demonstrations of Aquinas, given that she refers to these demonstrations as the "the way" of philosophical knowledge, and further relies on the inferences attained via these arguments in all subsequent investigations of Creator and creation, I have suggested that Stein's abridged reformulation of Aquinas's demonstrations bespeaks confident reliance on the metaphysics of Aquinas, rather than of any doubt in the philosophical cogency of his or similar demonstrations. Indeed, Aquinas's pattern of reasoning provides Stein with the conceptual apparatus necessary to rationally clarify the relational dependence of the personal I on God, a clarification that enables her to *rationally* satisfy her phenomenological approach to Divine Being. As a result, Stein comes to conceive of God in typically Thomistic terms, as Being Itself, and Pure Being or Pure Act, the *one* and *simple* being (n) in whom there is a perfect coincidence of essence and being (v). Yet, by so referring her phenomenological insights to the demonstrations of Aquinas, Stein also provides a new first premise for such arguments in the temporal

---

67   EES, 293.

finitude of personal life. In this way, Stein gives to Aquinas's reasonings a decidedly personalist slant that can rightly be described as the personalization of his demonstrations.

On the basis of this foundation in natural theology, Stein proceeds to detail the proper contours of the natural creaturely relation to God by employing the Thomistic conceptual apparatus of the analogy of being understood as an analogy of proportionality. Having already alighted on an ideational kind of analogy, which also provides an ideational basis for the actual analogy of being, Stein turns to the Thomistic presentation of analogy to achieve conceptual clarity over the actual relation of the finite creature to the infinite Creator. Following the lead of the Thomistic commentary of Gredt, Stein understands the analogy of proportionality to be the most appropriate way to capture the basic similitude of the creature to the Creator—a similitude grounded in their common possession of the actuality of being (v)—without ignoring the still greater dissimilitude of the creature from the Creator—a dissimilitude grounded in the contrasted manner the actuality of being (v) is possessed by the creature and the Creator, via its composition in the creature, versus its coincidence in God. Yet, given the coincidence of essence and being (v) in God as Being Itself, Stein suggests that something of a problem lies hidden at the heart of the Thomistic conception of the analogy of proportionality, namely: How can one speak of the actualization of the divine essence, or of the proportion of essence to being (v) in God, if essence and being (v) are really coincident in the Divine Being (n)? To solve this "riddling question," Stein proposes to investigate the analogy of proportionality from an entirely different perspective, that of the specifically personal.

Chapter Six

The Personal Form of the Analogy of Being

> An infinite distance obviously separates
> the being of the I from Divine Being,
> and yet it is more like him than anything else
> that lies in the realm of our experience,
> precisely through being an I, through being a person.
>
> —*Edith Stein*[1]

Stein begins her independent investigation of the analogy of being by approaching its meaning from the perspective of the divine name recounted in the book of Exodus (3:14), I Am Who I Am (אהיה אשר אהיה), noting that she follows Augustine in understanding this as the proper name of God.[2] Though she takes this theological point of departure for her investigations, and often has recourse to supporting theological reasonings as she proceeds, her ensuing investigation is not solely theological in kind or significance. Indeed, Stein chooses this particular theological starting point only as the most fitting place to begin her inquiry into the proportion of essence and being in God, precisely since God is here revealed not only as "He who is,"

---

1 EES, 295.
2 EES, 293. In EES, 293n21, Stein refers to an (earlier) referenced quotation of Augustine, *In Psalmos*, 134.6, cited in EES, 61. Aquinas also considers this name to be the most proper name of God, though he expressly formulates it as *Who Is* (qui est). See ST, I, 13.11.

but rather as "He who is personal." Since the God of Revelation *enunciates* "*I Am*," Stein argues that the essentially personal nature of God is revealed together with his unparalleled actuality in being.

Yet, notwithstanding this theological reflection and insight, Stein considers God to be knowable as personal also from a purely philosophical standpoint, has already outlined her philosophical conception of the personal God, and in this context needs only to recapitulate that earlier argument, pithily summarizing, "Only a person can create."[3] She reasons that since the finite things of the natural world are essentially determined, with teleological activities that are meaningfully ordered, the natural world bespeaks an *intelligent* being that meaningfully establishes the natural world with its teleological order. Moreover, and more basically, she reasons that since the finite things of the natural world actually exist, and evidently possess the undergirding actuality of being (v) as essence-being composites, the natural world bespeaks a *free-willing* being that actualizes certain essences (and only certain essences among all possible essences) in being.[4] According to these two fundamental givens, by way of essence and by way of being (v), Stein argues that creation provides the evidential basis for a philosophical conception of God as personal—who, precisely as personal, can most surely enunciate "I Am," since "the name with which every *person* designates himself as such is '*I*'."[5] With the personal nature of the Creator

---

3   EES, 293; compare EES, 99ff. In EES, Stein frequently supports her philosophical argumentation with faith-based theological claims and notes that recourse to theological data when dealing with the themes of creation and the person is especially fitting given that both concepts were philosophically refined, clarified, and deepened through Christian theological reflection.

4   See EES, 99–101, 293–94; PA, 150–51. Karl Schmidt contends that this is a "thin argument" that "relies on inductive claims." Yet there is no reason to think that Stein thinks this argument a form of induction, at least primarily, even if induction expands and substantiates what is basically a deductive argument, or that she considers it argumentatively thin, even if it is only restated by her in a highly abbreviated formulation. Schmidt continues by arguing that a philosophically developed personal form of analogy is "only possible based on the self-revelation of God" taken in tandem with the declaration in Genesis "that man is created in the image and likeness of God." With Schmidt's interpretation, as becomes apparent in what follows, I disagree. See Karl Schmidt, "Edith Stein, Apophatic Theology, and Freedom," in *Selected Papers on the Legacy of Edith Stein's Finite and Eternal Being*, ed. Sarah Borden Sharkey (= *Quaestiones Disputatae* 4, no. 1 (2013)), 21–30: 25–26.

5   EES, 294; emphasis on "person" (not "I") added. Thus, in contrast to Philip Gonzales, I do not find this appeal to Exodus to be a "detour" in Stein's analysis, but rather the use

thus established, both theologically and philosophically, Stein proceeds in her philosophical investigation of the analogy of being by expanding her earlier developed conception of the Creator to include the specifically personal, all in the hope that this will cast light on the "riddling question" arising from the perfect coincidence of essence and being (v) in God.

In what follows, in accord with my understanding of Christian philosophy, I prescind from the theological dimension of Stein's investigations by abstracting and examining only those elements of Stein's conception that are properly and purely philosophical in content.[6] Yet, since the term "person" is ordinarily used in a Christian theological context to identify the distinct supposits of the triune God, out of respect for this theological attribution of the term, care will be exercised in identifying the One God as personal. Hence, rather than predicating "person" of God, I restrict my attribution to the adjectival and adverbial form "personal," as a signifier of *that which pertains* to the One God as a being (n) both intellectual and volitional; and any attribution of "I" as personal pronoun to the One God should also be taken in the very same sense.[7]

---

of a theological datum that ratifies and strengthens the foundationally philosophical insight of Stein. See Philip Gonzales, *Reimagining the* Analogia Entis: *The Future of Erich Przywara's Christian Vision* (Grand Rapids, MI: Eerdmans, 2019); and below, 225n36. I note here that Maritain also reflects on the divine "I" and presents a similar understanding to Stein with respect to the personal in God. See Jacques Maritain, *Degrees of Knowledge*, trans. Gerald B. Phelan (Notre Dame, IN: University of Notre Dame Press, 1998, repr. 2014), 245–50.

6   For my understanding of Christian philosophy, see above xxxiiin15.
7   Though this abstract rendering of Stein's thought presents certain difficulties, both methodological and analytical, it is concordant with Stein's and Aquinas's philosophical understanding of the God as personal in nature. That this mode of predication is not only philosophically valid but theologically coherent is evinced by the fact that the divine enunciation "I Am" revealing the One God as personal is temporally and notionally antecedent to the completed Revelation of God as a Trinity of Persons. See EES, 10–11, 28–29, 42, 303. For a general attribution of "person/personal" of God in a philosophical context, without identifying the triune distinction of Persons, see also Karol Wojtyła, "Thomistic Personalism," in *Person and Community: Selected Essays*, trans. Theresa Sandok (New York: Peter Lang, 1993, repr. 2008), 165–75: 166–67; and for a detailed treatment of Stein's Trinitarian ontology, see Marian Maskulak, *Edith Stein and the Body-Soul-Spirit at the Center of Holistc Formation* (New York: Peter Lang, 2007), 79–83; and "Edith Stein's Trinitarian Ontology," in *Intersubjectivity, Humanity, Being: Edith Stein's Phenomenology and Christian Philosophy*, ed. Mette Lebech and Haydn Gurmin (Bern: Peter Lang, 2015), 269–88.

* * * * * *

Before proceeding with the analysis of Stein's investigation of the analogy of being, it is worth taking a brief aside on Stein's consideration of being (*Sein*) and her alignment with Aquinas in this area. This is especially important given the centrality of being (*esse*) and the act of being (*actus essendi*) in Thomistic metaphysics. Although Stein nowhere provides a direct investigation of being, as noted above, she does state that "the question of the meaning being [*den Sinn des Seins*]" is the primary concern of metaphysics, the philosophical discipline that bears fruit in a fully developed conceptual worldview.[8] Stein's recognition of the centrality of being (v) is borne out through the entire investigation of *Finite and Eternal Being* (and other mature works) and is especially patent in the manner she treats of the actual (*Wirklich*): first, (1) in her understanding that the finite beings of the natural world, which as essence-being composites have received the actuality of being (v); then, (2) in her contrast of actual being with the mode of being she identifies as essential being, a mode for which she recognizes existence (*Existenz*) but not actuality; and finally, (3) when she presents the analogy of being in typically Thomistic terms, as an analogy grounded in the proportion of essence to being (v) in creaturely and Divine Being (n). Given these features of Stein's thought, especially the last listed priority of the analogy of being, it is easy to deduce that Stein, in complete accord with Aquinas and the Thomistic tradition, gives pride of place to actuality and being (v) in her metaphysical account of the structure and meaning of reality. Therefore, notwithstanding the paucity of direct treatment of being (v) in Stein's works, which we should note is also absent in Aquinas,[9] we must

---

8   As earlier quoted, in engaging "Aquinas's metaphysics," Stein recognizes that "as a core inventory of the Thomistic organon, we may well regard the idea of being [*Sein*] and the basic forms according to which it is determined," and in WP has Aquinas say, "Foundationally, all questions are reduced to questions of being [*Seinsfragen*], and all philosophical disciplines become parts of a great ontology or metaphysics." EES, 489–90; cf. PA, 7; and WP, 104. See above, xlvn21 and lviiin51.

9   The absence of any thematized treatment of being (*Sein*, *esse*) in Stein and Aquinas could well follow upon the *inconceivability* of being (v)—that is, in their shared position that no concept of being (v) can be formed by the human intellect. Whereas concept formation is correlated with essence as something content-full, the intellectual act correlated with being (v) is the act of judgment. In contrast to the act of concept formation, which gives definition to the cognition of essence, the act of judgment gives proposition to the cognition of being, by first affirming the factuality of being (n), in an explicit manner, while simultaneously affirming the undergirding actuality of being

hold that being (v) stands at the very heart of Stein's mature philosophy, both in its practice and in its product, and this centrality should be acknowledged as an area of deep accord with Aquinas and the Thomistic tradition.[10]

The Person: An Analogue of Divine Being

As shown above, Stein initially approaches the analogy of being from a purely phenomenological perspective by reflecting on paired sets of contrasted ideas—those of finite, temporal, and mutable being, versus those of infinite, eternal, and immutable being—and has thereby delivered an ideal kind of analogy of being and a corresponding ideational basis for the actual analogy of being. As argued above, this ideational basis is immediately transposed into the actual when considered together with the demonstration of the existence and attributes of God, all of which is brought forth by Stein from a first-person perspective via her Augustinian way of proceeding. In just this way, Stein provides an initial understanding of the analogy of being, and does so already from a first-person perspective. Upon this basis, Stein proceeds to unveil a further dimension to the analogy of being from a specifically personal perspective, by observing that the first member of each pair qualifies the being of the *personal* self, which opens the way toward recognizing the personal dimension of the analogy. Through

---

(v), in an implicit judgment that later can be brought to explicit awareness by analysis of the so cognized being (n) into its metaphysical principles of essence and being (v). Therefore, since intellectual judgement cannot be conceived and defined, and since it is itself "simple" even while it bears fruit in propositional knowledge, the thematized treatment of being presents real difficulties toward any kind of analysis and expression.

10 I disagree with Przywara's interpretation of Stein, especially when he accuses her of developing a philosophy that "transfers all real existents to the level of the 'essential,'" and thereby provides a philosophy of pure essentialism, something he believes follows upon her employment of phenomenology. See Erich Przywara, "Edith Stein and Simone Weil: Two Fundamental Philosophical Themes," included in "Part II" of the English translation of *Analogia Entis: Metaphysics—Original Structure and Universal Rhythm*, trans. John R. Betz, and David Bentley Hart (Grand Rapids, MI: Eerdmans, 2014), 596–612. In contrast to Przywara, and in line with the interpretation of Gricoski, I hold that Stein avoids the either-or dichotomy of essentialism and existentialism through her prioritization of *Sein* and her correlated frequent thematic consideration of the actuality of beings (n)—and, I note again, in a way reminiscent of Aquinas's use of *esse* and his attention to the real. Compare Thomas Gricoski, *Being Unfolded: Edith Stein on the Meaning of Being* (Washington, DC: The Catholic University of America Press, 2020), 60ff., 129ff.

negating the limitations that determine the actual being of the personal self, the idea of a personal being that is not so limited is encountered in experience, the idea of an infinite, eternal, and immutable personal I. And since the idea of such a being is manifestly no mere idea but patently coincides with the actual Creator already shown to exist—through Stein's own reasonings in tandem with the supporting demonstrations of Aquinas—the personal I is given an intimate sphere of analogical access to God as *personal* Creator.

Early in *Finite and Eternal Being* Stein alludes to this specifically personal approach to analogy, there saying,

> But because [the finite personal I] is only for a moment, he is also not the fullness of being [*Sein*] in the moment, his frailty still remains in momentary being [*Sein*], this *self* is merely an "analogue" of Eternal Being [*Sein*], which is immutable, and therefore at every moment the fullness of Being [*Sein*], that is, an "image [*Abbild*]" which has a similarity [*Ähnlichkeit*] to its archetype [*Urbild*] but yet a still greater similarity [*Unähnlichkeit*].[11]

---

11   EES, 42; emphasis added. Stein here cites a dogmatic definition of the Fourth Lateran Council (1215) identifying the basic similarity and dissimilarity of creature and Creator (here given in its Latin original with English translation): "*Quia inter creatorem et creaturam non potest tanta similitudo notari, quin inter eos maior sit dissimilitudo notanda*; For between Creator and creature no similitude can be expressed without implying a greater dissimilitude." *Denzinger*, § 806, 269; translation provided. Given Stein's express recognition of the dogmatic constraints (for Catholic thinkers) surrounding the analogy of being, as well as the interpretation of Stein's thought here given (both above and below), I disagree with Przywara when he says, "In Edith Stein one does not find the Lateran analogy of a 'similarity, however great,' between finite and eternal being, intersected by an 'ever greater dissimilarity' in a true 'rhythm *in infinitum*.'" This claim of Przywara is evidently related to his claim that Stein's use of phenomenology leads to a foreshortened metaphysics by developing a kind of essentialism unbalanced by a fitting existentialism (which balance he finds in the fractional thought of Simone Weil), precisely inasmuch as Przywara understands the "still greater dissimilarity" to be found in the identity of *essentia* and *esse* in God in contrast to their real distinction in creatures. Consequently, Przywara continues, "Rather, what she sees in any given case are primarily 'other' (that is, 'dissimilar') 'given essences,' which she compares with one another in order to investigate their possible 'similarity.'" And again, a little later, "Since the formal principle of phenomenology, regarded purely as a method, is one of 'identity'—that is, an immediate, noetic encounter with a given essence—the phenomenologist Edith Stein duly investigates the given essences of 'finite' and 'eternal' being with regard to their specifiable differences."

However, only much later in the text does Stein fully examine the *meaning* of this personal mode of approach to analogy. Having achieved a conception of the Creator as both *actual* and *personal*, Stein develops her initial phenomenological insights alongside her adoption of the Thomistic conception of analogy by following the same pattern of negation through which the analogical ideas were earlier encountered in conscious experience. This negation includes the negation of any relational dependence on transcendent spheres of being—the inner and outer worlds, as well as the world above—the negation of any temporal transitioning of experiential acts—any coming to be of units of experience and their passing away—and the negation of any limitation of experiential contents—any limitation in time or meaning of the contents of experience. Thus, the being (n) of God the Creator is given as a fully actual personal kind of being (n), one who always already encompasses the essential fullness of being (v) in one eternally present actuality of spiritual living. This means that for Stein God is unveiled possessing a perfectly simple and fully actual *personal* mode of being and life as "the *fullness of being personally formed* [*die Fülle des Seins persönlich geformt*]"—which can then be perfectly signified by the divine enunciation "I Am."[12]

Stein explains more fully what "*being personally formed*" means by employing her already developed conception of the empty-form "personal I" (or "thing"), as that intrinsic and foundational principle that encloses the formal (and material) fullness of each and every finite being. Whereas in the sphere of finite personal being (or finite being in general), the empty-form "personal I" (or empty-form "thing") encompasses and encloses the being's essential fullness, the infinite personal God is without any such formal complexity and corresponding formal structuration of being, precisely since "the [divine] I implies *form and fullness at once*."[13] So considered, form and fullness come together in God in the perfect simplicity signified by the divine name, since everything included in the Divine Being is fully embraced and borne by this all-encompassing act of the personal Creator. To further describe what "*being personally formed*" means, Stein employs her already developed conception

---

Przywara, *Analogia Entis*, 602–4. See below, 210n35, for further clarification and defense of Stein's conception of analogy with reference to Przywara's criticisms.

12 EES, 295. Because of this, Stein maintains that languages that possess a single word for the divine enunciation—such as the Latin *sum*, or the Hebrew היה, both of which include a first-person reference—better capture the simplicity of the divine name.

13 EES, 295; see also 307.

of the different modes of being—the actual and intentional in addition to the above-detailed essential—and argues that the completed fullness of all modes of being coincide in the personal God. Earlier Stein has made it clear that "the inseparability of *essential being and actual being* in God means *God's essential being is actual being, and indeed the most actual, Pure Act*."[14] Here she simply clarifies that intentional being also coincides with the essential and actual fullness in God, since the personal Creator is actually "transparent to himself" and can "comprehend himself spiritually" with the perfect intellectual embrace of complete self-understanding.[15] So considered, the essentially personal God at once includes the completed fullness and perfect coincidence of both actual and intentional modes of being in addition to the completed fullness of essential being. And so, for Stein, "*being personally formed*" means that God is given as the preeminent kind of personal being, a being in whom all modes of being—actual, essential, and intentional—coincide in the perfect simplicity of the divine "I Am."

Of this Divine Being, the human being is a natural created analogue. As one who can similarly enunciate "I am," the human person is given for himself as having an analogical relation to the personal God. The analogy includes both the basic similitude and still greater dissimilitude of human and Divine Being. Of this duality, Stein says, "An infinite distance obviously separates the being of the I from Divine Being, and yet it is more like Him than anything else that lies in the realm of our experience, precisely through being an I, through being a person. Through [being an I] we come to an apprehension of Divine Being—even if only by likeness [*gleichnishaften*]—when we remove everything that is non-being."[16] The human being has a likeness to Divine Being through

---

14 EES, 62.
15 EES, 296.
16 EES, 295; see also PA, 42, 86–88; and AMP, 102. Whereas Stein identifies the person as such as an analogue of God in EES, in PA she expressly identifies only the core of the person as such an analogue, there saying, "The core of the person is the being that he is in himself, and through which he is a *similitudo* of Divine Being; that which positively underlies the *analogia entis*" (PA, 146); yet, as earlier noted, Stein drops her use of core in EES, possibly out of concern for the substantial unity of the human being as a personal unity. Peter Schulz claims that the question which motivates Stein in the context of the analogy of being is "whether God can be known as a person also philosophically"; however, as seen above, I contend that Stein has already concluded to the personal nature of God and is here interested in examining the consequent (analogical) meaning of this conclusion, precisely so she can attain an appropriately full understanding of its meaning.

his essentially personal nature and stands in unparalleled analogical relation to God by virtue of this essentially personal nature. Though "an infinite distance" separates the finite personal I from the infinite personal I, the finite personal I is still that which lies closest to God the Creator in the natural created sphere. Moreover, as is evident throughout Stein's presentation, this personal likeness to God implies more than simply the perfection of the rational nature, which insight is already found in the thought of Aquinas and Thomism, since being a person for her includes the further perfection of possessing the rational nature in a properly personal way. Indeed, Stein conceives of the human being as a likeness of the Divine Being *primarily* from the perspective of the I that encompasses and bears the essential fullness of human nature. This means that the human being also possesses the further similarity to Divine Being by being "personally formed" through the personal formation wrought by the personal I, with a personal kind of unity that is also best signified by the human "I am" embracing the entire fullness of human nature. So considered, there is a dual interconnected personal likeness embraced by the analogy encompassing human and Divine Being, first according to the created perfection of the rational nature, something already granted by Aquinas and Thomism, then according to the further perfection of personally bearing that nature, something new to Stein.[17]

This dual interconnected likeness grounds the basic similitude of the analogy, while also opening upon the still greater dissimilitude found in the way the personal is present in human and Divine Being, whether as the essentially and actually limited form of the personal in human life, or as the essentially and actually unlimited fullness of the personal in the Divine. Through the cancellation of the manifold of limiting qualifiers of the finite personal I, the greater dissimilarity conceptually embraced by analogy is given outline definition and the finite I is grasped in his basic dissimilitude from the Creator. Unlike the Divine Being in whom there is a personal fullness without qualification, the human being is essentially limited, having an inner division of I and rational nature, in addition to the remaining structured manifold of human nature, qualified as temporal and mutable on all sides. Unlike the Divine Being in whom there is a completed fullness of life, human experience is an ever-flowing

---

See Peter J. Schulz, *Edith Steins Theorie der Person: von der Bewusstseinsphilosophie zur Geistmetaphysik* (Freiburg i. Br.: Alber, 1994), 170–78: 172.

[17] Aquinas's understanding of the analogous attribution of the term "person" is taken up below and treated in more detail in its comparison to Stein's developed position; see 228ff.

admixture of potentiality and partial actuality, successively grasping only finite meanings in transitory intentional acts, living an essentially limited form of personal life, while also possessing a finite essence that progressively unfolds only through the course of time. Finally, and most importantly, unlike Divine Being in whom there is a perfect coincidence of infinite essence and infinite act of being (v), all encompassed by the infinite intentional fullness of divine life, the human being is a composite of a finite essence and a finite act of being (v), with a distinct and derivative mode of intentional living conditioned by his finitude and essential temporality. Thus, the human being falls radically short of the Divine Being in all areas, essential, actual, and intentional, and this shortfall is entirely grounded in the radical creaturely dependence upon the continual reception of the actuality of being (v). And *yet*, this manifold of difference grounding the still greater dissimilitude of analogy does not destroy the fact that the human person remains an unparalleled created analogue of the personal God.[18]

Stein's description of God as "the *fullness of being personally formed*" is especially significant toward understanding her reconsideration of analogy. As shown above, this fullness implies that God includes the completed fullness of personal being in a perfectly simple unity of divine life, which means that God is the personal fullness of meaning, the personal fullness of the actuality of being (v), and the personal fullness of free spiritual living. As the signifying expression of this divine fullness, the enunciation "I Am" reveals itself to be the personal principle of the *unity* and *simplicity* of God, with the consequence that the proportion of essence to being (v) in God should be understood entirely from the perspective of the "I Am." Stein formulates her understanding in the following way, "But the fullness of [the divine 'I Am'] is *the fullness*

---

18   In contrast to the presentation here, where I abstract from theological considerations and focus only on the natural dimension of the analogy of being, Betschart details the personal form of analogy with a focus on revealing its Trinitarian and Christological import. In doing so, Betschart pays special attention to the significance of analogy for the human person as an individual, while also attending to the analogy Stein draws between Divine Being as a Trinitarian unity and human beings as a unity in humanity (the species) and in community; and, in terms of the corresponding dissimilarities, Betschart notes the oneness of the Divine Being versus the plurality of human beings, and the possession of the divine nature by Three Persons in unity versus the possession of human nature by many persons with distinction. See Christof Betschart, *Unwiederholbares Gottessiegel: Personale Individualität nach Edith Stein* (Basel: Reinhardt, 2013), 128–31, 345–51, and 295n185, 346, fig. 18.

of being [Sein] *in every sense of the word*. It is *essential being*, which indeed belongs inseparably to the what, and it is *actual being*, since the living of the I is the highest actuality, and both are one therein since the divine 'I Am' is the actual living essence."[19]

So considered, the proportion of the essence to being (v) in God is given as a specifically personal proportion, a proportion that is determined by the absolute simplicity of the divine "I Am" as the personal coincidence of the essential and actual being in the simplicity of God's intentional mode of living. In precisely this way, then, by refocusing the analogy of being on God's personal mode of spiritual living in light of the "I Am," Stein provides a resolution to the earlier problem raised in relation to the Thomistic conception of the analogy of proportionality—her so-called "riddling question" over the "missing proportion" of essence to being (v) in God—and concludes that "the solution" is to be found in the fact that both essence and being (v) "are contained undivided in God as the 'I Am.'"[20] The metaphysical ground of the analogy of being is then best captured by the concept of the *personal I* as *bearer*, inasmuch as the personal God bears the divine essence and the divine being (v) in a personal way according to the absolute simplicity signified by the divine enunciation.[21]

---

19 EES, 296. Because of the living relation of the Divine Being to his own being (n) and to the created world through the eternal divine Λόγος, and the corresponding living relation of the human being to his own being (n) and to the created world through the finite λόγος, Stein proposes that there is a further dynamic living "*analogia*, agreement and disagreement, between the Λόγος and the λόγος, the Eternal Word and the human word" (EES, 105). So considered, the analogy of being clearly reveals the person-centered structure of reality, where all reality is understood with reference to persons, as something having its source, coherence, and constancy in the personal God, as something then given for finite created persons, for their cognition, appetition, affection, and perfection. This dynamic and living aspect of the personal form of analogy deserves further exploration not here possible beyond brief reference in what follows. I also note that this novelty of Stein certainly does not represent any contradiction with Aquinas (and the Christian philosophical tradition), even if this person-centered approach is not attended to or highlighted in his writings (or much of the associated tradition). See Betschart, *Unwiederholbares Gottessiegel*, esp. 225–26; Alfieri, "The Question of Individuality," 95, 100; and Maskulak, *Body-Soul-Spirit*, 49–50, 70.

20 EES, 296. Maritain similarly regards the unity of the Divine Being as a personal unity, such that, he argues, "Metaphysics, therefore, knows demonstratively that the Divine Essence subsists in itself as infinite personality." Maritain, *Degrees of Knowledge*, 249; see also, 247–50.

21 Stein sees in the bearing of the Divine Being the "the archetype of these different forms

This personal bearing in God can be further elucidated by again introducing the distinction of the personal *kind* of bearing and the personal *mode* of bearing, and their corresponding relation of simple coincidence in God. Since the divine personal I includes the completed fullness of essential being as its *formal* bearer, God is essentially personal with a personal kind of bearing of the divine essence. And, since the divine personal I also includes the completed fullness of actual being as its *actual* bearer, God is actually personal with a corresponding personal mode of bearing of the divine act of being (v). This personal kind and mode of bearing is then directly related to the divine mode of intentional living, since the personal bearing of God includes the enduring fullness of spiritual living and necessarily involves the intentional bearing of the divine essence and Divine Being (v) in one simple spiritual act of free intellectual comprehension. One could relate this latter insight to the terminology of Aquinas by saying that whereas the personal kind of bearing signifies the divine "*essentia*," an essential or ontological kind of bearing, the personal mode of bearing signifies the divine "*esse*," an actual or real mode of bearing, while the divine *essentia* and divine *esse* are found to be united in the simplicity of the divine "I Am" as that which signifies God as "*esse subsistens*." So considered, the concept "bearer" neatly captures the manifold of dimensions of the personal proportion of the divine essence to the divine act of being (v) insofar as the personal kind and mode of bearing of the divine "I Am" reflects the supreme unity and absolute simplicity of the personal God.[22]

This understanding of bearer is then analogously attributable to the human being as a personal being, and in a more limited sense to all finite beings in general. Focusing first on the human being: Since the personal I as empty-form frames the formal and material fullness of human nature, the personal I *formally* bears the human essence as the final determination enclosing the human structure as one whole. Then, since the finite act of being (v) is received by the human essence finally enclosed by the personal I, the personal I *actually* bears the personal

---

of bearer" (EES, 307), that is, *all* the earlier enumerated forms of being a bearer (see above, 24–26).

22 Though Stein develops her understanding of the concept *bearer* in the context of detailing the distinction of Persons in the Triune God, this concept is transferrable in a limited way to Divine Being as personal in abstraction from such properly theological consideration. This abstraction is of particular significance in the context of clearly manifesting the general applicability of the personal form of the analogy of being, where the empty-form "thing" replaces "personal I" as bearer for finite being in general.

individual who stands in existence by this received act of being (v). Like the Divine Being, this bearing can be further elucidated by considering the distinction and relation of the personal kind and mode of bearing in human nature. Since the human I encloses the fullness of the human essence as its *formal* bearer, the human being is *essentially* personal and has a personal kind of bearing—an *ontological kind* of bearing. And since the human I stands in existence through a received act of being (v) as its *actual* bearer, the human being is *actually* personal and has a corresponding personal mode of bearing—an *actual mode* of bearing. The proportion of essence to being (v) in the human being is then also best captured by the concept of the person as bearer, since the human individual bears his personal essence and being (v) in a personal way in the unity of the human "I am." Yet, as indicated above, the human being is also greatly dissimilar to the personal Creator, since, in addition to distinction and composition of essence and act of being (v), the finite human essence has a formal and material complexity, and the personal life of the human being is a finite and fleeting mode of personal living that does not include the perfect comprehension of his own being and life or indeed, of anything else experienceable, including God. This manifold of complexity, then, essential, actual, and intentional, means that even while the human being has a basic similitude to the personal Creator, the human being has a still greater dissimilitude to the personal God through the characteristic finitude of his personhood.

This specifically personal form of bearing distinguishes the human being from all non-personal beings, and yet this bearing of essence and being (v) provides the way toward understanding how non-personal beings can be understood as various creaturely analogues of the personal Creator. Since the empty-form "thing" bears the essential and actual fullness in non-personal things, the proportion of essence to being (v) in non-personal beings is like its proportion in personal beings, except now with the differentiated kind of empty-formality provided by "thing" and their corresponding thingly kind and mode of bearing. In this way, Stein is able to reformulate the analogy of proportionality with a specifically personal foundation in the Divine Being, analogously represented in a special way by personal creatures, without thereby destroying its applicability to all creatures in general. And so, again here, through usefully employing the concept "bearer," Stein proffers a universally applicable reinterpretation of the thought of Aquinas and Thomism, by providing a form of analogy that relates all finite creatures to the personal Creator through the bearing of the empty-form, whether "personal

I" or "thing." In this way, bearer is shown to be a concept of unparalleled significance for Stein, not only because it clarifies the manner the "personal I" or "thing" is found to predominate in the structure, unity, and formation of the human person or finite being in general, in addition to clarifying the kind of being-individual of individuals, including with priority persons, but also because it clarifies the ontological ground of the analogy of being, the most universal and all-encompassing conceptual apparatus of the Thomistic tradition. So considered, the concept bearer represents something of an interpretive key to the meaning of being for Stein, a conceptual key of universal applicability that enables her to grasp the entirety of the world of experience, the inner and outer worlds, as also the world above, and comprehend in outline form how the *many* of creaturely *beings* are found to be inherently related to the *One* of the uncreated *Being*.[23]

Summarizing the Personal Form of the Analogy of Being

By reconsidering the analogy of being from the perspective of the specifically personal, Stein simultaneously casts light on the basic similitude and still greater dissimilitude conceptually embraced by the analogy of proportionality, as well as grounding and reframing the entire structure of this form of analogy in something specifically personal. The basic similitude of human and Divine Being is found in three interrelated areas—namely, in the possession of the intellectual perfection of being, in the personal bearing of the intellectual nature by the

---

23 See esp. EES, 306–7. It is worth noting that the term and concept bearer has defined theological significance in the Christian religion, inasmuch as the Christian faith presents Jesus Christ as "bearer" of the cross, "bearer" of human sinfulness, "bearer" of redemption, "bearer" of the Gospel, and "bearer" of eternal life, the Blessed Virgin Mary as "God-bearer [*Theotokos*]," and consequent "bearer" of good fruit and the Gospel, and the Christian faithful as "bearers" of their crosses, and consequent "bearers" of good fruit and the Gospel. It is further worth noting that this term and concept helps one to understand Stein's own person and life together with her many sacrifices and eventual martyrdom, inasmuch as it clarifies the manner she freely assumed her own sufferings and those of others together with Christ—that is, as their personal bearer. Indeed, in accord with her understanding of Christian philosophy, Stein's philosophical attention to and development of the term and concept may well have arisen from her reflection on the meaning of personal existence from this specifically Christian perspective; accordingly, I believe it is not easy to overstate the significance of this term and concept in Stein's philosophical thought.

conscious I, and in the corresponding personal proportion of essence to act of being (v) in both human and Divine Being. The still greater dissimilitude is found in the imperfect way the personal perfection of being is had by the human being, the imperfect way the human personal I bears the rational nature, and in the corresponding real distinction of finite human essence and finite act of being (v)—all of which must also be taken together with the further range of complexities in human nature. Accordingly, the pithy statement of Gredt capturing the Thomistic conception of the analogy of being—namely, "as the creature relates to its being, so God relates to his Being"—can usefully be reformulated in the following distinctively Steinian ways: first, in general, (1) "as the creature bears his being, so God bears his being"; then, with personal specificity, (2) "as the personal creature personally bears his personal being, so the personal God personally bears his personal being."[24]

The Thomistic conception of the analogy of being together with Stein's personalized reformulations can then be represented in the paired propositions in the following two tables. *Table 1* provides the founding Thomistic formulas, in their basic meaningfulness, and in their corresponding metaphysical foundation, with the second member of each pairing expressly identifying the proportion included in the meaning of the analogy; and *Table 2* provides the Steinian reformulations of the same.[25]

Assessing Stein's "Personalized" Conception of the Analogy of Being

How does Stein's independently developed understanding of the analogy of being in its personal form compare with the conception of Aquinas and the Thomistic tradition? Exactly how is Stein's understanding different from that of Aquinas and Thomism? Does this difference stand directly opposed to the conceptualization of Aquinas and Thomism? Or rather is Stein's reconsideration of analogy a development of the received teachings in a way that is basically consistent with Thomism?

---

24 Notwithstanding this specifically personal reinterpretation, an interpretation that reveals the ultimate ground of the analogy of proportionality in the divine "I Am," as above noted, the general significance of the analogy of proportionality is not thereby disrupted since all finite beings can also be understood as thingly bearers of their essence and being (v).

25 In both tables, "being" obviously denominates the verbal noun, German "*Sein*," Latin "*esse*."

Table 1

Thomistic Formulation of the Analogy of Being
creature : creaturely being :: God : Divine Being
proportion (creature, creaturely being) ≅ proportion (God, Divine Being)
The Foundation of the Analogy of Proportionality in its Thomistic Formulation
creaturely essence : creaturely being :: divine essence : Divine Being
proportion (creaturely essence, creaturely being) ≅ proportion (divine essence, Divine Being)

Table 2

Steinian Reformulation of the Analogy of Being
personal creature : creaturely being :: personal God : Divine Being
personal proportion (personal creature, creaturely being) ≅ personal proportion (personal God, Divine Being)
The Foundation of the Analogy of Proportionality in its Steinian Reformulation
creaturely personal essence : creaturely being :: divine personal essence : Divine Being
personal proportion (creaturely personal essence, creaturely being) ≅ personal proportion (divine personal essence, Divine Being)

I argue that Stein's understanding of analogy is basically coherent with that of Aquinas and Thomism (notwithstanding the controverted character of the analogy of being in Thomism, and indeed Scholasticism more broadly), even while she presents an expanded conception of the analogy of proportionality to expressly include the personal perfection of being in a structural way. Moreover, I suggest that this is true notwithstanding the presence of certain disagreements when it comes to considering the proportion of essence to being (v) in finite beings (n), and with respect to the complexity and relation of the principles in finite beings (n). The basic coherence is seen initially when considering Stein's recourse to Aquinas's demonstrations of the existence and attributes of God. Though the analogy of being is the predominating concept in Stein's mature metaphysics, she underpins the whole conceptual structure with the conclusions provided by Aquinas's pattern of reasoning. Indeed, the metaphysical supporting structure of the conclusions is that without which Stein's further investigation of the analogy of being cannot be undertaken in a properly philosophical context, inasmuch as the conclusions of Aquinas's demonstrations are both necessary for and presupposed to the analogy of being. Four of these conclusions in particular are needed to correctly understand the analogy of proportionality—namely: (1) the radical distinction and concomitant relation of creature and Creator established by the act of creation; (2) the identification of the author and ground of finite being as Being Itself; (3) the supreme unity and absolute simplicity of God as Being Itself in whom there is no composition of essence and being (v), or indeed, any other actual or ontological composition; and (4) the actual or real complexity of creatures as finite beings receptive of the act of being (v), in whom there is always at least the distinction of essence and being (v), in addition to many further ontological complexities. Evidently, Stein's conception of the analogy of being includes deep areas of conceptual alignment with the understanding of Aquinas and Thomism, and this conceptual alignment can be traced back to Stein's brief but decisive recourse to Aquinas's demonstrations and their conclusions.

The essential consistency of Stein's conception with that of Aquinas is even more manifest when considering her recourse to the thought of Aquinas before and during her reconsideration of analogy. As shown above, Stein's investigation takes place in the broader context of an exploration of the Thomistic conception of the analogy of proportionality, and only after achieving basic clarity over its meaning and import does Stein proceed with her own investigation of its personal form, which she completes through an extended reflection on the Boëthian definition of the person as presented by Aquinas.[26] Moreover,

---

26   EES, 288ff.; see above, 24ff.

as mentioned above, of central significance toward understanding Stein's incorporation of the analogy of proportionality is the principle of Gredt's, which she quotes in the context of investigating the Thomistic conception, now here quoted in full:

> As the creature relates [*verhält*] to its being [*Sein*], so God relates [*verhält*] to his being [*Sein*]: created being [*geschaffene Sein*] is the act of the created essence and that through which it exists, and divine being [*göttliche Sein*] is the act of the divine essence and that through which it exists; for so it is conceived by us in this way (*concipitur enim a nobis ut quo* [for it is conceived by us as that by which]), although in God it is the same as the essence and is being [*Sein*] bearing itself (*esse subsistens* [subsistent being]).[27]

As detailed by Gredt, the analogy of creature and Creator rests upon the likeness of the proportions of their respective essences to their respective acts of being (v), whether the finite and essentially limited being (v) of the creature or the infinite and essentially unlimited being (v) of the Creator. In the Latin original, while Gredt expressly calls this agreement of creature and Creator the analogy of proportionality, "*ita proportionaliter analogice*" (in contrast to the German translated "*entsprechend* [accordingly]"), he notes that this is *merely our way of understanding*, since there is actually no distinction

---

27 EES, 290, citing Josef Gredt, *Die aristotelische-thomistische Philosophie*, 2 vols. (Freiburg i. Br.: Herder, 1935), 2:7. The corresponding text is actually not found in its precise formulation (or location) in the German translation of Gredt's work, and the closest formulation (found on 5–6) reads: "*Denn wie sich das Geschöpf zum Geschöpflichen Sein verhalt, so verhalt sich Gott zum göttlichen Sein. Wie das Geschöpflichen sein die Wirklichkeit des geschaffenen Wesens ist, das, wodurch es ist, so ist das göttliche Sein die Wirklichkeit des göttlichen Wesens, das, wodurch es ist. Auch das göttliche Sein, obschon eins mit dem göttlichen Wesen, wird dennoch notwendig von unserem unvollkommenen Denken gedacht als das, wodurch Gott ist.*" Given the difference in German formulation, in addition to the inclusion of Latin in brackets, it appears that Stein is translating directly from Gredt's Latin original text (which she also cites in other locations of EES), which reads as follows: "*Sicut enim se habet creatura ad suum esse, ita proportionaliter analogice Deus se habet ad suum esse: Esse creatum est actus essentiae creatae, et id quo exsistit; et esse divinum est actus essentiae divinae, et id quo existit concipitur enim a nobisut quo, quamquam in Deo identiñcatur cum essentia et est esse subsistens.*" Josef Gredt, *Elementa philosophiae Aristotelico-Thomisticae*, 13th ed. (Rome: Desclée, Lefebvre et Soc., 1899; Freiburg i. Br.: Herder, 1961), 2, no. 618, 2.

of essence and being (v) in the Creator. Rather, for Gredt, as for Thomism more broadly, God is simply subsisting Being (*esse subsistens*). This Thomistic understanding of the coincidence of essence and being (v) in God, even to the point of their identification, which culminates in describing God as "*esse subsistens*," is key to understanding Stein's critical questioning and corresponding personal development of the analogy of proportionality.

Indeed, the recognized coincidence of essence and being (v) in God is the exact location where Stein mounts her critique of the Thomistic understanding and proceeds to introduce her own expanded conception of analogy. According to the conception of Aquinas, since God is *esse subsistens*, his being is without any inner division and corresponding complexity, whether actual or ontological, and so is supremely one and absolutely simple. Thus, for Stein, "the divine I is the *actual living essence*" of God, where the divine "I Am" represents the perfect enunciation of the completed fullness of Being Itself, both of which imply that the Divine Being as *esse subsistens* is also "Being-In-Person," or more simply, "Being-Person."[28] This innovative proposal certainly represents a clear and explicit difference from the received teachings of Aquinas and Thomism. Whereas Aquinas signifies the simplicity of God by noting the absence of every composition in God, and thereby provides a fundamentally negative notion of simplicity, even if positive in referent, in recognizing the role of the divine enunciation in accounting for divine simplicity, Stein's signals that divine simplicity can actually be identified with something notionally positive.[29] More precisely, through reinterpreting the analogy of being, Stein simultaneously captures the *positive* perfection of divine simplicity with a *positive* notion—and indeed the most positive notion possible—the divine "I Am."[30] Yet, this contrast with Aquinas need not be interpreted as indicating

---

28 EES, 296; emphasis added.
29 The difference between Stein and Aquinas here obviously parallels their earlier difference over the related notion and definition of unity, where the contrast was also one of positive versus negative (see above, 110–12, 123–24). As is the case with unity, though now more clearly with simplicity, Aquinas is considering it from a specifically human perspective, according to a human mode of knowing that is naturally correlated with the composite things of the natural world, and certainly doesn't regard divine simplicity as something negative in itself. That is to say that despite the epistemologically conditioned character of the human notion of simplicity, Aquinas regards divine simplicity as a positive perfection of Divine Being, inasmuch as it names the actual indivision of God, and indeed his indivisibility.
30 The positive character of this notion is theologically confirmed in Stein and Aquinas's

contradiction. Given Aquinas's recognition of divine simplicity as a perfection, and his further recognition that God the Creator is personal, in addition to his theological assent to the enunciation of Exodus 3:14, it is reasonable to regard Stein's proposal as basically coherent with the conceptual framework of Aquinas and Thomism.[31] Therefore, I submit that Stein's insights regarding divine simplicity should be taken to represent a conceptual development in continuity of the Thomistic understanding, with the further consequence that Stein can provide a significant conceptual deepening of the analogy of being.

Stein's conception of the proportion of essence to being (v) in God provides the apposite foundation for understanding the proportion of essence to being (v) in finite creatures, including with priority the finite personal I. As indicated above, the simplicity of God means that the divine "I Am" transcends the distinction of form and fullness—all formal, content, and material distinctions—all categorizations and classifications of being—the distinction of substance and accidents, and all generic and specific distinctions, together with their corresponding perfections—and the universal notional distinctions of being—the various transcendental categories of being as such. Yet, Stein maintains that all distinctions together with their corresponding complexities are prefigured

---

identification of the divine "I Am" as the proper name of God. Moreover, this positive notion remains true even though the idea of the divine "I" is forged by negating the various complexities of the finite personal I, and even while its meaning lies infinitely beyond the human creature's ability to comprehend it.

31 Aquinas recognizes the attribution of both positive and negative notions of God, and all such attributions can be considered divine attributes (*attributa divina*) even while only the positive signify attributes of God strictly understood. Positive notions are formed on the basis of directly known positive perfections of creatures, such as truth, wisdom, goodness, etc., and analogously attributed of the Creator according to their proper meaning but with an altered mode of signification, i.e., a preeminent mode of signification with all creaturely limitations removed by negation so that the perfection can be attributed of God as absolutely simple. Negative notions are formed by the negation of specifically creaturely modes of being, such as materiality, composition, finitude, etc., and directly attributed of God according to their proper meaning and mode of signification, i.e., involving a simple denial of God, where what is proper to creatures is directly negated of God. For Aquinas's reasoning, together with various examples of positive and negative notions, see esp. SCG, 1.31–36; and ST, I, 13. See also Brian T. Carl, "Knowing God as He Who Is," at Summer Philosophy Workshop: "Aquinas on Divine Attributes," Soundcloud, streaming audio, 01:08 (June 14th, 2018), https://soundcloud.com/thomisticinstitute/knowing-god-as-he-who-is-dr-brian-carl.

in the simplicity of the personal God, so that the manifold of distinct and complex creatures should be understood as various imperfect likenesses of the one Divine Being. Indeed, Stein accounts for the contrast of divine simplicity and creaturely complexity in terms that resonate deeply with the presentation of Aquinas, by arguing that the personal mode of divine living not only involves the complete intentional comprehension of the transparent fullness of God himself, but also includes the comprehension of all actual (and possible) creatures as various imperfect similitudes of his Divine Being. In this way, all creatures are understood to be derived representations of God, each of which possess analogical agreement with God through their possession of the actuality of being (v), while simultaneously falling short of the perfection of equality with God through manifold limitations, the first of which is the essence-being (v) complexity of finite beings. Stein presents this intentional comprehension of creaturely being from the perspective of the divine "I Am," summarizing her understanding by saying, "The relation of the divine 'I am' to the manifoldness of finite beings is the most primordial *analogia entis*."[32] Thus, Stein shows that the intentional life of the divine "I Am" not only embraces the fullness of the Divine Being itself, but concomitantly embraces all creatures as various analogues of his own Being, truly representing the Divine Being by bearing the actuality of being (v), while also falling infinitely short by the imperfect manner they bear this actuality.[33]

Up to this point, there is not yet found any direct contradiction of the received teachings of Aquinas and Thomism. Indeed, the presentation of

---

32   EES, 296.
33   Stein interprets the distinction and relation contained in analogy according to the correlated concepts of archetype (*Urbild*) and image (*Abbild*), according to which the "primordial *analogia*" of the proportional likeness of all finite creatures to the Creator comes to be understood "as an image relation [*als ein Abbildverhältnis*]" (see EES, 296–97). At first sight this may appear to stand in some contrast to the position of Aquinas, who reserves the term image (*imago*) for personal creatures who possess a "similitude of form [*similitudinem formae*]," and grants to non-personal creatures only a trace (*vestigium*) of the creative causality of God. Yet, notwithstanding this apparent difference, it should be noted that Stein uses the phrase image character (*Abbildlichkeit*) rather than simply image (*Bild*) and clearly recognizes the special and distinctive way personal beings image God, while Aquinas also grants that all creatures are made similar (*assimilantur*) to their Creator cause and are thus a similitude or likeness (*similitudo*) of him "according to analogy alone [*secundum analogiam tantum*]." See EES, 296–302, esp. 303n1; and ST, I, 4.3 co.; I, 45.7.

Stein clearly mirrors Aquinas's presentation of the act of creation through the divine ideas while also recognizing the ultimate basis of the analogy of being in the imitability of God.[34] Yet, when considering the metaphysical ground of the analogy of proportionality in the complexity of the proportion of essence to being (v) in creaturely beings (n), both personal and non-personal alike, a number of differences with Aquinas and Thomism surface. As would be expected, these differences relate to Stein's understanding of the formal structure of finite being, and the ultimate priority she gives to the empty-form as bearer of the essential and actual structure of the individual. As indicated above, when critically questioning the Thomistic conception, Stein is concerned with the way Thomism accounts for the relation of the individual to the individual essence and the self-dependence of that essence. In particular Stein is concerned about the self-dependence of the individual essence of form-matter composites "resting upon" or "being borne" by the material principle, and she does not accept this recourse to matter for the self-dependence of the essence, especially when considering the human individual.[35] Though Stein acknowledges that matter is a condition of the possibility of the self-dependence of the individual essence, in contrast to Thomism she argues that the self-dependence of the essence is grounded in the individual essential-form, and that this self-dependence is further rooted in the empty-form "personal I" or "thing." This reconceptualization of the individual directly impacts Stein's understanding of the proportion of the individual essence to its received act of being (v), with the consequence that her understanding of the grounding of the analogy of proportionality in the proportion of essence to being (v) is also adjusted. With her flipping of the ontological polarity of self-dependence, now resting on the form rather than the matter, understood as the perfection of "being-a-bearer," Stein's account differs substantially from the Thomist conception.[36]

---

34 See esp. QDV, 3; QDP, 7.1, ad 8; and ST, I, 4.3; I, 15; I, 44.3; and I, 47.1.

35 Of Aquinas's position, Stein pointedly asks, "whether matter is to be regarded as the 'bearer' of the 'nature'" (EES, 292).

36 As should now be clear, Przywara's claim that Stein's understanding of analogy is constrained by her alleged essentialism and consequent disregard for the real distinction, taken together with her alleged recognition of a natural capacity to have an intuition of the divine essence—both of which he argues follow upon her use of phenomenology, with the result that she does not pay due regard to the "still greater dissimilarity" of the analogy of being—cannot be taken as an accurate reading of Stein. Given that Stein follows Aquinas in recognizing the real distinction and consequent

proportion of essence to being (v) in creaturely beings (n), in contrast to their perfect coincidence in Divine Being, while finally grounding the analogy of being in the difference of proportion of creature and Creator to their respective acts of being (v), and given that she also argues that one cannot have an intuition of the Divine Essence in this life, whether mediated or unmediated, Stein manifestly does not fall foul of Przywara's claims and their *sequelae*. Thus, in contrast to Przywara, I argue that Stein's understanding of analogy does not betoken any contradiction of the Lateran declaration that secures divine otherness in the *maior dissimilitudo*. In *Reimagining the* Analogia Entis, favorably contrasting Przywara's understanding with that of Stein's, Gonzales proffers a similar reading to Przywara that renders problematic Stein's conception of analogy, a problem Gonzales locates in a number of interrelated areas, the primary of which are the following: (1) in Stein's continued use of the phenomenological method in a decidedly Husserlian way, with transcendental constraints and immediacy of insight, and to the exclusion of metaphysical reasoning as its necessary complement; (2) in her phenomenological point of departure in the indubitable givenness of the I, which inevitably tends to force all thinking about God through the constricted lens of the ego; (3) in her proposing a univocal conception of being by presenting a conception that embraces both finite and eternal being with the common concept *ens commune* (being in common or general); and (4) in her anthropocentric prioritization of the creaturely similarity of the finite self to the Creator, at the cost of the still greater dissimilarity. The upshot of this array of problems for Gonzales—problems rooted in Stein's overly ambitious "Christian philosophy" together with her egological point of departure—is that Stein's presentation is unhelpfully anthropocentric in contrast to Przywara's rightly focused theocentric vision. See Gonzales, *Reimagining the* Analogia Entis, 137ff. As should be apparent from the analysis above (and again below), the following should be clear: (1) though Stein uses the phenomenological method to understand the creaturely relation of the personal I to Divine Being, she does not fall into transcendental idealism and nor does she regard intuition as immediate for human beings (see WP), and she further relies upon metaphysical reasoning in a Thomistic vein to provide the general metaphysical conclusions and parameters needed to proceed with her phenomenological investigations; (2) though she departs from a phenomenological and Augustinian starting point in the indubitably given self, she integrates an Aristotelian mode of investigation of the outer world to supplement and complement this first-person perspective, and thus includes, through her use of the concept bearer, all finite beings within her finally completed conception of the analogy of being; (3) though she does predicate being (n) of creature *and* Creator, she does not do so univocally (and makes no mention of *ens commune*, a Thomistic conception of the primary unity of all finite beings), but rather refers the "common stock of meaning" of the *analogia entis* in being (*Sein, esse*) itself and expressly states, "We must hold firmly before our eyes that both essence and being [*Sein*] have a different meaning in God than in the creature" (EES, 290), and further, that "'*ens*'—like all transcendental

In the case of the human being in particular, which is here of interest, rather than the individual essence having self-dependence via the bearing of the material principle, where the individual essence in some real sense "rests upon" the material principle, Stein argues that the individual essential-form finally determined by the personal I bears the individual essence of the human being, with the consequence that the proportion of essence to being (v) in the human being is grounded in the personal form. Evidently, as with material being in general, this conclusion of Stein contradicts the presentation of Aquinas, for whom the relation of essence to being (v) in the material individual is mediated by the designated matter of the body. Yet, according to the previously sketched lines of rapprochement with the thought of Aquinas, when it comes to the special kind of being of the human being, Stein's proposition need not be interpreted as diametrically opposed to that of Aquinas and Thomism. Since the human being is a rational and spiritual creature, the human soul receives its individuated act of being (v) directly and immediately from the Creator, through which it becomes something subsistent and naturally capable of individuated existence in separation from the material body, even while its continued individuation retains a (transcendental) relation to the *post-mortem*

---

names—is valid for [God] only in an analogous sense" (EES, 288); and finally, (4) while attending to analogy from the perspective of the creaturely similarity of the finite self to the Creator, Stein does so at the outset by following a kind of *via negativa* (finite vs. *in*finite, etc.), and continues to hold to the utter incomprehensibility of the divine essence, being (v), and being (n), throughout EES, without ever exhausting the mystery of the divine otherness embraced by the analogy of being.

However, notwithstanding this defense of Stein's project, inspired by Przywara's and Gonzales's criticisms it can still be asked: Does not Stein's recognition of a "common stock of meaning" finally referred to being (v) inevitably imply both the essentialization of being (v) and the rendering of being (n) univocal at its core? In spite of the express intention of Stein? This problem obviously relates to Stein's understanding of metaphysics as the study of the meaning of being (*den Sinn des Seins*), a reformulation of the fundamental question of metaphysics that highlights the meaningfulness, and thus the intelligibility of the act of being (v). However, despite Stein's recognition of this meaningfulness and her further recognition of a commonality of meaning across the infinite divide of the analogy of being, it seems to me that Stein is here simply acknowledging the intelligibility of being (v) as the ground of all intelligibility, and is not establishing its ability to be formulated in concepts, and the closely correlated intelligibility that renders finite being similar to Eternal Being even if still more greatly dissimilar.

matter of the body. Aquinas then evidently holds that the substantial form of the human individual has a special relation to its received act of being (v), and subsists in relation to this individuated act of being (v) in a properly personal and spiritual manner—that is, as a subsistent rational individual, even if imperfect in nature. If this be granted, we see that for Aquinas and Thomism the human being can be understood to have a proportional likeness to the personal God according to the manner the human individual has a personal relation to his individuated act of being (v), possessing it in a personal way through the enduring subsistence of the spiritual soul. However, even if such an avenue of partial reconciliation be granted, as indicated above, Stein and Aquinas's differences over the formal structure of being remain outstanding, as does their already detailed contradiction over the role of the material principle in bearing the individuation of the human individual.

Notwithstanding this difference, does the specifically personal dimension of the analogy of being have any counterpart in the thought of Aquinas? As noted by Stein in the course of her investigation, "person" is conceived and attributed by Aquinas in an analogous manner.[37] Indeed, in *Finite and Eternal Being* Stein quotes a lengthy section from *Summa theologiae* where Aquinas is discussing the analogous attribution of the term "person" of God, in addition to its attribution to creatures, whether human or angelic.

> *Person* designates what is most perfect in the whole of nature, namely, something that has subsistence in itself and a nature endowed with reason (*subsistens in rationali natura*). Now, since everything that belongs to perfection must be attributed to God, since his essence includes all perfection in itself, it is fitting to give the name *person* to God, not however in the self-same sense as with creatures, but rather in a preeminent sense.[38]

---

37   Though Aquinas does not expressly refer to analogy in this question, he evidently does maintain that the term "person" is neither univocal nor equivocal and should be interpreted in light of the other divine names that are analogously predicated.

38   Translated from EES, 304–5, citing ST, I, 29.3, co. From this text of Aquinas, it is clear that "person" is predicated of human and Divine Being not as signifying a common property or component possessed of both, but rather as signifying a specific perfection of being, and that the personal is predicable of God without reference to the distinct Persons of the Trinitarian God.

Aquinas indicates that this analogous form of attribution is of the same kind as other perfections attributed to God, and he immediately concludes the body of the same article, saying, "as other names also, which while given by us to creatures we attribute to God, as shown above when treating of the names of God." The above-mentioned treatment of the "names of God" is found in *Summa theologiae*, I, 13.2, where Aquinas details the analogous attribution of all true perfections of the finite creaturely realm primarily and preeminently of God, perfections such as "truth," "goodness," "wisdom," etc.[39] This clarification by Aquinas of the kind of attribution in use when predicating "person" is important when considering Stein's personal form of analogy. For Aquinas, the divine names attributed to God identify the one and simple Divine Being as *esse subsistens*, and not merely a property or accident of the Divine Being, precisely since each term signifying the divine essence simultaneously signifies the divine act of being (v), and, with that, the Divine Being (n). So considered, as indicated above, God does not so much have "truth," "goodness," "wisdom," etc., but rather is "*Truth*," "*Goodness*," "*Wisdom*," etc., and all other perfections in the absolute simplicity of Being Itself.[40] Then, since the perfection "person" is attributed to God in the same way as these other terms—that is, as directly entailed by the proportion of essence to being (v)—the term "person" must be attributable according to this form of analogical attribution, that is, according to the analogy of proportionality, at least according to the Thomist position mediated by Gredt.

---

39 The translation of the English Dominican Fathers indicates that the text to which Aquinas is referring is ST, I, 13.2, where he treats of the naming of God as substantial and essential rather than as accidental or incidental. In the subsequent articles Aquinas then progressively argues for an analogous form of predication, and in aa. 5–6 he argues that the attribution of perfections of God is by way of primacy and preeminence. In the above and following, I take this particular question as illustrative of the way Aquinas understands the order of knowing (*ordo cognoscendi*) to correspond to the order of being (*ordo essendi*).

40 On this point, see, ST, I, 6.3, co.: "This triple perfection [of the good] coincides with no creature according to its own essence; but to God alone, in whom alone essence is being [*esse*]; and to whom no accidents are superadded; but that which is said of others accidentally, coincides with Him essentially, as to be powerful, wise, and the like"; and also, QDV, 2.11. In agreement with Brian T. Carl, I understand Aquinas to mean that names are predicated analogously of God not because of their transcendental character, but rather because of the perfection of being indicated in their signification, which predictability is then applicable to the transcendentals as perfections. See Brian T. Carl, "The Transcendentals and the Divine Names in Thomas Aquinas," in *American Catholic Philosophical Quarterly* 92, no. 2 (2018): 225–47.

So understood, the term "person" signifies a certain fullness of the actuality of being, namely, subsistence in an intellectual nature, which precisely as such represents a perfection of being that can be analogously attributed to both human and Divine Being (as also that of angelic being). The identity of essence and being (v) in God implies that God is the essential fullness of the personal, whereas their nonidentity in the human person implies a limited form of participation in the personal. Since God is being by essence, and since the Divine Being is the completed fullness of being (v), insofar as one can say that God is the essential fullness of "Truth," "Goodness," "Wisdom," etc., so too one can say that God is the essential fullness of the "Personal." In contrast, since the human being is not being by essence, and since his being (n) possesses a received and limited act of being (v), insofar as the human being falls short of "truth," "goodness," "wisdom," etc.—namely, as merely possessing participated "truth," "goodness," "wisdom," etc.—so too the human being falls short of the fullness of the "personal." And so, in a way similar to all other created perfections, the human being merely participates in the perfection of personhood as a finite representation of the personal. Whereas God is the essential fullness of the personal, and thus is *the Personal Itself*, the human being is not this essential fullness and is rather only *a* person. So considered, we find clear alignment between Stein and Aquinas on the analogous attribution of "person" of human and Divine Being, even while Stein introduces the further perfection of the personal I possessing the rational nature as its personal bearer. And though Stein attends with much greater focus to the personal form of analogy, coming to see in the personal dimension the key that unlocks the analogy of proportionality, the personal analogy of human and Divine Being is found already in Aquinas, and indeed in the very writings upon which Stein relies to develop her own personal restructuring of analogy.

Thus, we can conclude that Stein's innovation in this sphere should not be understood in terms of the analogous attribution of the term "person," inasmuch as Aquinas already attributes this term analogously via the analogy of proportionality. Rather, her unique contribution should be understood in terms of the expansion of this analogous attribution to include the *personal I* as *bearer*, and in her further foundational restructuring of analogy to include the *personal proportion* of essence to act of being (v) in human and Divine Being, together with her grounding identification of divine simplicity in the personal I. And since this collage of innovations does not signal any contradiction of Aquinas and Thomism, at least as here presented, I submit that we can understand Stein's reconsideration of the analogy of being as an original organic development of the Thomistic tradition that stands in interior continuity with this tradition, as also with that of the *philosophia perennis* more broadly. Moreover, in tandem with the conclusions of all proceeding analyses, I propose that this Steinian development can again be identified as a "personalization" of the teachings of Aquinas and Thomism. Yet, in this particular case, Stein's personalization represents a radical transposition of the received conceptual apparatus in personal terms, inasmuch as the whole range of being, both finite and infinite, comes to be understood from the coordinating centrality of the person. This is perhaps the most important contribution of Stein to the metaphysics of Aquinas, an anthropological and personalist insight that foundationally restructures the Thomistic conception of the analogy of being, the most universal conceptual apparatus of Aquinas and Thomism, which enables us to embrace the whole of being, both finite and eternal.

In contrast to my presentation, Karl Schmidt maintains that the "uniqueness of Stein's approach is that the place of contact is not in the will or in reason but in the unknowable center of individuality."[41] However, as is evident from my analysis, Stein shows that the personal referent of the analogy of being is personal in its entirety, inasmuch as she attends to analogy in terms of the perfection of rationality as well as the specific personal kind and mode of bearing the rational nature via the personal I as empty-form. Though Stein certainly recognizes the human individual to be an analogue of God in terms of the *ineffability* of human uniqueness (as shown in chapter 4 above), this is not to the exclusion of the features here elucidated, and neither is it a statement that human individuality is *unknowable*. Indeed, while Stein argues that the human individual represents a unique likeness of God via the personal quality, this *quale* is evidently a qualification of an already extant substantive likeness to God as a personal spirit, a likeness anchored in the "I am" that embraces the rational nature and establishes the human individual in being with proportional likeness to God. The personal quality then simply qualifies the distinct analogy of the individual person, by rendering each personal analogue unique and unrepeatable through the distinctness of the *quale*. And though the *quale* does so in a manner that is ineffable, its ineffability does not signal any unknowability but rather only the impossibility of grasping in human language (via the formation of a concept) this divine feature of human individuality.

---

41 See Schmidt, "Apophatic Theology," 26, and also 27–28.

In this way, our understanding of the human being is simply further refined through the completing feature of the personal quality, a feature that enables the personal analogue of Divine Being to "shine" forth in all its radiance, as a unique and unrepeatable "ray" of the divine "I Am."

The Human Being's Personal Relation to the Personal God

Before concluding our analysis of Stein's adoption and development of analogy, it is worth explicitly considering the *relational* significance of the analogy of being as it is presented in Thomistic thought in tandem with the conceptual expansion provided by Stein. As shown above, Stein's conception of the relation of the human being to the world above is initially given from a first-person perspective via the Augustinian way of philosophizing. Yet her conception of the relation of the personal I to this vertically transcendent world is clarified as an actual relation of the self to the Creator only through recourse to the demonstrative reasoning of Aquinas. This means that, on the one hand, Stein's phenomenological investigation of this relation is conceptually supported by assistance she receives from Aquinas, and, on the other hand, Aquinas's demonstrations are expanded to include the personal I as a new first premise. Accordingly, Stein's mature philosophy elucidates a relation of creature to Creator that is both phenomenologically rich and metaphysically robust, phenomenologically rich inasmuch as it is permeated by experiential insight of the personal subject, and metaphysically robust inasmuch as it is supported by firm metaphysical inference. When the analogy of being is introduced to comprehensively clarify the contours of this creaturely relation, a further density of meaning and conceptual precision is achieved insofar as the creature is given as sharing a community of being (n) with God the Creator—a community of being that reaches its apex in the personal perfection of being (v). In light of the above analysis, I proposed that the Thomistic conception can thus be reformulated in the following way: "As the personal creature personally bears his personal being, so the personal God personally bears his personal being." So understood, the human person not only bears his own being (v) in a properly personal way, but in and through this bearing also *bears his own relation to the personal God in himself.*

How so? Since the finite personal I is the foremost analogue of the personal God, the primary natural locus of an exalted created similitude of the Creator, the personal I is immediately established in an exalted form of creaturely relation to the personal God. More precisely, inasmuch as the personal creature is established in a being through his personal likeness to God, and inasmuch as the personal creature bears his being in like manner to the way the God bears his being, with a proportional likeness mediated by the act of being (v), the personal creature not only bears likeness to God, but precisely as likened *to* God simultaneously bears this likeness with creaturely relativity *toward* God. When we further consider that the personal I is that which is closest to each one of us, the intimate core of the personal self from which the life of consciousness radiates, we grasp in Stein's reconsideration a proposal with defined personal significance. As a person who potentially enunciates "I am," the human individual has a unique relativity that bears immediate reference to the divine "I Am." Thus, the personal Creator is made accessible to the created person via the mediation of his own personal being, via his personal kind and mode of being, as well as his personal bearing. Access to the personal God is then not at all distant from the lived experience of the personal subject, since it is mediated by nothing else than the being he possesses by nature, something always already given for the personal subject, which also conditions each and every personal experience whatever it may be. Moreover, this fundamental form of personal relation embraces all other kinds of human relations, personal and non-personal alike, since nothing in the human person stands separate, or separable, from this foundational relation to God mediated by the reception of being (v) borne personally. The personal being of the self can then be understood as the locus of an exalted form of creaturely relation to God, a kind of relational self-transcendence toward God that is entirely mediated by the being of the person himself.

This idea of the human being's relation to God through the self can be compared with a parallel idea in the writings of Joseph Ratzinger, who presents the human self as the site of a profound relation to God through the experience of conscience, in light of its foundation in what he calls "anamnesis" (the Platonic analogue of the Scholastic "synderesis").[42] Ratzinger argues that conscience points beyond itself toward the absolute goodness of God, and thus provides a natural "window" that opens outward toward God as origin and end of the human person. Ratzinger beautifully expresses this notion by saying, "Nothing belongs less to me than I myself. My own I is the site of the profoundest surpassing of self and contact with Him from whom I came

---

42 See Joseph Ratzinger, *On Conscience* (San Francisco: Ignatius Press, 2007).

and toward Whom I am going."[43] Though Ratzinger meets the good God via conscience, and Stein the personal God via the perfection of personhood, both show that the human individual stands in being with unique relativity toward God. This means that rational reflection on his own personal being is the precise location where the individual can most adequately and comprehensively, in a natural way, encounter God. Moreover, in a way not found in Ratzinger, since access to God via conscience is most defined from a first-person perspective, Stein shows that such reflection can include the personal being of the human other with whom one lives in genuine personal engagement, which is possible with all who stand in one's orbit of life and thereby become one's "neighbor." Thus, for Stein, rational reflection reveals that personal being is a most exalted place of encounter with God. And this natural reflection includes the general creaturely relation—that is, the gift of creaturely being (n) inclusive of the proportion of essence to being (v)—and the specifically personal dimension of this creaturely relation—that is, the gift of the perfection of personhood, the gift of being a personal I who bears his own personal nature, with a personal proportion of essence to being (v).

Does Aquinas not deny this relational dimension of the human being as a person when he says, "In the signification of the Divine Person relation is contained, but not in the signification of angelic or human persons"?[44] Though Aquinas makes this statement in a theological setting, it is worth exploring this apparent contradiction with the above presentation of Stein. This further reflection will draw out more fully the relational import of Stein's novel approach, as well as its deeper significance for the Thomistic conception of analogy.

Though the human person is certainly not *essentially* relational in the thought of Aquinas—unlike the Divine Persons of the Trinity, whom he

---

43 Ratzinger, *On Conscience*, 40. This insight of Ratzinger, which I frequently reflect upon while teaching the Foundations of Ethics course at Franciscan University, may well have initially helped me to perceive the proper depth of Stein's thought in this area. Although Ratzinger's reasoning moves through conscience to the reality and presence of *the supremely good God*, while Stein's moves through the personal I to the reality and presence of *the personal God*, both present the human person in his entire being and nature as a unique point of creaturely contact with God.

44 ST, I, 29.4, ad 4; emphasis added. For Aquinas, the relation contained in the divine signification of the term "person" bears immediate and essential reference to the Trinitarian communion of Persons, and is not found in created persons, whether angelic or human.

describes as *subsisting relations*, saying, "a Divine Person signifies a relation as subsisting"—nevertheless in his thought the human person is *actually* relational, as are all creatures precisely as such.[45] Since the act of creation involves the actualization of the creaturely essence via a created act of being (v), the created and received act of being (v) is obviously something superadded to the creaturely essence rather than inherent to the essential structure, even while the essential structure is brought to existence via the reception of this act of being (v). Though not proper to the essence, the received act of being (v) is still inherent to the being (n) of the creature, since it is the very existential actuality of the creature itself, establishing the creature in existence and actualizing everything further that pertains to the creature, all accidental qualifications, relations, activities, etc. Stated in the negative, there is nothing in the creature, and by extension in all of creation, that does not follow upon the received act of being (v) as the ground of any and all actuality whatsoever. Thus, the created act of being (v) has absolute priority within the structure of creation, for Aquinas, a priority that is succinctly captured by him when he says, "Being [*esse*] is the most perfect of *all* things, for it is compared to *all* things as their act"; and again, "Being [*esse*] is the actuality of *all* acts and, because of this, the perfection of *all* perfections."[46] Now, while the act of creation actively considered is proper to God as an exclusively divine act, inasmuch as God is the actor executing the act of giving being (v), the act of creation passively considered is nothing else than the creature itself, inasmuch as the creature is the priorly nonexistent recipient of the creative act of being (v). Accordingly, Aquinas concludes that "creation is *in* the creature and *is* the creature [*est* in *creatura, et* est *creatura*]."[47] And, as a consequence of this understanding, he further concludes, "Creation posits something in the creature according to *relation only* [*secundum* relationem tantum]," and "it follows that creation in the creature is *only a certain relation* to the Creator [*non sit* nisi relatio quaedam *ad creatorem*], as to the principle of its being [*esse*]."[48]

---

45 ST, I, 29.4, co.
46 ST, I, 4.1, ad 3; and QDP, 7.2 ad 9; emphasis added.
47 ST, I, 45.3, ad 2; emphasis added.
48 ST, I, 45.3, co.; emphasis added; see also, SCG, 2.18. Even though Aquinas considers the creature to be the subject of this relation, and in a manner analogous to the various accidental categories of being and predication, as something outside the creaturely essence and superadded to that essence, this relation of the created subject is obviously unique in kind since it identifies the act of being (v) through which the subsistent

Thus, we see that all creatures have a natural creaturely relation to the Creator that is nothing other than the creature itself, established by the bestowal and corresponding reception of being, by God as active giver, by the creature as passive receiver. Moreover, we can see that this creaturely relation is one of

---

finite essence is established as something existent, rather than merely furnishing an accidental attribute inhering in the already existent creaturely substance. Evidently, even if the creature is the subject of this natural creaturely relation, it is subject precisely as essence, not as existent, meaning that it is a unique kind of created relation that is foundational for the creature as such. See ST, I, 45.3, ad 3; and Quodl, 12.4.1. co. Much of this analysis is inspired by W. Norris Clarke's "creative retrieval" of the thought of St. Thomas in his short book, *Person and Being*, and a corresponding series of articles in *Communio: International Catholic Review*, here listed in chronological order: W. Norris Clarke, "Person, Being, and St. Thomas," in *Communio* 19, no. 4 (1992): 601–18; David L. Schindler, "Norris Clarke on Person, Being, and St. Thomas," in *Communio* 20, no. 3 (1993): 580–92; W. Norris Clarke, "Response to David Schindler's Comments," in *Communio* 20, no. 3 (1993): 593–98; Steven A. Long, "Divine and Creaturely 'Receptivity': The Search for a Middle Term," in *Communio* 21, no. 1 (1994): 151–161; George Blair. "On *Esse* and Relation," in *Communio* 21, no. 1 (1994): 162–65; W. Norris Clarke, "Response to Long's Comments," in *Communio* 21, no. 1 (1994): 165–69; W. Norris Clarke, "Response to Blair's Comments," in *Communio* 21, no. 1 (1994): 170–71; David L. Schindler, "The Person: Philosophy, Theology, and Receptivity," in *Communio* 21, no. 1 (1994): 172–90; John Grabowski, "Person: Substance and Relation," in *Communio* 22, no. 1 (1995): 139–63; and, later, Stanislaw Grygiel, "'Existence Precedes Essence': Fear of the Gift," in *Communio* 26, no. 2 (1999): 358–370. See also the notionally related, Adrian Walker, "Personal Singularity and the *Communio Personarum*: A Creative Development of Thomas Aquinas' Doctrine of *Esse Commune*," in *Communio* 31, no. 3 (2004): 457–79. Finally, see also another series of *Communio* articles on the human person and the gift of being, though now treating specifically of the *embodied* person and *self-gift*, again listed in order of appearance: David L. Schindler, "The Embodied Person as Gift and the Cultural Task in America: Status *Quaestionis*," in *Communio* 35, no. 3 (2008): 397–431; Michael M. Waldstein, "'Constitutive Relations': A Response to David L. Schindler," in *Communio* 37, no. 3 (2010): 496–518; David L. Schindler, "Being, Gift, Self-Gift: A Reply to Waldstein on Relationality and John Paul II's Theology of the Body (Part One)," in *Communio* 42, no. 2 (2015): 221–51; David L. Schindler, "Being, Gift, Self-Gift (Part Two)," in *Communio* 43, no. 3 (2016): 409–83. The theological writings of Pope St. John Paul II also capture the relativity of creaturely being from the perspective of "the hermeneutics of the gift," when he employs this interpretive key to understand the meaning of marriage and family, and the undergirding meaning of sexual difference—which for both is that of self-gift. See John Paul II, *Man and Woman He Created Them: A Theology of the Body*, trans. Michael Waldstein (Boston, MA: Pauline Books and Media, 2006).

radical and absolute dependence upon the Creator, a dependence that traces its "roots" into the very depth of creaturely being and encompasses all that the creature is, was, and will be. And since being (v) is that which is "most intimate [*magis intimum*]" to finite creatures, this radical dependence on God is that which is innermost to the creature *qua* finite being.[49] Though God is distinct from creatures by the excellence of his being as Being Itself, nothing is distant from his creative gift and corresponding providential care, together with his undergirding and all-knowing intellectual gaze and corresponding affirming love. Thus, Aquinas says, "God is in all things, and intimately [*intime*]."[50] When this understanding of the general creaturely relation is extended to include the specifically human and personal, we see that while the human person is not essentially relational, like the Persons of the Trinity, in like manner to other creatures, the human person is *actually* relational—and this is to be relational at the most foundational level of being, that of the actuality of being (v) itself. This means that the relation of the human creature to the personal God is nothing else than the very being of the person himself. And this is simply to say that the personal individual "is" his relation to the Creator, and this natural creaturely relation is the most fundamental truth of his being *qua* creature. The human person is then God's gift to himself, and he stands in being in radical relation to God through this gift—that is, through his very self—and hence has the capacity to say with Augustine, "[God] is more inward to me than my innermost self [*interior intimo meo*]."[51]

Though Stein does not expressly refer to this understanding of Aquinas in her development of the analogy of being, her phenomenological insight into the radical dependence of the personal self on the transcendent world above evidently mirrors this coordinate metaphysical presentation. Should the Thomistic understanding then be considered together with Stein's further development of analogy, the human person is revealed as relational in a way entirely unmatched by non-personal creatures. Since the human creature possess the personal perfection of being and a corresponding personal proportion of essence to act of being (v), the human creature is given as something *personally* related to the Creator through the created act of being (v). And since the human person bears his created being (v) in a personal way, the human individual

---

49 ST, I, 8.1, co.
50 ST, I, 8.1, co.
51 Augustine, *Confessions*, trans. F. J. Sheed (London: Sheed and Ward, 1944, repr. 1954), 3.6.11.

necessarily "encounters" the personal God in and through his own personal being, and encounters him precisely as the *personal* ground and author of his own finite being. Moreover, since this relational encounter with God is mediated at its apex by the personal perfection of being, the human individual has the further capacity to embrace this personal relation to the Creator with rational freedom, by first coming to recognize the character of this relation in all its radicality, and by following this recognition with conscious acceptance and joyful gratitude. It then becomes possible, together with Stein, to say, "I know I am held and therein have peace and security—not the self-assured security of the one who stands on solid ground according to his own power, but the sweet and blessed security of the child who is borne by a strong arm."[52]

Stein is here responding to Heidegger's hypothesis that we are "*thrown* into existence," laboring with "anxiety" in the face of "the nothing," an hypothesis with which Stein fervently disagrees. Stein rather interprets the very same phenomena—that of being suspended between being and non-being in the temporal finitude of *Dasein*—as an experience of the enduring reception of being (v). If this reflective insight is followed through with rational reflection, the inchoate given of the conserving presence of the world above begins to unfold into a deeply felt appreciation of being held in being by the faithful hand of God.[53] Indeed, Stein argues that the experience of being gripped by anxiety described so vividly by Heidegger accompanies only unredeemed humanity, and she argues against this stance that recognition of God's faithfulness is a more rational interpretation of the very same experience of temporal finitude.[54]

If embraced, the natural creaturely relation then opens the space within which a personal relationship with the personal God in contrast to a mere relation can gradually begin to take shape—that is, a knowing and free

---

52   EES, 59–60.
53   See Heidegger, *Sein und Zeit*, 179, 266, emphasis added, cited by Stein, EES, 56, 59, nn. 43, 49, respectively. In *Being Reconfigured*, after first detailing the phenomenology of Stein's insights by showing the convergence of Stein's thought with that of Heidegger, before then highlighting her decisive divergence from him, Leask proceeds to discuss the "pathology" of such a nihilistic interpretation of experience while also noting that Stein's insights here cannot be divorced from her engagement with Scholastic thought regarding the creation and conservation of being. See Ian Leask, *Being Reconfigured* (Newcastle upon Tyne: Cambridge Scholars, 2011), esp. 87–91, and 100–104, respectively.
54   See EES, 60: "Or would the child living in constant fear that his mother might drop him be 'rational'?"

dialogical relationship. Since relationship requires some commonality of being and life, and since it is only by being personal that the further development of a personal relationship is possible, this relationship is evidently grounded in the analogical community of being and life that the human person shares with God. Indeed, in the likeness of the human "I am" to the divine "I Am," the human individual has the natural capacity in his own being to come to know the "proper name" of God, and upon this basis enter into dialogical engagement with God. This personal engagement can be considered the full and proper development of the analogy of being, since the formation of such a relationship would undoubtedly complete in the individual's ever-greater degree of likeness to the personal God, the primary analogate of the analogy of being. Yet, such a personal relationship can be brought about for the human individual *only* through freely chosen dialogue, dialogue that has its natural ground in the shared community of being personal, but which rises to consciousness for the individual through reflective awareness of the meaning of his own finite being within the rest of created reality. Such engagement with God would reach its natural apex in the life of prayer, even while it need not be wholly confined to the domain of deliberately expressed thought directed toward God. Indeed, given that prayerful dialogue is itself grounded in the personal perfection of being, it is reasonable to conclude that such personal dialogue already includes the very dynamism of personal life itself, where simply *living* a personal life comes to be included in the particular individual's dialogue with God—a living personal dialogue that embraces all that it means to *be* and *live* as a person.[55]

---

[55] Analysis of this dimension of human relationality—as the capacity to enter into personal relationship—opens outward in several directions, a number of which Stein details in outline form in EES and PA. In particular, she develops the relational potential of the person for self-gift, a self-giving that is made possible by the personal kind and mode of being a bearer, and which can refer either directly to God himself, or to another human person and indirectly to God. Stein develops both kinds of self-giving in a primarily theological context by highlighting the radical potential for self-gift that follows upon the human person's likeness to the Persons of the Triune God. See esp. PA, 113–22, 252–55; EES, 355, 382–88. Further exploration of Stein's thought in this area would likely show areas of deep agreement with the writings of Wojtyła/St. John Paul II, who it must be noted developed his understanding of personal self-gift also through phenomenological investigations enlightened by the metaphysics and anthropology of Aquinas. See Karol Wojtyła, *Love and Responsibility*, trans. Grzegorz Ignatik (Boston, MA: Pauline Books and Media, 2013); and John Paul II, *Man and*

Otherwise stated, the "story" that takes shape in each individual's personal life, the unfolding history of a life in the sphere of created reality under the providential hand of God, can be understood as the precise setting of an ongoing dialogue with God. Insofar as all that happens in the life of an individual is something meaningful, and insofar as all that is chosen by the individual is a meaningful response to this already given meaning, the unfolding story of each individual's life can be taken to represent a dialogical give-and-take with the Creator. The foundation of this dialogical relationship with God is to be found in the dramatic interchange that unfolds as the individual wrestles with God over the course of life with all its vagaries. The stage of the drama is creation and its immediate scene is providence, and on this stage and in this scene, together with all other *dramatis personae*, the individual plays out the drama of his life.[56] The individual thereby assumes his already given personal nature together with his unique individuality and chooses to be a dramatic protagonist in the unfolding narrative of life.[57] All this is acutely grasped when the individual comes to a recognition of this dialogical setting, when he recognizes that God expresses his intellect and will in speaking forth the *word* of creation and providence and begins to intentionally respond with his own word, through his own life with all his thoughts and choices. Yet, as already emphasized, it should be recognized that such a living dialogue is always already underway for the creaturely person, even if it falls to the individual

---

Woman He Created Them. See also Maskulak, "Trinitarian Ontology," 274–84; and Betschart, *Unwiederholbares Gottessiegel*, 308–10.

56 Perhaps this is a founding meaning of Augustine's *Confessions*, when he narrates the story of his life to God, before the audience of Christian and non-Christian witnesses, as he unfolds the outer drama of his life together with the interior drama taking place in the core of his soul, where he wrestles with truth and discovers that his "one delight was to love and be loved." Augustine, *Confessions*, 2.2.2.

57 This conception of persons as dramatic characters traces its roots into the origin of the term (Latin *persona*, Greek πρόσωπον) in ancient drama, where "person" originally designated the mask, and consequently the role, of characters in plays or dramatic narratives. In "Concerning the Notion of Person in Theology," Ratzinger sketches the theological and philosophical development of the concept as it becomes absolutely central to the Christian religion—employed in the two fundamental mysteries of the Christian faith, the Trinity and the Incarnation, while also capturing the *imago Dei* in its attribution to the human being—and simultaneously shows that the remote mundane origin of the term remains significant for our present understanding of its import. See Joseph Ratzinger, "Concerning the Notion of Person in Theology," in *Communio: International Catholic Review* 17, no. 3 (1990): 439–54.

himself to embrace the truth of this dialogue and to consciously live it out with personal authenticity. Should life be embraced in this way, before the face of God, the person discovers that his relationship to God is appropriately completed in the progressive unfolding of his unique likeness to the Creator. In living from the depth of his spiritual soul, the individual progressively learns to express his unrepeatable character ever more fully, whereby the "hue" of this personal quality can become the mark of an eminently personal way of living, a story that uniquely represents the individual and establishes the history of his life—a story of wrestling with God while the creative love of God simultaneously becomes manifest in the telling of his story.[58]

Conclusion: The Personal Form of the Analogy of Being

To develop her understanding of the relation of the human creature to the Creator, Stein approaches the analogy of being primarily from the perspective of the personal I. The personal being of God is initially given for Stein through a kind of *via negativa*, when the personal I subtracts from its being all limitations so that the Divine Being comes to be understood as "the *fullness of being personally formed.*" This conception of the divine aids Stein in overcoming a problem she finds in the Thomistic presentation of the analogy of proportionality with regard to the "missing proportion" of essence to being (v) in the Creator. To resolve this difficulty, Stein argues that the divine "I Am" should be understood as the personal principle of the absolute simplicity of the divine essence and being (v), where the divine "I Am" is understood to be the intentional bearer of the essential and actual fullness of God. Then, since the human person has a corresponding personal proportion of essence to being (v) in the unity of the human "I am," a basic similitude metaphysically grounding the analogy of proportionality is established for the human person precisely as personal. The still greater dissimilitude is found in the way the human creature falls short of the absolute simplicity of God, first through the distinction and composition of essence and being (v), then

---

[58] Perhaps this understanding furnishes something of a key toward understanding the above-referenced prayer of St. Augustine, "O God, ever the Selfsame: may I know myself, may I know Thee," what he calls his *most brief* and *perfect* prayer. See Augustine, *Soliloquies*, 2.1.1, in *St. Augustine's Cassiciacum Dialogues*, vol. 4, trans. Michael P. Foley (New Haven, CT: Yale University Press, 2020), 53.

through the finitude and complexity of the human essence, all of which can be borne only by the personal I in temporally conditioned, discrete intentional acts. Thus, Stein expands the analogical attribution of the term "person" by attending not only to the likeness of personhood in human and Divine Being, something already granted by Aquinas and Thomism, but by highlighting the personal I as bearer, and thereby restructuring the analogy of proportionality in correspondence with this personalized perspective.

Evidently, Stein's personal reconsideration of analogy represents a radical reinterpretation, where the analogy of proportionality is now shown to have a personal grounding in the relative simplicity of the human "I am" in analogical likeness of the absolute simplicity of the divine "I Am." Yet, as indicated above, this reinterpretation need not be understood as contrary to the received teachings of Aquinas and the Thomistic tradition, but rather should be understood as an original development of the analogy of proportionality in continuity with its adopted foundation. The coherence of Stein's position with Thomism is first seen in the way Stein relies upon Aquinas in developing the personal form of analogy, and in the way she relies on the Thomistic conceptual framework to proceed with her expansion of the personal form of analogy. Even though she critiques the Thomistic presentation for failing to adequately describe the proportion of essence to being (v) in the Divine Being, she does so only to provide a point of departure for her own solution to this "riddling question" in the personal coincidence of essence and being (v) in God. So considered, the critique of Stein is not so much a contradiction of Aquinas and Thomism but rather a constructive criticism undertaken for the sake of the attaining greater clarity. Stein's personal mode of approach to the problem not only casts light on the traditional concept of the simplicity of God—as also on the proportion of essence to being (v) in finite persons, and finite beings (n) in general—but also provides new philosophical access to conceiving of the natural creaturely relation of the human being to God. As a result, the being and life of the human person comes to be understood as the precise location of analogical access to God as Creator, which analogical access is duly completed by ongoing dialogue with the personal Creator as the drama of life unfolds for each *dramatis persona*.[59]

---

59   In terms of further potential benefits following upon Stein's conceptual expansion, we could consider her presentation as a way to bridge the gap between the Thomistic conception of divine simplicity and contemporary philosophical conceptions of God as personal among certain philosophers of religion. Alvin Plantinga and William Lane

Conclusion to Part III:
A Personal Relation to the Personal God

As with her investigation of human nature, and her investigation of the human individual, so too in her investigation of the human being's creaturely relation to God, Stein continues to focus on the personal I as she progressively incorporates the metaphysics of Aquinas and Thomism. Again here, Stein first phenomenologically confirms the received teachings before performing a fresh phenomenological investigation and concluding to her matured positions. The principal teaching she adopts and incorporates in this sphere is Aquinas's conception of the analogy of being, understood as an analogy of proportionality, undergirded by certain conclusions about God mediated by Aquinas's demonstrations of the existence and attributes of God. I have argued that Stein first accepts the essential core of these conceptual apparatuses unchanged in their content, while also identifying and highlighting a potential problem with the analogy of proportionality, a problem that she proposes to resolve by investigating the Divine Being from the perspective of the "I Am." Thus, Stein comes to conceive of the analogy of being not primarily from the perspective of the things of the outer world, a typically Thomistic conception with clear metaphysical objectivity, but above all in light of the conscious experience of the personal subject, a characteristically Augustinian conception with phenomenological insight and attention to human subjectivity.

First, Stein's personal mode of approach to the doctrine of creation leads to a "personalized" form of the demonstrations of the existence and attributes of God, since the conscious experience of the personal I becomes the first premise

---

Craig maintain that the strong conception of divine simplicity proposed by Aquinas and Thomism (especially considering the coincidence of divine attributes in God) is fundamentally incoherent with a conception of God as personal. Though this debate rests more on ontological positions presupposed to an explanation of divine simplicity rather than on the analogy of being, I submit that Stein's reconsideration of the divine basis of the analogy of proportionality in specifically personal terms provides a fresh avenue of approach to the question of divine simplicity that could prove fruitful in overcoming certain impasses in this debate. See Alvin Plantinga, *Does God Have a Nature?* (Milwaukee, WI: Marquette University Press, 1980); William Lane Craig, *God over All: Divine Aseity and the Challenge of Platonism* (Oxford: Oxford University Press, 2016). For a clear Thomistic response to Plantinga's concerns, see Lawrence Dewan, "Saint Thomas, Alvin Plantinga, and the Divine Simplicity," in *The Modern Schoolman* 66 (1989): 141–51.

grounding the diverse forms of rational inference. Whereas phenomenological reflection opens on the possibility of an enduring completed fullness of being as the radically transcendent other, the rational satisfaction of this insight is accomplished only by inferential reasoning of a metaphysical kind. For this rational accomplishment, Stein all but entirely, even if only cursorily, relies on the prior demonstrations of Aquinas by following the pattern of his reasoning in her own summary formulations. I propose that this use of phenomenology and metaphysics in tandem is precisely what capacitates Stein to outline and substantiate the fundamental creaturely relation of the human creature to the Creator from a personal perspective, and I further propose that this is best understood as her "personalization" of the inferential reasonings of Aquinas. Having in this way reached basic agreement with Aquinas over the reality of God, Stein employs the Thomistic conception of the analogy of being to attain conceptual clarity over the precise relation of the human creature to the Creator. Though she has already attained an ideal kind of analogy of being, and a corresponding ideational basis for the actual analogy of being, and has thereby remotely confirmed the analogy of being from the perspective of the ideal and possible (as well as the essential), only after relying on Aquinas's demonstrations does Stein surpass this ideal analogy for one understood in metaphysical terms, as a description of the actual distinction and relation of the creature and the Creator. Through this mode of approach, Stein deepens the conceptual content of the analogy of proportionality by reflecting on the personal proportion of essence to being (v) in human and Divine Being, and thereby gives to the entire structure an appropriately "personalized" turn.

Yet, here we see more than a mere "personalized" enhancement of an already completed teaching, and rather find a considerable reconceptualization of the teaching. In showing that the human person bears his personal being (v) like the personal God bears his personal being (v), in the unity and simplicity of the "I am," Stein radically restructures the analogy of being by giving to the whole structure a personal basis. The analogy of being is then both an analogy of being and an analogy of person, with being and person holding coequal and complementary priority—both of which are neatly signified by the "I am": *in the "am" signifying being; and in the "I" signifying person.* The relational import of this deepening is extensive. The human person is disclosed as the kind of being which does not so much "*have*" a relation to the Creator but rather "*is*" the place of his relation to the Creator, the site where he not only encounters himself but simultaneously encounters the personal God in and through himself. Thus, in his own being, the human person "meets" the personal Creator via the way his being opens analogically upon the personal God. Having received the gift of being from the Creator, now bearing a personal likeness to the personal Creator, all that which the human person is—his essential kind of personal being, his actual mode of personal being, his intentional mode of personal living, all rooted in the personal proportion of essence to being (v)—is discovered as the place of encounter with God. Moreover, since such analogical access to God is not only given via the being of the self, but can also be accessed via the personal being of the human other, the human individual can also encounter the personal God in all genuinely personal encounters.

All of this can be understood as fittingly capped by the presence of the personal quality as a unique reflection of the personal God. In living life in a properly personal way, from the depth of the spiritual soul, and in the consequent unfolding of the personal quality throughout the being and life of the individual, the relation of each person to the personal God is rendered qualitatively unique, as is the unrepeatable path of their life. This means that an irreplaceable sphere of relational intimacy is made possible for each person in their relation to God—both through the uniqueness of the individual self, and through the uniqueness of the beloved other—as the story of life unfolds through time with its dramatic character together with the unfolding of creation. In this way, the stage of life is set for the personal drama of existence, an existential narrative that includes many *dramatis personae*, those of God, oneself, and the human other, all of which can become conscious and knowing protagonists of the unfolding drama of creation when embraced in a personal way. The narrative plays out over the course of history in the unfolding of creation via the divine hand of providence, and it includes the providential care of the individual for himself and all those entrusted to his care. The drama is completed as something properly dialogical when the individual protagonist turns toward God and embraces the story of his life in ongoing dialogue with the personal Creator. This dialogue is nothing else than the wrestling of the individual with God in the course of life itself with all its meaningfulness. This wrestling is then duly elevated by cognizance of its condensed meaningfulness and a corresponding turn toward the creative expression of God with one's own creative response. In this way, the personal individual speaks forth his own finite λόγος in response to the Eternal Λόγος, and in so doing begins his entry into a relationship of friendship with him from whom we came and to whom we are going.

Conclusion

Being a Person

> The person is a hypostasis distinct
> by a property pertaining to dignity.
>
> —*Thomas Aquinas*[1]

After her conversion to Catholic Christianity and subsequent encounter with the thought of St. Thomas Aquinas, St. Edith Stein entered into sustained in-depth engagement with his teachings and those of the Thomistic tradition, an engagement that spanned the remainder of her life and directly impacted the shape of her mature thought. She continued to use the phenomenological method in her "own modification" while performing an objective investigation of the human person, and she progressively incorporated a number of key conceptual apparatuses of Aquinas's metaphysical anthropology, and thus situated her anthropology against this backdrop and in living engagement with

---

1   ST, I, 29.3, ad 2. This definition is not original to Aquinas and is referred to by Aquinas and other late medieval authors as *"magistralis*—magisterial, i.e., that of a master." See Jadwiga Guerrero van der Meijden, *Person and Dignity in Edith Stein's Writings* (Berlin: De Gruyter, 2019), 3nn8–9. Michael Smith traces the definition to Peter Lombard, who defines the person as "a hypostasis distinct by a property pertaining to nobility" (*In I Sent.*, 25.1.1). Michael A. Smith, *Human Dignity and the Common Good in the Aristotelian-Thomistic Tradition* (New York: Edwin Mellen Press, 1995), 49n2. Walter Principe traces it to Alexander of Hales, who also mentions unnamed *magestri* for its source, and, at least for certain details of the definition, to Alan of Lille. Walter H. Principe, *Alexander of Hales' Theology of the Hypostatic Union* (Toronto: Pontifical Institute of Medieval Studies, 1967), 66–71. I am grateful to Jadwiga Guerrero van der Meijden and a blind reviewer for bringing this research to my attention.

the Thomistic tradition. In each area of exploration—human nature, the human individual, and the human being's relation to God—Stein's incorporation of Thomistic teachings decisively informs and structures her mature anthropology, while her reconsideration of Thomistic teachings and principles brings about a corresponding conceptual deepening of the received anthropology. I argue that Stein's engagement with Aquinas represents a fundamental "personalization" of Thomistic anthropology, a personalization that is worked out differently in each area of exploration, but which always bears foundational reference to the "personal I" as "bearer."

Stein begins her investigation with the self-evidence of one's own being as it is given in conscious experience: the always present and inescapable "I am" of first-person inner awareness. This point of departure is the foundation of Stein's wide-ranging investigations and remains so as her investigations progress and open outward toward the outer world as she proceeds to supplement her "Augustinian way" of philosophizing with the complementary "Aristotelian way." After concluding to the personal kind of substantial being of the conscious I, and thereby having moved beyond the confines of the immanence of consciousness, Stein adopts the classical definition of the person as "an individual substance of a rational nature" and assimilates it through an extended examination of Aquinas's presentation of its meaning. In this way, Stein receives valuable assistance from Aquinas's exposition of the objective structure of the human being as a personal substance, while at the same time achieving confirmation of his presentation of the classical definition from a phenomenological perspective. By expressly approaching the meaning of the classical definition from the perspective of her starting point in the conscious I, Stein reinterprets its conceptual content by identifying the preeminent place of the I within the completed structure of the human being. In light of this attention to personal subjectivity, Stein changes the focal point of the conceptual content of the definition and reorients our understanding of the person as classically conceived. Accordingly, I suggest that the classical definition can be reformulated in the following distinctively Steinian way: "The person is an individual substance of a rational nature *borne by a conscious I*." The personal I is thus given as the actual and ontological bearer of the rational, personal nature, with the further potential to become the dynamic bearer of that same personal nature through the course of a life lived in a genuinely personal way. This altered perspective coordinates all further considerations of the human being for Stein, with an import both theoretical and practical, and comes to impress much, if not most of her further adoption of Thomistic anthropology.

Stein proceeds to disclose these dimensions by attending to the way primordial experience announces a transcendent depth of the self that is both spiritual and material, revealing the complex nature of the person as a composite of spiritual soul and living-body. Given this initial disclosure, Stein proceeds to adopt two further interconnected teachings of Aquinas's anthropology, those regarding the substantial unity of the human being via the rational soul, and the rational soul as form of the material body, in addition to their common basis in a hylomorphic understanding of the composition of natural substances. Here, yet again, Stein does not merely assimilate Aquinas's teachings without first making them her own through a thorough investigation of the nature of human unity and bodily formation. According to an abstractive analysis of material, organic, animal, and spiritual formation, Stein proposes that the human soul is a "formal structure" with unity provided by the "spiritual soul" as "ruling form" of the complex whole, the "formal framework" into which all formal subdeterminations are arranged and lawfully regulated. And since the personal I abides in the spiritual soul as the final determination of the soul itself, Stein concludes that the personal I provides the ultimate formal integration of the substantial whole of human nature and the final formal grounding of human unity and bodily formation. She further proposes that the living-body is formed in a layered fashion in direct correspondence to the formal layering of the soul, so that the Thomistic teaching, *anima forma corporis*, is understood to have manifold closely interrelated meanings—namely: (1) the one and unified human soul is the "living inner form" of the material body, organizing and animating an already-formed elemental and molecular matter as an organic, animal, and spiritual living-body; (2) the sensitive dimension of the soul is the sensitive form of the organized and animated living-body, dynamically impressing the body with its distinctive sensitive character in all affective, appetitive, and motile living; and (3) the spiritual dimension of the soul is the spiritual form of the already organized, animated, and sensitized body, dynamically impressing the body with its distinctive spiritual character, and potentially forming the body in a properly personal way through all personal expression and action via the living-body—duly completed with the impress of the unique personal quality of the individual on the whole of human nature inclusive of the living-body.

Yet, notwithstanding this manifold meaningfulness of human formation, with a corresponding manifold meaningfulness of soul, the various meanings proposed by Stein are not conceived in isolation from one another, but rather are understood as lawfully integrated under the personal I as the ultimate formal principle within the human structure. This means that the intrinsic τέλος of the human being as a natural being is to be found in the personal formation of the human whole inclusive of the living-body, in a personal and ethical unfolding that fittingly completes the already-given ontological unity of the human being as a personal substance. In taking her lead from Aquinas's defense of the substantial unity of the human being, while simultaneously exploring the diverse ways the human being is formed, Stein provides an original proposal that satisfies the fundamental reasons Aquinas argues for the substantial unity of the human being via the rational soul, while simultaneously furnishing an elegant solution to the problem of human unity and bodily formation, especially when considering the ordinary experiential given of human complexity. Indeed, Stein's multifaceted solution accounts for the many varied dimensions of formation that take place in human nature without in any way destroying the fundamental unity of the human being via the spiritual soul's immediate formation of the living-body—an absolutely decisive anthropological notion for the Catholic intellectual tradition. Though Stein eventually departs from Aquinas's conclusion regarding the ontological simplicity of the human soul, she nonetheless grants Thomistic teaching regarding the substantial unity of the human being and the spiritual soul's direct formation of the material body, and moreover, she does so in a way that does not contradict their basic propositional formulation in Thomistic thought, even while she significantly adjusts their meaning. Through repeatedly attending to the personal in human nature in this way, while also holding her independent investigations in tension with Aquinas's teachings, Stein successfully reinterprets the whole of human nature from a thoroughly personal perspective, which she then fittingly embeds in the received anthropology of Aquinas. This personalization enables Stein to integrate her insights regarding the classical definition with her understanding of human unity and bodily formation, so that both come to be understood from the perspective of the personal I as bearer. This personalization represents a clear benefit for the *philosophia perennis*, inasmuch as it integrates the personalistic insights of phenomenology regarding human subjectivity into the traditional conception of human nature, the unity of the human being, and the formation of the living-body.

Just as she situates her investigation of human nature against the background of Aquinas's teachings and those of the Thomistic tradition, Stein also positions her analysis of the human individual against the backdrop of the conceptual apparatus of Aquinas, the Thomistic tradition, and that of the *philosophia perennis*. This "situating" includes consideration of the hylomorphic structure of the material individual, the identification of the individual as a τόδε τί, the definition of the individual as "in itself undivided yet divided from all else," and the recognition that the individual is foundationally determined by incommunicability. However, beyond this basic agreement, Stein reaches conclusions regarding the "being-individual" and "qualitative individuality" of the material individual in general and the human individual in particular that expressly contradict Aquinas and the Thomistic tradition. The decisive reason for this contradiction is found in Stein's focus on the primordially given personal I, a phenomenological focal point that enables her to surmount a problem she perceives in the Thomistic account of human individuation. Yet, prior to treating the question of the human individual directly, Stein mounts a critique of Aquinas's position on Thomistic grounds and according to Thomistic metaphysical principles—the most important of which is the ontological priority of form in the hylomorphic structure of material substances. Though Stein continues to grant a role to matter in the becoming and being of the material individual, given the priority of form in the structure of the composite, Stein reverses the individuating polarity of the "transcendental relation" and argues that the actual individual is constituted as such through the individual "essential-form." By further proposing that the ultimate principle grounding the individual essential-form is the empty-form "thing" as the formal framework of the whole, setting it apart as something distinct and separate from all else and radically incommunicable to another, Stein not only completes her explanation of the material individual but provides a universal explanation of individuation that traverses all regions of being. Stein then further argues that the material individual is rendered qualitatively distinct from all other specifically identical individuals through the formative "history" of its incorporated matter, the variable impact of material-environmental factors upon the individual, and the essential variability of the common form of the species in the individual essential-form of this or that thing.

Building on this critique, Stein then reasons that being-individual and individuality are elevated and intensified in the human individual, and indeed in all personal kinds of individual. Given the personal structure of human nature, Stein argues that the being-individual of the human individual is finally rooted in the personal I encompassing and bearing the formal (and material) fullness of the human structural whole, setting the individual apart as a preeminent personal kind of unity, a being that is in himself undivided and distinct from all others, and absolutely incommunicable to another. Yet, notwithstanding this personal basis of being-individual—where the empty-form "personal I" replaces the empty-form "thing"—only when the human personal I is completed as a self-dependent structural whole of soul and living-body is it possible for him to come into being as an actual individual with his own distinctive being and action in the world. Stein thus discloses that the actual human individual is rendered individual in both kind and mode through the personal I bearing the essential and actual fullness of human nature, so that the whole formal and material fullness of the human being is thoroughly integrated with the individual being of the personal I. The ultimate rationale behind Stein's solution to the question of human individuation is found in the indubitable cognitive givenness of the being-individual of the person, who has the inherent capacity to enunciate "I am"—or indeed, with focus on the identity of the individual, "I am who I am"—in an evidently infallible way. Simply, the human individual discovers himself to be an individual being together with the discovery of his very being.

Upon this basis, Stein then argues that the human individual is rendered qualitatively distinct from all others in manifold interrelated ways as a material living-body, and yet is also qualitatively distinct from all others in a properly spiritual way via the personal *quale* or ποῖον of the personally determined spiritual soul. Stein regards the personal quality as the proper possession of the human individual, something that makes him unique and unrepeatable from the very core of his being—thus becoming a second ground of ontological distinctness and incommunicability. Yet, notwithstanding the spiritual basis of human individuality, Stein maintains that the personal quality is naturally apt to be impressed upon the human structural whole inclusive of the living-body, through the progressive unfolding of this uniqueness in all personal expression and action via the soul and living-body. In this way, the material living-body, already qualitatively distinct through various interlocking material and environmental factors, all genetically grounded, is rendered absolutely unique through its progressive personal formation—but, importantly, only inasmuch as the personal I bears his particular living-body in a genuinely personal way. Simply, the human individual discovers his individuality at the very center of his being and ideally comes to embrace this individuality as it unfolds in personal action and expression, through which it comes to impress the human whole in a unique way.

In so proposing that the being-individual and individuality of the human individual is ultimately rooted in the personal spirit, Stein provides an independently developed solution to the question of the human individual that expressly contradicts Aquinas's conclusions and those of the Thomistic tradition, a contradiction that is directly traceable to her phenomenological starting point and corresponding Augustinian mode of investigation. Yet, despite this dissonance with the prevailing tradition, Stein's conclusions meet all the requirements of the material individual enumerated by the *philosophia perennis*—namely, that the individual be a τόδε τι, something in itself undivided yet divided from all else, and established in being as inherently incommunicable to another. When consideration is then also made for the subtlety of Aquinas's presentation of the *post-mortem* subsistence of the spiritual soul and the special way persons stand in being as individuals, Stein and Aquinas need not be understood as standing squarely opposed on all issues relating to the spiritual and personal significance of the human individual. Accordingly, I have proposed certain limited avenues toward their partial rapprochement. Inasmuch as Aquinas argues that the personal soul receives its individuated being immediately from God and survives bodily death as a spiritual substance, and inasmuch as he also argues that the personal individual stands in being in an eminently individual way, the positions of Stein and Aquinas are seen to be closely aligned on decisive anthropological notions. And yet, even given this narrow domain of conceptual agreement, their respective accounts of the ontological bases of the human individual are clearly contradictory, with individuation rooted in the personal spirit versus the designated matter of the body—that is, in the form versus the matter. However, notwithstanding this express contradiction, I submit that Stein's original presentation of the human individual represents a positive phenomenological development of the anthropological tradition of the *philosophia perennis*, precisely inasmuch as it fittingly accounts for Aquinas's insight that "the individuation fitting for human nature is personality," and robustly grounds the Christian teaching that the individual soul is directly and immediately created by God and endures death of the living-body as a self-subsistent spiritual individual.[2]

---

2   See above, 156n70, referencing SCG, 4.41, no. 6.

Stein focuses with comparable attention on the relationality of the human being, a relationality that spans the broad range of relations proper to human beings—those associational, communal, and personal. Yet for the mature Stein, the most significant human relation, and that which grounds all other human relations, is the natural creaturely relation of the human person to the personal Creator. As shown above, Stein accounts for the basic structure of this foundational relation with help from the Thomistic conception of the analogy of being understood as an analogy of proportionality. The Thomistic conception of analogy provides Stein with the appropriate rational support for that which is already seminally disclosed in conscious experience—namely, the fact that the frail being and fleeting life of the self is received from and upheld by the "ground and author" of all being. In her attempt to conceive of the relation of the self to the transcendent "world above"—already ideationally disclosed in the finitude and temporality of experience—Stein relies on Aquinas's pattern of reasoning to demonstrate the actuality of the being of the Creator, and she comes to describe God in typically Thomistic terms as Being Itself and Pure Act, the first, self-necessary Being (*Seiend, ens*), in whom there is a perfect coincidence of essence and being (*Sein, esse*) precisely as Being Itself Subsisting (*Ipsum Esse Subsistens*). Though Stein turns to Aquinas's demonstrations only briefly, referencing and reformulating his arguments in highly abridged form, his conclusions are decisive for her in all further investigations of Creator and creation, since they provide the necessary underpinning of the analogy of being. The import of Stein's recourse to Aquinas in this sphere is twofold: on the one hand, Aquinas's demonstrations provide Stein with the conceptual apparatus needed to describe the relation of the human being to God as a one of radical ontological dependence; on the other hand, Stein's Augustinian starting point enables her to conceive of the Thomistic doctrine of creation primarily from the perspective of the personal—and, indeed, the first-personal—inasmuch as the personal I becomes the evident "first premise" grounding the diverse forms of rational inference. Since this newly introduced first premise is patently closest to the uninterrupted experience of every human individual, the Thomistic manner of conceiving of God and the radicality of the creaturely relation is given its fitting personal ground in the being of the self—*that which is perpetually closest to the experience of each one of us*.

To elucidate the proper conceptual depth of this creaturely relation, Stein turns to Aquinas's understanding of the analogy of being, the conceptual apparatus that simultaneously captures the basic similitude and still greater dissimilitude of creature and Creator. After attaining initial confirmation of the analogy of being via phenomenological reflection, Stein turns to the Thomistic commentary of Josef Gredt and his presentation of the analogy of proportionality to detail the proper contours of this form of analogy. According to Gredt, the ontological ground of the analogy of proportionality is found in the likeness of the proportions of essence to being (v) in creaturely and Divine Being (n), a likeness that Gredt formulates: "As the creature relates to its being, so God relates to His being."[3] Yet, since there is a perfect coincidence of essence and being (v) in God, as proven in Aquinas's reasoning to God as Being Itself, Stein identifies a "riddling question" that lies at the heart of the analogy of being, that of the "missing proportion" of essence *to* act of being (v) in the divine analogate. This prompts Stein to investigate the analogy of proportionality from the perspective of the specifically personal, since God is revealed in personal experience as "the *fullness of being personally formed.*" That is, when we negate all limitations of the being and life of the finite personal self, and consider this in connection with the creation of finite being by the Creator, we come to understand the Creator as a personal reality best signified by the divine "I Am." Since "the name with which every *person* designates himself as such is '*I*,'"[4] Stein concludes that the absolute simplicity of God should be understood as a personal simplicity, with the further consequence that the proportion of essence to being (v) in God should be understood as a personal proportion. Thus, in contrast to Aquinas's negative concept of divine simplicity, where simplicity is understood as the absence of all actual and ontological compositions, Stein interprets the simplicity of God in a notionally positive way, proposing that divine simplicity is best understood from the perspective of the personal, as signified by the enunciation "I Am." And since the human being has actual and ontological unity in the human personal I—even if he is not actually or ontologically simple in being—the "personally formed" human being also possesses a personal proportion of essence to being (v) in the human "I am." This then opens the space for conceiving of God as the completed fullness of personal being.

In this way, Stein reveals the proportional similitude of human and Divine Being in the personal bearing of essence and being (v) in human and Divine Being (n), with the consequence that the analogy of proportionality can be

---

3   See above, 196n52, referencing EES, 290, citing Josef Gredt, *Die aristotelische-thomistische Philosophie*, 2 vols. (Freiburg i. Br.: Herder, 1935), 2:7.
4   See above, 205n5, referencing EES, 294.

reformulated in the following specifically personal way: "As the personal creature personally bears his personal being, so the personal God personally bears his personal being." This personal reconsideration of analogy represents a radical restructuring of the analogy of being, a restructuring that shifts its conceptual foundation. And yet this shift need not be understood as contradictory to Aquinas's teachings. Indeed, Stein's attention to the specifically personal can be taken to represent a fitting expansion of the conceptual content of the analogy of proportionality by identifying its properly personal basis in human and Divine Being, while simultaneously providing an innovative resolution to the "riddling question" of divine simplicity. Moreover, this conceptual expansion highlights the unique analogy of the personal creature to the personal God, inasmuch as it now encompasses the personal I bearing the rational nature in a way that is entirely coherent with the Thomistic schema. As noted above, the relational import of this conceptual expansion is profound and extensive. By presenting the analogy of being in specifically personal terms, Stein has drawn attention to the preeminent position of the human creature in the natural created world and within the hierarchical order of natural kinds, a preeminence that shows the human creature's incomparable creaturely relation to God. Not only is the personal self the first premise of rational inference that concludes to the existence and attributes of God, but the personal self now becomes the innermost ground of a natural understanding of God as personal Creator, and the location of an elevated form of natural creaturely relation to this personal God. So considered, the human person does not so much *have* a relation to the personal God, but rather *is* this relation to the personal God. Having received the gift of personal being from the Creator, now bearing a personal likeness to the Personal God, all that constitutes the human creature—the essentially personal kind of being, the actually personal mode of living, all encompassed by a personal proportion of essence to being (v) in the human "I am"—is revealed as the precise location of an all-encompassing relation to the personal God.

This *being-in-personal-relation* to God helpfully clarifies the proper depth of Stein's starting point in the first-person experiences of the personal I. Far from leading to any radicalized individualism, or indeed to an isolated solipsism, the intimacy of Stein's first-person perspective unveils the immediate transcendence of the self with respect to Divine Being. Consequently, Stein's Augustinian point of departure in the indubitably given self is not at all disfigured by the problems of the modern turn toward the subject, but rather immediately opens outward in profound and far-reaching ways, the most exalted of which is the personal relation of the human person to the radically transcendent other, God the personal Creator. In *The Structure of the Human Person*, Stein beautifully summarizes her position in the following way: "As irrefutably certain as the knowledge of the fact of one's own being is for Augustine, still more certain is the fact of the Eternal Being who stands behind his own frail being. *This* is the truth upon which the human being alights when he goes down into the ground of his interior. *If the soul knows its own self, then it knows God in itself.*"[5] Thus, in and through the person himself, in the depth of his personal spirit, in the expanse of the spiritual soul's interior castle, the personal I encounters the personal Creator, and in so meeting the ground of his own being immediately transcends the confines of his own finite and fleeting existence. The personal being of the self becomes, so to speak, the natural creaturely "window" that opens outward on the vast expanse that is the personal God, the Eternal completed fullness of Being Itself, the Great "I Am."[6] By entering into this experience, the personal "I am" immediately gives way to the all-encompassing presence of the divine "I Am" and surrenders his being to the One who upholds his frail personal existence, all that he is, all that he has, and all that he will be. This means that the being of the personal self can become the place of a personal relationship with the personal God— not mere *relation* but *relationship*—when the human individual thoughtfully takes hold of his being and consciously refers himself to his personal Creator.

I have suggested that this personal relationship is best understood as a form of dialogue with the personal God, a dialogue that takes place in the very life of the personal I—that is, in the kind and mode of free rational life borne by the personal I. I have further suggested that this dialogue is always already underway in every person's wrestling with the joys and sorrows of life, but only becomes properly personal when one begins to embrace the meaning of life as expression and response, when one freely and rationally embraces the mystery of life before the face of God in ongoing dialogue with their Creator. The recognition and development of such a dialogical relationship naturally

---

5   AMP, 12. Emphasis added.

6   This metaphor of a window, I owe to Joseph Ratzinger and his reflections on conscience and anamnesis in *On Conscience*, cited above, 234n43. It might be of interest to note that Stein and Ratzinger's parallel insights seem to be shaped by their common Augustinian heritage, in Stein's Augustinian point of departure in the personal subject, and in Ratzinger's Augustinian-like reflections on Platonic anamnesis.

completes the human person in their being further likened to the primary analogate of the analogy of being, the personal God, through the relational conformity wrought by knowledge and love. This growing in likeness to God can then usefully be considered also from the perspective of the unity and simplicity of God, inasmuch as the human individual becomes ever more unified and simple as a personal spirit through this relationship. That is, in completing one's substantial unity through formation of the human self as a spirit-soul-body composite, the human individual thereby becomes ever more vividly the simplified analogue of the *"fullness of being personally formed."*

* * * * * *

By way of conclusion, we should note that in all areas of investigation Stein retains the basic conceptual content of the Thomistic teachings she receives and incorporates—notwithstanding significant differences over the formal structure of being and the principle of material individuation—while simultaneously adjusting and developing this conceptual content to fit her own developed and developing anthropology. This results in a body of work that is inwardly nourished by the teachings of Aquinas, but which is also Stein's own intellectual *corpus*, a body constituted by integration of Thomistic teachings that are duly transformed through their invigoration by Stein in the new soil of phenomenology. As I have repeatedly shown, this Steinian transformation of the intellectual matter of Thomistic teachings is most apparent in the personal innovation she accomplishes in the Thomistic teachings she assimilates. Throughout her wide-ranging investigations, Stein mounts an increasingly compelling case that the personal I is indeed the predominating formative feature in the structure of human nature, and she thus reconsiders all received teachings by passing them through this personalizing lens. This reconsideration leads to a refocusing of their conceptual content according to which each teaching is understood from the perspective of the personal I as the interior pole of personal subjectivity and the objective ground of personal being. Through her phenomenological investigations, Stein then achieves something of a synthesis of Thomistic teachings with her phenomenological insights and a corresponding deepening of their metaphysical significance, a deepening I have identified as a fundamental personalization of Thomistic anthropology. All of this can be summarized here by attending to the way the human person is a microcosm of the cosmos, but now reinterpreted from the perspective of the personal subject. In Stein's rereading of Thomistic anthropology, not only does the objective structure of human nature recapitulate the whole of the hierarchically ordered cosmos, but each human individual has the potential to progressively encompass the whole of the created cosmos in acts of knowledge and love duly completed, a meaningful recapitulation that structures the spiritual interior of the personal subject and becomes "his most personal property, an integral part of his very self [...] 'his flesh and blood.'" And it is precisely in this recapitulation that the individual stands as a finite personal representative of the divine in the created cosmos, a finite personal analogue of the infinite personal Creator.

Epilogue

Stein's "Thomistic Personalism"?

> St. Thomas found a reverent and willing pupil in me
> —but my mind was no tabula rasa.
>
> —*Edith Stein*[1]

In what sense—if any—can Stein be read as a "Thomist" who presents a "Thomistic anthropology"?

First, is Stein a "Thomist"? Stein engages with Aquinas's thought extensively in her later works, eventually coming to understand this as her "proper mission." Since she adopts metaphysical teachings and principles of the Thomistic tradition and progressively incorporates them into her mature conceptual worldview, it may well seem that Stein can be regarded as a Thomist without further ado. Yet, as evident from the above analysis, Stein also reinterprets many of these received teachings from her Augustinian starting point and corresponding phenomenological mode of testing, and she occasionally draws conclusions that contrast with and at times outright contradict Aquinas and the Thomistic tradition. Therefore, any simple identification of Stein as a Thomist runs aground, and one should exercise appropriate caution when evaluating the Thomistic character of Stein's mature thought and the content of her later writings, giving due regard to the considerable debt she owes to Aquinas and Thomism while recognizing the differences she introduces to the Thomistic conceptual schema. These differences are most defined in her conclusions regarding the complex structure of essential-forms (= *forma substantialis* of

---

1   EES, 3.

Aquinas) and her understanding of the relation of the material individual to its material principle, understanding it as a necessary but insufficient principle of the becoming and being of the individual—and the many consequent differences that these two differences have throughout the completed conceptual schema. Consequently, I agree with Borden Sharkey's assertion "any claim that Stein is a Thomist or Thomistic thinker need[s] to be approached with care"—and one could even say, great care.[2]

However, Stein evidently receives the teachings of Aquinas as those of a philosophical master of the *philosophia perennis* and finds in his thought the conceptual clarity and precision needed to proceed confidently with her own metaphysical investigations. Indeed, it is precisely because of this clarity and depth that Stein can incorporate the conceptual content of Aquinas's teachings together with their associated principles and inferential reasonings, and thereby engage with many complex and involved metaphysical problems throughout her mature thought. Yet, while so incorporating this Thomistic conceptual schema, Stein repeatedly returns to "the things themselves" as they are given in conscious experience phenomenologically investigated and performs her own objective investigations—an objectivity she considers absolutely essential to the work of a philosopher *qua* philosopher. When through such objective investigation, Stein considers the truth of the matter to lie beyond the expressly stated views of Aquinas and the Thomistic tradition, she pursues the voice of truth in drawing her conclusions, rather than mechanically adhering to Aquinas and Thomism. Though Stein recognizes the voice of truth echoing in the thought of Aquinas and resonating down through the living tradition of Thomism, the truth itself remains her primary philosophical allegiance in any critical engagement, including with Thomism, and it is precisely this pursuit of truth that leads her toward certain conclusions that diverge from the express position of Aquinas and Thomism.

Of course, this fidelity to truth is eminently Thomistic, as is clear in the way Aquinas himself enters into disagreement with the intellectual heritage bequeathed to him—as do many scholars in the Thomist tradition, insofar as it is a living movement of thought that continues to query and develop the conceptual apparatuses provided by Aquinas and his commentators/interpreters. This shared orientation to truth enables Stein to intellectually

---

2   Sarah Borden Sharkey, *Thine Own Self: Individuality in Edith Stein's Later Writings* (Washington, DC: The Catholic University of America Press, 2010), xix.

"live through" the received teachings of Aquinas and Thomism with trust and receptivity, a posture of investigation that first enables her to grasp the various conceptual apparatuses provided by the Thomistic tradition before proceeding toward her own developed conclusions. According to this trustful yet critical stance Stein is able to integrate the conceptual apparatuses of the Thomistic tradition into her own developing worldview while making needed clarifications and adjustments to each particular apparatus as the truth of the investigation demands—or, at least, as the truth of the matter appears to Stein herself. Thus, while teachings inform Stein's conceptualization, the truth remains the fixed focal point of her searching gaze. In this way, Stein remains true to the vocation of a philosopher, as one oriented toward truth in first-person engagement with the world of experience, while receiving the teachings of Aquinas and the Thomistic tradition with the humility of "a reverent and willing pupil."

On the one hand, then, one can say that Stein is thoroughly Thomistic in her philosophical disposition, insofar as truth remains ever at the center of her philosophical investigations; and moreover, in her basic metaphysical commitments and positions, insofar as she incorporates an extensive array of key Thomistic conceptual apparatuses. On the other hand, Stein is strikingly unThomistic in her willingness to stand apart from Aquinas and the Thomistic tradition in certain ways, insofar as she is willing to disagree on a number of significant positions; disagreements that invariably ripple outward throughout the entire conceptual schema. Therefore, rather than broadly classifying Stein as a "Thomist," I suggest it is better to consider her "Thomis*tic*," since she is undoubtedly a Thomistically *informed* philosopher, even while not a "pure" Thomist presenting a "pure" Thomistic philosophy. This qualified attribution identifies the profound impact of Aquinas on Stein's mature thought, while simultaneously recognizing her divergence from the standard Thomist presentation (at least insofar as certain Thomistic positions have most often been understood and presented). This qualified assessment bears reference to the proper assessment of Stein's mature thought, precisely so as not to conflate her philosophical contribution with Thomistic commentary or interpretation, and to the proper assessment of her engagement with Aquinas and Thomism, so as not to negatively evaluate her understanding of Aquinas and the Thomistic tradition.

What sense—if any—can Stein's anthropology be understood as a "Thomistic anthropology"? Granted that Stein can be read as "Thomis*tic*" in the above-detailed sense, we immediately gain clarity regarding the "Thomist" character of Stein's mature anthropology. As her thought in general is influenced by Aquinas and Thomism, so too her mature anthropology is shaped by Aquinas and the Thomistic tradition and lies in decisive continuity with its central anthropological teachings—none more significant than the Thomistic commitment to substantial unity via the spiritual soul. However, inasmuch as her mature anthropology is also formed by a living encounter with the reality of the human person—"the *personal* thing in itself"—while she continues to employ the phenomenological method, with its defined attention to the I and consciousness, Stein's mature anthropology diverges from that of Aquinas and the standard Thomist position in notable ways. As a result of her Augustinian approach, Stein does not simply receive and recapitulate Thomistic anthropology, but rather presents a conceptually expanded and deepened understanding of the essentially personal structure of human nature, and she shows that this personal structure powerfully permeates and pervades the whole of human nature, inclusive of the material living-body. Though Stein's later anthropology can be understood as one deeply informed by Aquinas and the Thomistic tradition, it is also distinctively her own, at times subtly contrasting, at times surpassing, and at times outright contradicting the stated position of Aquinas and Thomism. Therefore, in like manner to the measured attribution of "Thomistic" to the mature Stein, Stein's mature anthropology should be described as a "Thomistically informed anthropology." And since her anthropology is also decidedly personalist in its leanings, her Thomistic anthropology is best conceived as a "Thomistically informed personalism." This attribution partially reveals how Stein's particular brand of Thomistic personalism is quite different from that of St. Karol Wojtyła. Whereas Wojtyła develops Aquinas's anthropology by introducing the significance of personal subjectivity and consciousness without fundamentally altering the received conceptual apparatus, Stein reinterprets the apparatus from the perspective of the personal subject as bearer and thereby crucially restructures the whole apparatus.

We can now summarize Stein's relation to Thomistic thought by considering the precise meaning of the "Thomist" attribute. If by "Thomist" one means: (1) one who studies the works of Aquinas and the Thomistic tradition in an historical mode, expounding on the thought of Aquinas and Thomism with historical accuracy and concern for its chronological development; or (2) one who utilizes and develops the thought of Aquinas and the Thomistic tradition in view of handling philosophical problems in strict continuity with the teachings of Aquinas, then Stein cannot be identified as a Thomist philosopher. If, however, by "Thomist" one means: (1) one who receives the thought of Aquinas and Thomism as a living intellectual heritage and inwardly appropriates its teachings as a willing pupil, prepared to hand on the wisdom of this intellectual tradition to future generations of philosophers; and (2) one who creatively develops these teachings in dialogical engagement with Thomistic thinkers, informed by genuine philosophical developments since the time of Aquinas while solving problems old and new, then I suggest that the mature Stein can indeed be read as a Thomist—but, again, only in the above-qualified senses. The same qualifications then apply *mutatis mutandis* to the sphere of anthropology and personalism.

Stein's engagement with the teachings of Aquinas and the Thomistic tradition should thus be understood as her definitive entry into to the broad stream of the *philosophia perennis*, understood as a tradition of philosophizing that finds its exemplary form in Aquinas's thought, yet is not unduly confined to it. Moreover, we can simultaneously conclude that Stein's input in the sphere of anthropology in particular represents a significant original contribution to this tradition, a significance that is seen in her focused attention to the human being as a personal subject. Under Stein's investigative gaze, we discover that the human person is one who bears human nature in an eminently personal way, an individual who can enunciate "I am who I am" in analogical likeness to God, with a potency for perpetual dialogue with his personal Creator, speaking that finite λόγος that is himself, in reflective response to the Eternal Λόγος from which he came—dealing "out that being indoors each one dwells [...] Crying *Whát I do is me: for that I came*."[3]

---

3 These are lines of Hopkins's poem included at the front of the book: "As Kingfishers Catch Fire," which succinctly captures the central thread of the collective analyses here presented, where all being is understood to simultaneously proclaim itself and the divine, simply by being *what it is*, what the Creator made it to be.

... καὶ ἡ χάρις αὐτοῦ ἡ εἰς ἐμὲ οὐ κενὴ ἐγενήθη.
—*1 Corinthians 15:10*

BIBLIOGRAPHY

Primary Sources

Stein

German

Stein, Edith. *Aus dem Leben einer jüdischen Familie*, ESGA 1, 3rd ed. (Freiburg i. Br.: Herder, 2010).
———. *Beiträge zur philosophischen Begründung der Psychologie und der Geisteswissenschaften*, ESGA 6 (Freiburg i. Br.: Herder, 2010).
———. *Bildung und Entfaltung der Individualität*, ESGA 16, 2nd ed. (Freiburg i. Br.: Herder, 2004).
———. *Der Aufbau der menschlichen Person*, ESGA 14, 2nd ed. (Freiburg i. Br.: Herder, 2010).
———. *Die Frau, Fragestellungen und Reflexionen*, ESGA 13, 4th ed. (Freiburg i. Br.: Herder, 2010).
———. *Eine Untersuchung über den Staat*, ESGA 7 (Freiburg i. Br.: Herder, 2006).
———. *Endliches und ewiges Sein*, ESGA 11/12, 2nd ed. (Freiburg i. Br.: Herder, 2013).
———. *Einführung in die Philosophie*, ESGA 8, 2nd ed. (Freiburg i. Br.: Herder, 2010).
———. *"Freiheit und Gnade" und weitere Beiträge zu Phänomenologie und Ontologie*, ESGA 9 (Freiburg i. Br.: Herder, 2014).
———. *Geistliche Texte I*, ESGA 19 (Freiburg i. Br.: Herder, 2009).
———. *Kreuzeswissenschaft*, ESGA 18, 4th ed. (Freiburg i. Br.: Herder, 2013).
———. *Miscellanea thomistica. Übersetzungen—Abbreviationen—Exzerpte aus Werken des Thomas von Aquin und der Forschungsliteratur*, ESGA 27 (Freiburg i. Br.: Herder, 2014).
———. *Potenz und Akt*, ESGA 10 (Freiburg i. Br.: Herder, 2005).
———. *Selbstbildnis in Briefen I: 1916–1933*, ESGA 2, 2nd ed. (Freiburg i. Br.: Herder, 2005).
———. *Selbstbildnis in Briefen II: 1933–1942*, ESGA 3, 2nd ed. (Freiburg i. Br.: Herder, 2006).
———. *Selbstbildnis in Briefen III: Briefe an Roman Ingarden*, ESGA 4, 2nd ed. (Freiburg i. Br.: Herder, 2005).
———. *Übersetzung III: Thomas von Aquino, Untersuchungen über die Wahrheit* (Freiburg i. Br.: Herder, 2008).
——— and Hedwig Conrad-Martius, *Übersetzung V: Alexandre Koyré, Descartes und die Scholastik*, ESGA 25 (Freiburg i. Br.: Herder, 2005).

———. *Übersetzung V: Thomas von Aquino, Über das Seiende und das Wesen*, ESGA 26 (Freiburg i. Br.: Herder, 2010).
———. *Was ist der Mensch? Theologische Anthropologie*, ESGA 15 (Freiburg i. Br.: Herder, 2005).
———. *Wege der Gotteserkenntnis*, ESGA 17, 3rd ed. (Freiburg i. Br.: Herder, 2013).
———. *Zum Problem der Einfühlung*, ESGA 5, 3rd ed. (Freiburg i. Br.: Herder, 2016).

English

Stein, Edith. *An Investigation Concerning the State* (Washington, DC: Institute of Carmelite Studies, 2006).
———. *Finite and Eternal Being*, trans. Kurt F. Reinhardt (Washington, DC: Institute of Carmelite Studies, 2002).
———. *Finite and Eternal Being*, trans. Walter Redmond (unpublished, [2015]).
———. "Husserl and Aquinas: A Comparison," in *Knowledge and Faith*, trans. Walter Redmond (Washington, DC: Institute of Carmelite Studies, 2000).
———. *Knowledge and Faith* (Washington, DC: Institute of Carmelite Studies, 2000).
———. *Life in a Jewish Family*, trans. Josephine Koeppel (Washington, DC: Institute of Carmelite Studies, 1986).
———. *On the Problem of Empathy* (Washington, DC: Institute of Carmelite Studies Publications, 1989).
———. *Essays on Woman* (Washington, DC: Institute of Carmelite Studies Publications, 1996).
———. *Philosophy of Psychology and the Humanities* (Washington, DC: Institute of Carmelite Studies, 2000).
———. *Potency and Act*, trans. Walter Redmond (Washington, DC: Institute of Carmelite Studies, 2009).
———. *The Science of the Cross*, trans. Josephine Koeppel (Washington, DC: Institute of Carmelite Studies, 2002).

Aquinas

Latin

Aquinas, Thomas. *Compendium theologiae* (Rome: Editori di San Tommaso, 1979).
———. *De principiis naturae, De aeternitate mundi, De motu cordis, De mixtione elementorum, De operationibus occultis naturae, De iudiciis astrorum, De sortibus, De unitate intellectus, De ente et essentia, De fallaciis, De propositionibus modalibus* (Rome: Editori di San Tommaso, 1976).
———. *De substantiis separatis. Super Decretalem* (Rome: Sanctae Sabina, 1968).
———. *In duodecim libros Metaphysicorum Aristotelis expositio* (Rome: Marietti, 1971).
———. *In libros Posteriorum Analyticorum expositio* (Rome: S. C. de Propaganda Fide, 1882), 137–403.

Bibliography

———. *Quaestiones de quolibet* (Paris: Éditions du Cerf, 1996).
———. *Quaestio disputata de spiritualibus creaturis* (Paris: Éditions du Cerf, 2000).
———. *Quaestiones disputatae de anima* (Paris: Éditions du Cerf, 1996).
———. *Quaestiones disputatae de potentia* (Rome: Marietta, 1953).
———. *Quaestiones disputatae de veritate* (Rome: Sanctae Sabina, 1970–76).
———. *Sentencia libri De anima* (Paris: Librairie Philosophique J. Vrin, 1984).
———. *Summa contra gentiles* (Rome: Typis Riccardi Garroni, 1918, 1926, 1930).
———. *Summa theologiae* (Rome: S. C. de Propaganda Fide, 1888–1906).
———. *Super Boetium De Trinitate* (Paris: Éditions du Cerf, 1992).
———. *In librum Beati Dionysii De divinus nominibus expositio* (Rome: Marietta, 1950)

English

Aquinas, Thomas. *Aristotle's De anima in the version of William of Moerbeke and the Commentary of St. Thomas Aquinas*, trans. Kenelm Foster (New Haven, CT: Yale University Press, 1951, repr. 1965).
———. *Commentary on Aristotle's Physics*, trans. Richard J. Blackwell, Richard J. Spath, and W. Edmund Thirlkel (New Haven, CT: Yale University Press, 1963).
———. *Commentary on the Metaphysics*, trans. John P. Rowan (Chicago: Henry Regnery Company, 1961).
———. *Commentary on the Posterior Analytics of Aristotle*, trans. F. R. Larcher (New York: Magi Books, 1970).
———. *Compendium of Theology*, trans. Cyril Vollert (London: Herder, 1952).
———. *Disputed Questions on Truth*, trans. Robert W. Mulligan, and Robert W. Mulligan, Robert W. Schmidt (Chicago: Henry Regnery Company, 1952–54).
———. *Faith, Reason and Theology, Questions I-IV of his Commentary on the De trinitate of Boëthius*, trans. Armand Maurer (Toronto: Pontifical Institute of Medieval Studies, 1987).
———. *On Being and Essence*, trans. Armand Maurer, 2nd ed. (Toronto: Pontifical Institute of Medieval Studies, 1968).
———. *On Spiritual Creatures*, trans. Mary C. Fitzpatrick and John J. Wellmuth (Milwaukee: Marquette University Press, 1949).
———. *On the Power of God*, trans. Fathers of the English Dominican Province, (London: Burns Oates & Washbourne, 1932–33).
———. *Questions on the Soul*, trans. James H. Robb (Milwaukee: Marquette University Press, 1984).
———. *Summa contra gentiles*, trans. Fathers of the English Dominican Province (New York: Benziger Bros., 1923–29).
———. *Summa theologica*, trans. Fathers of the English Dominican Province (New York: Benziger Bros., 1947–48).
———. *Treatise on Separate Substances*, trans. Francis J. Lescoe (Carthagena, OH: The Messenger Press, 1963).

Reference Sources

Cairns, Dorion. *Guide for Translating Husserl* (The Hague: Martinus Nijhoff, 1973).
Denzinger, Heinrich. *Compendium of Creeds, Definitions, and Declarations on Matters of Faith and Morals*, ed. Peter Hünermann, 43rd ed. (San Francisco: Ignatius Press, 2012).
Drumond, John J. *Historical Dictionary of Husserl's Philosophy* (Lanham, MD: Scarecrow Press, 2008).
Knaup, Marcus, and Harald Seubert, eds. *Edith Stein-Lexikon* (Freiburg i. Br.: Herder, 2017).
Lewis, Charlton T., and Charles Short. *An Elementary Latin Dictionary* (Oxford: Oxford University Press, 1963).
Kasper, Walter, et al., eds. *Lexikon für Theologie und Kirche*, 4 (Freiburg i. Br.: Herder, 2006).
Ritter, Joachim, et al., eds. *Historische Wörterbuch der Philosophie*, vol. 8 (Basel: Schwabe 1971–2007), iv, ed., Karlfried Gründer (1976), vi, ed., Karlfried Gründer (1984), viii, ed., Karlfried Gründer (1992).

Secondary Sources

Abel, Donald C. "Intellectual Substance as Form of the Body in Aquinas," in *Proceedings of the American Catholic Philosophical Association* 69 (1995): 227–36.
Ales Bello, Angela. "Edmund Husserl and Edith Stein: The Question of the Human Subject," trans. Antonio Calcagno, *American Catholic Philosophical Quarterly* 82, no. 1 (2008): 143–59.
———. "Ontology, Metaphysics, and Life in Edith Stein," in *Contemplating Edith Stein*, ed. Joyce Avrech Berkman (Notre Dame, IN: University of Notre Dame Press, 2006), 271–282.
———. "Phänomenologie, Ontologie und Metaphysik Edith Steins," in *"Alles Wesentliche lasst sich nicht schreiben,"* ed. Andreas Speer and Stephen Regh (Freiburg i. Br.: Herder, 2016), 137–53.
———. "Thomas von Aquino in Edith Steins Interpretation," in *The Hat and the Veil: The Phenomenology of Edith Stein*, Ad Fontes: Studien zur frühen Phänomenologie, 3, ed. Jerzy Machnacz et al. (Nordhausen: Traugott Bautz, 2016), 15–25.
———. "What Is Life? The Contributions of Hedwig Conrad-Martius and Edith Stein," trans. Antonio Calcagno, *Symposium* 16, no. 2 (2012): 20–33.
Alfieri, Francesco. "Der Mensch baut sich nicht allein von sich aus auf!," in *Edith Steins Herausforderung heutiger Anthropologie*, ed. Hanna-Barbara Gerl-Falkovitz and Mette Lebech (Heiligenkreuz: Be&Be, 2017), 43–50.
———. "The Presence of Duns Scotus in the Thought of Edith Stein: The Question of Individuality," trans. George Metcalf, in *Analecta Husserliana*, 120 (Cham: Springer, 2015), eBook.

———. "Hin zu einer Lösung der Frage nach dem principium individuationis in den Untersuchungen von Edith Stein und Edmund Husserl," in *Husserl und Thomas von Aquin bei Edith Stein*, Ad Fontes: Studien zur frühen Phänomenologie, 2, ed. Peter Volek (Nordhausen: Traugott Bautz, 2016), 74–113.

Andrews, Michael F. "Edith Stein and Max Scheler: Ethics, Empathy, and the Constitution of the Acting Person," in *Selected Papers on the Early Phenomenology: Munich and Göttingen*, ed. Kimberly Baltzer-Jaray (= *Quaestiones Disputatae* 3, no. 1 (2013)), 33–47.

———. "Stein: Beyond Reason, Faith, and Ethics," in *Edith Steins Herausforderung heutiger Anthropologie*, ed. Hanna-Barbara Gerl-Falkovitz and Mette Lebech (Heiligenkreuz: Be&Be, 2017), 383–99.

Aristotle. *The Complete Works of Aristotle*, 2 vols, ed. Jonathan Barnes, trans. J. A. Smith et al. (Princeton, NJ: Princeton University Press, 1995).

Ashworth, E. J. "Suárez on the Analogy of Being: Some Historical Background," in *Vivarium* 33, no. 1 (1995): 50–75.

Augustine. *Soliloquies*, 2.1.1, in *St. Augustine's Cassiciacum Dialogues*, vol. 4, trans. Michael P. Foley (New Haven, CT: Yale University Press, 2020).

———. *Confessions*, trans. F. J. Sheed (London: Sheed and Ward, 1944, repr. 1954).

Baseheart, Mary Catherine. *Person in the World: Introduction to the Philosophy of Edith Stein* (Boston: Kluwer Academic, 1997).

———. *The Encounter of Husserl's Phenomenology and the Philosophy of St. Thomas Aquinas in Selected Writings of Edith Stein* (unpublished doctoral thesis, Notre Dame University, 1960).

Beckmann-Zöller, Beate. "Edith Stein's Theory of the Person in Her Münster Years (1932–1933)," trans. Amalie Enns, in *American Catholic Philosophical Quarterly* 82, no. 1 (2008): 47–70.

Betschart, Christof. "Edith Steins Vermittlung zwischen einem klassischen und einem modernen Personbegriff," in *The Hat and the Veil: The Phenomenology of Edith Stein*, Ad Fontes: Studien zur frühen Phänomenologie, 3, ed. Jerzy Machnacz et al. (Nordhausen: Traugott Bautz, 2016), 91–101.

———. "Edith Steins Verständnis der menschlichen Individualität in *Endliches und ewiges Sein*. Ein Beitrag zur kritischen Auseinandersetzung mit dem thomistischen Standardverständnis der Individuation," in *Husserl und Thomas von Aquin bei Edith Stein*, Ad Fontes: Studien zur frühen Phänomenologie, 2, ed. Peter Volek (Nordhausen: Traugott Bautz, 2016), 114–31.

———. "Kern der Person: (Meta-)Phänomenologische Begründung der menschlichen Person nach Edith Steins Frühwerk," in *Europa und seine Anderen*, ed. Hanna-Barbara Gerl-Falkovitz, René Kaufmann, and Hans R. Sepp (Dresden: Thelem, 2010), 61–72.

———. "The Individuality of the Human Person in the Phenomenological Works of Edith Stein," in *Edith Stein: Women, Social-Political Philosophy, Theology, Metaphysics and Public History*, ed. Antonio Calcagno (Cham: Springer, 2016), 73–86.

———. "Quid and Quale: Reflections on Possible Complementarity between Metaphysical and Phenomenological Approaches to Personal Individuality in *Potenz und Akt*," in *Intersubjectivity, Humanity, Being: Edith Stein's Phenomenology and Christian Philosophy*, ed. Mette Lebech and Haydn Gurmin (Bern: Peter Lang, 2015), 211–28.

———. "*Überlegungen zur Menschenwürde und zu ethischen Konsequenzen von Edith Steins Verständnis der menschlichen Individualität*," in *Edith Stein Jahrbuch*, 21, ed. Ulrich Dobhan (Würzburg: Echter, 2015), 87–109.

———. *Unwiederholbares Gottessiegel: Personale Individualität nach Edith Stein* (Basel: Reinhardt, 2013).

Betz, John R. "The *Analogia Entis* as A Standard Of Catholic Engagement: Erich Przywara's Critique of Phenomenology and Dialectical Theology," in *Modern Theology* 35, no. 1 (2019): 81–102.

Blankenhorn, Bernhard. "Aquinas on the Transcendental One: An Overlooked Development in Doctrine," in *Angelicum* 81, no. 3 (2004): 615–37.

Blair, George. "On *Esse* and Relation" in *Communio: International Catholic Review* 21, no. 1 (1994): 162–65.

Bobik, Joseph. *Aquinas on Matter and Form and the Elements* (Notre Dame, IN: University of Notre Dame Press, 1998, repr. 2006).

Boëthius, Anicius, *Liber de persona et duabus naturis contra Eutychen et Nestorium*, trans. H. F. Stewart and E. K. Rand (London: Heinemann, 1958).

Borden Sharkey, Sarah. "Capacity or Castle? Thoughts on Stein's Creative (Carmelite) Contribution to Discussions on the Soul," in *Edith Steins Herausforderung heutiger Anthropologie*, ed. Hanna-Barbara Gerl-Falkovitz and Mette Lebech (Heiligenkreuz: Be&Be, 2017), 203–14.

———. "Edith Stein and Individual Forms: A Few Distinctions regarding Being an Individual," in *Yearbook of the Irish Philosophical Society* (2006): 49–69.

———. "Eternal Rest: The Beauty and Challenge of Essential Being," in *Selected Papers on the Legacy of Edith Stein's Finite and Eternal Being*, ed. Sarah Borden Sharkey (= *Quaestiones Disputatae* 4, no. 1 (2013)), 45–64.

———. "How Can Being Be Limited?: W. Norris Clarke on Thomas's "Limitation of Act by Potency," in *The Saint Anselm Journal* 7, no. 1 (2009).

———. "The Meaning of Being in Thomas Aquinas and Edith Stein," in *Thomas Aquinas: Teacher and Scholar* (Dublin: Four Courts Press, 2012), 85–100.

———. "Reconciling Time and Eternity: Edith Stein's Philosophical Project," in *Intersubjectivity, Humanity, Being: Edith Stein's Phenomenology and Christian Philosophy*, ed. Mette Lebech and Haydn Gurmin (Bern: Peter Lang, 2015), 7–20.

———. *Thine Own Self: Individuality in Edith Stein's Later Writings* (Washington, DC: The Catholic University of America Press, 2010).

Brann, Eva. *The Logos of Heraclitus* (Philadelphia: Paul Dry Books, 2011).

Brown, Christopher M. "Aquinas on the Individuation of Non-Living Substances," in *Proceedings of the American Catholic Philosophical Association* 75 (2002): 237–54.

Brown, Montague. "St. Thomas Aquinas and the Individuation of Persons," in *American Catholic Philosophical Quarterly* 65, no. 1 (1991): 29–44.

Brown, O. J. "Individuation and Actual Existence in Scotist Metaphysics: A Thomistic Assessment," in *The New Scholasticism* 53, no. 3 (1979): 347–361.

Cajetan, Thomas de Vio. *De Nominum Analogia*, trans. Joshua P. Hochschild, appendix to unpublished dissertation, *The Semantics of Analogy According to Thomas De Vio Cajetan's De Nominum Analogia* (unpublished doctoral thesis, Notre Dame University, 2001).

Calcagno, Antonio. *The Philosophy of Edith Stein* (Pittsburgh: Duquesne University Press, 2007).

Callus, Daniel A. "The Origins of the Problem of the Unity of Form," in *The Thomist: A Speculative Quarterly Review* 24, no. 2 (1961): 257–85.

Cantens, Bernardo J. "A Solution to the Problem of Personal Identity in the Metaphysics of Thomas Aquinas," in *Proceedings of the American Catholic Philosophical Association*, 75 (2002): 121–34.

Carl, Brian T. "The Transcendentals and the Divine Names in Thomas Aquinas," in *American Catholic Philosophical Quarterly* 92, no. 2 (2018): 225–47.

———. "Knowing God as He Who Is," at Summer Philosophy Workshop: "Aquinas on Divine Attributes," Soundcloud, streaming audio, 01:08 (June 14th, 2018), https://soundcloud.com/thomisticinstitute/knowing-god-as-he-who-is-dr-brian-carl.

Chicoine, Glenn. "Present Potential in Edith Stein's *Finite and Eternal Being*, Chapter Two," in *Selected Papers on the Legacy of Edith Stein's Finite and Eternal Being*, ed. Sarah Borden Sharkey (= *Quaestiones Disputatae* 4.1 (2013)): 31–44.

Clarke, W. Norris. *Person and Being* (Milwaukee: Marquette University Press, 1993, repr. 2008).

———. "Person, Being, and St. Thomas," in *Communio: International Catholic Review* 19, no. 4 (1992): 601–18.

———. "Response to Blair's Comments," in *Communio: International Catholic Review* 21, no. 1 (1994): 170–71.

———. "Response to David Schindler's Comments," in *Communio: International Catholic Review* 20, no. 3 (1993): 593–98.

———. "Response to Long's Comments," in *Communio: International Catholic Review* 21, no. 3 (1994): 165–69.

Cohen, Marc, and Patricia Curd, CDC Reeve. *Ancient Greek Philosophy* (Indianapolis: Hackett, 1995).

Conn, Christopher. "Aquinas on Human Nature and the Possibility of Bodiless Existence," in *New Blackfriars* 93, no. 1045 (2012): 324–38.

Conrad-Martius, Hedwig. *Metaphysische Gespräche* (Halle: Max Niemeyer, 1921).

Crosby, John. *The Selfhood of the Human Person* (Washington, DC: The Catholic University of America Press, 1996).

Cross, Richard. *Duns Scotus* (Oxford: Oxford University Press, 1999).

Davies, Brian, and Eleonore Stump, eds. *The Oxford Handbook of Aquinas* (Oxford: Oxford University Press, 2012).

Decaen, Christopher. "Elemental Virtual Presence in St. Thomas," in *The Thomist: A Speculative Quarterly Review* 64, no. 2 (2000): 271–300.

De Haan, Daniel D. "A Mereological Construal of the Primary Notions Being and Thing in Avicenna and Aquinas," in *American Catholic Philosophical Quarterly* 88, no. 2 (2014): 335–60.

——— and Brandon Dahm. "Thomas Aquinas on Separated Souls as Incomplete Human Persons," in *The Thomist: A Speculative Quarterly Review* 83, no. 4 (2019): 589–637.

DeHart, Paul J. "What Is Not, Was Not, and Will Never Be: Creaturely Possibility, Divine Ideas and the Creator's Will in Thomas Aquinas," in *Nova et Vetera* 13, no. 4 (2015): 1009–58.

Descartes, René. *Descartes Philosophical Writings*, ed. and trans. Elizabeth Anscombe and Peter T. Geach, intro. by Alexander Koyré (Indianapolis: Bobbs-Merrill Educational Publishing, 1971, repr. 1983).

Dewan, Lawrence. "Saint Thomas, Alvin Plantinga, and the Divine Simplicity," in *The Modern Schoolman* 66 (1989): 141–51.

———. "St. Thomas and the Possibles," in *The New Scholasticism* 53, no. 1 (1979): 76–85.

———. "The Individual as a Mode of Being according to Thomas Aquinas," in *The Thomist: A Speculative Quarterly Review* 63, no. 3 (1999): 403–24.

Doolan, Gregory T. *Aquinas on the Divine Ideas as Exemplar Causes* (Washington, DC: The Catholic University of America Press, 2008).

———. "Aquinas on the Divine Ideas and the Really Real," in *Nova et Vetera* 13, no. 4 (2015): 1059–92.

Emery, Gilles. "The Dignity of Being a Substance: Person, Subsistence, and Nature," in *Nova et Vetera*, 9, no. 4 (2011): 991–1001.

Fabro, Cornelio. "The Intensive Hermeneutics of Thomistic Philosophy: The Notion of Participation," in *The Review of Metaphysics* 27, no. 3 (1974): 449–91.

Farmer, Linda L. "Human Individuation According to Aquinas: Resolving the Debate," in *The Modern Schoolman* 80 (2002): 55–61.

Íngrid, Vendrell Ferran. "Intentionality, Value Disclosure, and Constitution: Stein's Model," in *Empathy, Sociality, and Personhood: Essays on Edith Stein's Phenomenological Investigations*, ed. Elisa Magri and Dermot Moran (Cham: Springer, 2017), 65–85.

Finley, John. "The Problem of Individual Being," in *Selected Papers on the Legacy of Edith Stein's Finite and Eternal Being*, ed. Sarah Borden Sharkey (= *Quaestiones Disputatae* 4.1 (2013)), 107–20.

Flood, Anthony T. "Aquinas on Subjectivity: A Response to Crosby," in *American Catholic Philosophical Quarterly* 84, no. 1 (2010): 69–83.

Gabbe, Myrna. "Aristotle on the Starting Point of Motion in the Soul," in *Phronesis* 57 (2002): 358–79.

Galvani, Martina. "The Spiritual Dimension and the Complex Structure of the Human Person," in *"Alles Wesentliche lasst sich nicht schreiben,"* ed. Andreas Speer and Stephen Regh (Freiburg i. Br.: Herder, 2016), 307–20.

Gerl-Falkovitz, Hanna-Barbara. "Edith Stein zwischen Edmund Husserl und Thomas Aquinas," in *Husserl und Thomas von Aquin bei Edith Stein*, Ad Fontes:

Studien zur frühen Phänomenologie, 2, ed. Peter Volek (Nordhausen: Traugott Bautz, 2016), 12–34.

Gilson, Étienne. *John Duns Scotus: Introduction to His Fundamental Positions*, trans. James G. Colbert (London: T&T Clark, 2019).

———. *The Christian Philosophy of St. Thomas Aquinas* (New York: Random House, 1956; repr. Notre Dame, IN: University of Notre Dame Press, 1994).

———. *The Elements of Christian Philosophy* (New York: Mentor-Omega Books, 1963).

———. *The Spirit of Mediaeval Philosophy*, trans. A. H. C. Downes (New York: Charles Scribner's Sons, 1936; repr. Notre Dame, IN: University of Notre Dame Press, 1991, repr. 2008).

———. *Thomist Realism and the Critique of Knowledge*, trans. Mark A. Wauck (San Francisco: Ignatius Press, 1986, repr. 2012).

Gleeson, Gerald. "Exemplars and Essences: Thomas Aquinas and Edith Stein," in *Intersubjectivity, Humanity, Being: Edith Stein's Phenomenology and Christian Philosophy*, ed. Mette Lebech and Haydn Gurmin (Bern: Peter Lang, 2015), 289–308.

Gonzalez, Orestes J. "The Apprehension of Being in Aquinas," in *American Catholic Philosophical Quarterly* 68, no. 4 (1995): 475–500.

Gonzales, Philip. "*Analogia Entis* and Creatureliness: Stein and Przywara's Refutation of Heidegger," in *The Hat and the Veil: The Phenomenology of Edith Stein*, Ad Fontes: Studien zur frühen Phänomenologie, 3, ed. Jerzy Machnacz et al. (Nordhausen: Traugott Bautz, 2016), 119–30.

———. *Reimagining the* Analogia Entis: *The Future of Erich Przywara's Christian Vision* (Grand Rapids, MI: Eerdmans, 2019).

Goyette, John. "Thomas on the Unity of Substantial Form," in *Nova et Vetera* 7, no. 4 (2009): 781–90.

Grabmann, Martin. *Thomas Aquinas: His Personality and Thought*, trans. Virgil Michel (London: Longmans, Green, 1928; repr. LaVergne, TN: Kessinger Legacy Reprints, 2010).

Grabowski, John. "Person: Substance and Relation," in *Communio: International Catholic Review* 22, no. 1 (1995): 139–63.

Gracia, Jorge J. E. *Individuality: An Essay on the Foundations of Metaphysics* (Albany, NY: State University of New York Press, 1988).

———, ed. *Individuation in Scholasticism: The Later Middle Ages and the Counter-Reformation, 1150–1650* (Albany, NY: State University of New York Press, 1994).

Gredt, Josef. *Die aristotelische-thomistische Philosophie*, 2 vols. (Freiburg i. Br.: Herder, 1935).

———. *Elementa philosophiae Aristotelico-Thomisticae*, 13th ed. (Rome: Desclée, Lefebvre et Soc., 1899; Freiburg i. Br.: Herder, 1961).

Gricoski, Thomas. *Being Unfolded: Edith Stein on the Meaning of Being* (Washington, DC: The Catholic University of America Press, 2020).

———. "The Method of Stein's Realism," in *Intersubjectivity, Humanity, Being: Edith Stein's Phenomenology and Christian Philosophy*, ed. Mette Lebech and Haydn Gurmin (Bern: Peter Lang, 2015), 309–34.

———. "Towards a Steinian Neo-Essentialism," in *Edith Steins Herausforderung heutiger Anthropologie*, ed. Hanna-Barbara Gerl-Falkovitz and Mette Lebech (Heiligenkreuz: Be&Be, 2017), 234–44.

Grygiel, Stanislaw. "'Existence Precedes Essence': Fear of the Gift," in *Communio: International Catholic Review* 26, no. 2 (1999): 358–370.

Guerrero van der Meijden, Jadwiga. *Person and Dignity in Edith Stein's Writings* (Berlin: De Gruyter, 2019).

Haldane, John. "Is the Soul the Form of the Body," in *American Catholic Philosophical Quarterly* 87, no. 3 (2013): 481–93.

Heidegger, Martin. *Being and Time*, trans. J. Stambaugh, rev. by Dennis J. Schmidt (Albany, NY: State University of New York Press, 2010).

Herbstrith, Waltraud. *Edith Stein: A Biography* (New York: Harper, 1985; repr. San Francisco: Ignatius Press, 1992).

Hochschild, Joshua. "Form, Essence, Soul: Distinguishing Principles of Thomistic Metaphysics," in *Distinctions of Being: Philosophical Approaches to Reality*, ed. Nikolaj Zunic (Washington, DC: American Maritain Association, 2013), 21–35.

———. "Kenny and Aquinas on Individual Essences," in *Proceedings of the Society for Medieval Logic and Metaphysics* 6 (2006): 45–56.

———. "Proportionality and Divine Naming: Did St. Thomas Change His Mind about Analogy?," in *The Thomist: A Speculative Quarterly Review* 77, no. 4 (2013): 531–58.

———. *The Semantics of Analogy Rereading Cajetan's* De Nominum Analogia (Notre Dame, IN: University of Notre Dame Press, 2010).

Hopkins, Gerard Manley. *Selected Poems*, ed. Bob Blaisdell (New York: Dover, 2011).

Husserl, Edmund. *Cartesian Meditations*, trans. Dorion Cairns (The Hague: Martinus Nijhoff, 1960, repr. 1982).

———. *Ideas Pertaining to a Pure Phenomenology and to a Phenomenological Philosophy*, 2 vols., trans. W. E. Pohl, T. E. Klein, and F. Kersten (The Hague: Martinus Nijhoff, 1983, 1989).

———. *Logical Investigations*, 2 vols., trans. J. N. Findlay (New York: Routledge, 2001, repr. 2008).

Kerr, Gaven. *Aquinas's Way to God: The Proof in* De Ente et Essentia (Oxford: Oxford University Press, 2015).

———. "Essentially Ordered Series Reconsidered," in *American Catholic Philosophical Quarterly* 86, no. 4 (2012): 541–55.

———. "Essentially Ordered Series Reconsidered Once Again," in *American Catholic Philosophical Quarterly* 91, no. 2 (2017): 155–74.

King, Peter. "The Problem of Individuation in the Middle Ages," in *Theoria* 66 (2000): 159–84.

Knasas, John F. X. "The Intellectual Phenomenology of *De ente et essentia*, Chapter Four," in *Review of Metaphysics* 68, no. 1 (2014): 107–153.

———. "Making Sense of the *Tertia Via*," in *The New Scholasticism* 54, no. 4 (1980): 476–511.

———. "'Necessity' in the *Tertia Via*," in *The New Scholasticism* 52, no. 3 (1978): 373–94.

Klubertanz, George P. *Introduction to the Philosophy of Being*, 2nd ed. (New York: Appleton-Century-Crofts, 1963).

———. *St. Thomas Aquinas on Analogy: A Textual Analysis and Systematic Synthesis* (Eugene, OR: Wipf and Stock, 2009).

———. *The Philosophy of Human Nature* (New York: Appleton-Century-Crofts, 1953).

Kretzmann, Norman, and Eleonore Stump, eds. *The Cambridge Companion to Aquinas* (Cambridge: Cambridge University Press, 1993).

Leask, Ian. *Being Reconfigured* (Newcastle upon Tyne: Cambridge Scholars, 2011).

Lebech, Mette. "Edith Stein's Philosophy of Education in *The Structure of the Human Person*," in *Religion, Education, and the Arts* 5 (2005): 55–70.

———. *European Sources of Human Dignity: A Commented Anthology* (Oxford: Peter Lang, 2019).

———. "Study Guide to Edith Stein's Philosophy of Psychology and the Humanities," in *Yearbook of the Irish Philosophical Society: Voices of Irish Philosophy 2004* (2004): 40–76.

———. *On the Problem of Human Dignity: A Hermeneutical and Phenomenological Investigation* (Würzburg: Königshausen & Neumann, 2009).

———. *The Philosophy of Edith Stein: From Phenomenology to Metaphysics* (Oxford: Peter Lang, 2015).

Levering, Matthew, and Marcus Plested, eds. *The Oxford Handbook of the Reception of Aquinas* (Oxford: Oxford University Press, 2021).

Levinas, Emmanuel. *The Theory of Intuition in Husserl's Phenomenology*, trans. Andre Orianne (Evanston, IL: Northwestern University Press, 1995).

Lolordo, Antonio, ed. *Persons: A History* (Oxford: Oxford University Press, 2019).

Long, Steven A. "Divine and Creaturely 'Receptivity': The Search for a Middle Term," in *Communio* 21, no. 1 (1994): 151–161.

Lucas Lucas, Ramon. "The Anthropological Status of the Human Embryo," in *The Identity and Status of the Human Embryo: Proceedings of the Third Assembly of the Pontifical Academy for Life* (Vatican City: Libreria Editrice Vaticana, 1999), 178–205.

Lukasiewicz, Jan, G. E. M. Anscombe, and Karl R. Popper, "Symposium: The Principle of Individuation," in *Proceedings of the Aristotelian Society, Supplementary Volumes* 27 (1953): 69–120.

Machnacz, Jerzy. "Hedwig Conrad-Martius und Edith Stein. Husserls Schülerinnen und die aristotelische-thomistische Philosophie," in *Intersubjectivity, Humanity, Being: Edith Stein's Phenomenology and Christian Philosophy*, ed. Mette Lebech and Haydn Gurmin (Bern: Peter Lang, 2015): 393–416.

MacIntyre, Alasdair. *Edith Stein: A Philosophical Prologue* (London: Continuum, 2006, repr. 2017).

Manser, Gallus. *Das Wesen des Thomismus* (Fribourg: Paulusverlag, [1932], repr. 1949).

Maritain, Jacques. *An Essay on Christian Philosophy*, trans. Edward H. Flannery (New York: Philosophical Library, 1955, repr. 1995).

———. *Degrees of Knowledge*, trans. Gerald B. Phelan (Notre Dame, IN: University of Notre Dame Press, 1998, repr. 2014).

———. *Existence and the Existent*, trans. Gerald B. Phelan (New York: Paulist Press, 2015).

———. "The Person and the Common Good," in *The Review of Politics*, trans. John J. Fitzgerald, 8, no. 4 (1946): 419–55.

Maskulak, Marian. *Edith Stein and the Body-Soul-Spirit at the Center of Holistic Formation* (New York: Peter Lang, 2007).

———. "Edith Stein's Trinitarian Ontology," in *Intersubjectivity, Humanity, Being: Edith Stein's Phenomenology and Christian Philosophy*, ed. Mette Lebech and Haydn Gurmin (Bern: Peter Lang, 2015), 269–88.

Maurer, Armand. "Descartes and Aquinas on the Unity of a Human Being: Revisited," in *American Catholic Philosophical Quarterly* 67, no. 4 (1993): 497–511.

Maximos the Confessor. *On Difficulties in the Church Fathers: The Ambigua*, 2 vols., ed. and trans. Nicholas Constas (London: Harvard University Press, 2014).

McCarthy, John C. "How Knowing the World Completes the World: A Note on Aquinas and Husserl," in *Proceedings of the American Catholic Philosophical Association* 57 (1993): 71–86.

McCool, Gerald. *The Neo-Thomists* (Milwaukee, WI: Marquette University Press, 1994, repr. 2016).

McInerny, Ralph. *Praeambula fidei* (Washington, DC: The Catholic University of America Press, 2006).

McNamara, Robert. "Edith Stein's Thomistically Informed Understanding of Human Unity and Bodily Formation," in *American Catholic Philosophical Quarterly* 94, no. 4 (2020): 639–63.

———. "Essence in Edith Stein's Festschrift Dialogue," in *"Alles Wesentliche lasst sich nicht schreiben,"* ed. Andreas Speer and Stephen Regh (Freiburg i. Br.: Herder, 2016), 175–94.

———. "Human Individuality in Stein's Mature Works," in *Edith Steins Herausforderung heutiger Anthropologie*, ed. Hanna-Barbara Gerl-Falkovitz and Mette Lebech (Heiligenkreuz: Be&Be, 2017), 124–39.

———. "The Cognition of the Human Individual in the Mature Thought of Edith Stein," in *Philosophical News: "Dietrich von Hildebrand and Christian Personalism,"* ed. Elisa Grimi, 16 (2018): 131–43.

———. "The Concept of Christian Philosophy in Edith Stein," in *American Catholic Philosophical Quarterly* 94, no. 2 (2020): 323–46.

Meissner, William W. "Some Aspects of the *Verbum* in the texts of St. Thomas," in *The Modern Schoolman* 36 (1958): 1–30.

Merleau-Ponty, Maurice. *Phenomenology of Perception*, trans. Colin Smith (London: Routledge, 2012).

Moran, Dermot. "Edith Stein's Encounter with Edmund Husserl and Her Phenomenology of the Person." In *Empathy, Sociality, and Personhood: Essays on Edith Stein's Phenomenological Investigations*, edited by Elisa Magri and Dermot Moran, 31–48. Cham: Springer, 2017.

———. *Introduction to Phenomenology*. London: Routledge, 2000.

Morrison, James C. "Husserl and Brentano on Intentionality." *Philosophy and Phenomenological Research* 31, no. 1 (1970): 27–46.
Mortenson, John R. *Understanding St. Thomas on Analogy*. Rome: Aquinas Institute for the Study of Sacred Doctrine, 2006.
Nevitt, Turner C. "Aquinas on the Death of Christ: A New Argument for Corruptionism." *American Catholic Philosophical Quarterly* 90, no. 1 (2016): 77–99.
Nichols, Terence L. "Aquinas's Concept of Substantial Form and Modern Science." *International Philosophical Quarterly* 36, no. 3.143 (1996): 303–18.
Noone, Timothy B. "Individuation in Scotus." *American Catholic Philosophical Quarterly* 69, no. 4 (2010): 527–42.
O'Donnell, Robert A. "Individuation: An Example of the Development in the Thought of St. Thomas Aquinas." *The New Scholasticism* 33, no. 1 (1959): 49–67.
Ott, Hugo. "Die Randnotizen Martin Honeckers zur Habilitationsschrift "*Potenz und Akt*."" In *Studien zur Philosophie von Edith Stein: Internationales Edith-Stein-Symposium Eichstätt 1991 (Phänomenologische Forschungen, 26/27)*, edited by Reto Luzius Fetz, Matthias Rath, and Peter Schulz, 140–45. Freiburg i. Br.: Alber, 1993.
Owens, Joseph. *An Elementary Christian Metaphysics*. Milwaukee: Bruce, 1963; repr. Houston: Center for Thomistic Studies, 1986, repr. 2013.
———. "Aquinas on the Inseparability of Soul from Existence." *The New Scholasticism* 61, no. 3 (1987): 249–70.
———. "Thomas Aquinas." In *Individuation in Scholasticism: The Later Middle Ages and the Counter-Reformation, 1150–1650*, edited by Jorge J. E. Gracia, 173–94. Albany, NY: State University of New York Press, 1994.
Pascal, Blaise. *Pensées*, edited by Léon Braunschweig, translated by William F. Trotter. London: J. M. Dent and Sons, 1932, repr. 1947.
Pezzella, Anna Maria. "Bildung und Selbstbildung der menschlichen Person." In *Edith Steins Herausforderung heutiger Anthropologie*, edited by Hanna-Barbara Gerl-Falkovitz and Mette Lebech, 256–68. Heiligenkreuz: Be&Be, 2017.
Principe, Walter H. *Alexander of Hales' Theology of the Hypostatic Union*. Toronto: Pontifical Institute of Medieval Studies, 1967.
Przywara, Erich. *Analogia Entis: Metaphysics—Original Structure and Universal Rhythm*, translated by John R. Betz and David Bentley Hart. Grand Rapids, MI: Eerdmans, 2014.
Pseudo-Dionysius. *The Divine Names*. In *The Complete Works*, translated by Colm Luibheid. New York: Paulist Press, 1987.
Ramelow, Anselm. "The Person in the Abrahamic Tradition: Is the Judeo-Christian Concept of Personhood Consistent?" *American Catholic Philosophical Quarterly* 87, no. 4 (2013): 593–610.
Raschke, René. "Self Realization of the Human Being." In *Edith Steins Herausforderung heutiger Anthropologie*, edited by Hanna-Barbara Gerl-Falkovitz and Mette Lebech, 269-90. Heiligenkreuz: Be&Be, 2017.

———. "Selbstverwirklichung des Menschen. Edith Steins philosophisches Bildungsverständnis und ihr Beitrag zur pädagogischen Praxis." In *Alles Wesentliche lasst sich nicht schreiben*," edited by Andreas Speer and Stephen Regh, 512–37. Freiburg i. Br.: Herder, 2016.

Ratzinger, Joseph. "Concerning the Notion of Person in Theology." *Communio: International Catholic Review* 17, no. 3 (1990): 439–54.

———. *On Conscience*. San Francisco: Ignatius Press, 2007.

Redmond, Walter. "A Nothing That Is: Edith Stein on Being without Essence." *American Catholic Philosophical Quarterly* 82, no. 1 (2008): 71–86.

———. "Edith Stein on Evolution." *Logos: A Journal of Catholic Thought and Culture* 13, no. 2 (2010): 153–76.

———. "Edith Stein's Ontological Argument." In *Intersubjectivity, Humanity, Being: Edith Stein's Phenomenology and Christian Philosophy*, edited by Mette Lebech and Haydn Gurmin, 247–68. Bern: Peter Lang, 2015.

Reichmann, James. "Edith Stein, Thomas Aquinas, and the Principle of Individuation." *American Catholic Philosophical Quarterly* 87, no. 1 (2013): 55–86.

Reinach, Adolf. "Concerning Phenomenology." Translated by D. Willard, *The Personalist* 50 (1921): 194–211.

Ripamonti, Lidia. "Being Thrown or Being Held in Existence? The Opposite Approaches to Finitude of Edith Stein and Martin Heidegger." *Yearbook of Irish Philosophical Society* (2008): 71–83.

Salas, Victor M. "Edith Stein and Medieval Metaphysics." *American Catholic Philosophical Quarterly* 85, no. 2 (2011): 323–40.

Sanford, John J. "Scheler versus Scheler: The Case for a Better Ontology of the Person." *American Catholic Philosophical Quarterly* 79, no. 1 (2005): 145–61.

Sartre, Jean Paul. *The Transcendence of the Ego*. Translated by Andrew Brown. London: Routledge, 2004.

Sawicki, Marianne. *Body, Text, and Science: The Literacy of Investigative Practices and the Phenomenology of Edith Stein*. Dordrecht: Kluwer Academic, 1997.

Scarpelli Cory, Therese. *Aquinas on Human Self-Knowledge*. Cambridge: Cambridge University Press, 2015.

Schaeffer, Matthew. "The Thick-*Esse*/Thin-Essence View in Thomistic Personalism." *American Catholic Philosophical Quarterly* 89, no. 2 (2015): 223–51.

Scheler, Max. *Formalism in Ethics and Non-formal Ethics of Values*. Translated by Manfred S. Frings, and Roger L. Funk. Evanston, IL: Northwestern University Press, 1973, reprinted 1985.

Schindler, David L. "Being, Gift, Self-Gift: A Reply to Waldstein on Relationality and John Paul II's Theology of the Body (Part One)," in *Communio: International Catholic Review* 42, no. 2 (2015): 221–51.

———. "Being, Gift, Self-Gift (Part Two)," in *Communio: International Catholic Review* 43, no. 3 (2016): 409–83.

———. "Norris Clarke on Person, Being, and St. Thomas," in *Communio: International Catholic Review* 20, no. 3 (1993): 580–92.

———. "The Embodied Person as Gift and the Cultural Task in America: *Status Quaestionis*," in *Communio: International Catholic Review* 35, no. 3 (2008): 397–431.

———. "The Person: Philosophy, Theology, and Receptivity," in *Communio: International Catholic Review* 21, no. 2 (1994): 172–90.

Schmidt, Karl. "Edith Stein, Apophatic Theology, and Freedom." In *Selected Papers on the Legacy of Edith Stein's Finite and Eternal Being*, edited by Sarah Borden Sharkey (= *Quaestiones Disputatae* 4, no. 1 (2013)), 21–30.

Schulz, Peter J. *Edith Steins Theorie der Person: von der Bewusstseinsphilosophie zur Geistmetaphysik.* Freiburg i. Br.: Alber, 1994.

———. "Toward the Subjectivity of the Human Person: Edith Stein's Contribution to the Theory of Identity." In *American Catholic Philosophical Quarterly*, translated by Christina M. Gschwandtner, 8, no. 1 (2008): 161–76.

Sepp, Hans Reiner. "Edith's Stein [sic] Conception of the Person within the Context of the Phenomenological Movement." In *Empathy, Sociality, and Personhood: Essays on Edith Stein's Phenomenological Investigations*, edited by Elisa Magri and Dermot Moran, 49–62. Cham: Springer, 2017.

Siedentop, Larry. *Inventing the Individual: The Origins of Western Liberalism.* London: Penguin Books, 2015.

Simon, Yves. "Order in Analogical Sets." In *Philosopher at Work: Essays by Yves R. Simon*, edited by Anthony O. Simon, 135–71. Lanham, MD: Rowman and Littlefield, 1999.

Simpson, William M., R. Robert C. Koons, and Nicholas J. The, eds. *Neo-Aristotelian Perspectives on Contemporary Science.* New York: Routledge, 2017.

Smith, Garrett R. "The Analogy of Being in the Scotist Tradition," in *American Catholic Philosophical Quarterly* 93, no. 4 (2019): 633–73.

Smith, Michael A. *Human Dignity and the Common Good in the Aristotelian-Thomistic Tradition.* New York: Edwin Mellen Press, 1995.

Spaemann, Robert. *Persons: The Difference between "Someone" and "Something,"* translated by Oliver O'Donovan. Oxford: Oxford University Press, 1996, reprinted 2012.

Spencer, Mark K. "Aristotelian Substance and Personalistic Subjectivity," in *International Philosophical Quarterly* 55, no. 2 (2015): 145–64.

———. "Created Persons are Subsistent Relations: A Scholastic-Phenomenological Synthesis," in *Proceedings of the American Catholic Philosophical Association* 89 (2015): 225–43.

———. "The Personhood of the Separated Soul," in *Nova et Vetera* 12, no. 3 (2014): 863–912.

Sokolowski, Robert. *Phenomenology of the Human Person.* Cambridge: Cambridge University Press, 2008.

Staley Kevin M. "Norris Clarke and Sarah Borden on the Limitation of Existence or Why We Are Not God: A Response," in *The Saint Anselm Journal* 7, no. 1 (2009): 20–29.

Stump, Eleonore. *Aquinas.* New York: Routledge, 2005.

Svoboda, David. "The *Ratio* of Unity: Positive or Negative? The Case of Thomas Aquinas," in *American Catholic Philosophical Quarterly* 86, no. 1 (2012): 47–70.

———. "Thomas Aquinas on Whole and Part," in *The Thomist: A Speculative Quarterly Review* 76, no. 2 (2012): 273–304.

Teresa of Avila. *The Interior Castle*, translated by Kieran Kavanaugh, and Otilio Rodriguez. Washington, DC: Institute of Carmelite Studies, 1987.

Togni, Alice. "Edith Stein in Dialogue with Husserl: The Person as a Psycho-physical Unity." In *The Hat and the Veil: The Phenomenology of Edith Stein*, Ad Fontes: Studien zur frühen Phänomenologie, 3, edited by Jerzy Machnacz et al., 39–64. Nordhausen: Traugott Bautz, 2016.

Torrell, Jean-Pierre. *Saint Thomas Aquinas*, vol. 1: *The Person and His Work*, translated by Robert Royal. Washington, DC: The Catholic University of America Press, 1996, reprinted 2005.

Tullius, William. "Edith Stein and the Truth of Husserl's Ethical Concept of the 'True Self.'" In *"Alles Wesentliche lasst sich nicht schreiben,"* edited by Andreas Speer and Stephen Regh, 290–306. Freiburg i. Br.: Herder, 2016.

Varberg, Jordan T. "Stein's Critique of Heidegger. On Dasein's Orientation to Fullness," in *Edith Steins Herausforderung heutiger Anthropologie*, ed. Hanna-Barbara Gerl-Falkovitz and Mette Lebech (Heiligenkreuz. Be&Be, 2017), 245–54.

Von Hildebrand, Dietrich. *Christian Ethics*. New York: David McKay Co., 1953.

———. *The Heart: An Analysis of Human and Divine Affectivity*, trans. John F. Crosby (South Bend, IN: St. Augustine Press, 2007).

———. *The Nature of Love*, translated by John F. Crosby. South Bend, IN: St. Augustine Press, 2009.

Waldstein, Michael. "'Constitutive Relations': A Response to David L. Schindler," in *Communio* 37, no. 3 (2010): 496–518.

———. "Dietrich von Hildebrand and St. Thomas Aquinas on Goodness and Happiness," in *Nova et Vetera* 1, no. 2 (2003): 403–64.

———. "Personal Individuality According to Thomas" (unpublished article, [2005]).

Wall, Joseph B. "The Mind of St. Thomas on the Principle of Individuation," in *The Modern Schoolman* 18, no. 3 (1941): 41–44.

Wallenfang, Donald L. *Human and Divine Being: A Study on the Theological Anthropology of Edith Stein*. Eugene, OR: Cascade Books, 2017.

———. "*Geistwissenschaft*: Edith Stein's Phenomenological Sketch of the Essence of Spirit." In *Intersubjectivity, Humanity, Being: Edith Stein's Phenomenology and Christian Philosophy*, edited by Mette Lebech and Haydn Gurmin, 499–524. Bern: Peter Lang, 2015.

———. "The Heart of the Matter: Edith Stein on the Substance of the Soul," in *Logos: A Journal of Catholic Thought and Culture* 17, no. 3 (2014): 118–42.

Ward, Thomas. *John Duns Scotus on Parts, Wholes, and Hylomorphism*. Boston: Brill, 2014.

White, Kevin. "Individuation in Aquinas's *Super Boetium De Trinitate*, Q.4," in *American Catholic Philosophical Quarterly* 69, no. 4 (1995): 543–56.

———. "Act and Fact: On a Disputed Question in Recent Thomistic Metaphysics," in *The Review of Metaphysics* 68, no. 2 (2014): 287–312.

White, Roger M. *Talking about God: The Concept of Analogy and the Problem of Religious Language*. Surrey: Ashgate, 2010.

Wilk, Rafal Kazimierz. "On Human Being: A Dispute between Edith Stein and Martin Heidegger," in *Logos: A Journal of Catholic Thought and Culture*, 10, no. 4 (2007): 104–119.

Williams, Thomas D. "What Is Thomistic Personalism?," in *Alpha Omega* 7, no. 2 (2004): 163–97.

Wippel, John F. *The Metaphysical Thought of Thomas Aquinas: From Finite Being to Uncreated Being*. Washington, DC: The Catholic University of America Press, 2000.

Wojtyła, Karol. *Love and Responsibility*, translated by Grzegorz Ignatik. Boston: Pauline Books and Media, 2013.

———. (John Paul II) *Man and Woman He Created Them: A Theology of the Body*, translated by Michael Waldstein. Boston: Pauline Books and Media, 2006.

———. *Man in the Field of Responsibility*, translated by Kenneth W. Kemp and Zuzanna Maslanka Kieron. South Bend, IN: St. Augustine Press, 2011.

———. "Subjectivity and 'the Irreducible' in Man." In *Person and Act: And Related Essays*, translated by Grzegorz Ignatik. Washington, DC: The Catholic University of America Press, 2021.

———. *Person and Community: Selected Essays*, translated by Theresa Sandok. New York: Peter Lang, 1993, repr. 2008.

———. *The Acting Person*, translated by Anna-Teresa Tymieniecka. Dordrecht: Reidel, 1979.

Wolter, Allan B. "The Formal Distinction." In *Studies in Philosophy and the History of Philosophy, vol. 3: John Duns Scotus, 1265–1965*, edited by John K. Ryan and Bernardine M. Bonansea. Washington, DC: The Catholic University of America Press, 2018.

Woznicki, Andrew N. "Revised Thomism: Existential Personalism Viewed from Phenomenological Perspectives," in *Proceedings of the American Catholic Philosophical Association* 60 (1986): 38–56.

Zúñiga y Postigo, Gloria. "Phenomenological Ontology: Stein's Third Way." In *Intersubjectivity, Humanity, Being: Edith Stein's Phenomenology and Christian Philosophy*, edited by Mette Lebech and Haydn Gurmin, 139–67. Bern: Peter Lang, 2015.

INDEX

abstraction, xlvii, lv, 16, 20, 120–21, 125, 132, 138, 215

accident(s), lxxi, 13, 26–27, 35, 107, 162–63, 223, 229, 235; quantitative, 95. *See also* quality

act, xiv, xxiv, xxvii–xxviii, 6–7, 11–12, 29–30, 36, 40, 42, 72, 74, 119, 133, 154–56, 173, 183–84, 196, 221, 235; actual, lx, 31–32, 37, 96, 101, 136, 175, 184, 190, 210–11, 215–16; actuality, lix, lxiii, lxxii, 31, 107, 110, 136–37, 163, 166, 178, 180, 197–98, 205, 207, 235; *actus essendi*, 137, 207; *actus purus*, 176; act-matter, 57; act-quality, 57; essential, 180; existential, 198, 235; and perfection, 157–59, 161–62. *See also* being

affection, xxv, 7, 63, 140, 149, 162, 165, 214

Albert the Great, xlv, 21

analogy, 172, 174, 183–85, 187–98, 200–235, 237, 239, 241–45, 254–56, 258; analogue, xvi, 209, 211, 213, 216, 224, 231–32; essential, 190; four-term, 195; ideal, 190, 210, 244; of attribution, 193, 197; of being, 171–74, 188–93, 201–3, 206–8, 210–11, 213–15, 217–20, 222–28, 231–32, 239, 241, 243–44, 254–56; of proportion, 193, 195; of proportionality, 171–72, 185, 188, 191–93, 195–97, 199, 201–3, 214, 216–20, 222, 225, 229–30, 241–44, 254–56; personal form, 213–14, 229–30, 242–44; predication, naming, 173–74, 192, 197. *See also* proportion

anima, xx–xxi, xliv, 269; *forma corporis*, 62–64, 66; *rationalis*, 46, 49; *sensitiva*, 49; *separata*, 151; *vegetativa*, 49. *See also* body; soul

animal, 44, 47, 49–51, 53–54, 59, 68, 70–71, 75–78, 80–83, 127–30, 158, 163, 249

anthropology, xv, xxvi, xxxvii, lvii, lxix, 20, 22, 85, 239, 247, 264–65; apophatic, 149

Aquinas, Thomas, xix–xx, xxiii, xxv, xxviii–xxx, xxxii–xxxvii, xxxix–xlviii, xlix, liii, lvi–lviii, lxvii–lxxiii, 1–7, 20–24, 34–40, 44–53, 67–78, 81–85, 87, 91–95, 97–98, 107–11, 150–58, 178–88, 191–94, 222–25, 227–32, 236, 261–65. *See also* Thomism

Aristotle, xxi, xlii, lii, lvi, lix, lxii, lxx, 21, 71–72, 101–2, 191–92, 269

Augustine, xxii, xlii, 6, 21, 187, 204, 237, 240–41, 257

awareness, 6–7, 14–15, 36, 145–47, 175; explicit, l, 208; inward, 131, 139; outer, 170; reflective, 239. *See also* conscious; consciousness

285

bearer (*Träger*), xxxiv–xxxvi, 24–30, 32–33, 35–41, 38, 117–19, 122, 125, 200–201, 214–18, 225, 239, 242, 248, 250; bearing, 27, 29–32, 37, 39, 41, 79, 136, 212, 214–16, 221, 224, 227–28, 231–32, 252, 256; being-bearer (*Trägersein*), 117, 122; of conscious experience, 28, 35, 41; dynamic, 41, 84, 248; empty-formal, 30, 166; formative, 84; free and intentional, 29, 241; ontological, 41, 84, 248; personal, 147, 217, 230. *See also* I, personal I

becoming, 96, 101, 104, 109, 115, 160, 162, 164, 177, 184, 191, 197, 251–52

being, xi, lviii–lx, 119, 129, 180–92, 195–239, 241–45, 248, 251–58, 262, 265; act / actuality of, lix–lx, 101, 104, 122–23, 125, 136–37, 150, 153–54, 185, 196, 199, 216, 218, 220, 227, 230, 233, 235, 237; and action, 29, 100, 104, 108, 110, 132, 166, 252; and essence, 25, 118, 198, 201, 203, 208, 214, 216, 218, 222, 226, 230, 255; and life, 2, 4, 8, 18, 23, 28, 30, 139, 144, 175, 239, 242, 245; and nonbeing, 175, 177, 181; and unity, 45–46, 54–56, 68, 72–74, 102, 106, 108–10, 112, 115, 169; divine act of, 198, 215, 229, 235; *ens*, lviii, 123–24, 137, 185, 197–98, 200, 226, 254; *esse*, lviii–lix, 136–37, 152, 154, 176, 181, 184–85, 188, 196–99, 201, 207–9, 215, 221–22, 229, 235; meaning of, xi, xiii, xv, xxvii, xxix, xxxiii, lvii–lviii, lxxii–lxxiii, 91, 217, 227; mode of, lxv, lxix–lxxi, 9, 13, 133, 152, 154, 156, 198, 207, 211; non-personal, 127–28, 166, 216; personal, 28, 34, 103, 135, 147, 216

Betschart, Christof, xvii–xviii, 1, 15–16, 28, 31–32, 36–37, 42, 54, 88, 97, 115–17, 130, 132, 135, 138–39, 142, 149, 159–61, 166–67, 189, 213–14

body, 9, 16, 18–22, 45–46, 52, 54, 62–68, 76, 79–81, 122, 150–53, 155, 167–68, 227–29, 236, 249, 258; formation, vii, xviii, xxxiv, 23, 43–85, 129, 249–50. *See also anima*; soul

Borden Sharkey, Sarah, xviii, 54, 70, 88, 93, 102, 104, 108, 114–15, 117, 137, 146, 160–62, 164, 167, 189, 205, 262

capacity, lxviii, 40, 70, 141, 225, 237–39, 252

Christian Philosophy, xxxiii–xxxiv, xlii, lxxii, 153, 179, 183, 206

cognition, xlvii, lxi, lxvii, lxxii, 5–6, 10, 131, 140–41, 149, 156, 165, 207, 214

community, xii, xxiv, xxvi, xxxvii, 13, 30, 34, 42, 135, 206, 213

complexity, xxxii, xxxv, 17, 47, 52, 55, 58, 61, 69, 73, 75–76, 78, 82–83, 116–17, 121, 216, 218, 220, 223–25, 261; composition, 23, 45, 47, 52, 56, 67, 69, 94, 124, 203, 222–23, 249; formal, 73, 210; ontological, 201, 220; elemental, 103; substantial, 29, 84; of essence and being, 199, 220, 241. *See also* form, structure

concept, xxxiv, lii–liv, 3, 24, 26–27, 32–35, 37–38, 45, 117, 120, 173, 191–92, 205, 207, 214–17; conceptual apparatus, lii–lvii, lv–lvi, lxiv, 14, 22–23, 127–28, 150, 157, 161, 166, 185–86, 188, 191, 200–3, 217, 231, 251, 254, 262–64;

Index

conceptual content, xxxv, xxxvii, lii, liv, 1–2, 22–23, 37, 40, 84–85, 171–73, 248, 256, 258; concept formation, lii–liv, lvi, 207

conceptual schema, 83, 96, 112, 114, 125, 161, 168, 261–62; conceptual toolkit, lii, 150, 200

conscious, xiv–xvi, xxiv, xxxi, xlviii, l–lii, lxi, lxv–lxvii, 1, 5–17, 19–21, 28–33, 35–36, 40–41, 58–59, 131–34, 139–40, 174–78, 186, 189–90, 243, 248; consciousness, xxxi, xxxiv, xlvii–l, lxi–lxvi, lxix, 7–21, 25, 28, 30–32, 56, 59, 132–34, 136–37, 174, 264; perspective of, 56, 136; philosophy of, 9, 13. *See also* intellect; mind; reason

constitution, xxiv–xxv, l–li, lxi, lxvi, lxviii, 11, 19, 21, 96, 128; bodily, 65, 165. *See also* intersubjective

cosmos, xxvii, 2, 47–48, 80–81, 158, 258–59

creation, 179, 183, 185, 188, 191, 193, 202, 205, 220, 225, 235, 238, 240, 243, 245, 254–55; Creator, 147–48, 171–74, 179, 182–86, 188, 191–93, 195–203, 205–6, 209–10, 212, 220–24, 226–27, 232, 235–38, 240–42, 244–45, 254–57; personal Creator, 210–11, 216, 233, 242, 245, 254–57, 265; creature, 173–74, 183, 185, 188, 192–93, 195–203, 209, 216, 218–21, 223–24, 226, 228–29, 232, 235–37; personal creature, 147–49, 216, 218–19, 224, 232–33, 256. *See also* Divine Being; God

Dasein, 96, 187, 238

Descartes, René, xix, 5, 16–7, 22

determination, lxix, 3, 47–48, 55–57, 73, 75, 97, 99, 100–2, 113, 115, 117, 124, 144, 158, 195; accidental, 12–13, 138, 162; common, 94, 129; final, 52, 215, 249; generic, 68, 71, 99; inner principle of, 3, 102; structural, 140, 142; subordinate, 52, 68

dignity, ix–x, xvi, 24, 33, 26, 38–39, 44, 48, 92, 97, 166, 247

Divine Being, 34, 176–78, 198, 202–4, 207–8, 210–19, 222, 224, 226, 228–30, 232, 241–44, 255–56; divine, 58, 181, 206, 210–15, 218–19, 221–24, 232–33, 236, 239, 241–42, 255, 257, 259; divine ideas, lxxii, 58, 225; divine essence, 146, 196, 198, 201, 203, 214–15, 219, 221, 225–27, 229, 241; divine names, lix, 204, 210, 228–29; divine simplicity, 183, 222–24, 229–30, 242–43, 255–56. *See also* Eternal Being, God

Duns Scotus, li, 88, 105, 117

eidos (εἶδος), 3, 102; eidetic intuition and variation, lv, lxi, lxiv, 23. *See also* essence, form, morphe (μορφή)

epoché, xlix, li. *See also* method, phenomenology

essence (*Wesen, essentia*), xliii–xliv, lxiii–lxiv, lxx–lxxii, 2–4, 25–26, 29, 71, 94, 96, 122–23, 137, 140, 178–82, 185, 196–207, 209, 213–15, 216, 218–23, 225–30, 234–37, 241–42, 254–56; essentialism, 208–9, 225; essential being, lxix, 211, 214; essential-form (*Wesensform*), 3, 25–26, 28, 101–5, 107, 112–13, 115–22, 125, 128, 169, 225, 227, 251; finite, 196, 198–99, 213, 236; general, 92; individuated, 106, 136; personal, 30, 136, 162, 216,

essence *(continued)*
219; human, 71, 136, 142, 161, 215–16, 218, 241. *See also* form; nature
Eternal Being, xi, xxvii–xxviii, 5–6, 9–10, 60–61, 133–34, 173, 176–79, 183–84, 186–87, 189–92, 209–10, 227–28. *See also* Divine Being; God
existence, 6, 15, 96–97, 101, 115–16, 136–37, 151, 153–54, 175–76, 180, 182–83, 196, 198, 216, 235–36; existentialism, xxvii, xxxi, 208; personal, 217, 257
experience, xlvii–l, lv, lxi, lxiii–lxiv, lxvi–lxvii, 5, 9–12, 14–20, 22, 28–29, 32, 58–59, 70, 80–81, 84, 131–34, 137–41, 175–78, 238, 254; contents of, l, lxi, lxvii, 12–13, 17–18, 131, 177, 210; first-person experience, 1, 6, 13, 31, 51, 59, 61, 133–34, 138, 175, 185; given in, xxiv, xxxi, xlvii, xlix–l, lv, lxi, lxiii–lxiv, 1, 5, 7, 14–17, 19, 22, 58–59, 70, 76, 80, 139, 166, 174–75, 177–78, 248, 262; personal, 137, 139, 170, 233, 255; units of, 10–11, 13, 17, 20, 210; world of, xxiv, xxxiii, xlviii, xlix, li–lii, liv, lxi, lxiv, lxvi–lxvii, lxxii, 10, 51, 60, 217, 263. *See also* conscious, world

form, lxv–lxvi, lxviii–lxix, 43–46, 52, 54–59, 67, 71–72, 75–77, 94–99, 103–10, 113–18, 120–21, 151–53, 157–59, 161–63, 168–69, 194–95, 197, 223–25, 253–55; common, 104, 106, 110, 112, 251; corporeal, 49; formal determinations, 47, 52–55, 71–72, 77, 81, 99, 101–3, 116, 119, 121, 159; empty-form (*Leerform*), 25–26, 28–31, 37, 53–55, 116–25, 134–36, 138, 166, 169, 210, 215–16, 225, 251–52; essential-form (*Wesensform*), 3, 25–26, 28, 101–5, 107, 112–13, 115–22, 125, 128, 169, 225, 227, 251; formal structure, 47, 52–55, 57–58, 64, 69–70, 73–75, 77–79, 82, 84, 116–19, 121–25, 135, 150, 157, 159, 228, 258; formal framework, xxvii, 52–54, 57, 70–73, 77–78, 82, 84, 121, 124, 128, 150, 157, 215, 249, 225; formal notions, 57, 73, 120–21, 125; formation, 48–51, 62–65, 67–68, 76, 78–82, 85, 95, 98–101, 103, 114–16, 128, 130, 249–50; individual, 74, 88, 102, 120, 159; individuated, 106–9; individuating, 95, 105; of species, 102–6, 110, 112–13, 115, 129, 157–59, 161, 168–69, 251; ontological priority of, 105, 107, 115, 169, 251; preparatory formation, 100, 103, pure, 3, 102–4, 113, 115, 122; ruling (dominant), 53, 55, 68–71, 249; substantial form, 3, 44, 46, 48, 56–57, 67–69, 72–78, 101, 115, 121, 150, 155, 167, 169; self-subsisting, 151, 153–54
empathy, xi, xxiv, lxvi, 20–21, 140
freedom, xxv, xxvii, xlvi, 28–29, 36, 39, 49, 66, 144, 148, 189, 205, 238, 245
friendship, 161, 164, 245

gift, 83, 234, 236–37, 256; self-gift, 138, 164, 236, 239
Gilson, Étienne, xxxii, xliv, lxiv, lxv, 45, 94, 105, 117, 153
God, vii, xxvii, xxxiii–xxxvi, xl–xli, lxii, 33–34, 37–38, 58, 146–49, 151, 166, 171–206, 208–16, 218–45, 253–58; attributes of, 171–72, 174, 179, 181–183, 185–86, 188, 202, 208, 220,

223, 229, 243; personal, x, xvi, 205, 211, 213–16, 218–19, 224, 228, 232–34, 237–39, 243–45, 256–58. *See also* Divine Being; Eternal Being

Gredt, Josef, xxxii, xliv, 27, 36–37, 88, 93–99, 101, 104–8, 114–15, 122–23, 192, 194, 196–97, 200, 203, 218, 221–22, 255

heart, xxv, liii, 11, 19, 167, 170, 189, 191–92, 203, 208; perceiving with the, 143, 149

Hedwig Conrad-Martius, li, 21, 155, 184

Heidegger, Martin, xxxi, lviii, 10, 177–78, 186–87, 238

hierarchy, 129–30, 163; cosmic, 48, 99, 108, 116, 163; order, 158; distinctions, 160; gradation, 157–58; of being, 128–30, 138, 157–58

Hopkins, Gerard Manley, 265

human, xxv, 70, 138, 151–52; being, 65–66, 81, 123, 127, 130, 138, 142, 146, 148, 213, 226; nature, xxxiv–xxxvi, 1–4, 22–23, 33–35, 41–56, 58–59, 61, 64–65, 67–69, 71, 73–76, 78–85, 87, 135, 150–52, 165–68, 212–13, 215–16, 248–53, 264–65; person, ix–x, xiii–xvi, xxi, xxiii, xxv–xxviii, xxx–xxxi, xxxvi–xxxvii, 38, 42–44, 53–54, 64, 148–49, 159–61, 213, 232–37, 241–42, 244–45, 256–58

Husserl, x, xi–xii, xxix, xxxi, xlii, xlv, xlvii–xlviii, li, lv, lx, lxiii–lxv, 5, 8, 10–11, 16, 19, 52, 54, 226, 268

hylomorphism, xxxv, 45–46, 69, 72–74, 91, 97, 116, 145, 168, 170, 249, 251

hypostasis, 25–27, 35, 41, 247. *See also* subsistence; substance

I: personal I, xxxiv–xxxvi, 18–20, 29–43, 58–62, 64–65, 74–75, 78–80, 131–38, 166, 168–70, 173–79, 186, 209–10, 212, 214–18, 225–27, 230–34, 241–43, 248–52, 254–58; pure I, 10, 15–16, 20, 31, 60, 132, 140; life of the I, vii, xxiv, xxxiv, 5–41, 64, 174, 177, 189–90; spiritual I, 7. *See also* human; personhood

idea, lxx, 8, 37, 48, 58, 98, 176–78, 189–90, 209, 223, 233

identity, xxiv, 12–13, 74, 83, 92, 132, 134, 185, 209; numerical, 109

incommunicability (*Unmitteilbarkeit*), 91–94, 105, 109, 113–14, 117, 125, 129–30, 133, 135–36, 138, 145, 167, 251–52

independence, lxv, lxix, 16, 35, 50, 62, 81, 96, 132, 151

individual, xxiv–xxix, xxxiv–xxxvi, lxvii–lxxi, 2–4, 23–25, 27–34, 39–41, 64–69, 72–74, 79–84, 87–89, 91–171, 200–201, 225, 227–28, 231, 237–41, 245, 251–54, 256–59; being-individual, xvi, 79, 88–89, 91, 97–98, 101–5, 107, 110, 112–13, 115–16, 118, 120–30, 132–37, 142, 148, 155–57, 165–70, 251–53; qualitative individuality, 54, 64, 88–89, 91, 93, 98, 14–5, 107, 109, 115–17, 126–31, 137–39, 141–45, 148–49, 157, 161, 163, 167–68, 251–53; adjectival individuality, 162; and individuation, 74, 88, 92–94, 96–97, 105–6, 108–10, 112–13, 117, 119, 121–22, 152–55, 227–28; free-willed conditioning of individuality, 144; individual by reason of matter, 94, 97, 105, 114; individual essence,

individual *(continued)*
94–96, 101–2, 104, 116–17, 122, 162, 169, 200–201, 225, 227; individual form, 74, 88, 102, 120, 159; individual substance, xxxv, 2, 24, 40–41, 99, 107, 109, 115, 151, 248; material individual, vii, xxxiv, 87–89, 91–127, 150, 153–54, 159, 167, 169, 251, 253; material individuation, xxxv, 88–89, 91, 94, 96, 98, 108, 111–12, 124–25, 154, 258; human individual, vii, xxxiv, xlix, 3–5, 20, 64, 87, 89, 126–69, 148, 166; human individuality, 64, 131, 135, 140–42, 145, 148–49, 157, 161–63, 166–68, 170, 231; human individuation, 33, 109, 128, 137, 150, 154, 156, 251–52; personal individual, xxv, xxviii, 30, 127, 134–39, 141–44, 147, 149, 156, 159, 165, 168, 170; personal individuality, xxviii, 131, 149, 157; principle of individuation, 74, 92, 102, 108–10, 121, 153–54. *See also* person; substance

Ingarden, Roman, xix

intellect, lii–lv, lxi, lxiv, lxx, 119–20, 240; intellectual, xvii, xxviii–xxix, xlii, xlv–xlvii, li–lvi, lxx–lxxiii, 44–46, 67, 119–21, 150, 206–8, 217, 258, 262, 265. *See also* mind; reason; soul

intentionality, xlviii, 7, 139–40, 177; acts, xxxi, lxi, 6–7, 11, 14, 17, 56–57, 119, 131, 213; intention, 6, 227; modes, liii, 25, 120, 211, 214, 245; motivated, xxiv; reflexive, 6, 131. *See also* conscious, rational, intellect

interior castle, 59–60, 141, 257

intersubjective / intersubjectivity, li, 19, 131, 179, 206

irreducible(-ity), xiv, 30, 38, 42. *See also* irreplaceable, unique, unrepeatable

irreplaceable(-ity), 164–65, 167, 245. *See also* irreducible, unique, unrepeatable

judgment, liii–liv, lxii, 119, 199, 207; existential, xlix, liii; intellectual, 119

knowing, liii, lxii, lxv–lxvi, lxviii, lxix–lxxii, 6, 9, 73, 119, 149, 156, 222, 229; knowledge, xiv, xxvii, xxxiii–xxxiv, li, liii–liv, lxi–lxii, lxv, lxvii–lxviii, 6, 9, 58, 95–96, 164, 257–59

Koyré, Alexander, 17

Levinas, Emmanuel, xxxi, 10

logos (λόγος), xi–xii, xxiii, xxix, lix, 19, 192, 214, 245, 265

love, xiv, xxv, xxvii, 34, 146, 148, 164–66, 240–41, 258–59

Manser, Gallus, xxxii, xliv

Maritain, Jacques, xxxii–xxxiii, xliv, liii, lxv, 96, 188, 206

material, 15, 25–26, 29–30, 47–48, 53–55, 68, 74–78, 80–83, 87–89, 95–96, 98–119, 121–22, 124–30, 134–36, 150–51, 153–54, 166–67, 169, 200–201, 251–53; body, 18–19, 21, 44–45, 46–49, 62, 64, 67–68, 76, 79, 81–82, 85, 150, 152, 155, 249–50; composition, 49, 54, 56, 68–69, 71, 77, 79–81, 145; dimensive quantity, 74, 153; elements, 48–49, 56, 62–63, 77–78, 100, 129, 151; environment, 103, 105, 129, 251; extension, lxvi, lxx, 94–96, 98–99, 105–6, 113, 125,

128, 235; principle, 69, 94, 113, 115, 137, 153–54, 170, 225, 227–28, 261; substance(s), 45, 74, 76–77, 94–96, 98–99, 101, 103, 105–7, 109–10, 119, 169; substrate, 98, 101, 110. *See also* form, formal

matter, lxviii, 44–45, 48–49, 56–57, 72, 74, 76–77, 94–100, 102–10, 112–16, 150–55, 168–69, 225, 251, 262–63; designated matter (*materia signate*; *materia signata quantitate*), 74, 92, 94–96, 98, 105, 107, 109–10, 112, 114–15, 124–25, 137, 154–56, 167–68, 170, 251, 253; prime matter (*materia prima*), 45, 52, 62, 68, 74, 95, 98, 109, 114. *See also* form, material

meaning, xi–xii, xiv, xxxi, xxxv–xxxvi, lix–lxii, lxv, lxx, lxix–lxxii, 2–3, 23–28, 39, 44–46, 52, 63–66, 71–72, 91–92, 110–11, 176, 185–86, 207–8, 210–11, 213, 217–18, 227, 245, 248–50

Merleau-Ponty, Maurice, 20

metaphysics, xxvii–xxviii, xxxiv, xxxvi–xxxvii, xxxix, xlv, lviii–lx, lxii–lxv, lxix–lxx, 42, 150–51, 207–8, 227, 243–44, 269

method, x–xi, xxiii, xxviii–xxix, xxxi–xxxiii, xxxix–xl, xlvii–lii, lvii–lviii, lx–lxiv, 1, 9, 168, 206, 209, 226; Aristotelian way, 8–10, 23, 47, 84, 226, 248; Augustinian way, xxvii, 8–10, 23, 37, 40, 59, 84, 127, 137, 183, 187, 232. *See also* phenomenology, Scholasticism

microcosm, xxvii, 47, 258

mind, x, xii, xviii, xli, xliii, xlvi, lxvi, lxviii, lxx, 2, 7, 16. *See also* intellect; rational

morphe (μορφή), 3, 45, 101–2, 169. *See also eidos* (εἶδος); form

multiplicity, lxxi, 58, 96, 108–12, 142, 153. *See also* plurality

nature, ix–x, lxix–lxxi, 1–4, 14, 17–18, 20–24, 29–31, 36–41, 45, 47–49, 79, 135–36, 149, 154–55, 170–71, 180, 185–86, 228, 233–34. *See also* essence, form, world

necessary, liv–lv, 20, 23, 99–100, 103–4, 109–10, 152, 154, 180–83, 185, 197–98, 220, 254; necessity, 12, 76, 104, 180–82; actual necessity, 184; essential necessity, 145; logical necessity, 124, 147; notional necessity, 147. *See also* possible

negation, 123–24, 190, 198, 210, 223; negative (*negativa*), 176, 227, 241; negative notions, 110, 222–23. *See also* positive

object(s), xiv, xxiv, xxvii, xlvii–lv, lix–lxi, lxiii–lxvi, lxviii–lxix, lxxii, 9–12, 17, 25, 111, 117–18, 120, 131; object(s) of consciousness, xiv, xxxi, liii, xlvii, l, lxi, lv, lxiii–lxviii, lxx, lxxii, 9, 120. *See also* abstraction, constitution, intersubjective, subject

objective, xv, xlvi, lii, liv, 69; objectivity, l–li, lvi, 33, 79, 262; objective investigation, xlv–xlvii, lvii, xlix, liv, lxxii, 2, 5, 22, 69, 84, 97, 116, 124, 262; subject-object polarity, lxviii. *See also* subjective

ontology / ontological, ix, xxviii, xxxi, xlv, lix–lx, lxix, 37, 136, 207; comprehensive, 27 general, xxvii; formal, lix, 25; material, lix–lx; *See also* metaphysics

openness, l, lxxi, 141–42, 145–46, 157, 159, 163

order, of being, 67–68, 73, 229; of predication, 68, 70, 73; geometric, 157; hierarchical, 256; intentional, 73, 78; natural, lxxii; objective, lii; ontological, 73; political, 160; teleological, 205; temporal, 6. *See also* hierarchy

ousia (οὐσία), lix, 100. *See also* essence, substance

part(s), xxix, xxxiv, xxxvi, 1–2, 4, 15, 25, 52, 54–55, 59, 67, 69, 78, 82, 118, 236; formal, 54–55, 57, 71, 81; substantial, 25–26, 29

perfection, 74, 77, 155, 157–59, 161–63, 181–82, 196, 199–200, 212, 214, 222–25, 228–31, 235

personal perfection, 218, 220, 232, 237–39

person, ix–x, xiii–xv, xxiv–xxviii, 4, 14–24, 26–42, 85, 138–43, 150–56, 164, 167, 204–6, 209–17, 228–31, 233–34, 236–42, 244–45, 247–49, 264; *dramatis persona*, 240, 242, 245; personal action, 39, 64, 156, 253; personal depth, xii, xvi, liv, 9–14, 16, 18, 22–23, 27–28, 41, 59–60, 139–43, 143–45, 148, 170, 237, 241; personal encounter, 147, 149, 245; personal expression, 65, 143, 167, 249, 252; personal formation, vii, xv, xxxiv, 2, 33, 52, 61–62, 65, 83, 85, 204–245, 250; personal identity, 66, 83, 132, 151; personal kind, 34, 37, 128, 130, 134–36, 150, 167, 169, 215–16, 231, 233, 239, 248, 251, 256; personal life, xii–xiii, xv–xvi, 29–32, 36, 39, 64–65, 138, 141, 213, 216, 239–40; personal mode, 33, 37, 136–37, 152, 156, 210, 214–15, 224, 242–43, 256; personal nature, xxxv, 32–34, 36–37, 41, 78, 84, 127, 135–36, 205, 211–12, 248; personal possession, 40, 83, 144, 146; personal pronoun, 6, 32, 134, 206; personal proportion, 214–15, 219, 230, 234, 244–45, 255–56; personal quality, 140–49, 157, 159–63, 165, 167, 170, 231–32, 241, 245, 249, 252; personal relation, 146–47, 172, 228, 232–33, 238, 243, 257; personal relationship, 148, 160–61, 164, 238–39, 257; personal spirit, xxiv, 64, 81, 138, 140, 142–45, 157, 166–67, 231, 253, 257–58; personal structure, 16, 30, 40, 42, 89, 132, 134, 156, 163, 170, 264; personal subject, xxiii–xxvi, xxix, 17–18, 23, 28–30, 32, 35, 38–41, 103, 135, 137, 232–33, 257–59, 264–65; personal subjectivity, xv, xxviii, xxxvi, 2, 33–34, 38, 40–42, 79, 248, 258, 264; personal substance, 16–17, 19–20, 26, 28, 30, 32, 39, 43, 80, 84, 248, 250; personally determined spiritual soul, 47, 61–62, 68–72, 74–75, 80, 82, 84, 127–28, 130, 252. *See also* human; I; individual; soul; personhood

personhood, 33–34, 140, 150, 152, 156, 230, 234, 242. *See also* person

personalism, ix, xiii, xv, xxiii, xxvii, xxx, xxxvii, 34–35, 85, 160–61, 264–65. *See also* person

personalization, xxxvi, 35, 41, 83, 85, 186, 202, 231, 244, 248, 250, 258

Pfänder, Alexander, li

phenomenology, x–xi, xiii, xv–xvi, xxviii, xxxi, xxxix–xliii, xlv–li, lvi, lviii, lx–lxv, lxvii, lxxii, 10, 15, 19, 29, 42, 56–57, 132, 140, 175, 208–9; phenomena, xxxi, xlvii, xlix, lix, 61,

Index

192, 238; phenomenological, ix, xiv, xxxvii, xlix, 1, 7, 56–58, 120, 243, 251, 253; phenomenological analysis, 21, 130, 189, 191; phenomenological approach, 131, 174, 176, 187, 202; phenomenological attitude, xlix; phenomenological bracketing, lxiv; phenomenological investigation, 23, 39, 47, 82, 169, 172, 186, 226, 239, 243, 258, 261; phenomenological method, xi, xxiii, xxix, xxxiii, xxxix, xlvii–li, lviii, lx–lxiv, 37, 226, 247; phenomenological perspective, 23, 39, 57, 174, 208, 248; phenomenological reduction, xxxi, xlix, li, lxi, lxiii, lxv; practice of, xii, xlviii–xlix, lxiii. *See also* method, Scholasticism
philosophia perennis, xxix, xxxvii, xxxix, xli–xliii, lvi–lvii, 21, 33–34, 82, 85, 87, 125, 127, 250–51, 253, 262
philosophical theology, vii, xxxiv, xli, 172–205
philosophical traditions, xlvi, li–lii, 82, 102
phusis (φύσις), 2–3. *See also* nature
plurality, li, lxvi, 3, 69, 72, 94, 96, 100, 102, 106, 109–11, 113–14, 124, 138, 147, 149, 158–60, 181–82. *See also* multiplicity
pointing finger, 72, 92, 141
positive, 112, 222; notion, 123, 222–23; perfection, 96, 101, 123, 222. *See also* perfection
possible, 175, 178, 180, 189–90; possibility, lxii, lxiv, lxvi, 16, 92, 94, 99–100, 104, 150–51, 154, 177–79, 187, 190. *See also* necessary
potency (*potentia*), xx, xxvi, xliv, 45, 57, 74, 103, 106–10, 112, 115, 173, 175, 265; potentiality, 74, 158, 162–63, 175, 186, 213
power(s), 35–36, 61–63, 67, 70, 78, 141–42, 145–46, 151, 157, 159, 163; appetitive, xxv; formative, 48, 50, 62, 103; intentional, lxviii; motile, 63; of God; organic, 59; rational, 36, 78; sensitive, 59–60; of soul, 51, 79, 141–42; spiritual, 13, 32, 36, 59; volitional, 36
predication, 26–27, 67–68, 70–71, 73, 119–20, 162–63, 173–74, 194–95, 197, 229, 235; essential, 68, 71, 73
proportion, 192–97, 199, 201, 204, 214, 216, 218–21, 223, 225–27, 229, 234, 241–42, 255; of essence to being, 198, 200, 203–4, 207, 213, 216, 220, 223, 225–27, 229, 234, 242, 244–45, 255–56; proportionality, 171–72, 185, 188, 191–97, 199–203, 214, 216–22, 225, 229–31, 241–44, 254–56. *See also* analogy
Przywara, Erich, xli, 188–89, 192, 208–10, 225–27
Pseudo-Dionysius, xlii, lix
Pure Act, 158, 171, 176, 202, 211, 254; Pure Being, 176, 197, 202. *See also* Divine Being; God

qualitative, 160–61; difference, 103–4, 165; distinction, xvi, 64, 115, 130, 138–39, 142, 148; fullness, 88; singular, 147
quality (*quale*, ποῖον), 13, 140–46, 149, 153, 157, 162–64, 231, 252. *See also* accident(s); personal quality

rational (*rationalis*, *rationabilis*), xxxv, 7–9, 24, 26–31, 34–41, 44–49, 51–52, 67–68, 73–78, 81–82, 144–45, 150–53, 155–56, 186–87, 212, 230–31, 238, 243–44, 248–50, 256–57; nature, xxxv, 24, 28,

rational (continued)
30–31, 35–39, 41, 151, 155, 212, 218, 230–31, 248; reflection, 7–8, 174, 234, 238; soul, 45–48, 67–68, 73–78, 81–82, 109, 150, 153, 155, 249–50

Ratzinger, Joseph, 233–34, 240, 257

real, lx, lxv, 37, 190; distinction, 55, 137, 198, 209, 225; realism, lxv–lxxii; moderate realism, lxviii–lxx, lxxii; realist, lxv–lxvi, lxviii, 9, 57; reality, lxii, lxvi–lxvii, 16, 20, 23, 25–27, 84–85, 88, 101–2, 214, 234, 239–40, 244; world, xlviii, lxxii–lxxiii

reasoning, inferential, lxii, 6, 20, 22, 174, 176, 178–79, 183, 186–87, 226, 232, 244, 262

Reinach, Adolph, lxv

relation, xxv–xxvii, xxxiii–xxxiv, xxxvi, xlvii, lviii–lix, 25–26, 158, 160–62, 168–69, 171, 184–86, 188–89, 191–92, 194–95, 199–203, 224–28, 232–38, 241–45, 254, 256–57; relata, 146, 165; to God, vii, xxix, xxxiv, xxxvi, 148, 171, 185, 195, 197, 199–200, 220, 232–33, 243, 245, 248, 256; relationship, lviii, 54, 72, 104, 160–61, 169, 239, 241, 245, 257

Roland-Gosselin, Marie-Dominique, xxxii, xliv, 93

Sartre, 10
Scheler, 48
Scheler, Max, xxxi, li, lxv
Scholasticism, xix, xxxi, xli–xliii, xlvii–xlviii, lii, lvi–lviii, lxxi, 3, 56–58, 70, 92, 94, 108, 120, 193, 233
science, x, xxvii, xxxi, li, lix–lxi, 46, 72–73, 82–83, 100, 191
Scotus, John Duns, xlii, 69, 88, 93–94, 105, 112, 117, 121–22, 193

self, 1, 6–10, 12, 15, 17, 21, 43, 102, 104, 115, 117, 156, 174–75, 177–79, 181–82, 186–87, 190, 232–33, 237, 245, 254, 256–58; -awareness, 5–6; -consciousness, 136

self-dependence, 15, 26, 96–97, 101, 104, 115–16, 122, 125, 136, 168, 200–201, 225, 227; perfection of, 101, 115, 122, 125

self-subsistence, 151, 154–55, 170, 253

similitude (*similitudo*), 191, 195, 199, 203, 209, 211, 224, 232; basic, 195, 203, 211–12, 216–17, 241, 254; proportional, 255. *See also* analogy, proportion

simplicity, xlix, 6, 20, 44, 67, 74–75, 77, 82–83, 121, 124, 128, 141, 180–81, 183, 185, 202, 208, 210–11, 213–15, 222–23, 224, 242, 250, 255, 258; absolute, 185, 198–99, 201, 214–15, 229, 241–42

singular(-ity), 88, 145, 147. *See also* individual

solipsism, 256

soul (*seele*), 1, 16–23, 43, 45–46, 49–53, 55–56, 58–64, 66–68, 70, 72–80, 139, 141–43, 145–46, 148, 150–55, 249–50, 252; expansive, 18–19; individual, 151–55, 253; indwelling, 76; intellectual, 44–46, 49, 67, 150, 152; human, 44–45, 53–56, 58–59, 62, 64, 67–68, 74–75, 79, 82, 85, 150–52, 154, 249–50; personal, 64, 253; sensitive, 49, 59, 79; separated, 151–52, 155; simple, 45, 62; soul of the, 70; spiritual kind of, 56; substance of the, 70; substantial, 21, 25; vegetative, 49; spiritual, 52–56, 59, 61, 68, 71, 74–76, 78–80, 135, 139, 141–42, 151–52, 155–56, 165–66,

168, 249–50. *See also* anima, body, human, person

species, 92, 94, 97, 100–106, 108–10, 112–13, 115, 127, 129, 133, 157–63, 168–69; biological, 104; form of, 102–6, 110, 112–13, 115, 129, 157–59, 161, 168–69, 251; human, 4, 24, 34, 129, 142, 158, 160, 168, 170; intelligible, lii–liii; classification, 115. *See also* essence, form

spirit, xxiv, 2, 7, 15, 20, 43, 45, 58–59, 140, 145; spirit-soul-body, 258; spiritual, 7, 14, 19, 49; spiritual activity, xiv, 13, 14, 28–29, 41, 76, 131; spiritual faculties, 13; spiritual person, 48, 126–27, 129–31, 134–36, 138–39, 159, 161, 163; spiritual soul, 52–56, 59, 61, 68, 71, 74–76, 78–80, 135, 139, 141–42, 151–52, 155–56, 165–66, 168, 249–50; spiritual stirrings, 7–8, 14, 28–29, 31, 35, 40–41, 131–33. *See also* soul

structure, xxi, xxv–xxvi, 10–11, 40, 43–44, 48, 50–55, 57–58, 60–61, 75–77, 82–83, 114–17, 119–21, 123–24, 140–41, 143–44, 160–61, 169, 217, 244; completed, 21–22, 60, 71, 80, 114, 128, 144, 248; of human nature, xv, 33, 35, 42–43, 50, 55, 61, 68, 79, 81, 165–66. *See also* form, essence

subject, xiv, xlviii, li, lxvi–lxviii, 10–11, 14–15, 17–18, 23, 26, 28, 31, 131, 162, 235–36; conscious subject, xv, xxiv, xlviii, l, lii, lxi, lxvi, 9, 13–14, 24, 133; personal subject, xxiii–xxvi, xxix, 17–18, 23, 28–30, 32, 35, 38–41, 103, 135, 137, 232–33, 257–59, 264–65. *See also* conscious, object(s), person

subjectivity, xiv–xv, 12, 30, 33, 38, 42, 85, 132–33; personal subjectivity, xv, xxviii, xxxvi, 2, 33–34, 38, 40–42, 79, 248, 258, 264. *See also* objectivity

subsist, 15, 26–27, 38–39, 45, 150, 158, 228; subsistent (subsistentia) / subsistence, 13, 15, 19, 26–27, 29, 32, 35–39, 41, 151–52, 154–56, 184, 221, 227–28, 230, 235, 253; individuated soul, 153; subsistent spiritual substance, 13, 25; subsistent substance, 13, 25, 28–29, 32–33; subsisting (subsistens), 26, 37–39, 41, 107, 168, 184, 195, 215, 221–22, 228–29, 235, 254. *See also* substance; supposit

substance, 13–15, 19–20, 26–27, 29, 35–38, 52, 57, 69–70, 94, 96, 108–9, 112–13, 162, 236; human, 45, 56, 58, 68, 73–74, 77, 114, 154. *See also* subsist; supposit

supposit (*suppositum*), 26–27, 35–36, 41, 113. *See also* substance; subsist

teleology, 3, 65, 102, 205; *telos* (τέλος), 65, 192, 250

thing (*res*), 16, 25, 29–30, 116–21, 123–25, 134–35, 166, 169, 181, 210, 215–17, 251–52; individual, 29, 117; the thing itself, 22–23, 262

Thomism, xxix–xxx, xxxvi–xxxvii, xlii–xliii, xlv–xlvi, li–lii, lvi–lvii, lxviii, lxx, lxxii–lxxiii, 84–85, 94–97, 106–10, 112–16, 167–68, 200–201, 218–20, 222–25, 230–31, 242–43, 261–65; Thomist / Thomistic, xxix, xxxii, xxxv–xxxvii, lviii, lxxiii, 2, 35, 46, 93, 96, 98, 101, 124–25, 152, 154, 162–63, 168, 170, 201–3, 261–65; Thomistic Personalism, vii, xxix, xxxvii, 13, 30, 35, 42, 206, 261, 264

tode ti (τόδε τί), 89, 92, 96, 101, 104–5, 118, 125, 132, 167, 251, 253
transcendent, 7, 11, 13, 16, 20, 174–75, 182, 184–85, 190, 254, 257; transcendental relation, 95–96, 105–7, 116, 125, 155, 169, 251; transcendentals, 95, 111, 114, 123, 197, 226–27, 229; transcendent depth, 16–17, 24, 30, 84, 249
truth, x, xii–xiii, xxxiii–xxxiv, xl–xli, xliii, xlvii, 5–8, 45, 184–85, 199, 229–30, 240–41, 262–63

understanding, xxiv–xxvi, xxviii–xxix, xxxi–xxxiii, xl–xli, li–liv, lviii–lx, 7–8, 36–37, 39–41, 61–62, 72–74, 85, 87, 93, 119–21, 137–38, 149–52, 191–93, 215–16, 223–25
unfold(-ed/-ing), xiii, xxiv–xxviii, 1, 3, 6, 24, 36, 40, 44, 47, 60, 85, 141–45, 167, 186, 238, 240–42, 245, 250, 252–53
union, 22, 67, 122, 156, 164, 197; spousal, 161; of love, 164
unique, xiii–xvii, 28, 65–66, 145–49, 89, 161, 163–68, 170, 195, 230–36, 240–41, 245, 249, 252–53, 256; uniqueness, 145–48, 164–65, 231, 245, 252. *See also* irreducible; irreplaceable; unrepeatable
unity, 10–11, 21–23, 43–48, 52–56, 61–62, 67–68, 72–78, 80–84, 93, 106–12, 115–17, 123–25, 128–30, 134–36, 159–62, 169–70, 180–81, 212–14, 216–17, 222, 249–50; and incommunicability, 129, 135–36; and simplicity, 44, 121, 244, 258 dynamic, 70, 100; framed, 53, 69; human, vii, xviii, xxxiv, 19, 23, 53, 61–62, 65–66, 74–75, 82–83, 249–250; numerical, 110–12, 124, 182; of form, 45–46; personal, 61, 79, 81, 129, 212, 252; primitive, 111–12, 116, 121, 135; profound, 18–19, 74, 76, 79–81; progression of, 128; simple, 82, 213; substantial, 21, 43, 46, 61, 66–68, 71, 73–74, 77, 79, 81–84, 249–50, 258, 264; transcendental, 111–12, 123–24, 182; personal unity, xv, 58, 79, 82–83, 211, 214
universal(s), lxv, lxviii–lxx, lxxii, 120–21, 123, 197; notions-concepts-words, 121, 223; universal distinctions, 223; universality, li, lxviii–lxix, 134, 140, 149
unrepeatable(-ity), 147, 166. *See also* irreducible; irreplaceable; unique

virtual presence, 48, 76–78
von Hildebrand, Dietrich, xxv, lxv, 148

Weil, Simone, 188, 208–9
whole(s), 54, 69, 100; complex, 119; numerable, 112; substantial, 72
Wojtyła, Karol, xii–xv, xxxvii, 13, 30, 34–35, 38, 40, 42, 60, 66, 138, 148, 155, 164, 206, 236, 239, 264
word, xii, lii–liii, lxix, 109, 126, 148, 197, 214, 240; exterior, liii; inner, liii; interior, liii; mental, liii; single, 210; voiced, liii; of God, xxxiii
world, xxiv, xlix, liv, lvi, lx–lxi, lxiii, lxvi–lxviii, 7–8, 14, 28–31, 51, 59, 63, 141, 174–75, 178, 214; above, 7–8, 23, 175, 254; actual / real, lxiv, lxvi, lxx, 9, 103, 192; experienced, xxiv, xxxiii, xlviii, xlix, li–lii, liv, lxi, lxiv, lxvi–lxvii, lxxii, 10, 51, 60, 217, 263; inner, 7–10, 12, 14, 23, 59, 174–75, 187; meaningful, 18, 51, 63; natural, xxiii, xxvii–xxviii,

lxv–lxvii, lxix, lxxii–lxxiii, 3, 33–34, 39, 180–81, 186, 205, 207; objective, xxiv, xlviii, l, liii, lxvi, 14–15, 28; outer, lxvi, 7–10, 14, 18–19, 23, 28, 59–60, 174–75, 210, 217, 243, 248; transcendent, 60, 175, 178, 184, 232, 237; worldview, lvi, lxii, lxiv, lxxiii, 207, 261, 263

www.ingramcontent.com/pod-product-compliance
Lightning Source LLC
Chambersburg PA
CBHW071953290426
44109CB00018B/2007